THE DEVIL & THE GOOD LORD

and Two Other Plays

LE DIABLE ET LE BON DIEU

TRANSLATED FROM THE FRENCH BY KITTY BLACK

KEAN

BASED ON THE PLAY BY ALEXANDRE DUMAS
TRANSLATED FROM THE FRENCH BY KITTY BLACK

NEKRASSOV

TRANSLATED FROM THE FRENCH BY SYLVIA AND
GEORGE LEESON

THE DEVIL
& THE
GOOD LORD

and Two Other Plays

1368

by

JEAN-PAUL SARTRE

New York
VINTAGE BOOKS
A DIVISION OF RANDOM HOUSE

VINTAGE BOOKS

are published by ALFRED A. KNOPF, INC.

and RANDOM HOUSE, INC.

MANUFACTURED IN THE UNITED STATES OF AMERICA

CONTENTS

THE DEVIL

& THE GOOD LORD

(*Le Diable et le Bon Dieu*)

A PLAY IN THREE ACTS, ELEVEN SCENES

TRANSLATED FROM THE FRENCH BY KITTY BLACK

Le Diable et le Bon Dieu (The Devil and the Good Lord) *was presented for the first time at the Théâtre Antoine, Paris, in June 1951.*

CHARACTERS

GOETZ	A PROPHET
HEINRICH	THE BISHOP OF WORMS
NASTI	FRANZ
TETZEL	SCHULHEIM
KARL	NOSSAK }*Barons*
THE ARCHBISHOP	RIETSCHEL
	HERMANN
HEINZ	HILDA
SCHMIDT	CATHERINE
GERLACH	A WOMAN
THE BANKER	A WITCH

OFFICERS, SOLDIERS, CITIZENS, PEASANTS, *and* SERVANTS

THE ACTION *of the play takes place in Germany, around the town of Worms, in the middle of the Renaissance. Two violent crises shook the various German states at this period: two closely related events—the Peasants' Revolt, and the beginning of the Lutheran Reformation.*

ACT I

SCENE I

To the left, between heaven and earth, a hall in the ARCHBISHOP's palace. To the right, the BISHOP's palace and the ramparts of the city of Worms. For the moment, only the ARCHBISHOP's palace is visible, the rest of the stage being lost in darkness.

THE ARCHBISHOP [at the window]: Will he come? O Lord, on my golden coins the thumbs of my subjects have worn away my effigy; and now Thy terrible thumb is wearing away my flesh. I am now but the shadow of an archbishop. Should the end of this day bring news of my defeat, I shall be so worn down that I shall be transparent; and what, O Lord, canst Thou do with an archbishop that can be seen through? [A SERVANT enters.] Is it Colonel Linehart?

THE SERVANT: No, Your Grace. The banker Foucre. He is asking . . .

THE ARCHBISHOP: Later. [Pause.] What is Linehart doing? He should be here with fresh news. [Pause.] Do they talk of the battle in the kitchens?

THE SERVANT: They talk of nothing else, Your Grace.

THE ARCHBISHOP: What are they saying?

THE SERVANT: That our prospects are excellent. Conrad is hemmed in between the mountains and the river, and . . .

THE ARCHBISHOP: I know, I know. But if one battles, one may be beaten.

THE SERVANT: Your Grace . . .

THE ARCHBISHOP: Get out! [The SERVANT goes.] O God, why hast Thou permitted this? The enemy invaded

my lands, and while I was engaging Conrad in battle,
my faithful town of Worms revolted against me,
stabbing me in the back. I did not know, Lord, that
such great things were reserved for me. Must I
wander from door to door, a blind beggar, led by
a child? I am ready to obey, if such be Thy holy will.
But remember, Lord, that I am no longer young,
and that I never had a vocation to be a martyr.

[*In the distance can be heard cries of* "Victory!
Victory!" *The sounds draw near. The* ARCHBISHOP
listens, and lays his hand on his heart.]

THE SERVANT [*entering*]: Victory! Victory! We have
won, Your Grace. Colonel Linehart has arrived.

LINEHART [*entering*]: Victory, Your Grace. Victory,
complete and classic. An exemplary battle, an epoch-
making day. The enemy has lost six thousand men,
killed or drowned, the rest are in flight.

THE ARCHBISHOP: Thanks be to God. And Conrad?

LINEHART: Among the dead.

THE ARCHBISHOP: Thanks be to God. [*Pause.*] If he is
dead, then I forgive him. [*To* LINEHART]. I give you
my blessing. Go, spread the news.

LINEHART [*taking up a position*]: A little after sunrise,
we perceived a cloud of dust. . . .

THE ARCHBISHOP [*interrupting*]: No, no! No details!
Especially, no details. A victory described in detail
is indistinguishable from a defeat. At least, you're
sure it's a victory?

LINEHART: A pearl of a victory. Real style and elegance.

THE ARCHBISHOP: Leave me. I must pray. [LINEHART
goes out. The ARCHBISHOP *begins to dance.*] I've
won! I've won! [*He puts his hand to his heart.*] Ow!
[*He kneels on his* prie-dieu.] Let us pray.

[*Part of the stage lights up on the right: the ramparts,
and a sentinel's post.* HEINZ *and* SCHMIDT *are leaning
over the battlements.*]

HEINZ: I don't believe it. . . . I don't believe it. God
has certainly not permitted it.

SCHMIDT: Wait, they're beginning again. Look! One, two, three—three—and one, two, three, four, five . . .

NASTI [*appearing on the ramparts*]: What's the matter?

SCHMIDT: Nasti! We've some bad news.

NASTI: For God's Chosen the news is never bad.

HEINZ: For more than an hour, we've been watching the signal fires. Once every minute they repeat the message, and it's always the same. See! One, two, three—three and five. [*He points to the mountain.*] The Archbishop has won the battle.

NASTI: I know.

SCHMIDT: The situation is desperate. We are trapped here in Worms without allies and without supplies. You told us Goetz would finally lose patience and raise the siege, that Conrad would crush the Archbishop. Well, Conrad is dead, the Archbishop's armies can now join with Goetz's troops before our walls, and nothing remains for us but to die.

GERLACH [*entering, running*]: Conrad is beaten. The Burgomaster and the Aldermen are assembled at the Town Hall, deliberating on the situation.

SCHMIDT: I'll be damned! They must be thinking out a way to surrender the city.

NASTI: Do you have faith, my brothers?

ALL: Yes, Nasti, yes!

NASTI: Then, have no fear. Conrad's defeat is a sign.

SCHMIDT: A sign?

NASTI: A sign from God. Gerlach, hurry to the Town Hall and try to find out what the Council has decided. [*The ramparts disappear into the night.*]

THE ARCHBISHOP [*rising*]: Hallo, there! [*The* SERVANT *appears.*] Bring in the banker. [*The* BANKER *enters.*] Be seated, banker. You are splattered with mud. Where have you been?

THE BANKER: I have traveled for thirty-six hours without pause to prevent you from committing a folly.

THE ARCHBISHOP: Folly?

THE BANKER: You are about to kill a goose that every year lays a golden egg for you.

THE ARCHBISHOP: What are you talking about?

THE BANKER: Your city of Worms. I was told you are besieging it. If your troops sack the city, you will ruin yourself, and me besides. Is playing soldiers a fit game at your time of life?

THE ARCHBISHOP: It was not I who provoked Conrad.

THE BANKER: Perhaps not. But who tells me that you didn't provoke him to provoke you?

THE ARCHBISHOP: He was my vassal and he owed me obedience. But the Devil prompted him to incite the knights to revolt and to place himself at their head.

THE BANKER: Why didn't you accede to his demands before he lost patience?

THE ARCHBISHOP: He was demanding everything.

THE BANKER: Very well, enough of Conrad. He was obviously the aggressor, since he has now been defeated. But your city of Worms . . .

THE ARCHBISHOP: Worms, my jewel, Worms, my delight, Worms, the ungrateful, revolted against me the very day Conrad crossed the frontier.

THE BANKER: The city is greatly in the wrong. But three quarters of your revenues come from Worms. Who will pay your taxes, who will reimburse my loans if you massacre your citizens like an old Tiberias?

THE ARCHBISHOP: They have molested the priests and forced them to take refuge in the monasteries. They have insulted my bishop and forbidden him to leave his palace.

THE BANKER: Childish pranks! They would never have taken up arms if you had not forced them to it. Violence is only proper for those who have nothing to lose.

THE ARCHBISHOP: What do you want?

THE BANKER: I want you to pardon them. Let them

pay you a good indemnity and then forget the whole business.

THE ARCHBISHOP: Alas!

THE BANKER: What do you mean, alas?

THE ARCHBISHOP: I love my city, banker. Even without indemnity, I could heartily forgive it.

THE BANKER: Well, then?

THE ARCHBISHOP: I am not the one who is besieging Worms.

THE BANKER: Then who is?

THE ARCHBISHOP: Goetz.

THE BANKER: Who is this Goetz? The brother of Conrad?

THE ARCHBISHOP: Yes. The finest captain in all Germany.

THE BANKER: What is he doing outside the walls of your city? I thought he was your enemy?

THE ARCHBISHOP: To tell the truth, I don't really know what he is. First, he was Conrad's ally and my foe, then he was Conrad's foe and my ally. Now . . . He has a changing humor, which is the least one can say of him.

THE BANKER: Why take such doubtful allies?

THE ARCHBISHOP: What choice did I have? He and Conrad together invaded my territories. Luckily, I discovered there was a rift between them, and I promised Goetz in secret that he should have his brother's lands if he would join with us. If I had not won him away from Conrad, I should have lost this war long ago.

THE BANKER: So he came over to you with all his forces. And then?

THE ARCHBISHOP: I gave him command of the frontier posts. He must have grown tired of waiting; perhaps he does not like garrison life. One fine day he appeared with all his army before the walls of Worms and began the siege without a word from me.

THE BANKER: Command him. . . . [*The* ARCHBISHOP *smiles sadly and shrugs.*] He doesn't obey you?

THE ARCHBISHOP: What general in the field obeys political leaders?

THE BANKER: So we are at his mercy?

THE ARCHBISHOP: Yes.

[*The ramparts show.*]

GERLACH [*entering*]: The Council has decided to send a deputation to Goetz.

HEINZ: So that's it. [*Pause.*] The swine.

GERLACH: Our only hope now is that Goetz will demand impossible conditions. If he is the man they say he is, he won't even accept our unconditional surrender.

THE BANKER: Perhaps he will spare the city's treasures.

THE ARCHBISHOP: Not even the lives of the people, I'm afraid.

SCHMIDT [*to* GERLACH]: But why? Why?

THE ARCHBISHOP: He is a bastard of the worst kind— a son of a bitch. He takes no pleasure in anything but evil.

GERLACH: A bastard is a swine; he enjoys evil. If he wants to sack Worms, our citizens will have to fight to the finish.

SCHMIDT: If he intends to raze the city, he won't be fool enough to say so. He'll demand free entry, and promise not to touch a thing.

THE BANKER [*indignantly*]: Worms owes me thirty thousand ducats. We must put an end to all this. Set your forces in motion against Goetz.

THE ARCHBISHOP [*overcome*]: I'm afraid he may beat them for me.

[*The* ARCHBISHOP'*s palace disappears into the night.*]

HEINZ [*to* NASTI]: Then there is really no hope for us?

NASTI: God is with us, my brothers; we cannot lose. Tonight, I will leave Worms and try to cross the camp and reach Waldorf. In a week, I can have ten thousand peasants under arms.

SCHMIDT: But how can we hold out for a week? They are capable of opening the gates to him this very night.

NASTI: They must be prevented from opening them.

HEINZ: Do you want to seize command?

NASTI: No. The situation is too uncertain.

HEINZ: Well, then?

NASTI: We must compromise the citizens in such a way that they'll fear for their lives.

ALL: How?

NASTI: By a massacre.

[*Below the ramparts, the scene lights up. A* WOMAN *is sitting against the stairway which leads up to the sentinel's box. She is thirty-five and dressed in rags. She gazes ahead of her in stony silence. A priest passes, reading his breviary.*]

NASTI: Who is that priest? Why isn't he shut up with the others?

HEINZ: Don't you know him?

NASTI: Ah, yes. It's Heinrich. How changed he is. Nevertheless, he should have been locked up.

HEINZ: The poor people love him because he lives as they do. We were afraid to anger the poor people.

NASTI: He is the most dangerous of all.

THE WOMAN [*seeing the priest*]: Priest! Priest!
[*The priest tries to escape, she cries after him.*]
Where are you going so fast?

HEINRICH [*stopping*]: I have nothing left! Nothing! Nothing! I have given everything away!

THE WOMAN: That's no reason to run away when someone calls you.

HEINRICH [*coming back toward her, very wearily*]: Are you hungry?

THE WOMAN: No.

HEINRICH: Then what do you want?

THE WOMAN: I want you to explain.

HEINRICH [*quickly*]: I refuse to explain anything.

THE WOMAN: You don't even know what I want to ask you.

HEINRICH: Very well. Quickly. What do you want me to explain?

THE WOMAN: Why the child died.

HEINRICH: What child?

THE WOMAN [*laughing a little*]: My child. Don't you remember? You buried him yesterday. He was three years old, and he died of hunger.

HEINRICH: I am tired, my sister, and I didn't recognize you. To me, all you women seem alike, with the same face, the same eyes. . . .

THE WOMAN: Why did he die?

HEINRICH: I do not know.

THE WOMAN: And yet you are a priest.

HEINRICH: Yes.

THE WOMAN: Then who can tell me, if you cannot? [*Pause.*] If I were to let myself die now, would it be a sin?

HEINRICH [*forcefully*]: Yes. A great sin.

THE WOMAN: That's what I thought. And yet, I should so much like to die. You see, you really must explain. [*Pause.* HEINRICH *rubs his forehead, and makes a great effort.*]

HEINRICH: Nothing on earth occurs without the will of God. And God is goodness itself, therefore everything happens for the best.

THE WOMAN: I don't understand.

HEINRICH: God knows more than you can understand. What seems misfortune is a blessing in His eyes because He weighs all the consequences.

THE WOMAN: Can you understand that?

HEINRICH: No! No! I don't understand! I understand nothing! I neither can nor want to understand. We must believe—believe—believe!

THE WOMAN [*with a little laugh*]: You say we must believe and you don't look as though you yourself believe what you are saying.

HEINRICH: My sister, I have said the same words so
often these last three months that I no longer know
if I say them out of conviction or from habit. But
make no mistake. I believe. I believe with all my
strength and with all my heart. O God, I call upon
Thee to witness that not for one moment has my
heart been compromised by doubt. [*Pause.*] Woman,
your child is in heaven, and you will be reunited with
him there. [*He kneels.*]

THE WOMAN: Yes, priest, of course. But heaven is different. And I'm so tired, I shall never be able to
rejoice again. Not even in heaven.

HEINRICH: My sister, forgive me.

THE WOMAN: Why should I forgive you, good priest?
You have done me no harm.

HEINRICH: Forgive me. Forgive in me all the other
priests—those who are rich, as well as those who are
poor.

THE WOMAN [*amused*]: I forgive you with all my heart.
Does that satisfy you?

HEINRICH: Yes. Now, my sister, let us pray together.
Let us pray God to give us back our hope.
[*During the last lines,* NASTI *slowly comes down
from the ramparts.*]

THE WOMAN [*seeing* NASTI *and interrupting herself,
joyfully*]: Nasti! Nasti the baker!

NASTI: What do you want?

THE WOMAN: Baker, my child is dead. You must be
able to say why, you who know everything.

NASTI: Yes—I know.

HEINRICH: Nasti, I implore you, say nothing. Woe to
those through whom evil comes to pass.

NASTI: He died because the rich burghers of our city
revolted against the Archbishop, their very rich over-
lord. When the rich fight the rich, it is the poor who
die.

THE WOMAN: Was it God's will that they should wage
this war?

NASTI: God has forbidden them to wage it.

THE WOMAN: This man says nothing happens except by the will of God.

NASTI: Nothing, except evil, which is born of the wickedness of man.

HEINRICH: Baker, you lie. You are confusing the false and the true in order to betray the souls of men.

NASTI: Dare you assert that God permits this mourning and this useless suffering? I say that God is innocent of our sins.

[HEINRICH *is silent.*]

THE WOMAN: Then it was not the will of God that my child should die?

NASTI: If He desired his death, why should He have let the child be born?

THE WOMAN [*consoled*]: I think that is much better. [*To* HEINRICH] You see, when he says that, I understand. You mean, God is sad too, when He sees how I am suffering?

NASTI: Most terribly sad.

THE WOMAN: And He can do nothing for me?

NASTI: Of course He can. He can give you back your son.

THE WOMAN [*disappointed*]: Yes, I know. In heaven!

NASTI: No, not in heaven. Here on earth.

THE WOMAN [*surprised*]: On earth.

NASTI: You must first pass through the eye of a needle, and endure misfortune for seven years. Then the kingdom of God will be established on earth; our dead will arise, all men will love one another, and those who hunger will be filled.

THE WOMAN: Why must we wait seven years?

NASTI: Because we shall need seven years of endeavor to drive out the wicked.

THE WOMAN: That's a big undertaking.

NASTI: For that reason, God needs your help.

THE WOMAN: The Almighty God needs my help?

NASTI: Yes, sister. For seven more years, the Evil One

will reign on earth; but if each one of us fights valiantly we shall redeem ourselves and God with us. Do you believe me?

THE WOMAN [*rising*]: Yes, Nasti; I believe you.

NASTI: Your child is not in heaven, woman. He is within you, and you will bear him for seven long years, at the end of which time he will walk at your side, his hand in yours, and you will have brought him into the world a second time.

THE WOMAN: I believe you, Nasti. I believe you. [*She goes out.*]

HEINRICH: You have led her astray.

NASTI. If you believe that, why didn't you stop me?

HEINRICH: Ah! Because she seemed a little less unhappy. [NASTI *shrugs.*] O Lord, I lacked the courage to silence this blasphemer; I have sinned. But I believe, O Lord, I believe that nothing occurs except by Thy laws, even to the death of a little child, and that all is Good. I believe because it is absurd! Absurd! Absurd!

[*The whole stage lights up. Citizens with their wives are grouped around the* BISHOP's *palace, waiting for him to come out.*]

VOICES: Is there any news?
        No news.
        What are we doing here?
        Waiting.
        What are we waiting for?
        Nothing.
        Did you see?
        Over there to the right?
        Yes.
        The ugly brutes.
        When water is stirred, mud rises. . . .
        A man isn't safe in the streets any more. . . .
        We must end this war—we must end it soon.
            If not, we're in for disaster. . . .

I want to see the Bishop—I want to see the
    Bishop. . . .

He won't appear. . . . He is too angry. . . .

Who? Who?

The Bishop.

Ever since he has been imprisoned here, he
    comes from time to time to the window,
    draws aside the curtains, and watches us.

He doesn't look like a good man.

What do you expect him to say?

He may have had news.

[*Murmurs from the crowd, then isolated shouts.*]

A VOICE: Bishop! Bishop! Come out, show yourself!

ANOTHER VOICE: Advise us.

ANOTHER VOICE: What is going to happen?

FIRST VOICE: This is the end of the world!

[*A man emerges from the crowd, rushes to the façade
of the* BISHOP'S *palace and sets his back against it.*
HEINRICH *moves aside from him and rejoins the
crowd.*]

THE PROPHET: The world is doomed, is doomed!
               Beat the carrion flesh!
               Beat, beat, beat, beat!
               God is here.

[*Shouts, the beginning of a panic.*]

A CITIZEN: Quiet—quiet! It is only a prophet.

THE CROWD: Another prophet! We've had enough
prophets! We don't want to listen. They are springing up everywhere. What's the good of locking up
the priests?

THE PROPHET: Earth has its odors . . .
               The sun complained to God!
               O Lord, let me put out my light.
               I have suffered enough this putrefaction.
               The more I warm it, the more it reeks.
               Touching it, my beams are defiled.
               Alas! cries the sun. My fair golden mane
               is dragging in the mire.

A CITIZEN: Shut your trap!
[*Struck by the* CITIZEN, *the* PROPHET *falls to the ground. The window of the palace is flung open. The* BISHOP, *in full regalia, appears on the balcony.*]
THE CROWD: The Bishop!
THE BISHOP: Where are the armies of Conrad? Where are his armored knights? Where is the legion of angels to put the enemy to flight? You are alone, without friends, without hope, and accursed. Answer me, citizens of Worms, answer: if you believe you are serving God by imprisoning His ministers, why has the Lord abandoned you?
[*Groans from the* CROWD.]
Answer me!
HEINRICH: Do not deprive them of their courage.
THE BISHOP: Who speaks?
HEINRICH: It is I, Heinrich, the parish priest of Saint-Gilhau.
THE BISHOP: Swallow your tongue, priest apostate. Dare you look on the face of your bishop?
HEINRICH: If they have sinned against you, Your Grace, forgive them their trespasses as I forgive you these insults.
THE BISHOP: Judas! Judas Iscariot! Go hang yourself!
HEINRICH: I am no Judas.
THE BISHOP: Then what are you doing among those people? Why do you plead for them? Why are you not locked up with us, your fellows?
HEINRICH: They let me go free because they know that I love them. If I have not joined the other priests of my own free will, it was to ensure that masses be said and the Holy Sacraments given in this lost city. Without me, the Church would be absent, Worms delivered defenseless to the powers of heresy, and its people would die like beasts of the field. . . . Your Grace, do not deprive them of their courage.
THE BISHOP: Who fed you? Who brought you up? Who

taught you to read? Who gave you your knowledge? Who consecrated you priest?

HEINRICH: The Church, my holy Mother.

THE BISHOP: You owe the Church everything. You belong first of all to the Church.

HEINRICH: I belong to the Church, but I am also their brother.

THE BISHOP [*violently*]: The Church must be served first.

HEINRICH: Yes. The Church must be served first, but . . .

THE BISHOP: I shall speak to these men. If they persist in their errors and continue in their rebellion, I command you to rejoin the men of the Church, your true brothers, and to take your place with them at the monastery, or in the Seminary. Will you obey your bishop?

A MAN OF THE PEOPLE: Do not forsake us, Heinrich. You are the priest of the poor—you belong to us.

HEINRICH [*overcome, but in a firm voice*]: The Church must be served first. My Lord Bishop, I will obey.

THE BISHOP: People of Worms, behold your fair and flourishing city; look at it closely, for the last time. It will become an infected center of famine and plague; and as a last horror, the rich and the poor will massacre each other. When the soldiers of Goetz enter the city, they will find nothing but rotting corpses and ruins. [*Pause.*] I can save you, but you must know how to soften my heart.

VOICES: Save us—My Lord Bishop—save us!

THE BISHOP: On your knees, proud burghers, and ask pardon of God!

[*The burghers kneel down one after the other. The poor people remain standing.*]

Heinrich! Will you kneel?

[HEINRICH *kneels.*]

Lord God, forgive us our trespasses and soften the wrath of the Archbishop.

THE CROWD: Lord God, forgive us our trespasses, and soften the wrath of the Archbishop.

THE BISHOP: Amen. You may rise. [*Pause.*] First, you will free the priests and the nuns, then you will open the gates of the city. You will kneel in the square outside the cathedral and wait there in humble repentence. Meanwhile, we shall go in procession to Goetz to beg him to spare your lives.

A CITIZEN: What if he refuses to comply?

THE BISHOP: Above the power of Goetz is the power of the Archbishop. He is our holy father, and his justice will be paternal.

[*For some moments* NASTI *has been standing on the ramparts. He listens in silence, then on the last words he comes down two steps of the stairs.*]

NASTI: Goetz does not serve the Archbishop. Goetz serves the Devil. He swore an oath to Conrad his brother, and in spite of that, he betrayed him. If he promises to spare your lives today, will you be foolish enough as to believe him?

THE BISHOP: You, whoever you are, I command you . . .

NASTI: Who are you to give me orders? And you, citizens, do you need to listen? You need no orders from anyone, except from the leaders you have chosen.

THE BISHOP: And who chose you, ragamuffin?

NASTI: The people. [*To the others*] The soldiers are on our side. I have stationed my men at the gates. If anyone tries to open them—death.

THE BISHOP: Courage, unhappy man; drive them to perdition. They had only one hope of salvation and you have just taken it away from them.

NASTI: If there were no hope, I should be the first to counsel you to surrender. But who dare say God has abandoned us? Do they ask you to doubt the angels? My brothers, I tell you, the angels are with us. Do not lift your eyes—the heavens are empty. The angels are at work on this earth: they have attacked the enemy camp.

A CITIZEN: What angels?

NASTI: The angel of cholera and the angel of pestilence —the angel of famine and the angel of discord. Hold fast—the city is impregnable and God is on our side. The siege will be raised.

THE BISHOP: Citizens of Worms, those who listen to this heresy are doomed to perdition. I swear it by my place in Paradise.

NASTI: Your place in Paradise? A long time ago, God gave it to the dogs.

THE BISHOP: He is holding your place in the Hereafter ready for you, warm and waiting, till the moment you come to claim it. He must rejoice at this moment as He hears you insulting His priest.

NASTI: Who ordained you priest?

THE BISHOP: The Holy Church.

NASTI: Your Holy Church is a strumpet; she sells her favors to the rich. Why should I make confession to you? Why should I accept remission of my sins from you? Your soul is corrupted, God grinds His teeth when He beholds it. My brothers, we have no need of priests; any man can perform the rite of baptism; any man on earth can grant absolution; all men may preach. I tell you truly: all men on earth are prophets, or God does not exist.

THE BISHOP: Fie for shame! Anathema! [*He hurls his almoner's purse in* NASTI's *face.*]

NASTI [*pointing to the door of the palace*]: This door is worm-eaten; a single blow would split it in pieces. [*Silence.*] How patient you are, my brothers! [*Pause. To the people*] They are all in league against us: Bishop, the Council, the rich burghers. They would surrender the city because they are afraid of the people. And who will pay the price if they hand over the city? You! Always you! Come, arise, my brothers. We must kill in order to win our place in heaven.

[*The men of the people murmur.*]

A BURGHER [*to his wife*]: Come! Let's go.

ANOTHER [*to his son*]: We must bar the shutters and barricade the shop.

THE BISHOP: My God, Thou art my witness, I have done what I could to save my people. I shall die without regrets in Thy glory, for I know now that Thy anger will overwhelm Worms and grind the city to powder.

NASTI: This dotard will devour you alive. Why is his voice so strong? Because he eats his fill every day. Go and search his granaries; you will find there enough wheat to feed a regiment for six months.

THE BISHOP [*in a powerful voice*]: You lie. My storehouse is empty, and you know it.

NASTI: Why not go and see, my brothers? Why not? Will you take him at his word?

[*The* CITIZENS *withdraw hastily. The men of the people remain with* NASTI.]

HEINRICH [*going to* NASTI]: Nasti!

NASTI: What do you want?

HEINRICH: You know that his storehouses are empty. You know that he hardly touches food, that he gives all he receives to the poor.

NASTI: Are you for or against us?

HEINRICH: I am for you when you suffer, against you when you wish to shed the blood of the Church.

NASTI: You are for us when we are massacred, against us when we try to fight back.

HEINRICH: I belong to the Church, Nasti.

NASTI: Drive in the door!

[*A group of men attack the door. The* BISHOP *prays in silence, standing.*]

HEINRICH [*throwing himself in front of the door*]: You will have to kill me. . . .

A MAN OF THE PEOPLE: Kill you? Why?

[*They strike him and throw him to the ground.*]

HEINRICH: You struck me! I loved you more than my own soul, and you struck me. [*He rises and goes toward* NASTI.] Not the Bishop, Nasti, not the Bishop! Kill me if you will, but spare the Bishop.

NASTI: Why not? He has starved the people.

HEINRICH: You know that is false! You know it! If you want to free your brothers from oppression and falsehood, why begin by telling them lies?

NASTI: I never lie.

HEINRICH: You are lying. There is no grain in his storehouse.

NASTI: What does it matter? There are precious gems and gold in his churches. I say he is responsible for the deaths of all those who have died of hunger at the feet of his marble Christs and his ivory Virgins.

HEINRICH: It isn't the same thing. You may not be telling a lie, but you are also not telling the truth.

NASTI: You speak the truth of your people—I speak the truth of mine. And if God loves the poor, it is our truth which He will make His own on Judgment Day.

HEINRICH: Then let Him judge the Bishop. But do not shed the blood of the Church.

NASTI: I recognize but one Church: the community of men.

HEINRICH: All men, then, all Christians joined together by love. But you will inaugurate your community of men by a massacre.

NASTI: It is too early to love all mankind. We shall buy the right to do so by shedding blood.

HEINRICH: God has forbidden violence; it is an abomination.

NASTI: And Hell? Do the damned not suffer violence?

HEINRICH: God has said: He who takes the sword . . .

NASTI: By the sword shall he perish. . . . Very well—let us perish by the sword. We shall perish, but our sons will see His kingdom established on earth. Get out of here! You are like all the others.

HEINRICH: Nasti! Nasti! Why cannot you love me? What have I done to you?

NASTI: You are a priest, and a priest remains a priest whatever he may do.

HEINRICH: I am one of you. A poor man, and the son of a poor man.

NASTI: Well, that proves you are a traitor—nothing more.

HEINRICH [crying out]: They have broken down the door!

[The door has indeed given way, and men are pouring into the palace. HEINRICH falls on his knees.]

Dear God, if Thou canst still love mankind, if Thy face is not yet set against them, prevent this murder.

THE BISHOP: I have no need of your prayers, Heinrich! All you who know not what you do, receive my forgiveness. But may you, priest apostate, be accursed.

HEINRICH: Ah! [He falls to the ground.]

THE BISHOP: Halleluiah! Halleluiah! Halleluiah!

[He is struck down by the people and falls prostrate.]

NASTI [to SCHMIDT]: Now let them try and surrender the city!

A MAN OF THE PEOPLE [appearing in the doorway]: There was no grain in his storerooms.

NASTI: Then he has hidden it at the Monastery.

A MAN [shouting]: To the Monastery! To the Monastery!

[The crowd rushes after him, crying: "To the Monastery!"]

NASTI [to SCHMIDT]: Tonight, I shall try to cross the lines.

[They go out. HEINRICH rises, looks around him. He is alone with the PROPHET. He sees the BISHOP, staring at him wide-eyed.]

HEINRICH [trying to enter the palace. The BISHOP stretches out his arm to prevent him.]: I will not enter. Lower your arm—lower your arm. If you still have some life in you, forgive me. Rancor is heavy and belongs to the earth. Leave it on earth, and die the lighter. [*The* BISHOP *tries to speak.*] What? [*The* BISHOP *laughs.*] A traitor? I? Of course. They, too, call me traitor. But explain: how can I betray everybody at once? [*The* BISHOP *is still laughing.*] Why do you laugh? Come, come! [*Pause.*] I loved them. I loved them, but I lied to them. I lied to them by my silence. I held my peace! I held my peace! My lips were tight shut, my teeth clenched. They were dying like flies, and I still held my peace. When they asked for bread, I held out the crucifix. Can you feed a man with the cross? Ah! Lower your arm! We are accomplices. Ah! I wanted to share their poverty, suffer their cold, endure their hunger. They died all the same, didn't they? That was a way of betrayal. I made them believe the Church was poor. Now, rage has seized them, and they kill; they are lost; they will never know anything but Hell—first in this world, and tomorrow in the next. [*The* BISHOP *mutters unintelligibly.*] What could I have done? How could I have stopped them? [*He goes to the back and looks down the street.*] The square is swarming with people: they are hammering with benches on the door of the monastery. The door is solid. It will hold until morning. I can do nothing. Nothing, . nothing! Come, close your mouth, die bravely. [*The* BISHOP *drops a key.*] What key is this? What door does it open? A door in your palace? No? In the cathedral? Yes? In the sacristy? No? The crypt? . . . Is it the door of the crypt that is always shut? Well?

THE BISHOP: Underground.

HEINRICH: Where does it lead? . . . Don't tell me! May you die before telling me!

THE BISHOP: Outside.

HEINRICH: I will not pick it up. [*Pause.*] An underground passage leads from the crypt to outside the walls. You want me to find Goetz and let him enter

Worms by that passage? Do not count on me to do
that.

THE BISHOP: Two hundred priests. Their lives are in
your hands.

[A *pause*.]

HEINRICH: By heavens, I understand now why you
laughed. It is a rich joke. Thank you, good Bishop,
thank you. The poor will massacre the priests, or
Goetz will massacre the poor. Two hundred priests
or twenty thousand men, you leave me a fair choice.
The question is to know how many men equal a
priest. And I have to decide; after all, I belong to the
Church. I will not pick it up. The priests will go
straight to heaven. [*The* BISHOP *dies*.] Unless they
die like you, with rage in their hearts. Well, it's over
for you. Farewell. Forgive him, O God, as I forgive
him. I will not pick it up. That's that. No! No! No!
[*He picks up the key*.]

THE PROPHET [*rising*]: O Lord, let Thy will be done!
                          The world is doomed! Doomed!
                          Thy will be done!

HEINRICH: O Lord, Thou hast curst Cain and the children of Cain: let Thy will be done. Thou hast permitted men to have their hearts devoured, their intentions corrupted, their actions diseased and stinking;
Thy will be done. O Lord, Thou hast decreed that
my lot here on earth should be that of a traitor. Thy
will be done. Thy will be done! Thy will be done!
[*He goes out*.]

THE PROPHET: Beat the carrion flesh!
                    Beat, beat, beat, beat!
                    God is here!

THE LIGHTS FADE

SCENE II

The outskirts of GOETZ'S *camp. Night. In the background, the town. An officer appears and gazes toward the town. Another officer enters immediately behind him.*

SECOND OFFICER: What are you doing?

FIRST OFFICER: Watching the town. One fine day, it may fly off. . . .

SECOND OFFICER: It won't fly away. We shan't have such luck. [*Turning abruptly.*] What's that?
[*Two men pass, carrying a body on a stretcher, covered with a cloth. They are silent. The* FIRST OFFICER *goes to the stretcher, lifts the cloth and lets it fall back into place.*]

FIRST OFFICER: To the river! At once!

SECOND OFFICER: Is he . . . ?

FIRST OFFICER: Black.
[*Pause. The two stretcher-bearers move on again. The invalid on the stretcher groans.*]

SECOND OFFICER: Wait.
[*They stop.*]

FIRST OFFICER: What now?

SECOND OFFICER: He's alive.

FIRST OFFICER: I don't want to know. To the river!

SECOND OFFICER [*to the stretcher-bearers*]: What regiment?

STRETCHER-BEARER: Blue Cross.

SECOND OFFICER: What! One of mine! About turn!

FIRST OFFICER: Are you mad? To the river!

SECOND OFFICER: I refuse to let my men be drowned like a litter of kittens.

[*The two officers stare at each other. The two stretcher-bearers exchange amused looks, put down the dying man, and wait.*]

FIRST OFFICER: Dead or living, if we keep him here he'll spread cholera throughout the entire army.

THIRD OFFICER [*entering*]: And if not cholera, then blind panic. Hurry! Throw him into the river!

STRETCHER-BEARER: He's groaning.

[*Pause. The* SECOND OFFICER *turns toward the stretcher-bearers furiously, draws his dagger and stabs the body.*]

SECOND OFFICER: That'll stop him groaning. Away!

[*The stretcher-bearers go out.*]

Three. Three since yesterday.

HERMANN [*entering*]: Four. One has just dropped down in the middle of the camp.

SECOND OFFICER: Did the men see him?

HERMANN: In the middle of the camp, I tell you.

THIRD OFFICER: If I were in command, we'd raise the siege this very night.

HERMANN: Agreed. But you're not in command.

FIRST OFFICER: We must speak to him.

HERMANN: Who do you suggest for the job? [*Silence. They look at each other.*] You will do as he commands.

SECOND OFFICER: Then it's all up with us. If the cholera spares us, we'll get our throats cut by our own men.

HERMANN: Unless he should be the one to die.

FIRST OFFICER: What of? Cholera?

HERMANN: Cholera, or other causes. [*Pause.*] I've been told the Archbishop wouldn't be displeased to hear of his death. [*Silence.*]

SECOND OFFICER: I could not do it.

FIRST OFFICER: Nor could I. He sickens me so much I should be disgusted at the mere idea of touching him.

HERMANN: We're not asking you to do anything—except hold your tongue and not interfere with others who are less squeamish.

[*Silence.* GOETZ *and* CATHERINE *enter.*]

GOETZ [*entering*]: Have you any news for me? None? Not even that the troops are hungry? Or that cholera is decimating my ranks? Nothing to ask me? Not even to raise the siege and so avoid catastrophe? [*They are silent.*]

CATHERINE: How they stare at you, my precious! These men don't like you at all. I shouldn't be surprised if one day we found you on your back with a big knife stuck into your paunch.

GOETZ: Well, do you love me?

CATHERINE: For God's sake, no!

GOETZ: Even so, you haven't killed me.

CATHERINE: Not that I haven't wanted to!

GOETZ: I know. You have such lovely dreams. But I have no fear. The moment I die, you'll be set upon by twenty thousand men. And twenty thousand are rather too many, even for you.

CATHERINE: Better twenty thousand than one you detest.

GOETZ: What I like in you is the horror you feel for me. [*To the officers*] When would you like me to raise the siege? Thursday? Sunday? Well, my friends, it won't be Tuesday, Thursday, or Sunday. I'm taking the city tonight.

SECOND OFFICER: Tonight?

GOETZ: Almost immediately. [*Looking toward the town*] There, in the distance, do you see a little blue light? Every night I watch it, and every night, at this moment, it goes out. Look! What did I tell you? I have seen it go out for the hundred and first and last time. Good night; we must kill the thing we love. And there are others . . . other lights that disappear. My heavens, there are men who go to bed early because they wish to rise early tomorrow. And there will be no tomorrow. A fine night, eh? Not very much light, but teeming with stars; soon, the moon will rise. Just the kind of night when nothing happens.

They have foreseen everything, accepted everything, even a massacre; but not for tonight. The sky is so pure that it fills them with confidence, this night belongs to them. [*Abruptly*] What power! God, this city is mine, and I give it to Thee. In a moment I will make it blaze to Thy glory! [*To the officers*] A priest has escaped from Worms and says he will help us enter the city. Captain Ulrich is questioning him.

THIRD OFFICER: Hm!

GOETZ: What did you say?

THIRD OFFICER: I'm on my guard against traitors.

GOETZ: So? Personally, I adore them.

[*An officer enters, pushing the priest who is guarded by a soldier.*]

HEINRICH [*falling on his knees in front of* GOETZ]: Torture me! Tear out my nails! Skin me alive!

[GOETZ *bursts out laughing.*]

GOETZ [*falling on his knees in front of the priest*]: Rip out my guts! Break me on the wheel! Tear me in pieces! [*He rises.*] Well, that's broken the ice. [*To the* CAPTAIN] Who is he?

CAPTAIN: Heinrich, a priest from Worms. The one who is supposed to deliver over the city to us.

GOETZ: Well?

CAPTAIN: He says he won't tell us any more.

GOETZ [*going up to* HEINRICH]: Why?

CAPTAIN: He says he has changed his mind.

THIRD OFFICER: Changed his mind! Holy Jesus! Smash his teeth! Break his back!

HEINRICH: Smash my teeth! Break my back!

GOETZ: What a lunatic! [*To* HEINRICH] Why did you want to deliver the town to us?

HEINRICH: To save the priests the people want to murder.

GOETZ: And why have you changed your mind?

HEINRICH: I have seen the faces of your mercenaries.

GOETZ: So what?

HEINRICH: They are eloquent.

GOETZ: What do they say?

HEINRICH: That I should precipitate a massacre by trying to prevent a few murders.

GOETZ: You must have seen other soldiers. And you knew they never look kindhearted.

HEINRICH: The ones here look much worse than others.

GOETZ: Pooh, pooh! All soldiers look alike. What did you expect to find here? Angels?

HEINRICH: Men. And I would have asked those men to spare their fellow men. They should have entered the city after having sworn to me to spare the lives of the inhabitants.

GOETZ: So, you would have taken my word?

HEINRICH: Your word? [*He looks at* GOETZ.] Are you Goetz?

GOETZ: Yes.

HEINRICH: I . . . I thought I could trust you.

GOETZ [*surprised*]: Trust my word? [*Pause.*] I give it to you. [HEINRICH *is silent.*] If you let us enter the city, I swear I will spare the lives of the inhabitants.

HEINRICH: You want me to believe you?

GOETZ: Wasn't that your intention?

HEINRICH: Yes. Before I had seen you.

GOETZ [*beginning to laugh*]: Yes, yes, I know. Those who see me rarely trust my word; I must look far too intelligent to keep it. But listen to me: take me at my word. Just to find out! Merely to find out . . . I'm a Christian, after all; if I swore to you on the Bible? Let us go through with the stupid game of blind trust. Isn't it your role as priest to use Good to tempt the wicked?

HEINRICH: Use Good to tempt you? You'd enjoy it far too much!

GOETZ: You understand me. [*He looks at* HEINRICH *with a smile.*] Leave us, all of you.

[*The officers and* CATHERINE *go out.*]

[GOETZ *speaks with a kind of tenderness.*] You are sweating! How you are suffering!

HEINRICH: Not enough! Others suffer, but not I. God has allowed me to be haunted by the suffering of others without ever feeling those sufferings myself. Why are you looking at me?

GOETZ [*still tenderly*]: In my day I had just such a hypocrite's pan. I am looking at you, but I'm sorry for myself. We belong to the same race.

HEINRICH: That's not true! You betrayed your own brother. I shall never betray my own people.

GOETZ: You'll betray them this very night.

HEINRICH: Neither this night nor ever.

[*Pause.*]

GOETZ [*in a detached voice*]: What will the people do to the priests? Hang them from the butchers' hooks?

HEINRICH [*with a cry*]: Be quiet! [*He recovers himself.*] Those are the horrors of war. I am only a humble priest, unable to prevent them.

GOETZ: Hypocrite! Tonight you have power of life and death over twenty thousand men.

HEINRICH: I refuse to accept that power. It comes from the Devil.

GOETZ: You refuse it, but you possess it all the same. [HEINRICH *tries to escape.*] Hello! What are you doing? If you run away, it means you have agreed.

[HEINRICH *returns, looks at* GOETZ *and begins to laugh.*]

HEINRICH: You're right. Whether I kill myself or run away, it makes no difference. They are only ways of holding my peace. I am chosen by God.

GOETZ: Say, rather, that you are trapped.

HEINRICH: It's the same thing; to be chosen by God is to be pushed into a corner by the finger of God. [*Pause.*] O Lord, why hast Thou chosen me?

GOETZ [*gently*]: This is the moment of your agony. I wanted to shorten it for you. Let me help you.

HEINRICH: Help me? You? When God is silent? [*Pause.*] Very well, I lied; I am not His chosen one. Why should I be? Who forced me to leave the city? Who

ordered me to come and find you? I elected myself.
When I came to ask your mercy for my brothers,
I was already sure you would refuse. It wasn't the
wickedness in your faces that made me change my
mind, it was their reality. I dreamed of doing Evil,
and when I saw you I understood I was going to do
it in fact. Do you know I hate the poor?

GOETZ: Yes, I know.

HEINRICH: Why do they turn away when I open my
arms? Why do they always suffer so much more than
I could ever suffer? O Lord, why hast Thou allowed
poor people to exist? Or else, why didst Thou not
make of me a monk? In a monastery, I should belong
only to Thee. But how can I belong to Thee alone
while there are men around me dying of hunger?
[*To* GOETZ] I came to deliver them all over to you,
and I hoped you would exterminate them and let me
forget they ever existed.

GOETZ: So?

HEINRICH: So I have changed my mind. You shall not
enter the city.

GOETZ: Supposing it were the will of God that you
should make us enter? Listen to me; if you hold your
tongue, the priests will die this very night, that's certain. But the people? Do you believe they will survive?
I shall not raise the siege; within a month, every
human being in Worms will have died of hunger. You
don't have to decide between their life or death, but
to choose for them between two kinds of death. Gut-
less coward—choose the swifter way. Do you know
what they'll gain by it? If they die tonight before they
kill the priests, they will keep their hands clean;
everyone will meet again in heaven. If you choose the
second way, after the pitiful weeks you leave them,
you'll send them, all besmeared with blood, to the
depths of Hell. Come now, priest: it was the Devil
who prompted you to spare their earthly lives merely

to give them time to damn their souls forever. [*Pause.*] Tell me how to get into the city.

HEINRICH: You are nonexistent.

GOETZ: What?

HEINRICH: You do not exist. Your words are dead before they reach my ears; your face is not like those faces a man can meet in daylight. I know everything you will say, I can foresee all your movements. You are my creature, and your thoughts come only at my bidding. I am dreaming, the world is dead, and the very air is full of sleep.

GOETZ: In that case, I, too, am dreaming. I can see your future so clearly, your present bores me. All we need to know now is which one of the two is living in the dream of the other.

HEINRICH: I never left the city! I never left it! We are actors playing before a painted backdrop. Come along, fine actor, let's have your comedy. Do you know your part well? Mine is to say no. No! No! No! No! You say nothing? This is no more than an ordinary temptation, without much truth about it. What should I be doing in Goetz's camp? [*He gestures toward the city.*] If only those lights could extinguish themselves! What is the town doing over there, since I am within its walls! [*Pause.*] A temptation exists, but I do not know where it can be. [*To* GOETZ] What I do know clearly is that I am going to see the Devil: when he is preparing to pull faces at me, the entertainment begins with a weird fantasy.

GOETZ: Have you seen the Devil before?

HEINRICH: More often than you have seen your own mother.

GOETZ: Do I look like him?

HEINRICH: You, my poor man? You are the jester.

GOETZ: What jester?

HEINRICH: There is always a jester. His role is to contradict me. [*Pause.*] I have won.

GOETZ: What?

HEINRICH: I have won. The last light has gone out; the devilish phantom of Worms has disappeared. Well, now! You will disappear in your turn, and this ridiculous temptation will come to an end. Darkness, darkness and night over the whole world. What peace.

GOETZ: Go on, priest, go on. I remember everything you are going to say. A year ago . . . Oh yes, brother mine, I remember. How you would like to bring all that darkness into your head! How often I have desired it myself!

HEINRICH [*murmuring*]: Where shall I be when I wake up?

GOETZ [*laughing suddenly*]: You are awake, you impostor, and you know it. Everything is real. Look at me, touch me, I am flesh and blood. Look, the moon is rising, your devilish city emerges from the shadows; look at the town. Is it a mirage? Come now! It is real stone, those are real ramparts, it is a real town with real inhabitants. And you—you are a real traitor.

HEINRICH: A man is a traitor only when he betrays. You can do what you like, I shall never betray the city.

GOETZ: A man betrays when he is a traitor; you will betray the city. Come now, priest, you are a traitor *already*; two paths lie before you, and you pretend you can follow both at the same time. So you are playing a double game; you are thinking in two languages. The suffering of the poor, you call that a test in Church Latin, and in common German you translate it as iniquity. What more can happen to you if you help me enter the city? You will become the traitor you already are, that is all. A traitor who betrays is a traitor who accepts himself.

HEINRICH: How do you know this if your words aren't dedicated by my will?

GOETZ: Because I am a traitor. [*Pause.*] I have already

covered the road you still have to take, and yet look
at me: don't I seem to be flourishing?

HEINRICH: You are flourishing because you have followed your nature. All bastards betray, it's a well-
known fact. But I am not a bastard.

GOETZ [*hesitates whether to strike him, then controls
himself*]: Usually those who call me bastard never
do it twice.

HEINRICH: Bastard!

GOETZ: Priest! Priest, be serious. Don't force me to cut
off your ears; it won't help in the least because I shall
leave you your tongue. [*Abruptly, he kisses* HEIN-
RICH.] Hail, little brother! Welcome to bastardy!
You, too, are a bastard! To engender you, the clergy
coupled with misery; what joyless fornication. [*Pause.*]
Naturally, bastards betray, what else should they do?
I have been two people all my life; my mother gave
herself to a no-account, and I am composed of two
halves which do not fit together; each of those halves
shrinks in horror from the other. Do you believe you
are better served? A half-priest added to a half-peas-
ant, that doesn't add up to a whole man. We *are*
nothing and we *have* nothing. Every infant born in
wedlock can inherit the earth without paying. But
not you, and not I. Since the day of my birth, I have
only seen the world through the keyhole; it's a fine
little egg, neatly packed, where everyone fits the place
God has assigned to him. But I give you my word
we are not inside that world. We are outcasts! Reject this world that rejects you. Turn to Evil; you
will see how lighthearted you will feel. [*An* OFFICER
enters.] What do you want?

THE OFFICER: An envoy from the Archbishop is here.

GOETZ: Send him in.

THE OFFICER: He brings news; the enemy leaves on the
battlefield seven thousand dead and is in full flight.

GOETZ: What about my brother? [*The* OFFICER *tries
to whisper in his ear.*] Keep your distance. Speak out.

THE OFFICER: Conrad is dead.

[*From this moment,* HEINRICH *watches* GOETZ *closely.*]

GOETZ: Good. Has his body been found?

THE OFFICER: Yes.

GOETZ: In what condition? Answer me!

THE OFFICER: Disfigured.

GOETZ: A sword-cut?

THE OFFICER: Wolves . . .

GOETZ: Wolves? Are there wolves?

THE OFFICER: The forest of Arnheim . . .

GOETZ: Very well. When I have settled this matter, I shall march against Arnheim with the entire army. I will skin alive every wolf in the forest of Arnheim. . . . Get out. [*The* OFFICER *goes. Pause.*] Dead without absolution; the wolves have eaten his face, but as you see, I am still smiling.

HEINRICH [*softly*]: Why did you betray him?

GOETZ: Because I like things to be clear-cut. Priest, I am a self-made man. I was a bastard by birth, but the fair title of fratricide I owe to no one but myself. [*Pause.*] It belongs to me now, to me alone.

HEINRICH: What belongs to you?

GOETZ: The house of Heidenstamm. The Heiden-stamms are finished, liquidated. I contain them all in myself, from Alberic the founder of the family, down to Conrad, the last male heir of the line. Look well at me, priest, I am a family mausoleum. Why are you laughing?

HEINRICH: I thought I should be the only one to see the Devil tonight, and now I know there will be two of us.

GOETZ: I don't give a damn for the Devil! He receives our souls, but it isn't he who condemns them. I refuse to deal with anyone but God. Monsters and saints exist only through God. God sees me, priest, He knows I killed my brother, and His heart bleeds. Yes indeed, O Lord, I killed him. And what canst Thou

do against me? I have committed the worst of crimes,
and the God of justice is powerless to punish me; He
damned me more than fifteen years ago. There—
enough for one day. This is a holiday. I'm going to
have a drink.

HEINRICH [*approaching him*]: Here. [*He takes a key
out of his pocket and holds it out.*]

GOETZ: What is this?

HEINRICH: A key.

GOETZ: What key?

HEINRICH: The key to Worms.

GOETZ: Enough for one day, I said. A brother, for the
Lord's sake! You don't bury a brother every day; I
have the right to give myself a holiday until tomorrow.

HEINRICH [*bearing down on him*]: Coward!

GOETZ [*stopping*]: If I take this key, I shall burn everything.

HEINRICH: At the bottom of this ravine, there is a white
boulder. At its base, hidden among brushwood, there
is an opening. Follow the passage underground, and
you will find a door you can open with this.

GOETZ: How they'll love you, the poor people! How
they're going to bless you!

HEINRICH: That's no concern of mine any more. I am
lost, by my own choice. But I leave my poor in your
hands! Now, bastard, it is you who must choose.

GOETZ: You said just now you had only to see my
face. . . .

HEINRICH: I had not seen it clearly enough.

GOETZ: And what do you see in it at this moment?

HEINRICH: That you hate yourself.

GOETZ: It's true, but don't put your trust in that! I have
hated myself for fifteen years. So what? Don't you
understand that Evil is my reason for living? Give
me that key. [*He takes it.*] Well, priest, you will
have lied to yourself to the very end. You thought you

had found a way of disguising your treason from yourself. But once and for all you have now betrayed.
You have betrayed Conrad.

HEINRICH: Conrad?

GOETZ: Don't worry: you resemble me so closely that
I mistook you for myself. [*He goes.*]

CURTAIN

SCENE III

GOETZ's *tent. Through the opening we can see the town
in the distance, bathed in moonlight.* HERMANN *enters
and tries to hide under the camp bed. His head and
body disappear, but we can still see his enormous behind.* CATHERINE *enters, goes to him and gives him a
kick. He rises, terrified. She springs away from him,
laughing.*

HERMANN: If you call out . . .

CATHERINE: If I call out, you'll be discovered, and
Goetz will have you hanged. Much better talk this
over. What are you going to do to him?

HERMANN: What you should have done, slut, a long
time ago, if you had had any blood in your veins.
Get out of here! And thank God that a man has
taken on your job for you. D'you hear?

CATHERINE: What will become of me, if he dies? The
whole camp will fall upon me.

HERMANN: We'll help you escape.

CATHERINE: Will you give me some money?

HERMANN: A little.

CATHERINE: Give me my dowry and I'll enter a convent.

HERMANN [*laughing*]: A convent—you! If you want to
live in a community, why not enter a brothel; with
the talent you have between your thighs, you'd earn

a fortune in no time. Make up your mind. I only
ask you to hold your tongue.

CATHERINE: My silence—you can count on that; at all
events, I shan't betray you. When it comes to cutting
his throat . . . that depends.

HERMANN: Depends on what?

CATHERINE: We don't share the same interests, captain.
A man's honor can be redeemed at the point of a
knife. But a woman—he has made me a whore, and
I am much more difficult to redeem. [*Pause.*] Tonight the city will be taken. The war will be over,
everyone can go home. When he arrives, in a few
minutes, I'll ask him what he intends to do with me.
If he keeps me . . .

HERMANN: Goetz keep you? You're mad. What do you
expect him to do with you?

CATHERINE: If he keeps me you shan't touch him.

HERMANN: And if he sends you away?

CATHERINE: Then he is yours. If I cry out: "You asked
for it," come out of hiding, and he'll be at your mercy.

HERMANN: I don't want my whole plan to depend on a
question of fornication.

CATHERINE [*who for a moment or two has been looking
outside*]: Then fall on your knees and ask him for
mercy. Here he is.

[HERMANN *runs to hide himself.* CATHERINE *begins to
laugh.*]

GOETZ [*entering*]: Why are you laughing?

CATHERINE: I was laughing at my dreams. I saw you
lying dead with a knife in your back. [*Pause.*] So,
he's talked?

GOETZ: Who?

CATHERINE: The priest.

GOETZ: What priest? Oh, yes! Yes, of course.

CATHERINE: And you'll do it tonight?

GOETZ: What's it to do with you? Take off my boots.
[*She takes them off.*] Conrad is dead.

CATHERINE: I know. Everyone in the camp knows.

GOETZ: Give me a drink. We must celebrate. [*She pours his wine.*] Drink, too.

CATHERINE: I don't want to.

GOETZ: For God's sake, drink! This is a holiday.

CATHERINE: A fine holiday that begins with a massacre and ends with a holocaust.

GOETZ: The finest holiday in my life. Tomorrow, I leave for my estates.

CATHERINE [*surprised*]: So soon?

GOETZ: So soon! For thirty years I have dreamed of this moment. I shall not wait a single extra day. [CATHERINE *seems upset.*] Don't you feel well?

CATHERINE [*pulling herself together*]: It was hearing you talk of *your* estates while Conrad's body is still warm.

GOETZ: They have been mine in secret for thirty years. [*He raises his glass.*] I drink to my lands and my castle. Drink with me. [*She raises her glass in silence.*] Say: to your estates!

CATHERINE: No.

GOETZ: Why not, bitch?

CATHERINE: Because they are not yours. Will you cease to be a bastard because you assassinated your brother? [GOETZ *begins to laugh, aims a blow at her; she dodges, and falls back on the bed, laughing.*] Estates pass from father to son by inheritance.

GOETZ: I'd have to be paid a good price before I'd accept them that way. Nothing belongs to me except what I take. Come, drink the toast or I'll lose my temper.

CATHERINE: To your estates! To your castle!

GOETZ: And may there be legions of outraged phantoms on the corridors at night.

CATHERINE: That's true, mountebank. What would you do without an audience? I drink to your phantoms. [*Pause.*] So, my sweetheart, nothing belongs to you except what you take by force?

GOETZ: Nothing.

CATHERINE: But, apart from your manors and your domains, you possess a priceless treasure, though you don't seem aware of it.

GOETZ: What treasure?

CATHERINE: Me, my darling, me. Didn't you take me by force? [*Pause.*] What are you going to do with me? Tell me.

GOETZ: [*looking at her reflectively*]: I'll take you with me.

CATHERINE: You will? Why? [*She takes a hesitating step.*] To set a harlot at the head of a noble house?

GOETZ: To set a harlot in the bed of my noble mother.

CATHERINE: And if I refused? If I didn't want to go with you?

GOETZ: I sincerely hope you don't want to come.

CATHERINE: Ah! You'll carry me away by force. That's better. I should have been ashamed to follow you of my own free will. [*Pause.*] Why do you always want to force what might perhaps be given you with good grace?

GOETZ: To make sure I should be given it with bad grace. [*He goes to her.*] Look at me, Catherine. What are you hiding?

CATHERINE [*quickly*]: Nothing!

GOETZ: For some time now I've seen a change in you. You still thoroughly hate me, don't you?

CATHERINE: Yes, indeed, thoroughly!

GOETZ: You still dream that somebody will kill me?

CATHERINE: Every night.

GOETZ: You aren't forgetting it was I who ruined and defiled you?

CATHERINE: I can never forget.

GOETZ: And you submit to my caresses with repugnance?

CATHERINE: They make me shudder.

GOETZ: Good. If you ever get the idea of enjoying yourself in my arms, I shall drive you away immediately.

CATHERINE: But . . .

GOETZ: I shall accept nothing ever again, not even the favors of a woman.

CATHERINE: Why?

GOETZ: Because I have been given enough. For twenty years, everything has been given to me most graciously, down to the very air I breathe; a bastard has to kiss the hand that feeds him. Oh! How I am going to give back in my turn! How generous I am going to be!

FRANTZ [*entering*]: The Envoy of His Excellency is here.

GOETZ: Send him in.

THE BANKER [*entering*]: I am Foucre.

GOETZ: I am Goetz. This is Catherine.

THE BANKER: Delighted to meet so great a captain.

GOETZ: And I to salute so rich a banker.

THE BANKER: I am the bearer of three excellent pieces of news.

GOETZ: The Archbishop is victorious, my brother is dead, his lands and fortune belong to me. Isn't that it?

THE BANKER: Exactly. And so, I . . .

GOETZ: Let us celebrate. D'you want a drink?

THE BANKER: Unfortunately, my stomach won't take wine. I . . .

GOETZ: Do you want this handsome slut? She is yours.

THE BANKER: I shouldn't know what to do with her. I am too old.

GOETZ: Poor Catherine, he doesn't want you. [*To the* BANKER] Do you prefer young boys? You'll find one in your tent this evening.

THE BANKER: No, no! No boys! Most definitely, no boys! I . . .

GOETZ: What d'you say to a hefty foot-soldier with a pike? I have a pikeman who is six feet tall, covered with hair . . . a real gorilla.

THE BANKER: No! No! Most certainly not . . .

GOETZ: In that case, we'd better give you glory. [*He*

shouts.] Frantz! [FRANTZ *appears.*] Frantz, take this
gentleman for a tour of the camp, and see to it that
the soldiers shout, "Long live the banker!" tossing
their caps in the air. [FRANTZ *goes out.*]

THE BANKER: I am much obliged, but I wanted to talk
to you immediately—in private.

GOETZ [*surprised*]: What have you been doing ever
since you came in? [*Nodding towards* CATHERINE]
Oh! That one . . . She's a domestic animal; speak
without fear.

THE BANKER: His Grace has always been most peaceful,
and you know your late brother was responsible for
beginning this war. . . .

GOETZ: My brother! [*Violently*] If that old idiot
hadn't driven him to extremes . . .

THE BANKER: Sir, sir . . .

GOETZ: Yes. Forget what I just said, but you'll oblige
me by leaving my brother out of this. After all, I am
wearing his mourning.

THE BANKER: Therefore, His Grace has decided to mark
the return of peace by measures of exceptional clemency.

GOETZ: Bravo! Is he opening the prisons?

THE BANKER: The prisons? Good heavens, no!

GOETZ: Does he wish me to remit the punishments of
any soldiers I myself have sentenced?

THE BANKER: He desires it, certainly. But the amnesty
he envisages has a much more general character. He
wants to extend it to his subjects in Worms.

GOETZ: Ah! Ah!

THE BANKER: He has decided not to punish them for
a momentary deflection.

GOETZ: It seems an excellent idea.

THE BANKER: Can we be in agreement so soon?

GOETZ: Entirely in agreement. [*The* BANKER *rubs his
hands.*]

THE BANKER: Well, well, that's perfect; you are a reason-
able man. When are you thinking of lifting the siege?

GOETZ: Tomorrow it will be all over.

THE BANKER: Tomorrow—that seems a little too soon. His Grace desires to enter into negotiations with the besieged. If your army remains under their walls a few days longer, the ambassadors will find their task facilitated.

GOETZ: I see. And who is going to negotiate?

THE BANKER: I am.

GOETZ: When?

THE BANKER: Tomorrow.

GOETZ: Impossible.

THE BANKER: Why?

GOETZ: Catherine! Shall we tell him?

CATHERINE: Of course, my precious.

GOETZ: Then you tell him. I dare not, it will cause him too much pain.

CATHERINE: Tomorrow, Banker, all those people will be dead.

THE BANKER: Dead?

GOETZ: All of them.

THE BANKER: All dead?

GOETZ: All dead. This very night. You see this key? It opens the city. One hour from now, the massacre begins.

THE BANKER: Of everyone? Including the rich?

GOETZ: Including the rich.

THE BANKER: But you approved the Archbishop's clemency. . . .

GOETZ: I still approve it. He has been sinned against, and he is a priest; two reasons to forgive the offenders. But why should I forgive them? The inhabitants of Worms haven't sinned against me. No, no, I am a soldier, therefore I must do a soldier's work. I will kill them according to my office, and the Archbishop will forgive them according to his own.

[*Pause. Then the* BANKER *begins to laugh.* CATHERINE, *then* GOETZ, *begin to laugh, too.*]

THE BANKER [*laughing*]: I see you like to joke.

GOETZ [*laughing*]: It's the only thing I do like.

CATHERINE: He's very witty, isn't he?

THE BANKER: Most witty. He's managing this business excellently.

GOETZ: What business?

THE BANKER: For thirty years I have run my business on one principle: that self-interest directs the world. When they come to see me, men justify their behavior by citing the most exalted motives. I listen to them absent-mindedly, and I say to myself—find where their interest lies.

GOETZ: And when you have found it?

THE BANKER: Then we talk.

GOETZ: Have you found mine?

THE BANKER: Oh, really!

GOETZ: What is it?

THE BANKER: Gently, gently. You belong to a category which is very difficult to handle. With a man like you, one has to proceed one step at a time.

GOETZ: What category?

THE BANKER: You are an idealist.

GOETZ: What is that?

THE BANKER: I divide men into three categories: those who have a great deal of money, those who have none at all, and those who have only a little. The first want to keep what they have; their interest is to maintain order. The second want to take what they have not; their interest is to destroy the present order and establish another which would be profitable to them. Both of them are realists, men with whom one can come to an understanding. The third category of men want to overturn our social order to take what they have not, while at the same time making quite sure no one takes away what they already have. Therefore, they conserve in fact what they destroy in desire, or else, they destroy in fact what they are only pretending to conserve. Those people are idealists.

GOETZ: What about the poor? How are we to cure them?

THE BANKER: By transferring them to another social level. If you were to make them rich, they would defend the established order.

GOETZ: Then you should make me rich. What do you offer?

THE BANKER: Conrad's possessions.

GOETZ: You've already given them to me.

THE BANKER: Exactly. Only, remember you owe them to the bounty of His Grace, the Archbishop.

GOETZ: Believe me, I shall not forget it. What else?

THE BANKER: Your brother was in debt.

GOETZ: The poor fellow! [*He crosses himself, and sobs nervously.*]

THE BANKER: What's the matter?

GOETZ: Very little; a touch of family feeling. So, you say he was in debt.

THE BANKER: We could pay those debts for you.

GOETZ: That is not to my interest because I had no intention of acknowledging them. You should address yourself to his creditors.

THE BANKER: An annual income of one thousand ducats?

GOETZ: And my soldiers? Supposing they refuse to go away empty-handed?

THE BANKER: Another thousand to distribute among them. Is it enough?

GOETZ: Far too much.

THE BANKER: Then we are agreed?

GOETZ: No.

THE BANKER: Two thousand ducats annually? Three thousand? I can go no higher.

GOETZ: Who is asking you to?

THE BANKER: Then what do you want?

GOETZ: To take and destroy the city.

THE BANKER: I don't mind if you take it, but good heavens, why should you want to destroy it?

GOETZ: Because everyone wants me to spare it.

THE BANKER [*stunned*]: I must have been wrong. . . .

GOETZ: Indeed, yes! You couldn't discover my interest!
Come now, what can it be? Think! Think hard! But
hurry; you must find it within the next hour; if between now and then you haven't discovered what
strings make the marionette move, I shall have you
dragged through the streets, and you will see the fires
of destruction lighted one after the other.

THE BANKER: You are betraying the Archbishop's trust.

GOETZ: Betrayal? Trust? You are all the same, you
realists; when you don't know what else to say, you
have to borrow the language of idealists.

THE BANKER: If you destroy the city, you will never
possess your brother's lands.

GOETZ: Keep them! My interest, banker, was to have
them and to live there. But I'm not so sure men
act only out of self-interest. Keep the lands, I tell you,
and let His Grace stuff them up his arse. I sacrificed
my brother to the Archbishop, and now you're expecting me to spare twenty thousand lives? I shall
offer up the inhabitants of Worms to the spirit of
Conrad; they will be roasted alive in his honor. As
for the domaine of Heidenstamm, let the Archbishop
go into retirement there, if he likes, and spend the
rest of his days studying agriculture; he will have need
to, for I intend to ruin him this very night. [*Pause.*]
Frantz! [FRANTZ *appears.*] Take this venerable realist,
see that all honors are shown him, and when he is in
his tent, make sure that his hands and feet are
securely tied.

THE BANKER: No! No, no, no!

GOETZ: What's the matter?

THE BANKER: I suffer from atrocious rheumatism. Your
cords will kill me. Shall I give you my word of honor
not to leave my tent?

GOETZ: Your word of honor? It's to your interest to
give it, but quite soon it will be to your interest not

to keep it. Take him away, Frantz, and see that the knots are pulled tight.

[FRANTZ *and the* BANKER *go out. Immediately there are cries of* "Hurrah for the banker," *at first near by, then dying away in the distance.*]

GOETZ: Hurrah for the banker! [*He burst out laughing.*] Farewell to the estates! Farewell the fields and rivers! Farewell to the castle!

CATHERINE [*laughing*]: Farewell the estates! Farewell to the castle! Farewell to the family portraits!

GOETZ: Don't regret a thing! We would have been bored to death there.

CATHERINE: Are you very unhappy?

GOETZ: Hold your tongue! [*Pause.*] To do Evil must in the long run harm everyone. Including the one who sets it in motion.

CATHERINE [*timidly*]: Supposing you didn't take the city?

GOETZ: If I don't take it, you'll be mistress of a castle.

CATHERINE: I wasn't thinking of that.

GOETZ: Of course not. You needn't worry; I shall take it.

CATHERINE: But why?

GOETZ: Because it is wrong.

CATHERINE: Why should you want to do wrong?

GOETZ: Because Good has already been done.

CATHERINE: By whom?

GOETZ: By God the Father. Me, I invent. [*He calls.*] Hello, there! Captain Schoene. At once.

[GOETZ *stands at the entrance to the tent, and looks out into the night.*]

CATHERINE: What are you looking at?

GOETZ: The city. [*Pause.*] I was wondering if that night there was also a moon. . . .

CATHERINE: When? Where? . . .

GOETZ: Last year, when I was about to take Halle. It was a night very like this one. I stood at the entrance to my tent and watched the belfry which showed

above the ramparts. In the morning we took the
place by assault. [*He comes back to her.*] In any
case, I'll get out of here before it begins to stink.
Saddle and spurs and away.

CATHERINE: You . . . you're going away?

GOETZ: Tomorrow, before midday, without a word to
anyone.

CATHERINE: And me?

GOETZ: You? Stop your nose and pray that the wind
doesn't blow from that quarter. [*The* CAPTAIN *enters.*] Two thousand men under arms: the Wolfmar
and Ulrich regiments. Have them ready to follow
me in half an hour. The rest of the army stand to
arms. Put out all lights, and make your preparations
in silence. [*The* CAPTAIN *goes out. Until the end of
the act, there are muffled sounds of preparation.*] So
then, sweetheart, you will never be mistress of a
castle.

CATHERINE: I'm afraid not.

GOETZ: Very disappointed?

CATHERINE: I never believed it would happen.

GOETZ: Why not?

CATHERINE: Because I know you.

GOETZ [*violently*]: You know me? [*He stops short and
laughs.*] After all, I suppose I am predictable too.
[*Pause.*] You must have your own ideas about how
to manage me; you watch me, you look at me. . . .

CATHERINE: A cat can look at a king.

GOETZ: Yes, but the cat sees the king with the head of
a cat. What do you see me as? A cat? A mackerel?
A cod? [*He looks at her.*] Come on the bed.

CATHERINE: No.

GOETZ: I said come. I want to make love.

CATHERINE: I've never seen you so pressing. [*He takes
her by the shoulders.*] Nor so pressed. What's the
matter?

GOETZ: The fish-eyed, fornicating Goetz is signaling to

me. He and I want to get together. Tension stirs up desire.

CATHERINE: You feel tense?

GOETZ: Yes. [*He goes to sit on the bed, turning his back on the hidden officer.*] Come here!

[CATHERINE *goes over to him, pulls him up roughly, and sits down in his place.*]

CATHERINE: I'm here, yes, and I belong to you. But first of all, tell me what is going to become of me?

GOETZ: When?

CATHERINE: After tomorrow.

GOETZ: How should I know? Whatever you like.

CATHERINE: In other words, I am to become a whore.

GOETZ: I'd say that's the best solution, wouldn't you?

CATHERINE: Supposing I don't want that?

GOETZ: Find some poor specimen to marry you.

CATHERINE: What will you do—after tomorrow?

GOETZ: Stick to my soldiering. They tell me the Hussites are restless. I'll go and give them a few knocks.

CATHERINE: Take me with you.

GOETZ: What for?

CATHERINE: There will be times when you'll need a woman; when the moon will be shining, and you'll have to take a city and you'll be tense, and you'll feel like making love.

GOETZ: All woman are alike. My men will bring them to me by the dozens if the urge should ever take me.

CATHERINE [*abruptly*]: I won't have it!

GOETZ: You won't have what?

CATHERINE: I can be twenty women, a hundred, if you like, all women. Let me go with you. I'll ride pillion. I weigh very little, your horse will never feel me. I want to be your brothel! [*She presses herself to him.*]

GOETZ: What's come over you? [*Pause. He looks at her. Then speaks bruskly.*] Get out. I'm ashamed for you.

CATHERINE [*imploringly*]: Goetz!

GOETZ: I won't allow you to look at me like that. You

must be completely rotten to dare love me after all
I have done to you.

CATHERINE [*crying out*]: I don't love you! I swear I
    don't love you! Even if I did, you'd never know of my
    love! What difference does it make if someone loves
    you, provided they don't tell you!

GOETZ: What business have I to be loved? If you loved
    me, you'd be the one who had all the pleasure. Get
    out of here, you bitch! I won't let anyone profit at
    my expense.

CATHERINE [*crying out*]: Goetz! Goetz! Don't send me
    away! I have nobody else in the world.

    [GOETZ *tries to throw her out of the tent. She clings
    to his hands.*]

GOETZ: Will you get out of here!

CATHERINE: You asked for it! Goetz! You asked for it!
    [HERMANN *rushes out of hiding and springs forward,
    his dagger raised.*]
    Look behind you! Ah!

GOETZ [*turning round and catching* HERMANN's *wrist*]:
    Frantz! [*Two soldiers enter. He laughs.*] At any rate,
    I have managed to drive someone to desperation.

HERMANN [*to* CATHERINE]: Rotten bitch! Filthy traitor!

GOETZ [*to* CATHERINE]: You knew about this? I like that
    better; I like that very much better. [*He strokes her
    chin.*] Take him away. . . . I'll decide what to do
    with him later.

    [*The soldiers go out, taking* HERMANN. *Pause.*]

CATHERINE: What will you do to him?

GOETZ: I can never be angry with anyone who tries to
    kill me. I understand their point of view too well.
    I'll have him broached like the big cask of wine
    that he is—that's all.

CATHERINE: And what will you do to me?

GOETZ: Yes. I suppose I'll have to punish you, too.

CATHERINE: There's no real obligation.

GOETZ: Oh, yes, there is. [*Pause.*] A great many of my
    soldiers feel thirsty when they see you. I'll make

them a present of you. Afterward, if you're still alive, we'll choose a nice, one-eyed, pock-marked rascal, and the priest of Worms can marry you to him.

CATHERINE: I don't believe you.

GOETZ: No?

CATHERINE: No. You're not . . . You'll never do it. I'm quite sure! I'm absolutely sure!

GOETZ: I'll never do it? [*He calls.*] Frantz! Frantz! [FRANTZ *appears with two soldiers.*] Take away the bride, Frantz!

FRANTZ: What bride?

GOETZ: Catherine. You'll marry her first to everyone, with tremendous pomp. Afterward . . . [NASTI *enters, goes to* GOETZ *and strikes him on the ear.*] Hey, peasant, what are you doing?

NASTI: I struck you on the ear.

GOETZ: I felt it. [*Holding him*] Who are you?

NASTI: The baker, Nasti.

GOETZ [*to the* SOLDIERS]: Is this Nasti?

THE SOLDIERS: Yes. That's him.

GOETZ: A fine prize, by God.

NASTI: I am not your prize. I surrendered myself.

GOETZ: Just as you like; it comes to the same thing. God is overwhelming me with presents today. [*He looks at* NASTI.] So this is the famous Nasti, lord of every beggar in Germany. You are exactly as I imagined you: as depressing as virtue.

NASTI: I am not virtuous; but our sons will be if we shed enough blood to give them the right to become so.

GOETZ: I see. You are a prophet.

NASTI: In common with all men.

GOETZ: Indeed? Then I, too, am a prophet?

NASTI: All words are God's witness; all words reveal all on all things.

GOETZ: The devil! I'll have to be careful what I say.

NASTI: To what end? You cannot prevent yourself from revealing everything.

GOETZ: I see. Very well, answer my questions and try not to tell me quite everything, or we'll never come to the end. So, you are Nasti, prophet and baker.

NASTI: I am.

GOETZ: I heard you were in Worms.

NASTI: I escaped.

GOETZ: This evening?

NASTI: Yes.

GOETZ: To talk to me?

NASTI: To find reinforcements and attack you in the rear.

GOETZ: Excellent idea. What made you change your mind?

NASTI: As I was crossing the camp, I learned that a traitor had betrayed the city.

GOETZ: You must have had a trying moment?

NASTI: Yes. Very.

GOETZ: So then?

NASTI: I was sitting on a rock behind your tent. I saw the tent light up and shadows move. At that instant, I received an order to go to you and speak to you.

GOETZ: Who gave you that order?

NASTI: Who do you suppose it could be?

GOETZ: Who indeed? Happy man: you receive your orders, and you know who has given them to you. Curiously enough, I have my orders, too—to take and burn Worms. But I have no idea who commanded me. [*Pause.*] Was it God who commanded you to strike me over the ear?

NASTI: Yes.

GOETZ: Why?

NASTI: I don't know. Perhaps to loosen the wax which prevents you from hearing.

GOETZ: You have forfeited your own head in consequence. Did God warn you of that?

NASTI: God had no need to warn me. I have always known how I should end.

GOETZ: Of course—you're a prophet. I had forgotten.

NASTI: I don't need to be a prophet; men like me have only two ways to die. Those who are resigned die of hunger. Those who are not resigned die by hanging. At the age of twelve you already know whether you are resigned or not.

GOETZ: Fine. Well, now, get down on your knees.

NASTI: What for?

GOETZ: To beg for mercy, I suppose. Didn't God command you to do that? [FRANTZ *puts on* GOETZ's *boots.*]

NASTI: No. You have no mercy, and God has none either. Why should I ask for your mercy when, by morning, I shall have no mercy for anyone?

GOETZ [*rising*]: Then what the hell did you come here for?

NASTI: To open your eyes, my brother.

GOETZ: Oh, night of wonders! All is in motion, God walks upon earth, my tent is a heaven filled with shooting stars, and here is the fairest of all, Nasti, the prophet from the bakehouse, sent here to open my eyes. Who would have believed that heaven and earth would make so much ado for one town of twenty thousand inhabitants? By the way, baker, who assures you that you aren't a victim of the Devil?

NASTI: When the sun dazzles your eyes, who proves to you that it isn't night?

GOETZ: At night, when you dream of the sun, who proves to you that it isn't light? Supposing I had seen God, too? Eh? Ah! It would be sunlight against sunlight. [*Pause.*] I hold you all in my hands, all of you: this whore who wanted to kill me, the envoy of the Archbishop, and you, the king of the ragamuffins. God's finger has revealed the conspiracy, the guilty are unmasked; better still, it was one of God's ministers who brought me the keys of the city with His compliments.

NASTI [*in a changed voice, imperative and brusk*]: One of God's ministers? Which one?

GOETZ: What do you care, since you are about to die? Come now, admit that God is on my side.

NASTI: On your side? No. You are not a man of God. At the very most, His hornet.

GOETZ: What do you know about it?

NASTI: Men of God destroy or construct. You conserve.

GOETZ: I?

NASTI: You bring about disorder. And disorder is the best servant of established power. You weakened the entire order of chivalry the day you betrayed Conrad, and you'll be weakening the burghers the day you destroy Worms. Who will profit by your action? The rulers. You serve the rulers, Goetz, and you will serve them whatever you do; all destruction brings confusion; weakens the weak, enriches the rich, increases the power of the powerful.

GOETZ: Therefore, I am doing the opposite of what I intend? [*Ironically*] Happily, God has sent you to enlighten me. What do you propose?

NASTI: A new alliance.

GOETZ: Oh! A new betrayal? Isn't that charming. At all events, I am used to it. It won't be much change for me. But if I must not ally myself with the burghers, the knights, or the princes, I don't quite see whom I am to join with.

NASTI: Take the city, massacre the rich and the priests, give everything to the poor, raise an army of peasants and drive out the Archbishop. Tomorrow the whole country will march behind you.

GOETZ [*amazed*]: You expect me to join the poor?

NASTI: With the people, yes! With the people from the city, and the peasants from the fields.

GOETZ: What an extraordinary idea!

NASTI: They are your natural allies. If you want to destroy in good earnest, raze the palaces and cathedrals erected by the power of Satan, shatter the obscene pagan statues, burn the thousands of books which spread diabolic knowledge, suppress gold and silver, come to us, be one of us. Without us, you are turning in a circle, you hurt no one but yourself. With us, you will become the scourge of God.

GOETZ: What will you do to the burghers?

NASTI: Take their possessions from them, to cover the naked and feed the hungry.

GOETZ: The priests?

NASTI: Send them back to Rome.

GOETZ: And the nobles?

NASTI: Cut off their heads.

GOETZ: And when we have driven out the Archbishop?

NASTI: It will be time to build the city of God.

GOETZ: On what foundations?

NASTI: All men are brothers and equals. All are in God and God is in all; the Holy Ghost speaks through all mouths, all men are priests and prophets, all men can baptize, conduct marriages, interpret God's will, and remit sins; all men live openly on earth in the sight of men, and solitarily within their souls in the sight of God.

GOETZ: It won't be easy to laugh in your city.

NASTI: Can you laugh at what you love? Our one law will be the law of Love.

GOETZ: And what shall I be within your city?

NASTI: The equal of all men.

GOETZ: Supposing I don't want to be your equal?

NASTI: The equal of all men or the lackey of princes. Choose.

GOETZ: Your proposition is honest, baker. Only, you see, the people bore me to death; they hate everything I enjoy.

NASTI: What do you enjoy?

GOETZ: Everything you want to abolish: statues, luxury, war.

NASTI: The moon is not yours, my poor misguided friend, and you've been fighting all your life so that the nobles may enjoy it.

GOETZ [*deeply and sincerely*]: But I love the nobles.

NASTI: You? You assassinate them.

GOETZ: Nonsense! I assassinate them a little, from time to time, because their wives are fertile and they make ten more for every one I may kill. But I won't let you hang them all. Why should I help you put out the sun and extinguish the earthly torches? That would mean to create a polar night.

NASTI: Then you will go on being nothing but a useless uproar?

GOETZ: Useless, yes. Useless to men. But what do I care for mankind? God hears me, it is God I am deafening, and that is enough for me, for He is the only enemy worthy of my talents. There is only God, the phantoms, and myself. It is God I shall crucify this night, through you, and through twenty thousand men, because His suffering is infinite, and renders infinite those whom He causes to suffer. This city will go up in flames. God knows that. At this moment, He is afraid, I can feel it; I feel His eyes on my hands, His breath on my hair, His angels shed tears. He is saying to Himself: "Perhaps Goetz will not dare. . . ." exactly as if He were a man. Weep, weep, angels; I shall dare. In a few moments, I will march in His fear and His anger. The city shall blaze; the soul of the Lord is a hall of mirrors, the fire will be reflected in a thousand mirrors. Then, I shall know that I am an unalloyed monster. [*To* FRANTZ] Bring me my sword.

NASTI [*in a changed voice*]: Spare the poor. The Archbishop is rich, you can amuse yourself ruining him, but the poor, Goetz, it isn't amusing to make them suffer.

GOETZ: No, indeed, it is far from amusing.

NASTI: Well, then?

GOETZ: I have my orders, I, too.

NASTI: I implore you on my knees.

GOETZ: I thought you were forbidden to pray to men.

NASTI: Nothing is forbidden when it is a question of saving lives.

GOETZ: It looks to me, prophet, as though God had led you into an ambush. [NASTI *shrugs.*] You know what is going to happen to you?

NASTI: Torture and hanging, yes. I told you I have always known.

GOETZ: Torture and hanging . . . hanging and torture . . . how monotonous. The boring part of Evil is that one grows accustomed to it—you need genius to invent. Tonight, I don't feel at all inspired.

CATHERINE: Let him have a confessor.

GOETZ: A . . .

CATHERINE: You cannot let him die without absolution.

GOETZ: Nasti! There's the stroke of genius. Of course, my dear man, of course you shall have a confessor! It's my duty as a Christian. Besides, I have a surprise for you. [*To* FRANTZ] Go and fetch the priest. . . . [*To* NASTI] There's an act such as I love: with facets. Is it good? Is it evil? The understanding is confused.

NASTI: No Papist is going to defile me.

GOETZ: You'll be tortured until you confess your sins —it will be for your own good.

[*Enter* HEINRICH.]

HEINRICH: You have done me all the harm you could. Leave me in peace.

GOETZ: What was he doing?

FRANTZ: Sitting in the dark, shaking his head.

HEINRICH: What do you want of me?

GOETZ: Put you to work at your profession. You must conduct the marriage of this woman immediately.

As for this man, you must give him the last sacraments.

HEINRICH: This man? . . . [*He sees* NASTI.] Ah! . . .

GOETZ [*pretending to be surprised*]: You know each other?

NASTI: Is this the minister of God who gave you the key?

HEINRICH: No! No, no!

GOETZ: Priest, aren't you ashamed to lie?

HEINRICH: Nasti! [NASTI *will not look at him.*] I couldn't let them massacre the priests. [NASTI *is silent.* HEINRICH *goes to him.*] Tell me, could I let them be killed? [*Pause. He turns and goes to* GOETZ.] Well? Why must I hear this confession?

GOETZ: Because he is going to be hanged.

HEINRICH: Then do it quickly! Hang him quickly! And find him another confessor.

GOETZ: It must be you, or no one.

HEINRICH: Then it will be no one. [*He turns to go.*]

GOETZ: Hey! Hey! [HEINRICH *stops.*] Can you allow him to die without confession?

HEINRICH [*returning slowly*]: No, jester, no; you are right. I cannot do that. [*To* NASTI] Kneel. [*Pause.*] You will not? My brother, my transgression does not reflect on the Church, and it is in the name of the Church that I can remit your sins. Would you like me to make public confession? [*To the others*] I betrayed my city out of spite and malice; I deserve to be scorned by everyone. Spit in my face, and let there be no more of this. [NASTI *does not move.*] You, soldier, spit!

FRANTZ [*gaily, to* GOETZ]: Shall I spit?

GOETZ [*with equal gaiety*]: Spit, my boy, and do a good job while you're at it!

[FRANTZ *spits at* HEINRICH.]

HEINRICH: Now all is over. Heinrich is dead of shame. The priest remains. An anonymous priest; and it is before him that you must kneel. [*After a moment of waiting, he strikes* NASTI *suddenly.*] Murderer! I must be mad to humiliate myself before you when everything that happened was your fault!

NASTI: My fault!

HEINRICH: Yes! Yes! You are responsible. You wanted to be a prophet, and here you are defeated, a prisoner waiting for the hangman, and everyone who trusted you is going to die. All! All of them! Ha! Ha! You pretended you knew how to love the poor, and that I didn't know the way; well, you see, you have done them more harm than I have.

NASTI: More than you, you dung-heap! [*He throws himself upon* HEINRICH. *They are dragged apart.*] Who betrayed the city? You or I?

HEINRICH: I did! I did! But I should never have done it if you hadn't murdered the Bishop.

NASTI: God commanded me to strike him because he was starving the poor.

HEINRICH: God, indeed? How simple it all is; then God commanded me to betray the poor because the poor wanted to murder the monks!

NASTI: God CANNOT command anyone to betray the poor—God is always on their side.

HEINRICH: If He is on their side, why do their revolts always fail? Why has He permitted your revolt to finish in despair today? Come along, answer me! Answer! Why don't you answer me? You cannot?

GOETZ: This is the moment. This is the agony, the sweating of blood. There! There! Agony is refreshing. How gentle you look; I see your face, and I feel that twenty thousand men are about to die. I love you. [*He kisses* NASTI *on the mouth.*] Come now, brother, the last word has not been said; I decided I would take Worms, but if God is on your side, something may happen to prevent it.

NASTI [*in a low voice, with conviction*]: Something will happen.

HEINRICH [*crying out*]: Nothing! Nothing at all! Nothing will happen. It would be much too unjust. If God had to work a miracle, why should He not have done it before I became a traitor? Why should He damn me if He saves you?

[*An* OFFICER *enters. All are startled.*]

THE OFFICER: All is ready. The troops are drawn up at the edge of the ravine, behind the chariots.

GOETZ: So soon? [*Pause.*] Tell Captain Ulrich I am coming.

[*The* OFFICER *goes out.* GOETZ *sinks into a chair.*]

CATHERINE: There's your miracle, sweetheart. [GOETZ *passes his hand over his face.*] Go! Pillage and slaughter! And so, good night.

GOETZ [*with a weariness which changes into simulated exaltation*]: This is the moment of farewell. When I return, I shall be covered with blood and my tent will be empty. A pity, for I had grown accustomed to you. [*To* NASTI *and* HEINRICH] You will spend the night together, like a pair of lovers. [*To* HEINRICH] Be sure to hold his hand tenderly while they are tearing his flesh with red-hot pincers. [*To* FRANTZ, *pointing to* NASTI] If he agrees to confess, stop the torture immediately; as soon as he has been absolved, string him up. [*As if suddenly remembering* CATHERINE's *existence*] Ah, the bride! Frantz, you will assemble the stable boys, and introduce them to Madam. Let them do what they like with her, short of killing her.

CATHERINE [*suddenly throwing herself at his feet*]: Goetz! Pity! Pity! Not that! Not that horror! Pity!

GOETZ [*recoiling, astonished*]: You were so proud and confident just now. . . . You didn't believe me?

CATHERINE: No, Goetz, I didn't believe you.

GOETZ: To tell you the truth, I didn't believe in it myself. You only believe in evil *afterward.* [*She clings to his knees.*] Frantz, relieve me of her.

[FRANTZ *pulls her away and throws her on the bed.*]
There we are. I have forgotten nothing. . . . No!
I really believe I have forgotten nothing. [*Pause.*]
Still no miracle; I'm begining to think God is giving
me a free hand. Thank you, God, thank you very
much. Thanks for the women violated, the children
impaled, the men decapitated. [*Pause.*] If only I
wanted to talk! I know so much, you dirty hypocrite.
Listen, Nasti, I'm going to give you the answer:
God is making use of me. You saw how it was tonight; well, He sent His angels down to start me up
again.

HEINRICH: His angels?

GOETZ: All of you. Catherine is very certainly an angel.
So are you, so is the banker. [*Returning to* NASTI]
What about this key? Did I ask God to send me this
key? I didn't even suspect its existence; but God had
to send one of His ministers to place it in my hands.
Naturally, you all know what He desires: that I
should spare His priests and rescue His nuns. Therefore, He tempts me, secretly, making opportunities
without compromising Himself. If I am caught, He
has the right to disown me; after all, I could easily
throw this key into the ravine.

NASTI: Yes, you could. You still can.

GOETZ: No, indeed, my angel. You know perfectly well
I cannot.

NASTI: Why not?

GOETZ: Because I cannot be other than myself. Listen,
I am going to take a nice little blood-bath to oblige
the Lord. But when it is all over, He will stop His
nose and cry that that wasn't at all what He wanted.
Do you really not want it, Lord? Then there is still
time to prevent me. I don't ask for the heavens to fall
on my head; a gob of spit would do; let me slip in
it, break my thigh, and that would be enough for
one day. No? Fine, fine. I don't insist. Look, Nasti,
look at this key; a key is a fine thing, a useful thing.

And look at these hands. There's workmanship! We should all praise the Lord for giving us hands. Then, if you hold a key in your hands, that cannot be wicked; let us praise the Lord for all the hands holding keys at this moment in all the countries of the world. But as for what the hand does with the key, the Lord declines responsibility, that doesn't concern Him at all, the poor fellow. Yes, Lord, you are completely innocent; how can You conceive Nothingness, You who are fullness itself? Your presence is light, and changes all into light; how are You to know the twilight of my heart? And Your infinite understanding? How can it enter into my arguments without shattering them? Hatred and weakness, violence, death, displeasure, all that proceeds from man alone; it is my only empire, and I am alone within it; what happens within me is attributable to me alone. There—there—I take everything upon myself, and I shall talk no more. On the Day of Judgment, silence, shut lips; I am far too proud, I shall let myself be damned without uttering a word. But doesn't it embarrass You a little, Lord, a very little, to have damned the man who does your work for you? I am going, the men are waiting, the fine key is luring me—it wants to go home to its keyhole. [*In the tent opening, he turns back.*] Do you know my equal? I am the man who makes the Almighty uneasy. Through me, God is disgusted with Himself. There are twenty thousand nobles, thirty bishops, fifteen kings, we've had three emperors at once, a Pope and an anti-Pope. But can you find another Goetz? Sometimes, I imagine Hell as an empty desert waiting for me alone. Farewell. [*He turns to go.* HEINRICH *bursts out laughing.*] What's the matter?

HEINRICH: But Hell is overflowing, you fool! [GOETZ *stops and looks at him. To the others*] This is the strangest of all visionaries; a man who believes he alone is doing evil. Every night the soil of Germany is illuminated by living torches; tonight, as on every night, cities are going up in flames by dozens, and the captains who pillage them don't make nearly so much fuss about it. They kill, on weekdays, and then on Sundays go to confession, humbly. But this man takes himself for the Devil incarnate, because he is carrying out his duties as a soldier. [*To* GOETZ] If you are the Devil, jester, who am I, I who pretended to love the poor, and delivered them up to you?

[GOETZ *stares at* HEINRICH, *almost fascinated, during this speech. When it is over, he shakes himself.*]

GOETZ: What are you demanding? The right to be damned as well? I grant it to you. Hell is big enough for me not to meet you there.

HEINRICH: And the others?

GOETZ: What others?

HEINRICH: All the others. All those who haven't the chance to kill, but who want to.

GOETZ: My wickedness is not their wickedness; they do Evil as a luxury, or out of interest; I do Evil for Evil's sake.

HEINRICH: What do reasons matter if it is proved that a man can *only* do Evil?

GOETZ: Has it been proved?

HEINRICH: Yes, jester, it has been proved.

GOETZ: By whom?

HEINRICH: By God Himself. God has made it impossible for man to do good on this earth.

GOETZ: Impossible?

HEINRICH: Completely impossible. Love is impossible! Justice is impossible! Why don't you try and love your neighbor? You can tell me afterward what success you have.

GOETZ: Why shouldn't I love my neighbor if I felt like it?

HEINRICH: Because if only one man should hate another, it would be sufficient for hatred to spread from one to another and overwhelm mankind.

GOETZ [*catching him up*]: This man here loved the poor.

HEINRICH: Yet he wittingly lied to them, he excited their lowest passions and forced them to murder an old man. [*Pause.*] What could I do? Tell me what could I have done? I was innocent, and yet the crime fell upon me, like a thief. Where was the good then, bastard? Where was the least Evil? [*Pause.*] You are taking a great deal of trouble for nothing, you vaunter of the ways of vice! If you want to deserve Hell, you need only remain in bed. The world itself is iniquity; if you accept the world, you are equally iniquitous. If you should try and change it, then you become an executioner. [*He laughs.*] The stench of the world rises to the stars.

GOETZ: Then all are damned?

HEINRICH: Ah no, not all! [*Pause.*] I have my faith, O God, I have my faith. I shall not fall into the sin of despair. I am infected to the very marrow, but I know Thou wilt deliver me if Thou hast so decided. [*To* GOETZ] We are all equally guilty, bastard, we are all equally deserving of Hellfire, but the Lord forgives us when it pleases Him to forgive.

GOETZ: He will never forgive me against my will.

HEINRICH: Miserable wretch, how can you struggle against His mercy? How can you exhaust His infinite patience? He will take you up between His fingers if He pleases, raise you to the level of His paradise; with a flick of His thumb He will break your ill-will, He will open your jaws and stuff you with His benevolence, you will become good in spite of yourself. Go! Set fire to Worms. Go, pillage, go, massacre— you're wasting your time; one of these days you'll wake up in Purgatory like everyone else.

GOETZ: Then everyone is doing Evil?

HEINRICH: Everyone.

GOETZ: And no one has ever done Good?

HEINRICH: No one.

GOETZ: Capital! [*He re-enters the tent.*] I will wager you that I shall.

HEINRICH: Shall what?

GOETZ: Do Good. Will you take the bet?

HEINRICH [*shrugging*]: No, bastard, I will wager nothing at all.

GOETZ: You are wrong. You tell me Good is impossible —therefore I wager I will live righteously. It is still the best way to be alone. I was a criminal—I will reform. I turn my coat and wager I can be a saint.

HEINRICH: Who will be the judge?

GOETZ: You yourself, in a year and a day from now. You have only to make your bet.

HEINRICH: You fool, you have lost in advance if you do Good merely to win a bet.

GOETZ: Quite right! All the same, let's throw dice on it. If I win, Evil triumphs. If I lose—ah! If I lose, I am not in the least doubt as to what I shall do. Well? Who plays against me? Nasti?

NASTI: No.

GOETZ: Why not?

NASTI: It is wrong.

GOETZ: Of course it is wrong. What else do you expect? Come along, baker, I am still wicked for the moment.

NASTI: If you want to do Good, you need only make up your mind. That is all.

GOETZ: I want to drive the Lord into a corner. This time it is yes, or no. If He lets me win, the city burns, and His responsibility is established. Come now, play; if God is with you, you should not fear. You dare not, coward? You prefer to be hanged? Who will dare?

CATHERINE: I will.

GOETZ: You, Catherine? [*He looks at her.*] Why not? [*He hands her the dice.*] Throw.

CATHERINE [*throwing the dice*]: A two and a one. [*She shudders.*] You'll find it very difficult to lose.

GOETZ: Who said I wanted to lose? [*He puts the dice back in the box.*] Lord God, this time You are caught. The moment has come to show Your hand. [*He throws the dice.*]

CATHERINE: One and one . . . You've lost!

GOETZ: I submit to the will of God. Farewell, Catherine.

CATHERINE: Kiss me. [*They kiss.*] Farewell, Goetz.

GOETZ: Take this purse, and go where you please. [*To FRANTZ*] Frantz, take word to Captain Ulrich to send the men to bed. Nasti—you will return to the city, there is still time to prevent a panic. If you open the gates at dawn, if the priests leave Worms safe and sound and place themselves under my protection, I will lift the siege at noon. Agreed?

NASTI: Agreed.

GOETZ: Have you recovered your faith, prophet?

NASTI: I never lost it.

GOETZ: Fortunate man!

HEINRICH: You can restore their liberty, you can give them back their life and hope. But me, you dog, me whom you forced into betrayal, can you ever restore my purity?

GOETZ: It's up to you to find it again. After all, there was no real harm done.

HEINRICH: What matters whether the harm was done? It is my intention that matters. I'll follow you, yes, I'll follow, step by step, night and day; you can rely on me to judge your actions. You can rest assured that in a year and a day, wherever you may be, I shall meet you at the appointed time and place.

GOETZ: Here is the dawn. How cold it is. The dawn and absolute Good have entered my tent, and we are none the happier. This woman weeps, that man hates me; it feels like the aftermath of disaster. Perhaps Good is a disaster. . . . Anyway, what does it matter? I don't have to judge it, but to do it. Farewell.

[*He goes out.* CATHERINE *begins to laugh.*]
CATHERINE [*laughing to the point of tears*]: He cheated!
  I saw it! He cheated in order to lose!

CURTAIN

ACT II

SCENE IV

The Castle of Heidenstamm.

FIRST PEASANT: Shouting their heads off, in there.

KARL: It's the barons. I'll bet they're wild with rage.

FIRST PEASANT: Supposing he loses his nerve and gives in?

KARL: Don't worry; he's as stubborn as a mule. Careful—hide. There he is.

GOETZ [*to* KARL]: Brother, will you bring us some wine? Three cups will suffice—I do not drink. Do this out of love for me, brother.

KARL: Out of love for you, brother, I will.

[GOETZ *goes out. The* PEASANTS *come out of hiding, laughing and slapping their thighs.*]

THE PEASANTS: Brother—little brother! Baby brother! Take that! Take that for the love of me!

[*They buffet each other joyously, laughing.*]

KARL [*arranging glasses on a tray*]: All the servants are his brothers. He says he loves us, he wheedles us, and kisses us too, sometimes. Yesterday he amused himself by washing my feet. The kind lord, the good brother! Pah! [*He spits.*] That word burns my lips, and I spit every time I have to say it. He'll be hanged because he called me brother, and when they put the rope round his neck, I'll kiss him on the lips and say: "Good night, little brother. Die for the love of me." [*He goes out, carrying the tray with the glasses.*]

FIRST PEASANT: There goes a real man. No one ever gets round him.

SECOND PEASANT: They say he knows how to read, too.

FIRST PEASANT: I'll be buggered!

KARL [*returning*]: These are the orders. Visit everyone
on the estates of Nossak and Schulheim. Spread the
news in the smallest hamlet: "Goetz is giving the
peasants the lands of Heidenstamm." Give them
time to digest that, and then say: "If that bastard,
that son-of-a-bitch has given his lands away, why
doesn't the high and mighty lord of Schulheim give
you his?" Work them all up, work them up into a
rage, spread trouble everywhere. Go. [*They go out.*]
Goetz, my darling brother, you'll see how I'll spoil
your good works. Give away your lands, give them
all away: one day you'll be sorry you didn't fall dead
before you gave them away. [*He laughs.*] For love!
Every day I dress you and undress you. I see your
navel, your toes, your behind, and you expect me
to love you! Ho! I'll show you what love is! Conrad
was hard and brutal, but his insults offended me less
than your kindnesses. [*Enter* NASTI.] What do you
want?

NASTI: Goetz sent for me.

KARL: Nasti!

NASTI [*recognizing him*]: It's you!

KARL: So you know Goetz? A fine friendship!

NASTI: Don't worry about that. [*Pause.*] I know what
you're planning, Karl! You'd do much better to lay
low and wait quietly for orders.

KARL: The country takes no orders from the town.

NASTI: If you try and pull this dirty trick, I'll have you
hanged.

KARL: Take care the one hanged doesn't turn out to be
you. To begin with, what are you doing here? Seems
fishy. You talk to Goetz, and then you tell us not to
revolt: who's to say you haven't been bribed!

NASTI: Who's to say you haven't been bribed to make
the revolt break out prematurely, and so have it
crushed the more easily?

KARL: Here comes Goetz.

[GOETZ *enters, backing away from the barons* SCHUL-

HEIM, NOSSAK, *and* RIETSCHEL, *who are pressing around him, shouting.*]

NOSSAK: You don't give a damn for the peasants: what you want is our hides.

SCHULHEIM: You're hoping to use our blood to wipe away the bitcheries of your mother.

NOSSAK: You're digging the graves of all the German nobility.

GOETZ: My brothers, my very dear brothers, I don't even know what you are talking about.

RIETSCHEL: You don't know that this gesture of yours will put the match to the powder? That our peasants will be raving mad if we don't immediately give them our lands, our possessions, down to our very shirts, and then our blessing on top of everything?

SCHULHEIM: I suppose you don't know they'll come and besiege us in our castles!

RIETSCHEL: And that it means ruin if we accept, and death if we refuse!

NOSSACK: Don't you know that?

GOETZ: My very dear brothers . . .

SCHULHEIM: No speeches! Will you renounce your plans? Answer yes or no.

GOETZ: My very dear brothers, forgive me: I say no.

SCHULHEIM: You're an assassin.

GOETZ: Yes, my brother, like everyone.

SCHULHEIM: A bastard!

GOETZ: Yes: like Jesus Christ.

SCHULHEIM: You sack of dung! You filth of the earth! [*He drives his fist into* GOETZ's *face.* GOETZ *staggers, then recovers, and advances on* SCHULHEIM. *They all shrink away. Suddenly,* GOETZ *flings himself full length on the ground.*]

GOETZ: Help, angels, help! Help me to overcome myself! [*He trembles all over.*] I won't strike him. I'll cut off my right hand if it wants to strike him. [*He writhes about on the ground.* SCHULHEIM *kicks him.*] Roses, rain of roses, gentle caresses. How God loves me! I accept everything. [*He rises.*] I'm a dog of a bastard, a sack of dung, a traitor; pray for me.

SCHULHEIM [*striking him*]: Will you give up your plan?

GOETZ: Don't strike me. You will soil yourself.

RIETSCHEL [*threateningly*]: Will you give it up?

GOETZ: O Lord, deliver me from the abominable desire to laugh!

SCHULHEIM: Good God!

RIETSCHEL: Come away. We're wasting our time.

[*The barons go off, and* GOETZ *becomes aware of the two men.*]

GOETZ [*joyfully*]: Greetings, Nasti! Greetings, brother. I am glad to see you again. Two months ago, before the walls of Worms, you offered me an alliance with the people. Today, I accept. Wait: I must speak. I have good news for you. Before doing Good, I told myself I had to know what it was, and I considered for a long time. Well, Nasti, now I know what Good is. It is love, of course; but the fact is that men don't love one another, and what is it that prevents them? Inequality of conditions, servitude and misery. Therefore, these things must be suppressed. Up till now, we are in agreement, are we not? Nothing surprising about that: I have profited by your lessons. Yes, Nasti, I have thought of you a great deal, these last weeks. Only, you want to postpone the kingdom of God; I am much more cunning: I have found a way of establishing it now, at least in a single corner of the world—here. Firstly: I give up my lands to the peasants. Secondly: on this very land, I shall organize the first truly Christian community: all equal! Ah, Nasti, I am a captain: I engage the battle of Good, and I think I shall be able to win it at once, and without bloodshed. Will you help me? You know how to speak to the poor. We two will be able to construct a Paradise, for the Lord Himself has chosen me to efface our original sin. Listen, I have found a name for my Utopia: I shall call it the City of the Sun. What's the matter? You're as stubborn as a mule! Ah, you kill-joy! What else have you found to reproach me with?

NASTI: Keep your lands for yourself.

GOETZ: Keep my lands! And it's you, Nasti, who are asking this? I expected everything except that.

NASTI: Keep them. If you want to help us, don't do anything, and above all, don't interfere.

GOETZ: Then you, too, believe that the peasants will revolt?

NASTI: I don't believe it, I know it.

GOETZ: I might have known this would happen. I should have foreseen that I should outrage your narrow, prejudiced soul. Those swine just now, and you, at this moment—I must be very right, or you wouldn't all be protesting so loudly. You are only encouraging me! I'll give them all away, these lands of mine—how happy I shall be to give them away! Good shall be done in spite of you all.

NASTI: Who asked you to give them away?

GOETZ: I know I have to give them away.

NASTI: But who asked you?

GOETZ: I know, I tell you. I see my way as clearly as I see you. God has bestowed His light upon me.

NASTI: When God is silent, you can make Him say whatever you please.

GOETZ: Ah! Admirable prophet! Thirty thousand peasants are dying of hunger, I ruin myself to relieve their misery, and you calmly tell me God forbids me to save them.

NASTI: You—save the poor? You can only corrupt them.

GOETZ: Then who will save them?

NASTI: Don't concern yourself with the poor: they will save themselves.

GOETZ: Then what will become of me, if you take away my means of doing Good?

NASTI: You have plenty to do. Manage your fortune, and watch it grow. That's a task to fill a lifetime.

GOETZ: Then to please you I have to become a wicked rich man?

NASTI: No rich man is wicked. He is rich. That is all.

GOETZ: Nasti, I am one of you.

NASTI: No.

GOETZ: Have I not been poor all my life?

NASTI: There are two kinds of poor—those who are poor in company and those who are poor alone. The first are the real poor, the others are the rich who've been unlucky.

GOETZ: And the rich who have given away their possessions—they aren't poor either, I suppose.

NASTI: No, they are merely no longer rich.

GOETZ: Then I was beaten in advance. Shame on you, Nasti, you condemn a Christian soul without appeal. [*He walks up and down in agitation.*] However proud those petty lords may be who hate me, you are even prouder, and I should find it less difficult to join their caste than to join yours. Patience! Thanks to Thee, Lord, I shall love them without return. My love will break down the walls of your intractable soul: it will disarm the peevishness of the poor. I love you, Nasti, I love you all.

NASTI [*more gently*]: If you love us, give up your plan.

GOETZ: No.

NASTI [*in a changed voice, more urgently*]: Listen. I must have seven years.

GOETZ: To do what?

NASTI: In seven years we shall be ready to begin the holy war. Not before. If you plunge the peasants into this brawl today, I don't give them more than a week. What you will have destroyed in eight days will need more than half a century to reconstruct.

KARL: My lord, the peasants are here.

NASTI: Send them away, Goetz. [GOETZ *is silent.*] Listen, if you really wish to help us, you can.

GOETZ [*to* KARL]: Ask them to wait, brother. [KARL *goes out.*] What do you propose?

NASTI: Keep your lands.

GOETZ: That depends.

NASTI: If you keep them, they can serve as a place of refuge, and a place of assembly. I shall establish myself in one of your villages. From here, my orders will radiate over Germany; from here, in seven years, will go out the signal for war. You can render us inestimable service. Well?

GOETZ: The answer is no.

NASTI: You refuse?

GOETZ: I cannot do Good by installment. Haven't you understood, Nasti? Thanks to me, before the year is out, happiness, love, and virtue will reign over ten thousand acres of this land. On my domains I wish to build the City of the Sun, and you want me to turn it into a hiding-place for assassins.

NASTI: Good has to be served like a soldier, Goetz, and what soldier can win a war by himself alone? Begin by being modest.

GOETZ: I will not be modest. As humble as you please, but not modest. Modesty is the virtue of the half-hearted. [*Pause.*] Why should I help you prepare your war? God has forbidden the shedding of blood, and you want to steep Germany with blood! I will not be your accomplice.

NASTI: You refuse to shed blood? Then, give away your lands, give away your castle, and you'll see if this land of ours does not bleed.

GOETZ: It will not bleed. Good cannot engender Evil.

NASTI: Good does not engender Evil, true: therefore, because your mad generosity will provoke a massacre, what you are doing cannot be good.

GOETZ: Can it be good to perpetuate the sufferings of the poor?

NASTI: I ask for seven years.

GOETZ: And for those who die before then? Those who

have spent their lives in hatred and fear will die of despair.

NASTI: God will receive their souls.

GOETZ: Seven years! And then in seven years will come seven years of war, and then seven years of repentence because we shall have to build our ruins up again. Who knows what will follow after? A new war, perhaps, and a new repentence, and new prophets who will ask for seven more years of patience. Charlatan! Will you make them wait till the Day of Judgment? I tell you Good is possible, every day at every hour, at this very moment even. I shall be the man who does good at once. Heinrich told me: "Two men have only to hate each other for hatred to spread throughout the world." And I tell you, it suffices for one man to love mankind with undivided love for that love to spread from one to another throughout humanity.

NASTI: And you will be that man?

GOETZ: Yes, with God's help, I will be that man. I know that Good is much more difficult than Evil. Evil was only myself, but Good is the whole world. I am not afraid. We must bring new warmth to the world, and I will bring that warmth. God has commanded me to be resplendent, and I will dazzle, I will bleed light. I am a glowing coal, the breath of God fans my flame, and I am being consumed alive. Nasti, I am infected with Good, and my malady must prove contagious. I shall be witness, martyr, and temptation.

NASTI: Impostor!

GOETZ: You shall not shake my resolution! I see, I know, the way is clear. I shall prophesy!

NASTI: False prophet—instrument of the Devil! You are the one who says: I shall do what I think right, though the world perish.

GOETZ: False prophet and instrument of the Devil is

the man who says: Let the world perish, and I will
then see if Good is possible.

NASTI: Goetz, if you stand in my way, I will destroy
you.

GOETZ: Could you kill me, Nasti?

NASTI: Yes, if you stand in my way.

GOETZ: I could not kill you. Love is now my lot. I am
going to give away my lands.

CURTAIN

SCENE V

*Before the portal of a village church. Two benches are
on the porch. On one of them is a drum, on the other, a
flute.* GOETZ *enters, disguised as a monk, followed by*
NASTI.

GOETZ [*calling*]: Hallo! Ho! Not a soul within thirty
leagues. They've all gone to ground. My bounty has
descended upon them like a disaster. The fools! [*He
turns on* NASTI.] Why are you following me?

NASTI: To be present at your failure.

GOETZ: There will be no failure. Today I lay the first
stone of my city. They are in the cellars, I suppose.
But patience. Let me only capture half a dozen, and
you'll see if I don't know how to win them over.
[*Cries, music of fifes.*] What's this?
[*Enter a procession of* PEASANTS, *half drunk, carrying
a plaster saint shoulder high on a litter.*]
You seem very gay. Are you celebrating the gracious
gift of your former Lord?

A PEASANT: God forbid, holy father.

GOETZ: I am no monk. [*He throws back his hood.*]

THE PEASANTS: Goetz! [*They recoil, frightened. Some of them cross themselves.*]

GOETZ: Goetz, yes, Goetz the bogeyman! Goetz the Attila who gave away his lands out of Christian charity. Do I seem so redoubtable? Come, I want to speak to you. [*Pause.*] Well? What are you waiting for? Come here! [*Silence from the* PEASANTS. *In a more imperious tone*] Who's in command?

AN OLD MAN [*unwillingly*]: I am.

GOETZ: Come here. [*The* OLD MAN *moves out from the group and goes to him. The* PEASANTS *watch them in silence.*]
Tell me, I saw sacks of grain in the castle barns. Haven't you understood? No more taxes, no more tithes.

THE OLD MAN: For a little while longer, we are leaving everything as it should be.

GOETZ: Why?

THE OLD MAN: To see what happens.

GOETZ: Very well. The grain will rot. [*Pause.*] What do you think of your new estate?

THE OLD MAN: Let's not discuss it, my lord.

GOETZ: I am no longer your Lord. Call me brother. Understand?

THE OLD MAN: Yes, my lord.

GOETZ: Your brother, I tell you.

THE OLD MAN: Oh no. Not that, no.

GOETZ: I com . . . I beg you.

THE OLD MAN: You can be my brother as much as you like, but I shall never be yours. Each one to his station, my lord.

GOETZ: Never mind! You'll grow used to it. [*Pointing to the flute and the drum*] What are those?

THE OLD MAN: A flute and a drum.

GOETZ: Who plays them?

THE OLD MAN: The monks.

GOETZ: There are monks here?

THE OLD MAN: Brother Tetzel has arrived from Worms with two minor friars. They have come to sell indulgences.

GOETZ [*bitterly*]: So that's why you seem so gay? [*Abruptly*] To the devil! I won't have such mummery here. [*Silence.*] Those indulgences are worthless. Do you believe God gerrymanders His forgiveness? [*Pause.*] If I were still your master and commanded you to drive these three scoundrels away, would you do it?

THE OLD MAN: Yes, I would.

GOETZ: Well, for the last time, it is your master who commands you . . .

THE OLD MAN: You aren't our master any more.

GOETZ: Get out; you are too old. [*He pushes the* OLD MAN *away, leaps up on the steps, and addresses the crowd.*] Have you even wondered why I made you a gift of all my lands? [*Pointing to a* PEASANT] Answer me.

THE PEASANT: I don't know.

GOETZ [*to a* WOMAN]: Do you know?

THE WOMAN [*hesitating*]: Maybe . . . maybe because you wanted to make us happy.

GOETZ: Well answered! Yes, that was what I wanted. But you see, happiness is only a means to an end. What do you expect to do with your happiness?

THE WOMAN [*frightened*]: With happiness? First, we've got to have it.

GOETZ: You will be happy, never fear. What will you do with it?

THE WOMAN: Never thought about it. Don't even know what it is.

GOETZ: I have thought about it for you. [*Pause.*] You know that God commands us to love one another. Only, you see, up till now it was impossible. Even yesterday, my brothers, you were much too unhappy for anyone to dream of asking you for love. Well, I wanted you all to be without excuse. I am going to make you big and fat, and you will love your neighbors. By heaven, I insist that you love mankind! I give up the command of your bodies, but I have come to guide your souls, for God has enlightened me. I am the architect, and you will be my workmen; all for all, the tools and the lands in common. No more poor men, no more rich men, no more laws except the law of love. We shall be an example to all Germany. What do you say, men, shall we give it a trial? [*Silence.*] I am not displeased to see you frightened in the beginning; nothing is more reassuring than a good old devil. But the angels, my brothers! It's the angels who are suspect!

[*The crowd smiles, sighs, and begins to stir.*]

At last! At last, you are smiling at me!

THE CROWD: Here they are! Here they are!

GOETZ [*turns round, sees* TETZEL, *and says bitterly*]: May the Devil take the monks!

[*The two minor friars pick up their instruments. A table is brought and placed on the top step.* TETZEL *lays his rolls of parchment on the table.*]

TETZEL: Well, now, old fellows! Come along! Nearer! Nearer! I've not eaten garlic! [*They all laugh.*] How's things in these parts? Is the land good?

THE PEASANTS: Not too bad.

TETZEL: And the wives? Just as unbearable?

THE PEASANTS: You know how it is. Like everywhere else.

TETZEL: You mustn't complain: they protect you against the Devil because they are bigger bitches than he is. [*The crowd laughs.*] Ah, my friends, that's not what we're here for; we're going to talk about serious things! Music! [*Drum and flute.*] Work all the time, is all very fine, but sometimes, a man leans on his hoe, looks away into the distance, and says to himself: "What's going to happen to me after I die?" It's not enough to have a nice grave, with plenty of flowers: a man's soul doesn't live in the tomb. Then where will the soul go? Down to hell? [*Drum.*] Or up to Heaven? [*Flute.*] Good people, you can be quite sure the good Lord has asked Himself that question. He is so worried about you, the good Lord, that He doesn't even sleep any more. You, over there, what's your name?

THE PEASANT: Peter.

TETZEL: Tell me, Peter, I expect you take a drop too much from time to time? Come along, don't lie to me!

THE PEASANT: It does happen.

TETZEL: And the wife? You beat her sometimes?

THE PEASANT: When I've been drinking.

TETZEL: And yet you fear God?

THE PEASANT: Oh yes, father!

TETZEL: And the Holy Virgin? Do you love her?

THE PEASANT: More than my own mother.

TETZEL: Then see how embarrassed the good Lord is. "That good man is not very wicked," He says to Himself. "And I don't want to hurt him very much. Nevertheless, he has sinned, and I must punish him."

THE PEASANT [*desolate*]: Alas!

TETZEL: But wait a moment. Luckily, there are the Saints! Each one of them has deserved Paradise a hundred thousand times, but what good is that since they can only enter once, each one of them? Then what does the good Lord say to Himself? He says: "Those hundred thousand entrances that haven't been used, we mustn't waste them, and I'm going to distribute them to those who haven't deserved them. That good Peter, if he buys an indulgence from Brother Tetzel, will enter into Paradise with one of the invitation cards signed by good St. Martin." Well? Well? Wasn't that a good idea? [*Acclamations.*] Come along, Peter, bring out your purse. My brothers, God is offering him an incredible bargain. Paradise for only half a ducat. Where is the curmudgeon, where is the miser who won't give half a ducat for his eternal life? [*He takes a coin from Peter.*] Thank you. Go home, and sin no more. Who buys? Look, here is a special bargain. When you give this little note to your own priest, he has to grant you absolution from any mortal sin of your own choosing. Isn't that true, father?

THE PARISH PRIEST: Quite true.

TETZEL: D'you see this? [*He brandishes a parchment.*] Ah, this, my brothers, is a special dainty from the good Lord. These indulgences have all been specially drawn up for people who have members of their family still in Purgatory. If you lay out the necessary, all your late relations will spread their wings and fly to Heaven. The price is two crowns per person transferred: the transfer is immediate. Who buys? Who buys? You there—whom have you lost?

THE PEASANT: My mother.

TETZEL: Your mother? Is that all? At your age, have you only lost your mother?

THE PEASANT [*hesitating*]: Well, I did have an uncle. . . .

TETZEL: And you'd leave your poor uncle in Purgatory? Come, come! Count out four crowns. [*He takes them, and holds them out above the poor-box.*] Attention, good people, attention. When the coins fall, the souls will fly away. [*He drops the coins into the box. Flourish from the flute.*] One! [*Another flourish from the flute.*] Two! There they go! There they go! They are flying over your heads: two lovely pure white butterflies! [*Flute.*] We'll meet you in heaven! We'll meet you in heaven! Pray for us and give our respects to the Saints. Come on, friends, a good hand for the little darlings. [*Applause.*] Who's next? [*The* PEASANTS *surge round him.*] For your wife and your grandmother? For your sister? [*Flute . . . flute.*] Pay up! Pay up!

GOETZ: Stand back! [*Murmurs from the crowd.*]

TETZEL [*to the* PARISH PRIEST]: Who's this?

THE PRIEST: Their former lord. Nothing to fear.

GOETZ: Fools—you believe yourselves absolved with a miserable donation! Do you think the martyrs allowed themselves to be burned alive so that you could walk into Paradise as if it were a flour mill? As for the Saints, you won't save your souls by purchasing their merits, but by working to acquire their virtues!

A PEASANT: Then I'd rather hang myself and be damned outright. A man can't become a saint when he has to work sixteen hours a day.

TETZEL [*to the* PEASANT]: Hold your tongue, you fat idiot! No one's asking you to be a saint. Buy a little indulgence from time to time, and God will make room for you through His infinite mercy.

GOETZ: Go ahead! Lay out your money on his trumpery rubbish. He'll make you spend a ducat or two for the right to return to your miserable vices, but God won't ratify the transaction! You're rushing headlong to Hell.

TETZEL: Take away their hope! Take away their faith! Their courage! What will you put in their place?

GOETZ: Love.

TETZEL: What do you know of love?

GOETZ: What do you know of love yourself? How could you love these men, whom you despise so much that you try to sell them Paradise?

TETZEL [*to the* PEASANTS]: Do I, my lambs, despise you?

ALL: Oh!

TETZEL: Do I not, my little chickens, love you?

THE PEASANTS: Yes, yes, of course you love us!

TETZEL: I am the Church, my brothers: and outside the Church, there is no love. The Holy Church is our universal mother: through her monks and her priests she dispenses the same maternal love to all her children, to the most unfortunate, as to the most pampered favorites of fortune.

[*A handbell rings, and a rattle sounds. The* LEPER
appears. The PEASANTS *huddle away at the far end of
the scene, terror-stricken.*]
Who's this?
[*The* PARISH PRIEST *and the minor friars rush into
the church.*]

THE PEASANTS [*pointing to the* LEPER]: There! There!
Take care! The leper!

TETZEL [*horrified*]: Sweet Jesus!

[*A pause.* GOETZ *goes toward the* LEPER.]

GOETZ [*to* TETZEL, *pointing to the* LEPER]: Embrace
him!

TETZEL: Pah!

GOETZ: If the Church loves without revulsion or recoil
the most despicable of her sons, why do you hesitate
to embrace him? [TETZEL *shakes his head.*] Jesus
would have taken him in His arms. I love him better
than you do. [*Pause. He goes to the* LEPER.]

THE LEPER [*between his teeth*]: Here comes another to
pull the trick of the leper's kiss.

GOETZ: Come here, my brother.

THE LEPER: I thought so! [*He goes to* GOETZ *unwillingly.*]
If it's a question of your salvation, I cannot refuse,
but do it quickly. You're all the same; you'd think
the good Lord had given me leprosy expressly to give
you a chance to earn your place in Heaven.
[*As* GOETZ *approaches him*] Not on the mouth!
[GOETZ *kisses him on the mouth.*] Pah! [*He wipes
his lips.*]

TETZEL [*beginning to laugh*]: Well? Are you satisfied?
Look at him wiping his lips. Is he less of a leper now
than he was before you kissed him? Tell me, leper,
how goes the world with you?

THE LEPER: It would be better if there were fewer
sound men and far more lepers.

TETZEL: Where do you live?

THE LEPER: With other lepers in the forest.

TETZEL: What do you do all day?

THE LEPER: Tell each other leper stories.

TETZEL: Why have you come down to the village?

THE LEPER: I came to see if I could pick up an indulgence.

TETZEL: Wonderful!

THE LEPER: Is it true that you sell them?

TETZEL: For half a ducat.

THE LEPER: I haven't a penny.

TETZEL [*triumphantly, to the* PEASANTS]: Watch this! [*To the* LEPER] Do you see this shiny new indulgence? Which would you rather have? That I give it to you, or that I kiss you on the lips?

THE LEPER: Well . . .

TETZEL: Oh, I will do whichever you like. Choose.

THE LEPER: Well, I'd rather you give me the paper.

TETZEL: Here it is, *gratis pro Deo*—it's a gift from your Holy Mother Church. Take it.

THE LEPER: Hurrah for the Church! [TETZEL *throws him the parchment. The* LEPER *catches it.*]

TETZEL: Now, go away quickly.

[*The* LEPER *goes. Sound of the bell and the rattle.*]

TETZEL: Well, which of us loves him the better?

THE CROWD: You do! You do! Hurrah for Tetzel!

TETZEL: Come along, my brothers! Who's next? For your sister who died in a foreign land? [*Flute.*] For your aunts who brought you up? For your mother? For your father and your mother—for your eldest son! Pay up! Pay! Pay!

GOETZ: Curs! [*He strikes the table, sweeping the drum off the top, and it rolls away to the foot of the steps.*] Christ drove the money-changers out of the Temple. . . . [*He stops, looking at the silent and hostile peasants, pulls the hood over his face and throws himself on his knees with his back against the wall of the church, groaning.*] Ah! Ah! Ah! Shame on me! Shame on me! I don't know how to speak to them. Lord, I implore Thee, show me the way to their hearts!

[*The* PEASANTS *watch him;* TETZEL *smiles; the* PEAS-
ANS *look at* TETZEL. TETZEL *winks, lays a finger on
his lips to impose silence, and jerks his head in the
direction of the church door. He enters the church
on tiptoe. The* PEASANTS *enter the church, carrying
the plaster saint. They all disappear. A moment of
silence, then* HEINRICH *appears in the doorway in lay
clothes.*]

HEINRICH [*making his way toward* GOETZ *without seeing*
NASTI]: You seem to think souls are like vegetables.

GOETZ: Who is speaking?

HEINRICH: The gardener can decide what is best for his
carrots, but no man can decide for others wherein
their goodness lies.

GOETZ: Who is that speaking? Heinrich?

HEINRICH: Yes.

GOETZ [*rising and throwing back his hood*]: I was sure
I should see you again after my first blunder. [*Pause.*]
What have you come to do? To indulge your hate?

HEINRICH: "He who sows Good shall reap Good." You
said that, didn't you?

GOETZ: Yes, I did say it, and I will say it again. [*Pause.*]

HEINRICH: I come to bring you the harvest.

GOETZ: It is too soon to reap. [*Pause.*]

HEINRICH: Catherine is dying: that is your first crop.

GOETZ: She is dying? May God receive her soul! What
do you want me to do? [HEINRICH *laughs.*] Don't
laugh, imbecile! You must be aware that you don't
know how to laugh.

HEINRICH [*excusing himself*]: He's making faces at me.

GOETZ [*turning round swiftly*]: Who? [*He understands.*]
Ah! [*Turning back to* HEINRICH] I see—you two are
always together, now.

HEINRICH: Yes, always.

GOETZ: He must be company for you.

HEINRICH [*passing his hand over his face*]: It is tiresome.

GOETZ [*going to* HEINRICH]: Heinrich, if I have hurt
you, forgive me.

HEINRICH: Forgive you? So that you can boast every-where of having changed hatred into love as Christ changed water into wine?

GOETZ: Your hatred belongs to me. I will deliver you from it and from the Devil.

HEINRICH [*in a changed voice, as if someone else were speaking through his mouth*]: In the name of the Father, the Son, and the Holy Ghost. I am the Father, the Devil is my son: hatred is the Holy Ghost. You could more easily divide the Holy Trinity than split our Trinity into three parts.

GOETZ: Then, that's the end of it. Go back and say your masses in Worms. We shall meet again in nine months.

HEINRICH: I shall never go back to Worms, and I will never again say a mass. I no longer belong to the Church, jester. I have been forbidden to celebrate the offices and administer the holy sacraments.

GOETZ: What reproach can they bring against you?

HEINRICH: Of having been paid to betray the city.

GOETZ: It's a monstrous lie.

HEINRICH: I told the lie myself. I stood up in the pulpit and confessed everything before them all: my love of money, my jealousy, my disobedience, and my carnal desires.

GOETZ: You were lying!

HEINRICH: Why not? Everywhere in Worms they were saying that the Church abominated the poor and that the Church had ordered me to yield them up to the sword. We had to find a pretext for the Church to repudiate me.

GOETZ: You have expiated your sin.

HEINRICH: You know very well that no one ever ex-piates a sin.

GOETZ: You are right. Nothing effaces anything. [*Pause. Suddenly, he goes to* HEINRICH.] What is happening to Catherine?

HEINRICH: Her blood is becoming corrupt, her body

is covered with sores. For three weeks she has neither slept nor eaten.

GOETZ: Why did you not stay with her?

HEINRICH: She is no concern of mine, nor I of hers.

[NASTI *enters and remains in the background.*]

GOETZ: She must be nursed.

HEINRICH: She cannot be cured. She will certainly die.

GOETZ: What is she dying of?

HEINRICH: Of shame. Her body revolts her because of all the men's hands that have been laid upon it. Her heart disgusts her even more because your image has remained within it. You are her mortal sickness.

GOETZ: All that happened last year, priest, and I no longer acknowledge the sins of a year ago. I will pay for this sin in the next world and for all Eternity. But in this world, it is over, and I have no time to waste.

HEINRICH: Then there are two men named Goetz.

GOETZ: Two, yes. A living Goetz who lives by Good, and a dead Goetz who lived by Evil.

HEINRICH: And you buried your sins with the dead Goetz?

GOETZ: Yes.

HEINRICH: Excellent. Only it isn't a dead man who is killing Catherine but the fine, brave Goetz himself, the one who is devoting himself to living by love.

GOETZ: You lie! It was the evil-doing Goetz who committed the crime.

HEINRICH: No crime has been committed. When you deflowered her you gave her far more than you possessed yourself: you gave her love. She really loved you, though I don't know why. And then, one fine day, divine grace touched you, so you pressed a purse into Catherine's hands, and drove her away. For this, she is dying.

GOETZ: Could I have gone on living with a whore?

HEINRICH: Yes, because you were the one who made her that.

GOETZ: I had to renounce Good or give her up.

HEINRICH: If you had kept her, you might have saved her, and yourself with her. But save one soul—save only one? How could a man like Goetz stoop to that? He had much more important projects.

GOETZ [*abruptly*]: Where is she?

HEINRICH: On your own lands.

GOETZ: She wanted to see me again?

HEINRICH: Yes. And then Evil struck her down.

GOETZ: Where is she?

HEINRICH: I will not tell you. You have done her enough harm.

GOETZ [*raising his fist, furious*]: I . . . [*He controls himself.*] Very well, I will find her again myself. Farewell, Heinrich. [*He bows in the direction of the Devil.*] My respects. [*He turns towards* NASTI.] Nasti, come with me.

HEINRICH [*amazed*]: Nasti!

[NASTI *tries to follow* GOETZ. HEINRICH *stands in his way.*]

HEINRICH [*timidly*]: Nasti! [*More loudly*] Nasti, I was looking for you. Stop! I must talk to you. Despise me as much as you like, provided you listen to me. I have come from Schulheim. Revolt is brewing.

NASTI: Let me pass. I know that.

HEINRICH: Do you want this revolt to break out? Tell me, is that what you want?

NASTI: Is that any concern of yours? Let me pass.

HEINRICH [*stretching out his arms*]: You shall not pass without answering me.

[NASTI *looks at him in silence, then makes up his mind.*]

NASTI: Whether I want it or not, no one can prevent it now.

HEINRICH: I can. In two days, I can build a dike to contain the sea. In exchange, Nasti, I want you to forgive me.

NASTI: Still playing the game of forgiveness? [*Pause.*]

It is a game that bores me. I am not concerned with this. I have no right to condemn or absolve. Those matters concern only God.

HEINRICH: If God allowed me to choose between His pardon and yours, it is yours that I would choose.

NASTI: Then you would choose wrongly: you would renounce Paradise for a whisper.

HEINRICH: No, Nasti: I should be renouncing the forgiveness of Heaven for the forgiveness of earth.

NASTI: The earth does not forgive.

HEINRICH: You weary me.

NASTI: What?

HEINRICH: I wasn't speaking to you. [*To* NASTI] You don't make my task easy: I am being driven to hatred, Nasti. I am being driven to hate and you render me no aid. [*He crosses himself three times.*] There, I am tranquil for a moment. So, listen to me. Quickly. The peasants are organizing themselves. They are going to negotiate with the barons. That will give us a few days.

NASTI: What will you do with them?

HEINRICH [*pointing to the church*]: You saw them: they will let themselves be cut to pieces for the Church. There is more piety in this countryside than in all the rest of Germany.

[NASTI *shakes his head.*]

NASTI: Your priests are powerless: the people love them, true, but if they condemn the uprising, they will find themselves preaching in the desert.

HEINRICH: I'm not counting on their sermons, but on their silence. Imagine: one fine day they wake up, the villagers find the door of their church open, and the church itself standing empty. The bird has flown. No one before the altar, no one in the sacristy, no one in the crypt, nor in the presbytery . . .

NASTI: Is this possible?

HEINRICH: All is prepared. Have you men?

NASTI: A few.

HEINRICH: Let them go through the land, shouting louder than anyone, and above all blaspheming. They must provoke scandal and horror. Then, at Righi, next Sunday, let them carry off the priest in the middle of the mass. Let them drag him into the forest and return with their swords stained with blood. All the priests of the region will secretly leave their villages the following night, and assemble at the castle of Markstein, where they will be expected. On Monday morning, God returns to Heaven. Children will no longer be baptized, sins will no longer be absolved, and the sick will fear to die without confession. Fear will stifle the revolt.

NASTI [*reflecting*]: That might well be . . .

[*The door of the church opens. Snatches of organ music. The* PEASANTS *come out, still carrying the saint.*]

[*Looking at them.*] If it might be, then it shall be . . .

HEINRICH: Nasti, I implore you, if this enterprise succeeds, tell me you will forgive me.

NASTI: I will say it if you like. The trouble is that I know who you are.

CURTAIN

SCENE VI

The interior of the church a fortnight later. All the villagers have taken refuge inside the church and now no longer leave it. They eat and sleep there. At this moment they are praying. NASTI *and* HEINRICH *are watching. Men and women are lying here and there on the floor: the sick and infirm have also been carried*

*into the church. Some are groaning and moving about
at the foot of the pulpit.*

NASTI [*to himself*]: I can't stand listening to them any
more! Alas! You had nothing but your anger, and
I blew upon it to extinguish it.

HEINRICH: What did you say?

NASTI: Nothing.

HEINRICH: You aren't content?

NASTI: No.

HEINRICH: Everywhere the people are crowding into the
churches: they are held in a grip of fear, and the
revolt has been nipped in the bud. What more can
you want? [NASTI *is silent.*] I shall rejoice for both of
us. [NASTI *strikes him.*] What's come over you?

NASTI: If you dare rejoice, I'll break your back.

HEINRICH: You don't want me to celebrate our victory?

NASTI: I won't allow you to rejoice because you have
brought people to their knees.

HEINRICH: What I have done, I did for you and with
your consent. Are you beginning to doubt your own
powers, prophet? [NASTI *shrugs.*] And yet this isn't
the first time you have lied to them.

NASTI: It's the first time I've brought them to their
knees to prevent them from defending themselves.
It's the first time I have compounded with super-
stition and formed an alliance with the Devil.

HEINRICH: Are you afraid?

NASTI: The Devil is God's creature; if God so wishes,
the Devil will obey me. [*Bruskly*] I'm stifling in this
church. Let us go.

[HEINRICH *and* NASTI *make a move to leave.* GOETZ
suddenly enters and strides up to HEINRICH.]

GOETZ: You swine! Anything to win your wager! You
made me waste a whole fortnight. I searched my
whole domain a dozen times to try to find her, and
now I learn that she was here, while I was hunting
for her miles away. Here, ill, lying on a stone floor.

And by my fault. [HEINRICH *shakes himself free and exits with* NASTI. GOETZ *repeats to himself*] By my fault . . . No, nothing . . . my words sound hollow. Thou wouldst have me feel ashamed, and I have no shame. It is pride that sweats through all my wounds; for thirty-five years I have been bursting with pride, it is my way of dying of shame. We must change all that. [*Abruptly*] Destroy my power of thought! Destroy it! Make me forget myself! Transform me into an insect! So be it!

[*The murmur of the* PEASANTS *at their prayers swells and dies down.*]

Catherine! [*He walks up and down among the crowd, looking at each face and calling.*] Catherine! Catherine! [*He goes to a dark figure stretched out on the paving, lifts the covering which hides it and lets it fall back, reassured. Then he disappears behind a pillar, and we hear him calling again.*] Catherine! [*A clock strikes seven.*]

A SLEEPER [*lying on the stones and waking with a start*]: What time is it? What day is it?

A MAN: Today is Sunday, and it is seven o'clock in the morning.

VOICES: No, it isn't Sunday. . . . No more Sundays, it's over, there'll never be another Sunday, the parish priest has carried them off with him. . . . He left us the weekdays, the cursed days of work and hunger.

THE PEASANT: Then go to the Devil! I'm going to sleep again. You can wake me for Judgment Day.

A WOMAN: Let us pray.

[HILDA *enters, carrying a truss of straw. She is followed by two peasant women, also carrying straw.*]

FIRST WOMAN: Hilda, it's Hilda!

SECOND WOMAN: We have missed you. What is happening outside? Tell us.

HILDA: There is nothing to tell. Silence everywhere, except for the animals crying because they are afraid.

A VOICE: Is the sun shining?

HILDA: I don't know.

A VOICE: Didn't you look at the sky?

HILDA: No. [*Pause.*] I brought back some straw to make
beds for the sick. [*To the two peasant women*] Help
me. [*She helps a sick man to rise and settle himself
on a bed of straw.*] There. This one, now. [*Same
business.*] And now this woman. [*They help lift an
old woman who begins to sob.*] Don't cry, I implore
you; don't take away their courage. Come, grandma,
if you begin to cry, they'll all start crying to keep
you company.

THE OLD WOMAN [*snivelling*]: My rosary, there . . .
[*She points to the ground where she had been lying.*]

HILDA [*exasperated*]: Take it! [*She picks up the rosary,
throws it in the old woman's lap, then, controlling
herself, speaks more gently.*] Pray for us! Prayers are
better than tears, they make less noise. Ah, no! You
mustn't pray and cry at the same time. [*She wipes
the old woman's eyes with her own handkerchief.*]
There, there! Dry your eyes! It's all over! Don't cry
any more; we are not guilty, and God has no right
to punish us.

THE OLD WOMAN [*still snivelling*]: Alas! my daughter!
You know He has the right to do anything He
pleases.

HILDA [*violently*]: If He has the right to punish the innocent, I will give myself directly to the Devil. [*They
are all startled and look at her. She shrugs and goes
to lean against a pillar. She stands for a moment with
fixed gaze, as if possessed by a memory, then suddenly, with disgust, exclaims*] Pah!

FIRST WOMAN: Hilda! What's the matter?

HILDA: Nothing.

FIRST WOMAN: You always know how to give us back
our hope . . .

HILDA: Hope in whom? In what?

THE WOMAN: Hilda, if you lose courage, we shall all
lose courage.

HILDA: Very well. Don't pay any attention to what I say. [*She shivers.*] It's cold. You are the only warmth left in the world. You must all cling together and wait.

A VOICE: Wait for what?

HILDA: To be warm again. We are hungry and thirsty, we are afraid, we are suffering, but the only thing that matters is to keep warm.

THE WOMAN: Then come here, close to me. Come! [HILDA *does not move. The* WOMAN *rises and goes to* HILDA, *whom she questions in an understanding way.*] Is she dead?

HILDA: Yes.

THE WOMAN: May God receive her soul.

HILDA: God? [*A short laugh.*] He will refuse it.

THE WOMAN: Hilda! How can you say that? [*Murmurs among the crowd.*]

HILDA: She saw the flames of hell before she died. Suddenly she sat up, crying that she could see them, and then she died.

THE WOMAN: Is anyone with her?

HILDA: No. Will you go and watch beside her?

THE WOMAN: Not for all the gold in the world.

HILDA: Very well. I'll go back there in a moment. Give me time to warm myself again.

THE WOMAN [*turning toward the crowd*]: Let us pray, my friends! Pray for the pardon of a poor dead girl, who saw the flames of Hell and is in danger of damnation.

HILDA [*in a low voice*]: Implore Thy pardon! What hast Thou to forgive us? Thou art the one who shouldst ask our forgiveness! I do not know what Thou hast in store for me, and I did not even know that girl, but if Thou dost condemn her, I shall refuse to enter heaven. Dost Thou believe a thousand years of Paradise would make me forget the terror in her eyes? I have only scorn for Thy elect—idiots, who have the heart to rejoice while there are damned

souls writhing in hell and poor people on earth. I
am on the side of humanity, and I will not desert
my fellow beings. Thou hast the power to let me
die without confession and summon me suddenly
before Thy bar of judgment; but we shall then see
who will judge the other. [*Pause.*] She loved him.
All night long, she cried his name aloud. What sort
of man is he, this bastard? [*She turns round abruptly
toward the crowd.*] If you must pray, ask that the
blood shed at Righi may be visited on the head of
Goetz!

A VOICE: Goetz?

HILDA: He alone is guilty!

VOICES: May God punish Goetz the bastard!

GOETZ [*with a short laugh*]: There you have it! Whether
I live by Evil or by Righteousness, I always find myself detested. [*To a* PEASANT] Who is that young
woman?

THE PEASANT: Why, it's Hilda.

GOETZ: Hilda who?

THE PEASANT: Hilda Lemm. Her father is the richest
miller in the village.

GOETZ [*bitterly*]: You listen to her as if she were an
oracle. She tells you to pray for the damnation of
Goetz, and you all throw yourselves on your knees.

THE PEASANT: Well, you see, we love her dearly.

GOETZ: You love her? She is rich and you still love her?

THE PEASANT: She isn't rich now. Last year, she was
going to take the veil, and then during the famine,
she gave up her vows to come and live among us.

GOETZ: What does she do to be beloved?

THE PEASANT: She lives like a good sister, denying herself everything. She helps everyone. . . .

GOETZ: Yes, yes. I can do all that, too. There must be
something else, surely?

THE PEASANT: Nothing that I know.

GOETZ: Nothing? Indeed!

THE PEASANT: She . . . She is kind.

GOETZ [*beginning to laugh*]: Kind? Thanks, my good
man, you have enlightened me. [*He walks away.*] If
she is really doing Good, I will rejoice, Lord, I will
rejoice as I should. Provided Thy kingdom is established, what matters whether it be through her or
through me? [*He looks at* HILDA *with hostility.*] Like
a good sister! And I? Do I not live like a monk? What
has she done that I have not done? [*He goes to her.*]
Greetings! Do you know Catherine?

HILDA [*startled*]: Why do you ask me that? Who are
you?

GOETZ: Answer me. Do you know her?

HILDA: Yes. Yes. I know her. [*She suddenly flings back
the hood from* GOETZ's *face.*] And I know you, too,
even though I have never seen you before. You are
Goetz?

GOETZ: Yes, I am.

HILDA: At last!

GOETZ: Where is she?
[*She looks at him without replying, with an angry
smile.*]

HILDA: You'll see her. There's no hurry.

GOETZ: Do you believe she wants to suffer five minutes
more?

HILDA: Do you believe her sufferings will cease when
she sees you? [*She looks at him. Pause.*] You will both
have to wait.

GOETZ: Wait for what?

HILDA: Until I have had a good look at you, in my own
time.

GOETZ: Madwoman! I neither know you nor wish
to know you.

HILDA: But I know you.

GOETZ: No.

HILDA: No? On your breast you have a tuft of curling
hair, almost like a patch of black velvet; to the left

of your groin there is a purple vein, that swells and darkens when you're making love. In the small of your back there is a birthmark like a strawberry.

GOETZ: How do you know?

HILDA: For five days and nights I've been nursing Catherine. There were three of us in that room—she, you, and I. We lived together for those five days. She saw you everywhere, and I ended up by seeing you, too. Twenty times a night the door opened and you came into the room. You would stand there, looking at her, lazy and complacent, and then lightly you would stroke the nape of her neck. Like this. [*She seizes his hand roughly.*] What power do they possess, these fingers? What power? They are only hairy flesh. . . . [*She flings his hand violently from her.*]

GOETZ: What did she say?

HILDA: Everything needful to make me hold you in abhorrence.

GOETZ: That I was brutal, coarse, repellent?

HILDA: That you were handsome, brave, intelligent; that you were insolent and cruel; that no woman could see you without desiring you.

GOETZ: She was talking about the other Goetz?

HILDA: There is only one.

GOETZ: Then, look at me with *her* eyes. Where's the cruelty? Where's the insolence? Alas, where is the intelligence? Before, I could see clear and far, because to do Evil is easy; but my sight has dimmed, and the world is filled with matters beyond my understanding. Hilda! I beg you! Please don't be my enemy.

HILDA: What can it matter to you, since I am without means to harm you?

GOETZ [*indicating the peasants*]: In their eyes, you have already harmed me.

HILDA: Those people belong to me and I to them: don't try to drag them into your problems.

GOETZ: Is it true they love you?

HILDA: Yes. It's true.

GOETZ: Why?

HILDA: I've never wondered about it.

GOETZ: Bah! It's because you are beautiful.

HILDA: No indeed, captain. You soldiers love fair women because you have nothing to do and you eat spiced dishes. My brothers here work all day long and they are hungry. They have no eyes for the beauty of women.

GOETZ: Then why is it? Because they need you?

HILDA: It is rather because I need them.

GOETZ: Why?

HILDA: You couldn't understand.

GOETZ [going to her]: Did they love you immediately?

HILDA: Immediately. Yes.

GOETZ [to himself]: That's just what I thought. Straight away or never. It's win or lose in advance: time and effort are of no avail. [Abruptly] God cannot desire that: it's unjust. You might as well say some people are born damned.

HILDA: Some people are. Catherine, for one.

GOETZ [without listening]: What did you do to them, sorceress? You must have done something to them to succeed where I failed?

HILDA: What did you do to infatuate Catherine? What did you do? [They stare at each other, fascinated.]

GOETZ [still staring at her]: You have robbed me of their love. When I look at you, it's their love that I see.

HILDA: When I look at you, it is Catherine's love that I see—and it fills me with horror.

GOETZ: What do you accuse me of?

HILDA: In Catherine's name, I accuse you of having driven her to despair.

GOETZ: That doesn't concern you.

HILDA: I reproach you, in the name of these men and women, for having flung your lands upon us in cart-loads, and burying us beneath them.

GOETZ: Get out and be damned to you! I don't have to justify myself before a woman.

HILDA: I reproach you, in my own name, for having slept with me against my will.

GOETZ [*stupefied*]: Slept with you?

HILDA: For five nights running you possessed me by cunning and by force.

GOETZ [*laughing*]: It must have been in your dreams.

HILDA: In dreams, yes. It was in dreams. Her dream: she drew me into it. I wished to suffer with her suffering as I suffer with these others, but it proved a snare; for I had to love you with her love. God be praised! I see you. I see you in the light, and am free! By daylight, you are no more than yourself.

GOETZ: Very well. Wake up from your dream. All this happened in your mind; I never touched you. Until today I never saw you; nothing has happened to you.

HILDA: Nothing. Absolutely nothing. She cried out in my arms, but what does it matter? Nothing happened to me because you neither touched my breasts nor kissed my mouth. Yes indeed, fine captain, you are as solitary as a rich man, and you've only suffered the wounds that have been dealt you—that is your misfortune. But I—I hardly feel my own body, I don't know where my life begins or ends—I do not always answer when my name is called—so much does it astonish me, sometimes, that I have a name. But I suffer with all bodies, I am struck on all cheeks, I die the death of everyone. Every woman you have taken by force, you have violated in my flesh.

GOETZ [*triumphantly*]: At last! [HILDA *looks at him, surprised.*] You will be the first.

HILDA: The first?

GOETZ: The first to love me.

HILDA: I? [*She laughs.*]

GOETZ: You already love me. For five nights I held you in my arms—my mark is still upon you. In me you love the love that Catherine had for me, and in you,

I love the love these people have for you. You will
love me. And if they're yours, as you claim, then they
must love me through you.

HILDA: If I thought that one day my eyes might look
at you with tenderness, I'd pluck them out immediately. [*He seizes her arm. She stops laughing and
looks at him malignantly.*] Catherine is dead.

GOETZ: Dead! [*He is stunned by the news.*] When?

HILDA: A few moments ago.

GOETZ: Did she . . . suffer?

HILDA: She saw the flames of Hell.

GOETZ [*staggering*]: Dead!

HILDA: She has escaped you, hasn't she? Why don't you
go and stroke her neck!

[*Silence, then a disturbance at the back of the church.
The peasants rise and turn toward the door. A moment of waiting. The noise of voices increases, then
HEINRICH and NASTI appear, carrying CATHERINE on
a litter. She is half-sitting, and is muttering as if to
herself.*]

CATHERINE: No! No! No! No! No!

GOETZ [*shouting*]: Catherine! [*To HILDA*] Slut! You lied
to me!

HILDA: I . . . I didn't lie to you, Goetz. Her heart had
stopped beating. [*She bends over CATHERINE.*]

HEINRICH: We heard her crying from the road. She said
the Devil was lying in wait for her. She implored us
to bring her here to the foot of the cross.

[*The crowd begins to gather round them, menacing.*]

VOICES: No! No! She is damned! Away with her! Outside! Away with her! At once!

GOETZ: By heaven, you swine, I'll teach you Christian
charity!

HILDA: Be quiet, you only know how to do harm. [*To
the PEASANTS*] It is only a corpse; the soul is surrounded by demons and clings to it for safety. The
Devil is lying in wait for you, too. Who will take
pity on you if you will not take pity on her? Who will

love the poor if the poor refuse to love each other
[*The crowd parts in silence.*] Carry her to the fee
of the Christ, since that is what she demands.
[HEINRICH *and* NASTI *carry the litter to the foot of the*
cross.]

CATHERINE: Is he here?

HILDA: Who?

CATHERINE: The priest.

HILDA: Not yet.

CATHERINE: Go and find him! Quick! I shall hold out
until he comes.

GOETZ [*approaching*]: Catherine!

CATHERINE: Is it he?

GOETZ: It is I, my love.

CATHERINE: You! Ah! I thought it was the holy priest
[*She begins to cry out.*] Find me the priest—please
find him, quickly. I don't want to die without confession!

GOETZ: Catherine, you have nothing to fear—they will
not do you any harm. You have suffered too much on
earth.

CATHERINE: I tell you I can see them.

GOETZ: Where?

CATHERINE: Everywhere. Sprinkle them with holy water.
[*She begins to cry out again.*] Save me, Goetz—please
save me. It was you who sinned—I am not guilty. If
you love me, save me!
[HILDA *holds her in her arms and tries to make her*
lie down again. CATHERINE *struggles, still crying out.*]

GOETZ [*imploringly*]: Heinrich!

HEINRICH: I am no longer of the Church.

GOETZ: She doesn't know it. If you will sign her forehead with the cross, you will save her from this horror.

HEINRICH: To what end? She will find horror on the
farther side of death.

GOETZ: Those are only visions, Heinrich!

HEINRICH: You think so? [*He laughs.*]

22914

GOETZ: Nasti—you who say all men are priests . . .
[NASTI *shrugs and makes a helpless gesture.*]

CATHERINE [*without hearing them*]: Can't you see that
I am dying? [HILDA *tries to make her lie down.*]
Leave me alone! Leave me alone!

GOETZ [*to himself*]: If only I could . . . [*Suddenly he
makes a decision and turns to the crowd.*] It was
through my sin that this woman was damned, and it
is through me that she shall be saved. Leave us, all of
you.
[*The* PEASANTS *go out slowly,* NASTI *dragging* HEIN-
RICH *with him.* HILDA *hesitates.*] You too, Hilda.
[*She gives him a long look and goes out.*] This time,
Thou art caught! However grudging Thou may'st be
of miracles, this time Thou must work a miracle for
me.

CATHERINE: Where are they going? Don't leave me
alone.

GOETZ: No Catherine, no, my love. I will save you.

CATHERINE: What can you do? You aren't a priest.

GOETZ: I am going to ask Christ to put the burden of
your sins upon me. Do you understand?

CATHERINE: Yes.

GOETZ: I shall bear them all in your stead. Your soul
will be as pure as on the day you were born. Purer
than if the holy father had absolved you.

CATHERINE: How shall I know if God has answered your
prayer?

GOETZ: I shall pray. If I return to you with my face
ravaged with leprosy or gangrene, will you believe me?

CATHERINE: Yes, beloved. I will believe you.
[*He draws apart.*]

GOETZ: Lord, these sins are mine—Thou knowest it.
Render to me what rightfully belongs to me. Thou
hast no right to condemn this woman since I alone
am guilty. Give me a sign! My arms are ready—my
face and my breast are prepared. Blast my cheeks—let

her sins become pus oozing from my eyes and ears;
let them burn like an acid into my back, my thighs,
and my genitals. Strike me with leprosy, cholera, the
plague, but redeem her!

CATHERINE [*more feebly*]: Goetz! Save me!

GOETZ: Canst hear me, God, or art Thou deaf? Thou
canst not refuse me this bargain, it is fair and just.

CATHERINE: Goetz! Goetz! Goetz!

GOETZ: Ah! I cannot endure that voice! [*He mounts
the pulpit.*] Didst Thou die for mankind, yes or no?
Look down on us: mankind is suffering. Thou must
begin to die again! Give! Give me Thy wounds! Give
me the wound in Thy right side, the two holes in Thy
hands. If a God could suffer for their sins, why cannot
a man? Art Thou jealous of me? Give me Thy stigmata! Give me Thy wounds! Give me Thy wounds!
[*He repeats this over and over like an incantation.*]
Art Thou deaf? Good heavens, how stupid I am!
God helps those who help themselves! [*He draws a
dagger from his belt, stabs the palm of his left hand,
then the palm of his right hand, and finally his side.
Then he throws the dagger behind the altar and,
leaning forward, marks the breast of the Christ with
blood.*] Come back, all of you!

[*The crowd returns.*]

The Christ has bled. [*Murmurs. He raises his hands.*]
See, in His infinite mercy, He has allowed me to bear
His stigmata. The blood of Christ, my brothers, the
blood of Christ is flowing from my hands. [*He comes
down the steps from the pulpit and goes to* CATHER-
INE.] Fear no more, my love. I touch your forehead,
your eyes and lips with the blood of our Lord Jesus
Christ. [*He marks her face with blood.*] Do you see
them still?

CATHERINE: No.

GOETZ: Die in peace.

CATHERINE: Your blood, Goetz, your blood. You have
shed it for me.

GOETZ: The blood of Christ, Catherine.

CATHERINE: Your blood . . . [*She dies.*]

GOETZ: Kneel, all of you. [*They kneel.*] Your priests are
curs; but you need have no fear. I shall remain with
you. As long as the blood of Christ flows from these
hands, no harm can touch you. Go back peacefully
to your homes and rejoice—this is a holiday. Today,
the kingdom of God begins for you all. We shall build
the City of the Sun.

[*Pause. The crowd begins to disperse in silence. A
woman passes close to* GOETZ, *seizes his hand and
smears her face with blood.* HILDA *is the last to go.
She approaches* GOETZ, *but he seems not to see her.*]

HILDA: Promise not to harm them.

[GOETZ *does not reply. She goes.* GOETZ *staggers and
leans against a pillar.*]

GOETZ: They are mine at last.

CURTAIN

ACT III

SCENE VII

A square at Altweiler. Peasants are gathered around a peasant woman who is acting as their teacher. She is a young, gentle-looking woman. She holds a rod, with which she points to certain letters drawn upon the ground.

TEACHER: What is this letter?

A PEASANT: An L.

TEACHER: And this one?

ANOTHER PEASANT: An O.

TEACHER: And these two?

A PEASANT: N E.

TEACHER: No!

ANOTHER PEASANT: V E.

TEACHER: And the whole word?

A PEASANT: Love.

ALL THE PEASANTS: Love, love . . .

TEACHER: Courage, friends! Soon you will know how to read. You will be able to tell good from bad, true from false. Now, tell me, you . . . over there . . . What is our primary nature?

A PEASANT GIRL [*replying as if to a catechism*]: Our primary nature is the nature we had before we knew Goetz.

TEACHER: What was that nature?

A PEASANT [*in the same tone*]: It was evil.

TEACHER: How must we combat our primary nature?

THE PEASANT: By creating a second nature.

TEACHER: How may we create a second nature?

A PEASANT GIRL: By teaching our bodies the gestures of love.

TEACHER: Are the gestures of love the same as love?

A PEASANT: No, the gestures of love are not. . . .
[HILDA *enters. The peasants stare at her.*]
TEACHER: What is it? [*She turns.*] Ah, Hilda! . . .
[*Pause.*] My dear sister . . . You upset us.
HILDA: How can I do that? I am not saying anything.
TEACHER: You say nothing, but you watch us, and we
know you don't approve.
HILDA: May I not think what I like?
TEACHER: No, Hilda. Here we all think aloud, in the
clear light of day. The thoughts of each one belong
to all. Will you not join us?
HILDA: No!
TEACHER: Then you do not love us?
HILDA: Yes, but in my own way.
TEACHER: Are you not glad to see our happiness?
HILDA: I . . . Ah, my friends, you have suffered so
much; if you can be happy, then I must be happy too.
[*Enter* KARL *with a bandage over his eyes, led by a
young woman.*]
TEACHER: Who are you?
THE YOUNG WOMAN: We are looking for the City of the
Sun.
TEACHER: You have arrived. This is the City of the
Sun.
THE YOUNG WOMAN [*to* KARL]: I might have known it.
What a pity you cannot see their happy faces; you
would be happy too.
[*The* PEASANTS *crowd round them.*]
THE PEASANTS: The poor things! Are you thirsty? Are
you hungry? Come and sit down!
KARL [*sitting down*]: You are very kind.
A PEASANT: Everyone is kind here, because everyone is
happy.
ANOTHER PEASANT: But in these troubled times, no one
travels any more. We've only got each other to love.
That's why your coming is such a joy!
A PEASANT WOMAN: It is sweet to be able to spoil a
stranger. What can we do for you?

THE YOUNG WOMAN: We want to see the man with the bleeding hands.

KARL: Is it true that he can work miracles?

THE PEASANT WOMAN: He does nothing else.

KARL: Is it true that his hands bleed?

A PEASANT: Every day.

KARL: Then I would like him to put a little blood on my poor eyes and give me back my sight.

A PEASANT WOMAN: Ah! Ah! He is just the man to do that. He will cure you!

KARL: How fortunate you are, to possess such a man. And none of you sins any more?

A PEASANT: No one drinks—no one steals.

ANOTHER PEASANT: Husbands are forbidden to beat their wives.

A PEASANT: Parents are forbidden to whip their children.

KARL [*sitting down on a bench*]: I hope it will last.

A PEASANT: It will last as long as it pleases God.

KARL: Alas! [*He sighs.*]

TEACHER: Why do you sigh?

KARL: This young girl here has seen armed men everywhere. The peasants and barons are going to fight.

TEACHER: Here in Heidenstamm?

KARL: No, but all round.

TEACHER: In that case, we are not concerned. We don't want to harm anyone, and our task is to establish the reign of love.

KARL: Bravo! Then let them kill each other! Hatred, massacres, the blood of others are necessary ingredients of your happiness.

A PEASANT: What do you mean? You're mad.

KARL: I only repeat what is being said everywhere.

TEACHER: What is being said?

KARL: That your happiness has made their sufferings more unbearable, and that despair has driven them to extremes. [*Pause.*] Bah! You're quite right not to concern yourselves with others: a drop or two of blood

sprinkled on your happiness, why not? It isn't too
high a price to pay!

TEACHER: Our happiness is sacred. Goetz has said so.
We are not happy for ourselves alone, but for everyone in the world. We witness to all and before all
that happiness is possible. This village is a sanctuary,
and all the peasants should turn their eyes toward us,
as Christians turn toward the Holy Land.

KARL: When I return to my village, I will testify to this
good news. I know whole families dying of hunger.
They will be able to rejoice when they learn that
you are happy for their sake. [*An embarrassed silence
falls over the peasants.*] And tell me, good people,
what will you do if this war breaks out?

A PEASANT WOMAN: We shall pray.

KARL: Ah! I'm afraid you may be obliged to join the
fight.

TEACHER: Oh, no!

ALL THE PEASANTS: No! No! No!

KARL: Is this not a holy war, this war of slaves fighting
for the right to become free men?

TEACHER: All wars are ungodly. We shall remain as
guardians of love and martyrs of peace.

KARL: The barons pillage, violate, kill your brothers at
your gates, yet you do not hate them?

A PEASANT WOMAN: We pity them for being wicked.

ALL THE PEASANTS: We pity them.

KARL: But if they are wicked, is it not just that their
victims should rebel?

TEACHER: Violence is unjust, no matter what the source.

KARL: If you condemn the violence of your fellow men,
then you approve the conduct of the barons?

TEACHER: No, of course not.

KARL: But you must, since you have no desire that it
should cease.

TEACHER: We want it to cease by the will of the barons
themselves.

KARL: And who will give them that will?

TEACHER: We shall.

THE PEASANTS: We shall!

KARL: And until then, what should the peasants do?

TEACHER: Submit, wait, and pray.

KARL: Traitors, now you are unmasked! You have no love except for yourselves. But take care: if this war breaks out, you will be called upon to render an account, and no one will tolerate your remaining neutral while your brothers are having their throats cut. If the peasants are victorious, beware lest they burn down the City of the Sun in order to punish you for having betrayed them. As for the lords, if they should win the battle, they would not allow a noble estate to remain in the hands of the serfs and peasants. To arms, boys, to arms! If you will not fight out of fraternity, then let it at least be in your own interest: happiness is something to defend.

A PEASANT: We refuse to fight.

KARL: Then you will be fought.

THE TEACHER: We will kiss the hand that strikes us, we shall die praying for those who kill us. As long as we live, we have always the possibility of letting ourselves be destroyed, but when we are dead, we will inhabit your souls and our voices will echo in your ears.

KARL: By heaven, you know your lesson well. Ah! You are not the ones most to blame, the criminal is the false prophet who has filled your eyes with that deranged look of placidity.

THE PEASANTS: He insults our Goetz! [*They advance upon him.*]

THE YOUNG WOMAN: Would you strike a blind man, you who maintain that you live to love your fellow men?

A PEASANT [*snatching the bandage from* KARL'S *eyes*]: Some blind man! Look! It is Karl, the lackey from the castle. His heart is devoured with hate, and for weeks he has been prowling round, preaching discord and rebellion.

THE PEASANTS: Hang him!

HILDA: My gentle sheep, are you grown so desperate? Karl is a swine because he is driving you into war. But he speaks the truth, and I will not allow you to strike anyone who speaks the truth, whoever he may be. It is true, my friends, that your City of the Sun is built on the misery of others; and for the barons to allow it, their peasants must resign themselves to slavery. My friends, I do not reproach you for your happiness, but I felt much more at ease when we were all suffering together, for our misery was the misery of mankind. On this earth that bleeds, all joy is obscene, and all happy men are solitary.

A PEASANT: You only love misery—Goetz wants to build for the future!

HILDA: Your Goetz is an impostor. [Murmurs] Well? What are you waiting for? Why don't you beat me? Or hang me?

[GOETZ enters.]

GOETZ: What are these threatening looks?

A PEASANT: Goetz, he . . .

GOETZ: Be quiet! I won't have these frowning brows. Smile first, then speak. Come along, smile!

[The peasants smile.]

A PEASANT [smiling]: This man has come to incite us to revolt.

GOETZ: So much the better—it is a test. We must learn how to listen to words of hate.

A PEASANT WOMAN [smiling]: He insulted you, Goetz, and called you a false prophet.

GOETZ: My good Karl, do you hate me so much?

KARL: Yes: enough.

GOETZ: Then it is because I haven't known how to make myself loved; forgive me. Escort him to the gates of the village, give him food, and the kiss of peace.

KARL: Everything will end in a massacre, Goetz. May the blood of these men be visited on your head.

GOETZ: So be it.

[*They go out.*]

Let us pray for their souls.

TEACHER: Goetz, there is one thing that torments us.

GOETZ: Speak.

TEACHER: It has to do with Hilda. We love her very much; but she makes us feel uneasy. She is not in accord with you.

GOETZ: I know.

HILDA: What can it matter to you, since I am going away?

GOETZ [*surprised*]: You're going away?

HILDA: Very soon.

GOETZ: Why?

HILDA: Because these people are happy.

GOETZ: Well?

HILDA: I can be of no service to happy people.

GOETZ: They love you.

HILDA: Of course, of course. But they'll manage.

GOETZ: They still need you.

HILDA: Do you think so? [*She turns toward the peasants.*] Is it true that you still need me? [*Embarrassed silence from the peasants.*] You see. What service could I be to them, since they have you? Farewell.

GOETZ [*to the peasants*]: Would you let her go without a word? Ingrates—who saved you from despair when you were desperate? Stay, Hilda—I am asking you in their name. And you, I order you to give her back your love.

HILDA [*with sudden violence*]: Keep your love: you have stolen my purse, and you shall not give me back my own money as charity.

TEACHER: Stay, Hilda, since he desires it. We shall obey him. I swear it, and we shall all love you as the Holy Man commands.

HILDA: Hush! Hush! You all loved me with a natural impulse of your hearts. Now it is over. Let's drop the

subject. Forget me, forget me quickly: the sooner the
better.

GOETZ [*to the peasants*]: Leave us.

[*All the peasants go out.*]

Where will you go?

HILDA: It doesn't matter. There's no lack of misery in
the world.

GOETZ: Always misery! Always unhappiness! Is there
nothing else?

HILDA: Nothing for me. That is my life.

GOETZ: Must you always suffer with their suffering?
Can't you also rejoice with their happiness?

HILDA [*violently*]: No, I cannot! A fine happiness! They
are bleating sheep. [*With despair*] Oh, Goetz, since
you came among us, I have become my own soul's
enemy. When my soul speaks, I am ashamed of what
it says. I know these people are no longer hungry,
and that they do not work so hard. If they desire this
sheep-like happiness, I should desire it along with
them. Well, I cannot, I cannot desire it. I must be
a monster; I have less love for them since they have
less suffering. And yet, I have a horror of suffering.
[*Pause.*] Can it be that I am spiteful?

GOETZ: You? No. You are jealous.

HILDA: Jealous. Yes. Full to bursting with jealousy.
[*Pause.*] You see, it's high time I went away; you
have corrupted me. It doesn't matter where I am;
whatever you undertake, you will arouse evil in
people's hearts. Farewell.

GOETZ: Farewell. [*She does not move.*] Well? What are
you waiting for? [*She makes a move to go.*] Hilda, I
implore you, don't abandon me. [*She laughs.*] What
is it?

HILDA [*without bitterness*]: You, you who have taken
everything away from me, you now implore me not
to abandon you?

GOETZ: The more they love me, the more I feel alone.

I am their roof, and I have no roof. I am their heaven, and I have no heaven. Yes, I have—that one, and see how far away it is. I tried to turn myself into a pillar and carry the weight of the celestial vault. You can have it! Heaven is an empty hole. I even wonder where God lives. [*Pause.*] I don't love the people enough; it all stems from that. I have made the gestures of love, but love has not followed; I suppose I am not very adroit. Why are you looking at me?

HILDA: You don't love them at all. You have robbed me for nothing.

GOETZ: Ah! It wasn't their love that should have been taken from you, it was your own love I should have taken. I should have loved them with your heart. You know, I envy you, envy even your jealousy. There you are, you look at them, you touch them, you are warmth, you are light, and YOU ARE NOT MYSELF. It's unbearable. I do not understand why we are two entities, and I should like, while remaining myself, to become you.

[NASTI *enters.*]

NASTI [*in a hollow voice*]: Goetz! Goetz! Goetz!

GOETZ [*turning round*]: Who is it? . . . Nasti! . . .

NASTI: Mankind is deaf.

GOETZ: Deaf? Deaf to your voice? That's new.

NASTI: Yes. It's new.

GOETZ: God puts you, like all others, to the test? We'll see how you will acquit yourself.

NASTI: Let God test me as much as He pleases. I shall never lose my faith in Him nor in my mission: and if God loses faith in me, then He's insane.

GOETZ: Speak.

NASTI [*pointing to* HILDA]: Send her away.

GOETZ: She is my own self. Speak, or go away.

NASTI: Very well. [*Pause.*] The revolt has broken out.

GOETZ: What revolt? [*Bruskly*] It wasn't I! It wasn't my fault! If they're killing each other, I'm not to blame!

NASTI: They were only held back by their fear of the Church: you proved that they didn't need their priests; prophets are now springing up everywhere. But they are prophets of anger who preach revenge.

GOETZ: And all that is my work?

NASTI: Yes, all.

GOETZ: Indeed! [*He strikes him.*]

NASTI: Strike! Strike again!

GOETZ: Ha! [*He wheels about.*] How sweet was Evil: I could kill! [*He walks up and down. Pause.*] Well! What do you want me to do?

NASTI: You can still prevent the worst.

GOETZ: I? [*A short laugh.*] Idiot, I have the evil eye. How could you dare use my services?

NASTI: I have no choice. . . . We have no arms, no money, no military leaders, and our peasants are too undisciplined to make good soldiers. In a few days, our reverses will begin; in a few months, the massacres.

GOETZ: So?

NASTI: There remains one hope. Today, I cannot control the revolt; in three months, I could. If we can win one pitched battle, only one, the barons will sue for peace.

GOETZ: What can I do?

NASTI: You are the finest captain in Germany.

GOETZ [*gazes at him, then turns away.*]: Ah! [*Pause.*] Redress wrongs! Always redress! You make me waste my time, the lot of you. Dear God, I have other things to do.

NASTI: You would let humanity destroy itself, provided you could build your City, your plaything, your model town?

GOETZ: This city is an arch. I have sheltered Love beneath it. What matters the deluge if I have saved brotherly love?

NASTI: Are you mad? You won't escape this war, it will

come here and seek you out. [GOETZ *is silent.*] Well?
Do you accept?

GOETZ: Not so fast. [*He returns to* NASTI.] There is no
discipline; I shall have to create it. Do you know
what that means? Executions.

NASTI: I know.

GOETZ: Nasti, I shall have to hang these people. Hang
them at random, to serve as examples; the innocent
with the guilty. What am I saying? They are all
innocent. Today, I am their brother, and I recognize
their innocence. Tomorrow, if I become their leader,
there will be none but the guilty, and I shall not
understand any more: I shall hang them.

NASTI: It must be done.

GOETZ: I shall have to turn myself into a butcher; you
have neither weapons nor skill. Force of numbers is
your one trump card. I shall have to waste lives.
Horrible war!

NASTI: You will sacrifice twenty thousand men to save
a hundred thousand.

GOETZ: If only I could be sure! Nasti, you can believe
me, I know what a battle is like. If we fight this one,
it's a hundred to one we shall lose it.

NASTI: Then I'll take that single chance. Come! Whatever may be the designs of God, we are named as His
elect: I am His prophet, and you are His butcher.
There is no longer time to hesitate.
[*Pause.*]

GOETZ: Hilda!

HILDA: What do you want?

GOETZ: Help me. What would you do in my place?

HILDA: I shall never be in your place, nor do I wish to
be. Men like you are leaders of men, and I am only
a woman. I have no advice to give you.

GOETZ: I have confidence only in you.

HILDA: In me?

GOETZ: Far more than in myself.

HILDA: Why should you want to make me an accomplice in your crimes? Why force me to decide in your place? Why give me power of life and death over my fellow men?

GOETZ: Because I love you.

HILDA: Be quiet. [*Pause.*] Oh! You have won. You have made me come over to the other side of the barricade. I was with those who suffered, now I am with those who decree the suffering. Oh, Goetz, I shall never sleep again. [*Pause.*] I forbid you to shed blood. Refuse.

GOETZ: We will make the decision together?

HILDA: Yes. Together.

GOETZ: And we will endure the consequences together?

HILDA: Together, whatever happens.

NASTI [*to* HILDA]: What business is this of yours?

HILDA: I speak in the name of the poor.

NASTI: No one other than I has the right to speak in their name.

HILDA: Why?

NASTI: Because I am one of them.

HILDA: You, one of the people? You ceased to be that long ago. You are a leader.

[GOETZ *has been lost in thought, and has not heard them. He raises his head abruptly.*]

GOETZ: Why not tell them the truth?

NASTI: What truth?

GOETZ: That they don't know how to fight and that they are lost if they begin this war.

NASTI: Because they will kill anyone who tells them so.

GOETZ: Supposing it was I who told them?

NASTI: You?

GOETZ: I have some credit with them because I am a prophet, and I gave them my possessions. What should one do with credit if not risk it?

NASTI: One chance in a thousand.

GOETZ: One chance in a thousand! Well! Have you the right to refuse?

NASTI: No. I have no right. Come.

HILDA: Don't go.

GOETZ [*taking her by the shoulders*]: Don't be afraid, this time God is on our side. [*He calls*] Come here, everyone!

[*The* PEASANTS *come back into the square.*]

There is fighting everywhere. Tomorrow, all Germany will be in flames. I am going back among men to preserve the peace.

ALL THE PEASANTS: Alas, Goetz, do not abandon us. What shall we do without you?

GOETZ: I shall return, my brothers; here is my God, here is my happiness, here is my love. I shall return. Here is Hilda. I entrust you to her. If, during my absence, anyone should try to enlist you on one side or the other, refuse to fight. If you are threatened, reply to the threats with love. Remember, brothers, remember all of you: love can drive back this war. [*He goes out with* NASTI.]

THE PEASANTS: What if he does not come back? [*Silence.*]

HILDA: Let us pray. [*Pause.*] Pray that love may drive back this war.

THE PEASANTS [*kneeling*]: O Lord, let our love drive back this war.

HILDA [*standing in their midst*]: Let my love drive back this war. Amen.

[*The scene blacks out and the first lines of the eighth scene follow immediately upon* HILDA's *prayer.*]

SCENES VIII AND IX

The peasants' camp. Murmurs, and cries in the darkness.

VOICES: Fie! Fie! Fie!

GOETZ'S VOICE [*dominating the tumult*]: You will die, all of you!

VOICES: Kill him! Kill him!

[*The lights come up on a clearing in the forest. It is night. Peasants armed with sticks and pitchforks. A few carry swords. Others hold torches.* GOETZ *and* NASTI *are standing on a rocky promontory, dominating the crowd.*]

VOICES: Fie! Fie for shame!

GOETZ: My poor friends, you haven't even the courage to look the truth in the face?

A VOICE: The truth is that you are a traitor.

GOETZ: The truth, my brothers, the blinding truth, is that you don't know how to fight.

[*A peasant of Herculean proportions strides forward.*]

THE HERCULES: I don't know how to fight? [*Laughter from the crowd.*] Hey, fellows, it seems I don't know how to fight! I can catch a bull by the horns and twist his ruddy neck off.

[GOETZ *jumps down from his rock, and comes to the man.*]

GOETZ: Well now, big brother, it seems you are three times as strong as I am?

THE HERCULES: Me, little brother? [*He gives* GOETZ *a light tap which sends him staggering.*]

GOETZ: Exactly. [*To one of the peasants*] Give me that stick. [*To the* HERCULES] And you, take this one. On guard. Come—*pique, taille, sabre, estoque.** [*He*

* Fencing terms for: prick, cut, slash, thrust.

parries and dodges the HERCULES's *clumsy thrusts.*]
You see! You see! You see! What good is your
strength? You only make the air-spirits moan and
the wind bleed! [*They fight.*] And now, my friend,
forgive me. I'm going to bash your head just a little.
It's for the common good. There! [*He strikes down
the* HERCULES.] Sweet Jesus, forgive me. Are you convinced? He was the strongest among you, and I am
far from being the most agile. [*Pause. The* PEASANTS
are silent, amazed. GOETZ *enjoys his victory for a
moment, then resumes his argument.*] Would you
like me to tell you why you are not afraid of death?
Each of you believes it will only strike the other
fellow. [*Pause.*] But now I am going to speak to God
the Father and ask Him a question. Father in Heaven,
if it is Thy desire that I help these men, send me a
sign to show which of them will perish in this war.
[*Suddenly he pretends to be afraid.*] Oh! Oh! Oh!
What do I see? Ah, my brothers, what is happening
to you! Oh, horrible vision! Truly, your fate is sealed!

A PEASANT [*worried*]: What's the matter? What's the
matter?

GOETZ: God is melting your flesh like sealing-wax: I
see nothing but your bones! Holy Virgin! All those
skeletons!

A PEASANT: What do you think that means?

GOETZ: God is against this revolt, and shows me those
who are marked down for death.

THE PEASANT: Who, for instance?

GOETZ: Who? [*He points at the peasant and thunders
in a terrible voice.*] You! [*Silence.*] And you! And you!
And you! What a ghoulish procession!

A PEASANT [*shaken, but still doubting*]: What proof
have we that you are a real prophet?

GOETZ: Oh, men of little faith, if you must have your
proof, behold this blood. [*He lifts his hands. Silence.
To* NASTI.] I have won.

NASTI [*between his teeth*]: Not yet. [KARL *advances*.]
    Take heed of that one—he's the toughest of the lot.

KARL: Oh, too-credulous brothers, when will you learn
    to be on your guard? Are you so tender and soft that
    you do not even know how to hate? Today, again, a
    man merely has to speak in the name of the Lord
    to make you bow your heads. What has he done?
    There are a few drops of blood on his hands! A fine
    proof! If a man has to bleed before he can convince
    you, I, too, can bleed.
    [*He raises his hands, and they begin to bleed.*]

GOETZ: Who are you?

KARL: A prophet like yourself.

GOETZ: Prophet of hate!

KARL: The only road that leads to brotherly love.

GOETZ: I recognize you now. You are Karl, my lackey.

KARL: At your service.

GOETZ: A lackey-prophet—it's ridiculous.

KARL: Not more ridiculous than a general-prophet.

GOETZ [*coming down the steps*]: Show me your hands!
    [*He turns them over.*] Good heavens, this man has
    bladders filled with blood concealed in his sleeves.

KARL: Let me see your hands. [*He examines them.*]
    This man scratches old wounds with his nails to
    squeeze out a few drops of pus. Come along, broth-
    ers, put us to the test, and decide which of us two
    is the true prophet.

MURMURS: Yes . . . Yes . . .

KARL: Can you do this? [*He makes a stick burst into
    flowers.*] Or this? [*He pulls a rabbit out of his hat.*]
    And this? [*He is surrounded by a cloud of smoke.*]
    Show me what you can do!

GOETZ: Conjuring tricks I have seen a hundred times
    in village fairs. I am no juggler.

A PEASANT: A prophet ought to be able to do anything
    a juggler does.

GOETZ: I shall not engage in a competition of miracles

with my own body-servant. My brothers, I was a general before I became a prophet. We are talking of war; if you will not believe the prophet, put your trust in the general.

KARL: You will be able to trust the general when the general has proved that he is no traitor.

GOETZ: Ingrate! It was for love of you and your fellows that I despoiled myself of my belongings.

KARL: For the love of me?

GOETZ: Yes, for you who hate me.

KARL: You mean, you love me?

GOETZ: Yes, my brother, I love you.

KARL [*triumphantly*]: He has betrayed himself, my brothers! He's lying to us! Look at my mug and tell me how anyone could love me. And you, my lads, each and every one of you, do you believe you are lovable?

GOETZ: Idiot! If I did not love them, why should I have given them my lands?

KARL: Exactly. Why? There's the whole question. [*Bruskly*] God! God who probes our hearts and loins, help me now! I will lend Thee my body and my voice: tell us why Goetz the bastard gave away his lands. [KARL *begins to utter horrible cries.*]

THE PEASANTS: God is here!
               God will speak!

[*They fall on their knees.*]

GOETZ: God! That's the last straw!

KARL [*with closed eyes, speaking in a strange voice that seems not to belong to him*]: Hallo! Earth ahoy!

THE PEASANTS: Hallo! Ahoy, ahoy!

KARL [*as before*]: I, God, behold you, men of earth. I behold you.

THE PEASANTS: Have mercy upon us.

KARL [*as before*]: Is the man Goetz among you?

A PEASANT: Yes, Our Father, to the right, a little behind Thee.

KARL [*as before*]: Goetz! Goetz! Why did you give them
   your lands? Reply.

GOETZ: To whom have I the honor of speaking?

KARL [*as before*]: I am the One who is.

GOETZ: Well, if you are who you are, then you know
   what you know and you must know why I did what
   I did.

THE PEASANTS [*threateningly*]: Fie, for shame! Answer!
   Answer!

GOETZ: I will answer you, my brothers. You, not him.
   I gave away my lands so that all men might be equal.
   [KARL *laughs*.]

THE PEASANTS: God is laughing!
                    God is laughing!
   [NASTI *has come down the steps and taken up a position behind Goetz*.]

KARL [*as before*]: You lie, Goetz, you lie to your God.
   And you, my sons, hear me!
   Whatever a Lord may do, he can never be your equal.
   That is why I command you to kill them all.
   This one gave you his lands,
   But in your turn, were you able to give him yours?
   He had the choice of bestowing or keeping,
   But had you the choice of refusing?
   To him who gives you a kiss or a blow,
   You should render a kiss or a blow;
   But to him who gives what you cannot render,
   Offer all the hatred within your hearts.
   For you were slaves, and he enslaved you;
   You were humiliated, and he increased your humilia-
        tion.
   Gift of the morning, grief!
   Gift of the noontide, care!
   Gift of the evening, despair!

GOETZ: Oh! A fine sermon! Who gave you life and
   light? It was the Lord God! To give is His law, and
   whatsoever He does, He bestows. And what can you

render Him, you who are nothing but dust? Nothing!
Conclusion: it is God you should hate.

THE PEASANTS: With God, it's different.

GOETZ: Why did He create us in His image? If God
is generosity and love, man, his creature, should be
love and generosity! My brothers, I conjure you:
accept my gifts and my friendship. I do not ask for
your gratitude, not at all. I ask only that you should
not condemn my love as a vice, nor reproach my
gifts as crimes.

A PEASANT: Talk away; as for me, I don't like charity.

KARL [*resuming his natural voice, and pointing to a
beggar*]: There's one who has understood. The lands
are yours; he who pretends to give them to you is
deceiving you, for he is giving away what is not his.
Take his lands. Take and kill, if you wish to become
men. We can only teach ourselves by violence.

GOETZ: Is there nothing but hate, my brothers? My
love for you . . .

KARL: Your love comes from the Devil, it corrupts
whatever it touches. Ah, lads, if you could see the
people of Altweiler; it only took him three months to
castrate them. He'll love you so well that he'll cut
off your balls and replace them with forget-me-nots.
Don't let yourselves be fooled: you were brute beasts
and hate has changed you into men. If they take hate
away from you, you will again fall down on all fours
and again will know the mute misery of beasts.

GOETZ: Nasti! Help me!

NASTI [*pointing to* KARL]: The case is judged. God is
with him.

GOETZ [*stupefied*]: Nasti!

THE PEASANTS: Get out! Get out! Go to the devil!

GOETZ [*suddenly enraged*]: Yes, I shall go away, never
fear. Run toward your death! If you get yourselves
done in, I'll dance for joy. How hideous you are!
Lemur-people! Larvae! I thank God for showing me

your souls; for I know now that I was mistaken; it is right that the lords should possess the land, for their souls are proud. It is right that you should again crawl on all fours, you thick-skinned clodhoppers, for you are nothing but swine!

THE PEASANTS [preparing to throw themselves upon him]: Kill him! Kill him!

GOETZ [snatching a sword from a peasant]: Come and take me!

KARL [raising his hands]: Enough. [Silence.] This man trusted your word. You must learn to keep it, even when it is given to an enemy.

[The stage empties little by little, and the shadows fall once more. The last torch is set up on the rock; NASTI takes it, and turns to go.]

NASTI: Leave this place, Goetz! Leave quickly!

GOETZ: Nasti! Nasti! Why have you forsaken me?

NASTI: Because you have failed.

GOETZ: Nasti, they are a pack of wolves. How can you remain with such people?

NASTI: All the love in the world is in them.

GOETZ: In them? If you have found a grain of love among these dunghills you must have good eyesight. I've seen nothing of it.

NASTI: That's true, Goetz: you've seen nothing. [He goes.]

[It is night. The sounds die away in the distance; far off, a woman cries out, then a faint light shows upon GOETZ.]

GOETZ [alone]: You are done for, curs! I shall wreak unforgettable harm upon you! Return, my wickedness! Render me light! [Pause.] What a joke! Good has purged my soul, there remains not one drop of venom. Very well. On the road to Good, on the road to Altweiler! I must either hang myself or do Good. My children are waiting, my capons, my farmyard-angels. They will rejoice to see me. O God, how they bore me! It's the others I love—the wolves. [*He begins to walk up and down.*] Very well, Lord, Thou must guide me through the dark night. Since we must persevere despite frustration, let every frustration be to me a sign, every misery a piece of luck, every accident a grace. Give me the good use of my misfortunes! Lord, I believe, I must believe, that Thou didst permit me to wind up outside the world because Thou didst desire to keep me for Thyself. Here I am, my God, here we are face to face again, as in the good old days when I was doing Evil. Ah! I should never have concerned myself with mankind: humanity is a nuisance, it is the brushwood that must be thrust aside in order to reach Thee. I come, Lord, I come. I am walking in Thy night: stretch out Thy hand. Tell me: art Thou, indeed, the night? Night, the tormenting absence of everything! For Thou art the One who is present in the universal absence, whom we hear when all is silence, whom we see when we can see no more. Ancient night, great night before the Creation, night of non-knowing, night of disgrace and misfortune, hide me, devour my foul body, slip between my soul and myself and prey upon me. I demand the destitution, shame, and loneliness of scorn, for man is made to destroy man in himself and to open up like a female to the huge, dark body of the night. Until I shall have tasted everything, I shall not have a taste for anything, until I shall have possessed all, I shall possess nothing. Until I shall have been everything, I shall be less than nothing. I shall abase myself before all people, and Thou, O Lord, wilt take me in the nets of Thy night and raise me up above them. [*He cries aloud in distress.*] This hatred of men, this disdain of myself, did I not seek them when I was still wicked? The loneliness of Good—how am I to distinguish it from the loneliness of Evil? [*The dawn light slowly grows.*] The dawn is breaking. I have come through Thy night. Blessed

art Thou for Thy gift of light: I shall be able to see
clearly.

[*He turns and sees Altweiler in ruins.* HILDA *is sitting
on a pile of stones and rubble, her head in her hands.
He cries out.*]

Ah!

HILDA [*raising her head and looking at him*]: At last!

GOETZ: Where are the others? Dead? Why? Because
they refused to fight?

HILDA: Yes.

GOETZ: Ah, give me back my night! Hide me from the
sight of men! [*Pause.*] How did it happen?

HILDA: Peasants came from Walsheim with weapons
in their hands; they asked us to join them, and we
refused.

GOETZ: Then they set fire to the village. Capital! [*He
bursts out laughing.*] Why didn't you die with the
others?

HILDA: Are you sorry?

GOETZ: No survivors—how much more simple!

HILDA: I am sorry, too. [*Pause.*] They shut us in a house
and then set fire to it. A good idea.

GOETZ: Yes, a good idea, a very good idea.

HILDA: At the last minute, a window opened. I jumped
out. I wasn't afraid to die, but I wanted to see you
again.

GOETZ: What for? You would have seen me again in
heaven.

HILDA: We shall not go to heaven, Goetz, and even if
we were both to go, we would have no eyes to see
each other, no hands to touch each other. In heaven,
there is no time for anything but God. [*She comes
to touch him.*] Here you are: a little flesh, worn-out,
rough, miserable—a life, a wretched life. It is this
flesh and this life I love. We can only love on earth,
and against God's will.

GOETZ: I love only God, and I am no longer on earth.

HILDA: Then you don't love me?

GOETZ: No. Nor do you, Hilda, love me, either. What you believe to be love is hate.

HILDA: Why should I hate you?

GOETZ: Because you believe that I have killed your people.

HILDA: It was I who killed them.

GOETZ: You?

HILDA: It was I who said no. I loved them better dead than alive as murderers. O God, what right had I to choose for them?

GOETZ: Bah! Do as I do! Wash your hands of all this blood. We are nothing; we have no power over anything. Man dreams he can act, but it is God who leads him.

HILDA: No, Goetz, no. But for me, they would still be alive.

GOETZ: Very well. So be it. But for you, perhaps. I am not concerned in this.

HILDA: "We decided together, and we shall take the consequences together." Remember?

GOETZ: We are not together. You wanted to see me? Well, look at me, touch me. Good. Now, go away. For the rest of my days, I shall look no more at a human face. I shall have eyes for nothing but the earth and the stones. [*Pause.*] I asked Thee a question, Lord, and Thou didst reply. Blessed art Thou, who hast revealed the wickedness of men. I shall chastise their sins in my own flesh, I shall torment this body with hunger, cold, and the scourge; but slowly, very slowly. I shall destroy the man, because Thou hast created man for destruction. They were my people: only a few—a single village, almost like a family. My subjects lie dead, and I, the living, am dead to the world. I shall spend the rest of my days meditating on dissolution. [*To* HILDA] Are you still there? Leave me. Go elsewhere to seek your life and your misery.

HILDA: You are the more miserable. This is my place.
I shall stay here.

SCENE X

*The ruined village, six months later. Sitting in the
same position as at the end of the previous scene,*
HILDA *is gazing toward the road. Suddenly, we realize
she sees someone approaching. She half-rises and
waits.* HEINRICH *enters, flowers stuck in his hat, a
bouquet in his hand.*

HEINRICH: Here we are. [*He turns to an invisible companion.*] Take off your hat. [*To* HILDA] My name is
Heinrich; in the old days I used to say mass. Today
I live on charity. [*To the* DEVIL] Where are you off
to? Come here. [*To* HILDA] When the smell of death
is around, he has to be about his business. But he
wouldn't really harm a fly.

HILDA: It's a year and a day, isn't it? A year and a day
since Worms?

HEINRICH: Who told you?

HILDA: I counted the days.

HEINRICH: They've talked to you about me?

HILDA: Yes. A long time ago.

HEINRICH: A beautiful day, isn't it? I picked these
flowers on the way; it's an anniversary bouquet. [*He
holds them out to her.*]

HILDA: I don't want them. [*She lays them down beside
her.*]

HEINRICH: You shouldn't be afraid of happy people.

HILDA: You aren't happy.

HEINRICH: I told you, this is a holiday; last night I even slept. Come along, little sister, give me a smile; I love all men except one, and I want everyone in the world to be happy. [*Bruskly*] Go and find him. [*She does not move.*] Run along! Don't keep him waiting.

HILDA: He isn't waiting for you.

HEINRICH: Isn't he? You surprise me. We are a couple of friends, and I'll wager he's smartened himself up to welcome me.

HILDA: Spare him. Pick up your bouquet and go.

HEINRICH [*to the* DEVIL]: D'you hear?

HILDA: Leave your Devil alone, I don't believe in him.

HEINRICH: Neither do I.

HILDA: Well, then?

HEINRICH [*laughing*]: Ha! Ha! Ha! You are a child.

HILDA: The man who harmed you is no more; he is dead to the world. He won't even recognize you, and I am sure you could never recognize him. You are looking for one man, and you will find another.

HEINRICH: I will take what I find.

HILDA: Spare him, I implore you. Why should you want to hurt me? I have done you no harm.

HEINRICH: I wasn't meaning to hurt you; I like you very much.

HILDA: I shall bleed through all the wounds you deal him.

HEINRICH: You love him?

HILDA: Yes.

HEINRICH: Then it is possible to love him? How strange. [*He laughs.*] Many people have tried to love me, but without success. Does he love you?

HILDA: He has loved me as much as he has loved himself.

HEINRICH: If he loves you, I shall regret less making you suffer.

HILDA: Forgive him his trespasses, and God will forgive you your own.

HEINRICH: But I don't want Him to forgive me, in the least. Damnation has its good sides—the whole thing is to adapt one's self. And I have done that. I am not yet in Hell, and already I have my little habits.

HILDA: Poor man.

HEINRICH [*angry*]: No! No! No! I am not a poor man. I am happy, I tell you I am happy. [*Pause.*] Come along! Call him. [*She is silent.*] It's better for you to call him; then he'll have a surprise when he sees me. Won't you call him? I'll call him myself, then. Goetz! Goetz! Goetz!

HILDA: He isn't here.

HEINRICH: Where is he?

HILDA: In the forest. Sometimes he stays there for weeks on end.

HEINRICH: Far from here?

HILDA: Twenty-five leagues.

HEINRICH [*to the* DEVIL]: Do you believe her? [*He closes his eyes and listens to what the* DEVIL *whispers.*] Yes, yes. Yes. [*He smiles maliciously.*] Well, how am I to find him?

HILDA: Go and look, good priest. Go and look. Your companion will know how to guide you.

HEINRICH: God keep you, my sister. [*To the* DEVIL] Come along. This way.

[*He disappears.* HILDA *is left alone, and watches him out of sight.* GOETZ *enters, carrying a whip in his right hand, a pitcher in the left. He seems exhausted.*]

GOETZ: Who was calling me? [HILDA *does not reply.*] Someone was here and called me. I heard his voice.

HILDA: You always hear voices when you are fasting.

GOETZ: Where did those flowers come from?

HILDA: I picked them myself.

GOETZ: You don't often pick flowers. [*Pause.*] What is today? What day of the year?

HILDA: Why ask me that?

GOETZ: Someone was to have come in the autumn.

HILDA: Who?

GOETZ: I don't know any more. [*Pause.*] Tell me. What is today? What day of what month?

HILDA: Do you think I count the days? We have only one now, that begins and begins again; it is given to us with the dawn and taken away with the night. You are a clock that has stopped and always tells the same time.

GOETZ: Stopped? No; I have gained. [*He shakes the pitcher.*] Can you hear? It gurgles. Water makes a heavenly music; I have Hell in my throat and Paradise in my ears.

HILDA: How long is it since you drank?

GOETZ: Three days. I have to hold out till tomorrow.

HILDA: Why until tomorrow?

GOETZ [*laughing like an idiot*]: Ha, ha! I must! [*Pause. He shakes the pitcher.*] Glug! Glug! Hey? I don't know any sound more unpleasant for a man dying of thirst.

HILDA: Amuse yourself, torment your desires. To drink when you're thirsty—that would be too easy! If you didn't harbor a temptation eternally in your soul, you'd run the risk of forgetting yourself.

GOETZ: How am I to conquer myself, if I don't give myself temptations?

HILDA: Oh, Goetz, do you really believe you are living this day for the first time? The pitcher, the sound of the water, the blanched skin of your lips, I know all that by heart. Don't you know what is going to happen?

GOETZ: I shall hold out till tomorrow; that's all.

HILDA: You have never held out to the end because you set yourself impossible tests. You are going to shake that pitcher until you collapse. When you have fallen, I will have to make you drink.

GOETZ: You want something new? Look. [*He tilts the pitcher.*] The flowers are thirsty. Drink, flowers, drink up my water, let Heaven visit your golden gullets. Look. They are reviving. Earth and plants accept my

gifts; it is only men who reject them. [*He overturns
the pitcher.*] See: now there is no possibility of
drinking. [*He laughs and repeats painfully*] It's impossible . . . impossible . . .

HILDA: Is it God's will that you should become childish?

GOETZ: Of course. Man has to be destroyed, hasn't he?
[*He throws away the pitcher.*] Now, see if you can
make me drink! [*He falls.*]

HILDA [*looks at him coldly, then begins to laugh*]: You
know quite well I always have water in reserve; I
know you. [*She fetches a jug of water, then returns
and lifts his head.*] Come, drink.

GOETZ: Not before tomorrow.

HILDA: God wishes you to be insane or childish, but
not dead. Therefore, you must drink.

GOETZ: I make all Germany tremble, yet here I lie on
my back like a suckling babe in the hands of his
nurse. Art Thou satisfied, Lord? Dost Thou know
any abjection worse than mine? Hilda, you who foresee everything, if I quench my thirst, do you know
what will happen afterward?

HILDA: Yes, I know. The great game: the temptation
of the flesh. You will want to go to bed with
me.

GOETZ: And even so you want me to drink?

HILDA: Yes.

GOETZ: Supposing I were to take you by force?

HILDA: In the state you're in? Now, now! Everything
is as carefully planned as in the mass. You will shout
obscenities and insults, and then end up by flogging
yourself. Drink.

GOETZ [*taking the jug*]: Another defeat! [*He drinks.*]
The body is disgusting. [*He drinks.*]

HILDA: The body is good. It's in your soul that there's
rottenness.

GOETZ [*setting down the jug*]: My thirst has gone; I
feel empty. [*Pause.*] I am tired.

HILDA: Sleep.

GOETZ: No, because I am tired. [*He looks at her.*] Show me your breasts. [*She does not move.*] Go on, show them, tempt me; make me burst with desire. No? Ah, bitch, why not?

HILDA: Because I love you.

GOETZ: Heat your love till it is white hot, plunge it into my heart, make it sizzle and smoke! If you love me, you must torture me.

HILDA: I belong to you; why should I make my body a rack for your torment?

GOETZ: If you could see into my mind, you would smash my face. My mind is a witches' sabbath, and you are all the witches.

HILDA [*laughing*]: You are boasting.

GOETZ: I wish you were a beast so I could mount you like a beast.

HILDA: How you suffer because you are a man!

GOETZ: I am not a man, I am nothing. There is only God. Man is an optical illusion. I disgust you, don't I?

HILDA [*calmly*]: No, because I love you.

GOETZ: Can't you see I am trying to degrade you?

HILDA: Yes, because I am your most precious possession.

GOETZ [*angrily*]: You are not playing the game!

HILDA: No, I am not playing the game.

GOETZ: As long as you remain beside me, I shall not feel altogether unclean.

HILDA: That is why I remain.

[GOETZ *rises painfully.*]

GOETZ: If I took you in my arms, would you shrink from me?

HILDA: No.

GOETZ: Even if I came to you with my heart filled with horrors?

HILDA: If you can bring yourself to touch me, it is because your heart is pure.

GOETZ: Hilda, how can we love each other without shame? The sin of lust is the most degrading of vices.

HILDA: Look at me, look at me well, look at my eyes, my lips, my breasts and my arms: am I a sin?

GOETZ: You are beautiful. Beauty is Evil.

HILDA: Are you sure?

GOETZ: I am no longer sure of anything. [*Pause.*] If I gratify my desires, I sin, but I free myself of desire; if I refuse to satisfy them, they infect the whole soul. . . . Night is falling; at twilight a man needs good eyesight to distinguish the good Lord from the Devil. [*He approaches her, touches her, then springs away.*] Sleep with you under the eye of God? No. I don't care for coupling in public. [*Pause.*] Oh, for a night deep enough to hide us from his regard. . . .

HILDA: Love is that deep night; when people love each other, they become invisible to God.

[GOETZ *hesitates, then springs away from her.*]

GOETZ: Give me the eyes of the Boetian lynx so that my gaze may penetrate this skin! Show me what is hidden in your nostrils and inside your ear holes. I who would shudder to touch dung with my finger tips, how can I desire to hold in my arms this bag of excrement?

HILDA [*violently*]: There is more filth in your soul than within my body. The ugliness and filth of the flesh is in the mind. I do not need to be lynx-eyed; I have nursed you, washed you, know the odors of your fever. Have I ever ceased loving you? Each day you grow a little more like the corpse you will become, and I still love you. If you die, I will lie down beside you and stay there to the very end, without eating or drinking; you will rot away in my embrace, and I will love your carrion flesh; for you do not love at all, if you do not love everything.

GOETZ [*holding out the whip*]: Whip me. [HILDA *shrugs.*] Come along, beat me, beat me, take vengeance upon me for dead Catherine, your lost youth, and all those people burned alive by my fault.

HILDA [*bursting out laughing*]: Yes, I will beat you,

filthy monk; I will beat you because you have ruined our love. [*She takes the whip.*]

GOETZ: Across the eyes, Hilda, across the eyes!

HEINRICH [*entering*]: Whip away! Whip away! Carry on exactly as if I were not here. [*He comes forward. To* HILDA] My friend here prompted me to take a little walk and then come back stealthily. You can't deceive him, you know. [*To* GOETZ] She wanted to prevent our meeting. Is it true you weren't expecting me?

GOETZ: What? I was counting the days.

HILDA: You were counting them? Oh! Goetz, you lied to me. [*She looks at him.*] What's the matter? Your eyes are shining, you are no longer the same.

GOETZ: It is the joy of seeing him again.

HILDA: A strange joy; he'll do you all the harm he can.

GOETZ: It is proof that he loves me. You are jealous, eh? [*She does not reply.*] [*To* HEINRICH] Was it you who picked the flowers?

HEINRICH: Yes. For you.

GOETZ: Thank you. [*He picks up the bouquet.*]

HEINRICH: Happy anniversary, Goetz.

GOETZ: Happy anniversary, Heinrich.

HEINRICH: Tonight, you are probably going to die. . . .

GOETZ: Indeed? Why?

HEINRICH: The peasants are looking for you to kill you. I had to come quickly to get here before them.

GOETZ: Kill me, by Christ! That's honoring me beyond my deserts; I thought I had been completely forgotten. And why do they want to kill me?

HEINRICH: Last Thursday, on the plain of Gunsbach, the barons cut Nasti's army to ribbons. Twenty-five thousand dead; it was a complete rout. In two or three months the revolt will be stamped out.

GOETZ [*violently*]: Twenty-five thousand dead! They should never have engaged in that battle! The idiots! They should have . . . [*He controls himself.*] The devil! We are all born to die. [*Pause.*] They put the whole blame upon me, of course?

HEINRICH: They say you would have avoided the butchery if you had accepted the leadership of the troops. Rest assured, you are the most hated man in all Germany.

GOETZ: And Nasti? Is he in flight? A prisoner? Dead?

HEINRICH: Guess.

GOETZ: Go to hell. [*He becomes lost in thought.*]

HILDA: Do they know he is here?

HEINRICH: Yes.

HILDA: Who told them? You?

HEINRICH [*pointing to the Devil*]: Not me. Him.

HILDA [*gently*]: Goetz! [*She touches his arm.*] Goetz!

GOETZ [*startled*]: Ha! What is it?

HILDA: You cannot stay here.

GOETZ: Why not? I must pay, mustn't I?

HILDA: You have nothing to pay for—you are not guilty.

GOETZ: Mind your own business.

HILDA: This is my business. Goetz, you must go.

GOETZ: Go where?

HILDA: No matter where, provided you are safe. You have no right to get yourself killed.

GOETZ: No.

HILDA: It would be cheating.

GOETZ: Ah yes: cheating. Well? Haven't I cheated all my life? [*To* HEINRICH] Begin your interrogation; this is the moment, I am ready.

HEINRICH [*meaning* HILDA]: Tell her to go away.

HILDA: You will have to talk in front of me. . . . I am not going to leave him.

GOETZ: He is right, Hilda, this trial must be conducted in private.

HILDA: What trial?

GOETZ: Mine.

HILDA: Why let him put you on trial? Drive away this priest and let us leave the village.

GOETZ: Hilda, I need to be put on trial. Every day, every hour, I condemn myself, but I can never convince myself because I know myself too well to trust myself. I cannot see my soul any longer, because it is under my nose; I need someone to lend me his eyes.

HILDA: Take mine.

GOETZ: You don't see me either; you love me. Heinrich hates me, therefore he can convince me; when my own thoughts come from his mouth, I will be able to believe.

HILDA: If I go away, will you promise to flee with me in a moment?

GOETZ: Yes, if I win my case.

HILDA: You know quite well you have decided to lose it. Farewell, Goetz. [*She goes to him, kisses him, and goes out.*]

GOETZ [*throwing aside the bouquet*]: Quickly, to our work! Do me all the harm you can.

HEINRICH [*looking at him*]: This wasn't how I imagined you.

GOETZ: Courage, Heinrich, the task is easy. Half of myself is your accomplice against the other half. Begin, search me to the depths of my being, since it is my being that is on trial.

HEINRICH: Is it true that you want to lose?

GOETZ: Of course not, no fear. Only I prefer despair to uncertainty.

HEINRICH: Well . . . [*Pause.*] Wait: it is a blank in my memory. I am subject to these lapses; it will soon come back. [*He walks up and down in agitation.*] Yet I had taken every precaution; this morning I went over everything in my mind . . . it is your fault. You aren't at all as you ought to be. You should be crowned with roses, with triumph in your eyes; in the end, you would have fallen on your knees. . . . Where is your pride? Where is your insolence? You are half dead—what pleasure can I find in finishing you off? [*In a rage*] Ah! I am not yet wicked enough!

GOETZ [*laughing*]: You are working yourself up, Heinrich. Relax, take your time.

HEINRICH: There isn't a moment to lose. I tell you they are on my heels. [*To the Devil*] Prompt me, prompt me; help me to hate him now I'm with him. [*Plaintively*] He is never there when you need him.

GOETZ: I'm going to prompt you myself. [*Pause.*] The lands.

HEINRICH: The lands?

GOETZ: Did I do wrong to give them away?

HEINRICH: Ah! Your lands . . . But you didn't give them away: you can only give what you have.

GOETZ: Well said! Possession is a friendship between man and objects; but possessions shrieked in my hands. I gave nothing away. I read a public act of donation, that is all. However, priest, though it is true that I didn't give away my lands, it is equally true that the peasants received them. How can you answer that?

HEINRICH: They didn't receive the lands since they were unable to keep them. When the barons shall have invaded the domain and installed a young cousin of Conrad's in the castle of Heidenstamm, what will remain of this phantasmagoria?

GOETZ: Capital! Neither given nor received; that is much simpler. The gold pieces of the Devil change into dead leaves when you try to spend them; my good deeds are like them: when you touch them, they turn into corpses. But what about the intention? Eh? If I really meant to do good, neither God nor the Devil can take that away. Attack the intention. Tear the intention to pieces.

HEINRICH: It's not worth the trouble; as you couldn't enjoy your possessions, you wanted to raise yourself above other men by pretending to despoil yourself.

GOETZ: Oh, brazen voice, proclaim, proclaim my thoughts; I no longer know if I am listening to you or hearing my own voice. So then, all was nothing but lies and make-believe? I have effected nothing; I merely went through the motions. Ah, priest, you are scratching me where I itch. But what then? What did the mountebank do? You run short of breath very quickly!

HEINRICH [*infected by* GOETZ's *frenzy*]: You gave only to destroy.

GOETZ: You're right! It wasn't enough for me to have murdered the heir. . . .

HEINRICH [*as before*]: You wanted to grind the inheritance to powder.

GOETZ: I lifted the ancient domain of Heidenstamm. . . .

HEINRICH [*as before*]: And you dashed it to the ground, smashing it to pieces.

GOETZ: I wanted my benevolence to be more destructive than my vices.

HEINRICH: And you succeeded: twenty-five thousand dead! In one day of virtue you killed more people than in thirty-five years of malice!

GOETZ: Don't forget that those dead were the poor; those very poor to whom I pretended to offer Conrad's possessions.

HEINRICH: Why, yes, you always detested the poor.

GOETZ [*raising his fist*]: You cur! [*He stops and begins to laugh.*] I wanted to strike you; that means you were right. Ha! Ha! So that's where the shoe pinches! Go on! Accuse me of detesting the poor and exploiting their gratitude to enslave them. Before, I violated souls by torture, now I violate them through the power of Good. I turned this village into a bouquet of faded souls. The poor creatures mimicked me, and I mimicked virtue; they have died as useless martyrs, without knowing why they perished. Listen, priest: I had betrayed everyone, including my own brother, but my appetite for betrayal was not yet assuaged; so, one night, before the ramparts of Worms, I

thought up a way to betray Evil, that's the whole
story. Only Evil doesn't let itself be betrayed quite so
easily; it wasn't Good that jumped out of the dice-
box; it was a worse Evil. What does it matter anyway? Monster or saint, I didn't give a damn, I wanted
to be inhuman. Say it, Heinrich, say I was mad with
shame, and wanted to amaze Heaven to escape men's
scorn. Come along! What are you waiting for? Speak!
Ah, it's true, you cannot speak any more; I have your
voice in my mouth. [*Imitating* HEINRICH] You didn't
change your skin, Goetz, you altered your language.
You called your hatred of men love, your rage for
destruction you called generosity. But you remained
unchanged; nothing but a bastard. [*Resuming his
natural voice*] My God, I bear witness that he speaks
the truth; I, the accused, acknowledge myself guilty.
I have lost my case, Heinrich. Are you satisfied? [*He
staggers, and leans against the wall.*]

HEINRICH: No.

GOETZ: You are very hard.

HEINRICH: O, my God, is this my victory? How sad it
is.

GOETZ: What will you do when I am dead? You'll miss
me.

HEINRICH [*meaning the Devil*]: He gives me plenty to
do. I shan't have time to think of you.

GOETZ: At least, you are sure they want to kill me?

HEINRICH: Sure.

GOETZ: The kind people! I shall stretch out my neck,
and all will be over; a good riddance for everyone.

HEINRICH: Nothing ever finishes.

GOETZ: Nothing? Ah yes, we still have Hell. Well, it
will be a pleasant change.

HEINRICH: It won't be any change for you; you are there
already. My companion here—[*Meaning the Devil*]—
tells me that earth is only an illusion; there is Heaven
and Hell, nothing more. Death is a booby trap for
families; for the dead man, it all goes on.

GOETZ: Then everything will go on for me?

HEINRICH: Everything. You will enjoy yourself for Eternity. [*Pause.*]

GOETZ: How near it seemed—Righteousness—when I was an evildoer. One had only to stretch out an arm. I stretched mine out and Good changed into a breath of wind. Is it then only a mirage? Heinrich, Heinrich, is Good possible for men?

HEINRICH: Happy anniversary, Goetz. A year and a day ago, you asked me the same question. And I replied, no. It was dark, you laughed as you looked at me, and you said: "You are trapped." And then, you wriggled yourself clear with a throw of the dice. Well, look about you: it is dark—another night like the first one, and who is caught in the rattrap?

GOETZ [*clowning*]: I am.

HEINRICH: Will you wriggle out?

GOETZ [*becoming serious*]: No. I shall not wriggle out. [*He walks up and down.*] Lord, if Thou dost refuse us the means of doing good, why hast Thou made us desire it so keenly? If Thou didst not permit that I should become good, why shouldst Thou have taken from me the desire to be wicked? [*He continues his restless pacing.*] Strange that there should be no way out of this.

HEINRICH: Why do you pretend to talk to Him? You know quite well He will not answer.

GOETZ: Then why this silence? He who manifested Himself to the ass of the prophet, why does He refuse to manifest Himself to me?

HEINRICH: Because you are unimportant. Torture the weak, or martyrize yourself, kiss the lips of a harlot or a leper, die of privation or excesses: God doesn't give a damn.

GOETZ: Then who is important?

HEINRICH: No one. Man is nothing. Don't pretend to be surprised; you have always known it, you knew it the night you threw the dice. If you didn't, why did you cheat? [GOETZ *tries to speak*.] You cheated, Catherine saw you: you raised your voice to cover the silence of God. The orders you pretend to receive, you send to yourself.

GOETZ [*reflecting*]: Myself, yes.

HEINRICH [*surprised*]: Yes, indeed. You, yourself.

GOETZ [*as before*]: I alone.

HEINRICH: Yes, I tell you, yes.

GOETZ [*lifting his head*]: I alone, priest; you are right. I alone. I supplicated, I demanded a sign, I sent messages to Heaven, no reply. Heaven ignored my very name. Each minute I wondered what I could BE in the eyes of God. Now I know the answer: nothing. God does not see me, God does not hear me, God does not know me. You see this emptiness over our heads? That is God. You see this gap in the door? It is God. You see that hole in the ground? That is God again. Silence is God. Absence is God. God is the loneliness of man. There was no one but myself; I alone decided on Evil; and I alone invented Good. It was I who cheated, I who worked miracles, I who accused myself today, I alone who can absolve myself; I, man. If God exists, man is nothing; if man exists . . . Where are you going?

HEINRICH: I am running away; I have no more to do with you.

GOETZ: Wait, priest. I am going to make you laugh.

HEINRICH: Be quiet!

GOETZ: You don't know what I'm going to tell you. [*He looks at* HEINRICH *and then speaks roughly*.] You do know!

HEINRICH [*crying out*]: It's not true! I know nothing, I don't want to know!

GOETZ: Heinrich, I am going to tell you a colossal joke: God doesn't exist.

[HEINRICH *throws himself upon* GOETZ *and strikes him. Under the rain of blows*, GOETZ *laughs and shouts*.] He doesn't exist. Joy, tears of joy. Halleluiah! Fool!

Don't strike me! I have delivered us. No more Heaven, no more Hell; nothing but earth.

HEINRICH: Ah! Let Him damn me a hundred times, a thousand times, provided He exists. Goetz, men have called us traitors and bastard; and they have condemned us. If God doesn't exist, there is no way of escaping men. My God, this man blasphemed, I believe in Thee, I believe. Our Father which art in Heaven, I would rather be judged by an Infinite Being than judged by my equals.

GOETZ: To whom are you talking? You've just said He is deaf. [HEINRICH *looks at him in silence.*] No way, now, of escaping men. Farewell monsters, farewell saints. Farewell pride. There is nothing left but mankind.

HEINRICH: Mankind will not accept you, bastard.

GOETZ: Bah! I'll manage somehow. [*Pause.*] Heinrich, I haven't lost my case: for lack of a judge, it was not heard. [*Pause.*] I am beginning again.

HEINRICH [*startled*]: Beginning what?

GOETZ: My life.

HEINRICH: That would be much too easy. [*He throws himself upon* GOETZ.] You shan't begin again. This is the end, today: the bolt must be shot.

GOETZ: Let me go, Heinrich, let me go. Everything is changed, I want to live. [*He struggles in the other man's arms.*]

HEINRICH [*choking him*]: Where is your strength, Goetz, where is your strength? How wonderful that you want to live: you'll die in despair!

[GOETZ, *weakened by his fast, tries vainly to shake himself free.*]

May your whole future in Hell be contained in this last moment.

GOETZ: Let me go. [*He struggles.*] By heaven, if one of us must die, it had better be you! [*He stabs* HEINRICH.]

HEINRICH: Ha! [*Pause.*] I don't want to stop hating,
I don't want to stop suffering. [*He falls.*] There will
be nothing, nothing, nothing. And tomorrow, you
will still see the light. [*He dies.*]

GOETZ: You are dead, and the world is as full as ever;
you will not be missed by anyone. [*He takes the
flowers and throws them on the corpse.*] The comedy
of Good has ended with a murder. So much the
better. I cannot go back on my tracks. [*He calls.*]
Hilda! Hilda!

[*Night has fallen.*]

God is dead.

HILDA: Dead or living, what do I care! I haven't given
Him a thought for a very long time. Where is Heinrich?

GOETZ: He has gone.

HILDA: Did you win your case?

GOETZ: There was no trial: I tell you, God is dead. [*He
takes her in his arms.*] We have no witness now, I
alone can see your hair and your brow. How REAL
you have become since He no longer exists. Look at
me, don't stop looking at me for one moment: the
world has been struck blind; if you turned away your
head, I should be afraid of annihilation. [*He laughs.*]
Alone at last!

[*Lights. Torches approach.*]

HILDA: Here they are. Come.

GOETZ: I will wait for them.

HILDA: They will kill you.

GOETZ: Bah! Who knows? [*Pause.*] Let us stay: I need
the sight of men.

[*The torches draw nearer.*]

CURTAIN

SCENE XI

The peasants' camp. A WITCH *is rubbing the peasants with a wooden hand, while* KARL *looks on.*

NASTI [*entering*]: What are you doing?

THE WITCH: Those I touch with this wooden hand become invulnerable; they can deal blows but receive none!

NASTI: Throw that thing away! [*He strides toward her.*] At once. Throw it away. [*The* WITCH *takes refuge behind* KARL.] Karl, are you in on this, too?

KARL: Yes. Leave her alone.

NASTI: As long as I command here, the captains shall tell no lies to their men.

KARL: Then the men will die with their leaders.

NASTI [*to the peasants*]: Get out of here!

[*They go. Pause.* KARL *crosses to* NASTI.]

KARL: You hesitate, Nasti; you dream, and while you dream, the men desert in hundreds! The army is losing its soldiers as a wounded man loses his blood. You must stop this hemorrhage. We no longer have the right to be fastidious in our methods.

NASTI: What do you want me to do?

KARL: Give orders that everyone is to let himself be touched by this pretty child. If they believe themselves invulnerable, they will stay.

NASTI: I was dealing with men, you are changing them into beasts.

KARL: Better have beasts that stand and let themselves be killed than men who run like rabbits.

NASTI: Prophet of error and abomination!

KARL: Very well. I am a false prophet. But you, what are you?

NASTI: I didn't want to fight this war. . . .

KARL: That's possible, but since you weren't able to prevent it, it must mean God was not on your side.

NASTI: I am not a false prophet but a man the Lord has betrayed. Do as you please. [KARL *goes out with the* WITCH.] Yes, God, You have betrayed me, for You allowed me to believe I was Your elect. But how can I reproach You for lying to your creatures, how can I question your divine love, I who love my brothers as I do, and lie to them as I am lying.

[GOETZ *and* HILDA *enter, with three armed* PEASANTS.]

NASTI [*with no surprise*]: So, here you are!

A PEASANT [*pointing to* GOETZ]: We hunted him to slit his throat for him, but he isn't the same man any more. He acknowledges his sins and says he wants to fight in our ranks. So here he is. We've brought him to you.

NASTI: Leave us. [*The* PEASANTS *go out.*] You want to fight in our ranks?

GOETZ: Yes.

NASTI: Why?

GOETZ: I need you. [*Pause.*] I want to be a man among men.

NASTI: Only that?

GOETZ: I know: it's the most difficult of all things. That's why I must begin at the beginning.

NASTI: What is the beginning?

GOETZ: Crime. Men of the present day are born criminals. I must demand my share of their crimes if I want to have my share of their love and virtue. I wanted pure love: ridiculous nonsense. To love anyone is to hate the same enemy; therefore I will adopt your hates. I wanted to do Good: foolishness. On this earth at present Good and Evil are inseparable. I agree to be bad in order to become good.

NASTI [*looking at him*]: You have changed.

GOETZ: Strangely! I lost someone who was dear to me.

NASTI: Who?

GOETZ: Nobody you know. [*Pause.*] I ask to serve under your orders as a simple soldier.

NASTI: I refuse.

GOETZ: Nasti!

NASTI: What do you expect me to do with ONE soldier when I lose fifty every day?

GOETZ: When I came to you, with the pride of a rich man, you rejected me, and it was right, for I alleged you needed me. But today I tell you I need you, and if you drive me away you will be unjust, for it is unjust to drive away beggars.

NASTI: I am not driving you away. [*Pause.*] For a year and a day, your place has been waiting for you. Take it. You shall command the army.

GOETZ: No! [*Pause.*] I was not born to command. I want to obey.

NASTI: Capital! So then, I order you to place yourself at our head. Obey.

GOETZ: Nasti, I am resigned to kill, I shall let myself be killed if I must; but I shall never send another man to his death. At last I know what death is. There is nothing afterward, Nasti, nothing: we have nothing but our life.

HILDA [*silencing him*]: Goetz! Be quiet!

GOETZ [*to* HILDA]: Yes. [*To* NASTI] Leaders are alone; I want men all around me. Around me, above me, and let them hide the sky from me. Nasti, allow me to be a nobody.

NASTI: You are not a nobody. Do you believe one leader is worth more than another? If you refuse the command, you must go.

HILDA [*to* GOETZ]: Accept.

GOETZ: No. Thirty-six years of loneliness are enough.

HILDA: I shall be with you.

GOETZ: You are myself. We shall be alone together.

HILDA [*in a low voice*]: If you are a soldier among soldiers, will you tell them God is dead?

GOETZ: No.

HILDA: You see.

GOETZ: What do I see?

HILDA: You will never be like other men. Neither better
nor worse: different. And if you ever agree, it will be
through misunderstanding.

GOETZ: I killed God because He divided me from mankind, and now I see that His death has isolated me
even more surely. I shall not allow this huge carcass
to poison my human friendships; I shall tell the whole
truth, if necessary.

HILDA: Have you the right to take away their courage?

GOETZ: I will do it little by little. At the end of a year of
patience . . .

HILDA [laughing]: In a year, we shall all be dead.

GOETZ: If God is not, why am I alone, I who wished
to live with all men?

[The PEASANTS enter, driving the WITCH before them.]

THE WITCH: I swear it does no harm. If this hand rubs
you, you become invulnerable.

THE PEASANTS: We'll believe you if Nasti lets himself
be rubbed.

[The WITCH goes to NASTI.]

NASTI: Go to the devil!

THE WITCH [whispering]: I come from Karl: let me rub
you, or the game is up.

NASTI [aloud]: Very well. Be quick.

[She rubs him with the wooden hand. The PEASANTS
applaud.]

A PEASANT: Rub the monk, too.

GOETZ: No, damn it!

HILDA [gently]: Goetz!

GOETZ: Rub away, my pretty, rub away. [She rubs him.]

NASTI [violently]: Get out! All of you!

[They go.]

GOETZ: Nasti, has it come to this?

NASTI: Yes.

GOETZ: Then you despise them?

NASTI: I despise only myself. [Pause.] Do you know of

a stranger comedy? I who hate lies, lie to my brothers to give them the courage to be killed in a war I detest.

GOETZ: Hilda, for heaven's sake, this man is as lonely as I am.

NASTI: Much more so. You have always been alone. But I was a hundred thousand, and now I am only myself. Goetz, I knew neither loneliness nor defeat nor distress, and I am helpless against them.

[A SOLDIER *enters.*]

THE SOLDIER: The captains ask to speak to you.

NASTI: Let them come in. [*To* GOETZ] They have come to tell me confidence is dead, and that they have no more authority.

GOETZ [*in a loud voice*]: No. [NASTI *looks at him.*] Suffering, anguish, remorse, are all very well for me. But if you suffer, the last candle goes out: darkness will fall. I take command of the army.

[*Enter the captains and* KARL.]

A CAPTAIN: Nasti, you must make an end of this war. My men . . .

NASTI: You will speak when I give you leave. [*Pause.*] I have news for you which is worth a great victory: we have a general, and he is the most famous military leader in Germany.

A CAPTAIN: This monk?

GOETZ: Everything except a monk! [*He throws off his robe and appears dressed as a soldier.*]

THE CAPTAINS: Goetz!

KARL: Goetz! For God's sake! . . .

A CAPTAIN: Goetz! That changes everything!

ANOTHER CAPTAIN: What does it change, tell me? What does it change? He is a traitor. He's probably drawing you into a fine ambush.

GOETZ: Come here! Nasti has named me chief and leader. Will you obey my orders?

A CAPTAIN: I'd rather die.

GOETZ: Then die, brother! [*He stabs him.*] As for you others, listen to me! I take up this command against my will, but I shall be relentless. Believe me, if there is one chance of winning this war, I shall win it. Proclaim immediately that any soldier attempting to desert will be hanged. By tonight, I must have a complete list of troops, weapons, and stores; you shall answer for everything with your lives. We shall be sure of victory when your men are more afraid of me than of the enemy. [*They try to speak.*] No. Not a word. Go. Tomorrow you will learn my plans. [*They go.* GOETZ *kicks the body.*] The kingdom of man is beginning. A fine start! Nasti, I told you I would be hangman and butcher. [*He has a moment of weakness.*]

NASTI [*laying his hand on* GOETZ's *shoulder*]: Goetz . . .

GOETZ: Never fear, I shall not flinch. I shall make them hate me, because I know no other way of loving them. I shall give them orders, since I have no other way of obeying. I shall remain alone with this empty sky over my head, since I have no other way of being among men. There is this war to fight, and I will fight it.

CURTAIN

KEAN

Based on the play by Alexandre Dumas

A PLAY IN FIVE ACTS

TRANSLATED FROM THE FRENCH BY KITTY BLACK

Jean-Paul Sartre's adaptation of Kean was presented for the first time at the Théâtre Sarah-Bernhardt, Paris, in November 1953.

CHARACTERS

KEAN

THE PRINCE OF
    WALES

COUNT DE KOEFELD

LORD NEVILLE

SOLOMON

A CONSTABLE

PETER POTT, *landlord of
the Black Horse*

DARIUS, *a hairdresser*

STAGE MANAGER *at Drury
Lane Theatre*

ANNA DANBY

ELENA, COUNTESS DE
    KOEFELD

AMY, COUNTESS OF GOS-
    VILLE

GIDSA, *Elena's maid*

MAJOR-DOMO, FOOTMEN, ACROBATS, STAGEHANDS,
    THEATER ATTENDANTS, FIREMEN, ETC.

ACT I

The hall of the Danish Embassy in London. When the curtain rises, the orchestra is playing a waltz. FOUR FOOTMEN *enter down the grand staircase, carrying candelabra, and line up, center. The* MAJOR-DOMO *enters, speaking to the orchestra, off.*

MAJOR-DOMO: Thank you, gentlemen. Your brilliance and tempo are sure to please His Excellency. Be ready to open the ball as soon as His Royal Highness arrives. [*He crosses to the* FOOTMEN, *inspecting each one in turn. To the first*] Serve tea and punch in the boudoir. [*To the second*] Set up the card tables in the conservatory—two of Whist and three of Boston. [*To the remaining two*] Announce the guests. To your places!
The FOOTMEN *turn back to the stairs and exit.* GIDSA *enters from Elena's room.*]

GIDSA: Mr. Matheson! Her Excellency. [*She draws aside a curtain.* ELENA *appears.*]

ELENA: Oh—Matheson—I hope you remembered the cigars.

MAJOR-DOMO: Yes, indeed, your ladyship. Nothing is lacking to make this the dance of the year.

ELENA: Very good. I shall expect you to be within call the whole evening.
[*The* MAJOR-DOMO *bows and turns to go. The* FOUR FOOTMEN *enter and take up their places on each side of the stairs.*]

1ST FOOTMAN: The Countess of Gosville!

ELENA [*aside*]: Good heavens! Already! [*She quickly takes up a graceful position on the sofa. The* MAID *hastens to arrange her train.* ELENA *dismisses her with a gesture, The* MAID *exits discreetly.*]

AMY *enters with a great rustle of skirts. A moment later, obeying a wave of the hands from* ELENA, *the* FOOTMEN *withdraw.*]

ELENA: Amy, my dear, how kind of you to come so early; I have a thousand things to say to you.

AMY: My dear, I wanted to have you to myself for a moment. It's impossible—we can no longer see our friends, we only meet them at parties. Those races at Newmarket—naturally, one had to be seen there. . . .

ELENA: I thought you had a horror of racing. . . .

AMY: So I have. It's absurd to drive dozens of miles behind one's own horses merely to watch other people's gallop. Horses gallop—what is surprising in that? It's natural. And most of the men one knows can do nothing but ride. Put a dozen men on the backs of as many horses, set the whole lot to whooping and shouting, naturally, one or the other will arrive at the finishing post before all the others. Still, one has one's obligations. You have them too, Elena, but I find you observing them less and less. . . .

ELENA: I'm not English, my dear, and I have no . . .

AMY: You may not be English, but your husband is an ambassador. How are we to remember we are no longer at war with Denmark if we never see the Danish Ambassador's wife at our receptions? I have had to endure four dinners, two balls, and three visits to the Opera this week alone. I tell you, Elena, I am not made of iron, and when I see my friends fail in their duties, I find my own courage ebbing.

ELENA: I was at Drury Lane last night.

AMY: Drury Lane—at least that is better than nothing. But the play is not fatiguing. You can relax, close your eyes, even go to sleep, in the privacy of your box. While you were enjoying a rest, I was dancing with the old Duke of Leinster. You know how lame he is, and when I reached home, I found I was limping myself. What was the play?

ELENA: *Hamlet.*

AMY: Again! The trouble with old authors is they never give us anything new.

ELENA: Their plays are renewed each time they are created by a new actor.

AMY: So they say. But when one has seen Othello stifling Desdemona twenty times with a pillow, they may change their Othello, or their leading lady, it is still the same pillow. The first time I saw *Hamlet,* when he cried "A rat, a rat!" I was so frightened, I screamed and jumped on my chair. Now the surprise has worn off, and whether Hamlet is Young or Kemble, I know quite well the rat is only Polonius!

ELENA: Last night you would have been frightened.

AMY: Enough to scream?

ELENA: And jump on your chair.

AMY: Then your Hamlet must have been Kean.

ELENA: It was Kean.

AMY: Why do you find him so wonderful?

ELENA: I don't know. I . . . I felt I was seeing Hamlet himself.

AMY: What a play! A man who need only draw his sword to kill off his uncle, and takes five acts to make up his mind! Your Hamlet is a bore, my dear. Why go to the theater to spend three hours with people one would refuse to receive in one's own home? Go to the theater to see Hamlet! Now if you told me you went to see Kean . . .

ELENA: Kean? Is there such a man as Kean? The creature I saw last night was the Prince of Denmark in person. . . .

AMY: Yes—as he was Romeo the night before, and the Thane of Glamis the night before that. How agreeable for his mistress—if he has one. Tonight she can sleep with the Prince of Denmark, and tomorrow in the arms of the Moor of Venice. The most fickle would find satisfaction. Elena—you won't be angry with me?

ELENA: Never with you. What is the matter?

AMY: Oh, the maddest story. I only tell you to make you laugh.

ELENA: Then I promise not to disappoint you.

AMY: No one can hear us?

ELENA: You're frightening me, my dear.

AMY: Do you know what they're saying?

ELENA: Who are they?

AMY: Everyone.

ELENA: I can guess. They say a husband is unfaithful to his wife, or a wife is unfaithful to her husband. Isn't that it?

AMY: Not altogether.

ELENA: And of whom are they saying this "not altogether"?

AMY [taking her hands]: Elena, my dearest Elena . . . [Pause.] Of you.

ELENA: Of me?

AMY: They say you have fallen in love with Shakespeare.

ELENA: If it were true, the English should be proud.

AMY: You may be sure of that.

ELENA: If Shakespeare is their god, why shouldn't he be mine?

AMY: But you see, they wonder if it is for the sake of the god that you visit the temple.

ELENA: What else?

AMY: For the priest.

ELENA: Young?

AMY: Pooh!

ELENA: Macready?

AMY: My dear!

ELENA: Kemble?

AMY: Ha! Ha! [A very slight pause.] Kean.

ELENA: A madcap story, as you said. Where do these rumors come from?

AMY: Who knows? Such stories fall from the sky.

ELENA: From the sky straight into the ears of our best

friends. [*She touches* AMY'S *ear.*] So? I am in love with him?

AMY: Passionately.

ELENA: What would I do for him?

AMY: Everything.

ELENA: Flattering. I have Italian blood and I neither love nor hate by half measures. What else do they say?

AMY: Everyone is sorry for you.

ELENA: A pity. I should prefer to be condemned.

AMY: To think of such a thing. In love with Kean!

ELENA: Not so fast, my dear, I have admitted nothing. Why should I not be in love with Kean?

AMY: The man's an actor.

ELENA: No doubt. And why not?

AMY: Those creatures are not received in our world. . . .

ELENA: And therefore should not be admitted to our beds. Amy, I met Edmund Kean in the company of the Prince of Wales.

AMY: A prince may be permitted his caprices. . . . Seriously, Elena, as a man he is utterly detestable.

ELENA: Indeed?

AMY: Good heavens—only you could be unaware of his reputation. Do you know he has had a thousand mistresses?

ELENA: A thousand?

AMY: A thousand.

ELENA: Neither one more nor less?

AMY: Exactly a thousand. He says that after the next he will be the equal of Don Juan.

ELENA: So according to your rumors I shall be the thousand and first. . . .

AMY: Yes—unless before then . . .

ELENA: I see. Poor man . . .

AMY: Oh, he has been famous for ten years. A thousand in that time . . .

ELENA: If it is true, where is the crime? The women

were willing, I suppose? Your Mr. Kean knows how to manage his life, that is all.

AMY: My Mr. Kean? I implore you, this is no joking matter. He is a lost soul, a monster of pride, driving himself mad because of his low birth, scattering his money in an endeavor to compete with the prodigalities of the Prince of Wales. He is crippled with debts —he should have been in prison months ago were it not for the kindness of certain great ladies . . . a parvenu whose vulgar habits proclaim his lack of breeding . . .

ELENA: Kean, vulgar?

AMY: Every night he leaves his kingly robes in the theater and frequents the lowest taverns dressed as a common sailor.

ELENA: Is that true?

AMY: Entirely true.

ELENA: Ah, my dear, I can see you're right—he is utterly detestable.

AMY: You see!

ELENA: A vile man!

AMY: Now you have learned reason!

ELENA: With revolting habits.

AMY: Alas!

ELENA: And it is this man you have decided to give me as a lover? How you protect my reputation!

AMY: Elena, I have never believed it!

ELENA: Of course not, my dearest. Believe me, I never believed that you could believe it. [*Pause.*] I do exactly the same for you. Wherever I go, I defend your reputation.

AMY: My reputation? Good heavens, against whom?

ELENA: Against vile slanders. The little stories that fall from heaven. How is Lord Delmours?

AMY: Lord Delmours . . . But . . . how should I know? I . . . I hardly know him.

ELENA: I always ask everyone how he is these days. He is so charming, don't you think? I like him so much

—so young, so handsome, so fragile one fears he may break at a touch. Every virtue, in fact, except one. He is not very discreet.

AMY: Not discreet?

ELENA: No, not altogether. But who can believe what he says? Everyone knows he is a fool and a coxcomb. You were saying?

AMY: I? Nothing at all.

ELENA: Then I have said nothing, either. [*They laugh.*] How time flies when one is saying nothing.

AMY: How time flies when one has said nothing. [*She picks up a fan.*] What a beautiful fan!

ELENA: It was a present.

AMY: From whom?

ELENA: A Don Juan who has loved a thousand women, a prodigal, crippled with debts. . . .

AMY: From . . .

ELENA: No, my friend; from the Prince of Wales.

AMY: Indeed!

ELENA: Will rumor now credit me with a tenderness for the Prince?

AMY: It credits him with a tenderness for you. But are we not to see His Excellency your husband?

ELENA: Your desires are his orders; here he comes. [*The* COUNT *enters.*]

COUNT: Tomorrow I bow to the crowned heads of Europe; tonight I only acknowledge one queen. [*He kisses* AMY's *hand.*]

AMY: How provoking that one can never believe you.

COUNT: And why not?

AMY: I know you diplomats too well—when you say yes, you mean no.

COUNT: Then I shall say your dress has been cobbled together, and you have been made to look a perfect fright. [*He laughs.*]

AMY: How am I to know you don't mean what you say?

COUNT [*startled*]: But, dear lady . . .

AMY: If I were as hideous as a scarecrow you would take

advantage of my lack of confidence in diplomats and tell me the truth to make me believe you were lying. That is diplomacy of the second degree.

ELENA: Yes, but supposing I were jealous and he wished to pay you compliments without arousing my suspicions? He could play on the different degrees of our belief. By telling you he thinks you ugly, he would make you believe he lied, while making me believe he was speaking the truth. That is diplomacy of the third degree.

AMY: Then this is the fourth; supposing he believes you fickle, and wishes to make you jealous. He will say I am ugly to make you think he wants to make you believe he does not like me. As for the fifth . . .

COUNT: Ladies, ladies, for pity's sake! I swear to you diplomacy was never so complex; if it needed so much reflection, we should have to appoint women as ambassadors.

AMY: Well, Count, what do you say? Am I fair, or ugly?

COUNT: Madame, I no longer know what to say. . . .

AMY: You have chosen the better part. I will believe in your silence.

ELENA: Are we not to see Lord Gosville?

AMY: I fear me not. He is helping Lord Neville ruin himself.

ELENA: I thought him ruined already?

AMY: This time it is tragic, my dear. He is getting married.

ELENA: Married?

AMY: A fortune—an heiress—a disaster.

ELENA: Surely the disaster has a name?

AMY: If you like. But it is a name without meaning—and utterly unmemorable. Annie . . . Anna . . .

COUNT: Danby.

ELENA: Danby? It has a meaning—at least for me. But what?

COUNT: Anna Danby, my dear, is the child who has the box at Drury Lane opposite ours.

ELENA: And never takes her eyes off Kean? She is delightful.

AMY: Indeed?

ELENA: I mean, she is quite pretty. My one complaint is her lack of manners; she never misses a single performance, and indeed it was her—persistence, which made me remark her.

COUNT: Be sure she has noticed you too, my dear.

ELENA: Why should she notice me? Do I lean over the edge of my box? Do I applaud till I split both my gloves?

AMY: Perhaps she likes Shakespeare?

COUNT [*with a glance at* ELENA]: Obviously!

ELENA: Shakespeare! Imagine! I hope for her sake that marriage will calm her down.

AMY [*aside*]: This gallant seducer begins to intrigue me. [*To the* COUNT] Your Excellency, may I be so bold as to ask for a seat in your box the next time he plays?

COUNT: What? You too wish to see him?

AMY: Yes, and at close quarters. From your stage box one must be able to see his every expression.

COUNT: With pleasure: but tonight you will be able to see him still closer.

AMY: Tonight?

COUNT: He is coming to the ball and will sup with us later.

ELENA: Did you invite him? Without asking me?

COUNT: Invite? Invite? Does one invite these people? Let us say I engaged a buffoon. He will give us Falstaff with the dessert.

ELENA: Without asking me!

COUNT: Elena, I must do my best for the royal prince who condescends to find him amusing. Ladies, ladies, I was keeping this for His Royal Highness, and you have surprised my secret. Now can you say I am a diplomat?

[*The* MAJOR-DOMO *enters with a letter.*]

Excuse me. [*He reads.*] A strange era when an actor refuses the invitation of an ambassador!

ELENA: From Kean?

COUNT: Yes.

ELENA: He declines?

COUNT: Yes. I can hardly believe my eyes.

ELENA: I hope your invitation was polite?

COUNT: Judge by the reply. [*He reads aloud.*] Your Excellency, I am deeply distressed. The rare honor you were gracious enough to do me was addressed, I have no doubt, to the actor. Although you had the delicacy not to put it into words, I am sure you would have been disappointed had I not played for your guests after supper, and I would have been delighted to give my best endeavors for your entertainment. Unfortunately, I know of no way of inviting the actor without the man, and the man is otherwise engaged at an appointment he cannot cancel. I beg you to be kind enough to accept my most sincere regrets, and to lay my respectful homage at the feet of the Countess your wife.

AMY: Insolence!

COUNT [*annoyed*]: Of course not.

AMY: No?

COUNT: No. If it had been insolence, I would have had to be angry, and my dignity as Ambassador forbids me to lose my temper.

[ELENA *sinks into a chair, almost fainting.*]

Elena, what is the matter?

[*The* MAJOR-DOMO *enters.*]

MAJOR-DOMO [*announces*]: His Royal Highness the Prince of Wales.

[*The* FOUR FOOTMEN *take their places on the stairs. The* PRINCE *enters, laughing.*]

PRINCE: Ha! Ha!

COUNT [*amused at seeing the* PRINCE *laugh*]: He! He!

PRINCE [*his laughter growing*]: Ha! Ha! Ha!

COUNT: He! He! He!

ELENA: Your Royal Highness is very gay.

PRINCE [*kissing her hand*]: You must forgive me, ladies, but the most extraordinary story is going round London.

ELENA: We will only forgive you, sir, if you tell us what it is.

PRINCE: Tell you! I would tell the reeds of the Thames if I had no other audience.

ELENA: I warn you I shall not believe a word.

AMY: I implore Your Royal Highness—we can repeat it without believing it.

PRINCE: Lord Neville . . . [*He begins to laugh.*] Ha! Ha!

COUNT [*laughing*]: He! He!

[*Everyone laughs.*]

AMY: Have pity on us, sir. . . .

PRINCE [*through his laughter, painfully*]: Left flat.

COUNT: Flat? But I thought . . .

PRINCE: That he was getting married? So did he, I suppose. The proof is that he bought a new wardrobe, refurnished his house, refilled his stables, and equipped himself with a host of new creditors. Then tonight, when he went to claim his bride . . . [*He laughs again.*] Gone!

COUNT: Gone?

AMY: Gone?

PRINCE: Flown! The door wide and the cage bare! [*He laughs.*]

ELENA: Poor child! Were they marrying her against her will?

[*The* PRINCE *is still laughing.*]

Sir, how can you laugh! Supposing some harm has befallen her!

PRINCE: Where's the harm in running away with the man you love?

ELENA: The man you love?

AMY: Then they know the name of her abductor?

PRINCE: Know it? It's the best-known name in London!

AMY: Tell us—tell us! I cannot endure the suspense!

COUNT: Ladies, don't press His Royal Highness—you may be embarrassing him.

PRINCE: I? No, no, dear friend, I never interfere with the middle classes. Ladies, the hero of the adventure is the man who wears his crown while I still wait for mine—long live the King!

ELENA: Tell us who it is!

PRINCE: Don Juan! Romeo! The Richelieu of three kingdoms! Edmund Kean.

ELENA: Kean!

PRINCE: At this very moment, madam, he is with her on the road to Dover.

ELENA: It's . . . it's impossible.

AMY: But why, Elena? You were saying yourself that the child never takes her eyes off him. . . .

COUNT: So this is the reason he declined my invitation.

PRINCE: Your invitation? To come here?

COUNT: I invited him, hoping to give you pleasure, sir.

PRINCE: It may be as well that he refused; otherwise you might have been taken for his accomplice and we'd have had a war between Denmark and England. . . . Ladies, we must celebrate this happening which has restored peace to our firesides. It is a victory for public morality, and I swear that half London will be illuminated tonight.

AMY: Was he so irresistible?

PRINCE: Ah! Ah!

AMY: They say that certain great ladies have been complacent enough to raise him up to their level.

PRINCE: Madam, they have been kinder still, for they have descended to his.

ELENA [*violently, in spite of herself*]: Your Royal Highness, I cannot allow . . .

COUNT: Elena . . .

ELENA: Forgive me, sir, and be good enough to think of me as a country girl. After all, I have only spent one season in London and our Danish husbands are barbaric enough to respect their wives. Be sure that by next autumn my foolish scruples will have drifted with the leaves; I shall laugh at my sex with the best of your wits, and I shall slander my best friends to cause you amusement.

PRINCE: Madam, it is I who should ask forgiveness, and give you my thanks.

ELENA: Thanks?

PRINCE: I know your smiles and your graces, but I thank you for giving me occasion to admire your anger. Your husband is fortunate—I hope you find many occasions to scold him.

COUNT: Yes, indeed—very many.

PRINCE: As for our great ladies, I have no desire to speak ill of them; I merely pity them. It isn't their fault if our court grows effeminate. If they lose their hearts to Kean, they are chasing a shadow.

ELENA: A shadow? Is Kean then not a man?

PRINCE: Indeed no, madam. He is an actor.

ELENA: And what is an actor?

PRINCE: A mirage.

ELENA: And our princes? Are they also mirages?

PRINCE: That is something you can only verify by touching them.

[*The* MAJOR-DOMO *and the* FOUR FOOTMEN *enter.*]

MAJOR-DOMO: Mr. Edmund Kean.

ELENA: Kean!

COUNT: Kean!

PRINCE: Kean? This is growing complicated. [*He rubs his hands.*] I adore complications.

COUNT: Let him come in.

[KEAN *enters.*]

KEAN: Ladies . . . Your Excellency . . . [*Seeing the* PRINCE] Your Royal Highness.

[*No one moves.*]

I ask you to forgive my erratic behavior. I did think I should be unable to accept your gracious invitation, but an unexpected happening altered my plans and forced me to come here and ask for your help.

COUNT: We were no longer expecting you, sir.

KEAN: Alas, Your Excellency, I was sure of that myself. For one moment you honored me by desiring my presence, and I, to my shame, was unable to take advantage of your kindness. Believe that I regret most sincerely having to appear when no one wishes to see me.

[*Pause. No one replies.*]

I find myself in a false position, but after all, false positions are a part of my profession—I live through them every night. The man I meet is the one who wishes me a thousand miles away—the woman to whom I declare my passion grasps the knife with which she intends to kill me. You have no idea of the situations our authors imagine; sometimes I declare my passion to my brother, not knowing he is my rival, and he hears me in silence, as you are doing now. Another time, the woman I love believes me false, and I must prove my innocence before her very husband. Yesterday, the King of Denmark—your country, Excellency—decreed my banishment and death. I escaped his vengeance, though it was this same king who had killed my father. It seems I am unfortunate in my relations with Denmark. Today I have mortally offended the Danish Ambassador—but I shall survive your scorn, Excellency, and do you know why? I have become impregnable. We actors, when we have to demonstrate scorn, must make it perceptible to a thousand eyes. It must flame and blaze, it must dazzle the spectator. Falstaff endures the scorn of the King without the flicker of an eyelid. That is why, Excellency, I can survive your reprobation without sinking into the earth; your disdain is terrible, of course, but it has the drawback of being real. Sometimes I wonder if real emotions are not merely false emotions badly acted. Come, Excellency, and you too, sir, will you trust me? In a moment we shall be laughing at this together. Our playwrights plunge me into a false situation every night—but every night they extricate me. I shall know how to get us out of this one as easily as all the others.

COUNT: I can see only one way of doing that, sir—your immediate departure. The rumors attendant on your name, which His Royal Highness has related to us, must certainly make you feel . . .

KEAN: That my presence here is unwelcome? Excellency, I am deeply aware of my indiscretion—nevertheless, it was those rumors that brought me here.

AMY: Are they false, sir?

KEAN: No, madam, they are true; Miss Anna Danby came to my house this evening.

ELENA: Well, sir, and what has it got to do with us? Do you expect my husband to condone your love affairs?

KEAN: Madam, everything is true, except one point; the lady left again without seeing me.

PRINCE: Yet I was told . . .

KEAN: That she had stayed? Ah, sir, the spy who saw her come in did not have the patience to see her leave. [*With vehemence*] The result of his fine work is that her reputation is compromised.

PRINCE: What vehemence! I thought you were not always so prompt in defending a woman's honor!

KEAN: Sir, I enact—consequently I have to experience —every feeling. Every morning I put on the one that matches my coat. Today I decided on a generous mood. [*To the* COUNT] Excellency, my one hope is in you.

COUNT: In me? What the devil do you expect? If you are innocent, you need only deny the story.

KEAN: Deny the story? Ah, Excellency, you are unaware of what people think of me? [*He turns to* ELENA.] If I were to say to you, madam, quite simply: "The story is false, I do not know Miss Danby, and I could never love her," would you believe me?

ELENA: Without further proof?

KEAN: Without further proof than my word of honor.

AMY: Elena, you wouldn't believe him!

ELENA: No, I should not believe you.

KEAN: You see, Excellency, Madam de Koefeld herself cannot discern the honor of the man behind the habiliments of the actor. Kean's honor—that makes you laugh. But you, Your Excellency, you who have a natural right to command respect, if you were to say . . . No, to silence gossiping tongues requires more than respect, it demands veneration. Madam, all London venerates you. Would you condescend to utter this denial yourself?

ELENA: Mr. Kean, I cannot deny the story unless I believe you sincere.

KEAN [*holding out a letter*]: Deign to glance at this letter. You can declare to the whole world that Miss Danby's honor is without stain.

COUNT: Read it yourself, sir, we will hear you.

KEAN: Pardon me, Excellency, we must allow each of us to keep his station; honor to men of the world, intelligence and talent to actors, delicacy of feeling to the ladies. A secret on which the happiness, the future, and perhaps the very life of a woman depends can only be revealed to another woman. Read, madam, I implore you.

PRINCE: Does my rank give me the right to enjoy this confidence?

KEAN: Sir—before a secret all men are equal.

PRINCE [*drawing* KEAN *aside*]: Kean, what game are you playing?

KEAN: What game? Sir, what else do you expect of a player? I am playing a part, that is all. [*To* ELENA] Madam, I urge you to hear my prayer.

COUNT [*growing impatient, tapping his foot, loudly*]: I cannot decide. . . .

AMY [*taking his arm*]: Come, Count, you are a diplomat: as soon as your wife knows, you will be able to guess at this secret.

PRINCE [*taking his other arm*]: And when you have guessed it, you will be able to tell us.

ELENA [KEAN *draws her aside*]: This letter alone will justify you?

KEAN: Read!

ELENA [*reading*]: "Sir, I came to see you and found you away from home. I have not the honor of your acquaintance, but when you learn that my whole life depends on the advice you alone can give me, I am sure you will not refuse to see me tomorrow. Anna Danby." Thank you, Mr. Kean, thank you a thousand times. But what reply have you given?

KEAN [*in a low voice*]: Turn the page, madam.

ELENA [*reading in a low voice*]: "I did not know how to see you, Elena, I dared not write to you; an opportunity has arisen and I have seized it. The rare moments you steal from those who surround you are so brief and tormenting they are marked in my life only by their remembrance. . . ." [*She stops.*]

KEAN: I beg you to read to the end, madam.

ELENA [*reading*]: "I have often wondered how a woman of your world, who loved me truly, could grant me one hour without compromising herself. . . . If this woman loved me enough to accord me this hour, in exchange for which I should give my life, she would come to Drury Lane, stop her carriage, and enter the theater as if to purchase a ticket. The man she would find there is devoted to me, and I would instruct him to open the secret door to my dressing room if a woman veiled and dressed in black might perhaps condescend to visit me tomorrow night. . . ." Here is your letter, sir.

[*She kisses the letter lightly and holds it out to him, but, gazing at him passionately, slips it into her dress before he can take it.*]

KEAN [*bowing*]: A thousand thanks, madam—Your Excellency—my lady . . . Your Royal Highness . . .

[*He makes as if to go, but remains a little apart.*]

AMY [*close to* ELENA]: Well, Elena?

PRINCE: Well, madam?

COUNT: Well, my dear?

ELENA: Mr. Kean has been wrongfully accused of abducting Miss Anna Danby.

[KEAN *bows.*]

PRINCE [*taking* AMY's *arm and going upstairs*]: Ah, Mr. Kean, you have been acting a charade—but I swear on my honor I shall have the last word.

[ELENA *turns and smiles at* KEAN *as she passes him with the* COUNT.]

KEAN [*in a murmur*]: Thank you, madam.

[*A* FOOTMAN *blows out the candles on one side, throwing* KEAN *into shadow.* ANOTHER *extinguishes the candles on the other side, putting the forestage into darkness. In the shadows,* KEAN *watches the* COUNTESS *disappear; then, in the light coming from the ballroom, we see the silhouettes of the two couples beginning to waltz.* KEAN *blows a kiss in the direction of his beloved while the music swells and the curtain falls.*]

CURTAIN

ACT II

KEAN's *dressing room.* KEAN *and his factotum,* SOLOMON.

SOLOMON: Guv'nor!

KEAN: Eh?

SOLOMON: Can I have a word with you?

KEAN: Later, later. What time is it?

SOLOMON: Six o'clock.

KEAN: She will not come.

SOLOMON: Of course she will!

KEAN: You'll see—you'll see.

SOLOMON: Then she will be the first, sir.

KEAN: I wasn't in love with any of the others. There's no one in the world more punctual than a woman one does not love. . . . The door opens easily, I hope?

SOLOMON: I oiled it myself this morning.

KEAN: Suppose she was here and tried to open it, and couldn't get in?

SOLOMON: Impossible.

[*He goes to the secret door, opens it. It squeaks badly. He closes it again.*]

A child could open it with one finger.

KEAN: Very well. There's nothing to do but wait. I hate waiting.

[*A* street musician *is playing outside and the noise gets on* KEAN's *nerves. He picks up a purse.*]

Throw the fellow this and tell him to leave me in peace.

[SOLOMON *pulls a few coins from the purse, throws half to the musician, and puts the rest back in the purse, which he lays on the table.*]

KEAN: What are you doing?

SOLOMON: Dividing the spoils; half for you, and half for him.

KEAN: What's the matter with you? I detest half-measures.

SOLOMON: Then you should have kept the lot.

KEAN: *You* trying to stop my charitable impulses?

SOLOMON: Yes, when you perform them with other people's money.

KEAN: Those miserable guineas . . .

SOLOMON: Those guineas, we earned them last month, but for nearly three years we've been spending them with all the others we will earn for the next six years to come.

KEAN: You mean the money belongs to my creditors?

SOLOMON: Alas!

KEAN: All the more reason to give it away. I'm saving their souls. [*He moves to throw the purse from the window.* SOLOMON *stands in his way.*]

SOLOMON: Over my dead body. [*Clutching the purse*] Guv'nor, it's all we've got left.

KEAN: All?

SOLOMON: All the ready, that is.

KEAN: So we're flat broke.

SOLOMON: Cleaned out—plucked like a chicken.

KEAN: Well, I'll be able to pull in my belt. It's all good for the figure, Solomon.

SOLOMON: Not so good when you have to go round mother-naked.

KEAN [*severely*]: Solomon!

SOLOMON: I must make you see sense, Guv'nor.

KEAN: Why should I trouble myself about money? What good does it do?

SOLOMON: It pays for what you buy.

KEAN: Why do I need it when I buy everything without paying?

SOLOMON: Why do you need it? You'll know in a moment even if you won't listen to me.

KEAN: I always listen to you, Solomon.

SOLOMON: In the end.

KEAN: But not today.

SOLOMON: I might have known. Tomorrow?

KEAN: Yes, tomorrow.

SOLOMON: We'll never get a better chance! You can't keep still—you're yawning your head off—you're bored and restless.

KEAN: I'm expecting a woman, simpleton. . . .

SOLOMON: That's what I said.

KEAN [continuing]: And I'm bored because love is a boring experience.

SOLOMON: Let me give you a statement of your financial position, and I promise you won't find it boring—the time will slip by like a dream.

KEAN: And if I want to be bored, eh?

SOLOMON: What for?

KEAN: For the love of love. Seriously, when do you expect me to meditate on the charms of my beloved?

SOLOMON: Heavens! When she arrives.

KEAN: When she arrives, I shan't have a moment to see her; I shall be very much too busy watching her. Come now, let me rest. [He stretches on the divan and closes his eyes.] Elena!

SOLOMON [approaching on tiptoe and shouting in his ear]: The game's up!

KEAN [startled]: Eh?

SOLOMON: You're bankrupt.

KEAN: You shouldn't have told me. How do you expect me to make love to her now? [Pause.] Bankrupt. Charming! It's been going on for thirty-five years— d'you think I don't know? Twenty times I've thought of hanging myself; a hundred times I thought I should die of starvation. When I was a child . . .

SOLOMON [protesting]: Oh, no, no, no! Everything, but not your childhood. I haven't deserved it.

KEAN: Not my childhood? What's wrong with my childhood?

SOLOMON: I respect it, I pity it, but I know your childhood by heart. We'll never get anywhere if you insist on telling me the story every time I want to discuss money matters. We're not talking about the child now, but the man. The child lived in poverty and thought of nothing but how to grow rich. The man has lived in luxury for ten years . . . and we've got to find a way of keeping him in it. Guv'nor, you've got to listen to me.

KEAN [*indignant*]: Luxury? What on earth are you talking about?

SOLOMON: All this . . . your house, your carriage, your six servants. . . .

KEAN: But that isn't my concern, idiot! The house is crumbling under a mortgage, the bill for the carriage has been outstanding for years; the servants are owed three months' wages. This divan belongs to poor Gregory McPherson, dealer in antiques. This dressing gown . . . You want to see the likeness between the man and the child; the child owned nothing but the holes in his Harlequin jacket and the man owns nothing but his debts, which are the holes in his budget. If all my creditors took it into their heads to take back their wares, I should find myself naked in Piccadilly, feeling a dozen years younger.

SOLOMON: To listen to you, anyone would think you desired it.

KEAN: I want to be free. They are keeping my place for me—old Bob and his troupe of acrobats. I should put on my mask, pick up my bat, and get into my Harlequin jacket.

SOLOMON: When?

KEAN: Whenever I wish. I have nothing, nothing keeps me here. Everything is provisional—I live from day to day in a fabulous imposture. Not a farthing, nothing in my hands, nothing in my pockets, but I need only snap my fingers to summon spirits of the air who bring me Orient pearls, jewels, and bouquets of rare flowers.

[*He snaps his fingers. There is a knock at the door.*]
Who is it?

SOLOMON [*who has gone to open*]: Flowers.

KEAN: Well? What d'you say? Am I a magician or an illusionist? Put them down—they are for her. [*Pause.*] You're looking very sour.

SOLOMON: They must cost a guinea apiece.

KEAN: What?

SOLOMON: Those flowers.

KEAN: Where do you see flowers?

SOLOMON: There.

KEAN: Nothing but illusion. Have I paid for them?

SOLOMON: Certainly not.

KEAN: Then who is the legitimate owner?

SOLOMON: The florist of Soho Square.

KEAN: Is he a prodigal? A ninny? A fool?

SOLOMON: He is the meanest of skinflints, who gives nothing for nothing.

KEAN: You see: having given nothing, I have received nothing: therefore, they are still in his shop and you are the victim of an optical illusion. Shadows of roses, all hail! Enter into fantasy. I prefer to rule over mirages, and I love you all the more because you do not exist in truth. See how they open, how they unfold themselves: if I had bought them, I should already be tired of them: but I still desire them because they will fade without ever belonging to me. Play, Solomon.

SOLOMON [*startled*]: Eh?

KEAN: Play the game.

SOLOMON: What game?

KEAN: Everything that doesn't belong to you. The wind of the skies, the wives of other men, these flowers. [*He throws him a rose.*] Enjoy but never possess.

SOLOMON: To enjoy without possession is to lay up debts for the future.

KEAN: Very well, let us have debts. Look, am I not adored if my admirers send me such flowers? As long as you don't pay your debts, they are gages of love, proofs of human generosity. Ah, the good florist—

the noble heart—it is too much—very much too much—he is spoiling me—I shall have to scold him! And be sure he prays God every day to send me long life. Solomon, do you love me?

SOLOMON: You know I do!

KEAN: Then you must love those who love me. Instead of reproaching me for my debts, help me to multiply them.

SOLOMON: Impossible.

KEAN: What? What is impossible?

SOLOMON: The multiplication of your debts.

KEAN: Why?

SOLOMON: Credit exhausted.

KEAN: Exhausted? But even yesterday . . .

SOLOMON: That was yesterday.

KEAN: Can the hearts of men change in a night?

SOLOMON: The hearts of men, no: but we're speaking of creditors. They have passed round the word. No more dealings except for ready money.

KEAN: And this is the moment you choose to tell me?

SOLOMON: For an hour I've been trying to get in a word.

KEAN: Let them all go to the devil! Moneylenders at least will never lack.

SOLOMON: A word concerning you has been sent round all London.

KEAN: What word?

SOLOMON: "Not a penny to the actor Kean."

KEAN: But what do they all want?

SOLOMON: To be paid.

KEAN: The sharks! [*He strides up and down.*] Will they allow me to continue my work? Do these people imagine I can rehearse *Richard III* in a hovel? Assassinate the greatest actor of the age and see how tedious your evenings become. [*To* SOLOMON] What do you think you are doing? I'm being strangled, stabbed to the heart, and you stand there yawning your head off! Run! Find us some money!

SOLOMON: Where?

KEAN: That's your affair. My business is to spend it and yours is to find it. [*Abruptly*] Just a moment . . . Come here! What has been happening? What is all this about? If they have stopped my credit, it must be because they don't trust me any more. And if they have lost faith, it must mean I have lost my reputation. . . . Go to the manager at once and ask to see the house returns. . . .

SOLOMON: What do you care about the receipts? The money doesn't belong to you.

KEAN: I want to know if business has gone down. . . . Because if it has, Solomon, then it means I have gone down as well.

SOLOMON: Yesterday we turned away six hundred people.

KEAN: And the day before?

SOLOMON: Seven hundred and fifty. ·

KEAN: You see! You see! Why this discrepancy?

SOLOMON: Because of the difference of opinion between our Government and the Kingdom of Holland.

KEAN: To the devil with politics! Politics fill prisons and empty theaters. Solomon, you swear the people love me still?

SOLOMON: Passionately.

KEAN: Listen to me, my brother, my friend—you who teach me my parts and hold the book every evening, tell me frankly, am I slipping? Don't be afraid to hurt me; I want to leave the stage before I cover myself with disgrace.

SOLOMON: You never acted better in your life.

KEAN: Never better. But have I been as good?

SOLOMON: Well . . .

KEAN: I understand. [*He walks about in a frenzy.*] I am not slipping, but I am not rising either. That means I am lost; in the theater as in love, there is only one law: improve, or slip back. But good heavens, what do they expect of me? That I should surpass myself? How? Our authors are all dwarfs. If you want a Super-Kean you must give me a Super-Shakespeare. Solomon, I am Aladdin, my lamp is my genius. If one day it were to go out . . .

SOLOMON: It will never go out; that lamp will shine till the day of your death.

KEAN: It . . . touch wood, fool! Touch wood! [*He grasps the arm of a chair. In a changed voice*] Well, what must we do?

SOLOMON: Firstly; economize.

KEAN: On that point, I am adamant. Never. Go on to the next.

SOLOMON: It would be so easy!

KEAN: How the devil do you expect me to economize?

SOLOMON: You care so little for the company of men: do not give these supper parties.

KEAN: I have given none for a very long time.

SOLOMON: You are giving one tonight. The dresser told me.

KEAN: Tonight? It isn't a party. I'm going to Peter Pott, to the Black Horse—the haunt of cutthroats, down by the river.

SOLOMON: What for?

KEAN: A christening party.

SOLOMON: How many guests?

KEAN: How should I know? Two or three dozen.

SOLOMON: Not counting the thieves and murderers you will collect on your way.

KEAN: Solomon, what do you want? To stop me treating my friends?

SOLOMON: Those beggars were never your friends.

KEAN: Not beggars, you fool! Acrobats! Old Bob and his company. To me, they are sacred. I touched the depths of poverty with them, I begged, I danced at street corners, they taught me everything. Do you expect me to forget them? All my childhood, Solomon. Do you insist I renounce my childhood? . . .

SOLOMON: For the love of heaven, leave your childhood in peace.

KEAN: Good. I will never mention it, if you won't mention my debts. Come with me, Solomon, you are warmly invited. Old Bob has just had his twelfth, and I am the godfather. Why don't you come!

SOLOMON [*mournfully*]: It will only mean one more mouth to feed.

KEAN: Peter Pott still gives us credit. Come along, Solomon, why don't you laugh? Why do you always look so sour? Why won't you smile? What else is there to tell? Holding something back? Another question of money, eh?

SOLOMON: The . . .

KEAN: I won't hear a word—I won't hear a word! You are going to spoil my good humor! Solomon, she is a countess, I shall need all my patience. [*Pause.*] Very well. Tell me; what is the matter?

SOLOMON: It's the jeweler. You gave him your note for £400. For the necklace you gave Miss Fanny Hearst.

KEAN: How can you speak of it! . . . They are things one does without thinking.

SOLOMON: Yes, but you haven't honored your signature.

KEAN: My signature? When and what did I sign?

SOLOMON: Your note of hand, six months ago.

KEAN: Since then I have played Hamlet, Romeo, Macbeth, Lear, and you say I haven't honored him.

SOLOMON: I mean you haven't paid him.

KEAN: Are you mad? You choose the moment I love Elena to make me pay for a necklace I gave Fanny? It would be the worst of betrayals.

SOLOMON: But the jeweler lives on such betrayals. . . .

KEAN: What has he done?

SOLOMON: Your lawyers told me he has asked for a warrant for your arrest.

KEAN: My arrest! He'll never obtain it.

SOLOMON: They say they are quite sure it will be granted.

KEAN: And if they obtain it?

SOLOMON: You will be arrested, certainly—and imprisoned, most probably.

KEAN: We'll see if the people of London will leave me to be imprisoned. Kean, in prison? All the theaters of the world will close in sign of mourning. [*Changing his tone, sadly*] So it has come! You have spoiled it at last!

SOLOMON: What?

KEAN: My good mood. I know I am ruined—lost—cleaned out—flat broke. Only I have the good manners not to talk about it.

SOLOMON: I thought . . .

KEAN: What now?

SOLOMON: That you might . . . ask the Prince of Wales.

KEAN: Good heavens! His debts are three times greater than mine.

SOLOMON: He might be able to intercede with the King.

KEAN: We'll see. Now I won't hear another word!

SOLOMON: A very little money . . .

KEAN [*violently*]: From today, I forbid you to pronounce that obscene word in my presence. What am I to say to Elena? How shall I open my arms to her? You have besmirched me.

SOLOMON [*sticking to his idea*]: If the King would pay half your debts—only half, with the money you earn . . .

KEAN: I, earning money! I'd rather die!

SOLOMON: All the same, you . . .

KEAN: What are you talking about? Do you believe I am paid to act? I am a priest; every evening I celebrate mass, and every week I receive the offerings of my public, that is all. Money stinks, Solomon. You may steal it, or if you must, inherit it. But the money you earn, there is only one way to use it. [*He has crossed to the window. The musician has started to play again.*] Throw it out of the window. [*He throws his purse to the musician.*]

SOLOMON [*with a great cry*]: Oh, my God!

KEAN [*a little disconcerted by his own gesture, shrugs his shoulders*]: Oh, well, can't be helped. [*Charmingly*] You'll lend me a guinea tonight, for my cigars.

SOLOMON: Yes, Guv'nor.

[*There is a knock at the door.*]

KEAN: Again? Is this a public house? I can see no one. [SOLOMON *has opened the door.*]

SOLOMON: It's . . .

KEAN [*impatiently*]: Well? Who?

SOLOMON: The Prince of Wales.

KEAN: Tell His Royal Highness that I cannot see him.

PRINCE [*entering*]: Why cannot you see me, Mr. Kean?

KEAN [*continuing, as* SOLOMON *goes out*]: That I cannot see him without the greatest pleasure.

PRINCE: Naturally. But you find this visit inconvenient and you would like to see me in Hades.

KEAN: Your Royal Highness can never inconvenience me.

PRINCE: You flatter from force of habit, but your teeth are so tightly clenched the words can scarcely get past your lips.

KEAN: Imperfect diction? That is serious. [*He repeats —articulating as if at an elocution lesson*] Your Royal Highness is never inconvenient.

PRINCE: Never?

KEAN [*smiling*]: Never.

[*The* PRINCE *picks up a cigar.*]

Please . . .

PRINCE: Thank you. But if you expected a woman? Kean, you must tell me at once, and I will retire.

KEAN: Sir, I am expecting nobody.

PRINCE: Liar! And these flowers?

KEAN: Bouquets sent by admirers.

PRINCE: And this elegant dressing gown?

KEAN: Every night I have to dress to please my audience. May I not dress in private to please myself?

PRINCE: Who made it for you?

KEAN: Perkins.

PRINCE: I shall order one like it tomorrow morning.

KEAN: Again?

PRINCE: What do you mean?

KEAN: This is the sixth time Your Royal Highness has been pleased to copy my taste. . . .

PRINCE: What harm is there in that?

KEAN: In a week's time, all Europe will be wearing this identical garment.

PRINCE: In your place I should be very proud.

KEAN: Sir, for a long time my voice and features have belonged to the world, and the actors of the United Kingdom have copied my style of acting. At least in the old days I had a few rags I could call my own—behind locked doors, this mirror could reflect the image of the true Kean that I alone could be said to know. When I survey myself today, I see only a fashion plate. Thanks to the condescension of Your Royal Highness, I have become a spectacle down to the last detail of my private life.

PRINCE: And you complain? It is the price you pay for my friendship. [*Pause.*] What do you play tonight?

KEAN: Romeo.

PRINCE: Romeo? At your age? My poor Kean—he was eighteen when he died, was he not?

KEAN: More or less.

PRINCE: So you have survived him by twenty years?

KEAN: For twenty years I have kept him from dying.

PRINCE: And your Juliet—who is she?

KEAN: Miss MacLeish.

PRINCE: Good heavens! She was my father's first mistress. Between you, you must be a hundred years old. The stage will bend beneath the weight of your combined years. I cannot imagine how the public can endure the sight of an old couple enacting middle-aged amours.

KEAN: Where is my talent if I cannot persuade them I am eighteen?

PRINCE: Oh, you—you can always manage. But what about MacLeish?

KEAN: Where is my genius if I cannot convince them she is a child?

PRINCE: How will you do that?

KEAN: By insuring they see no one but me—that they see her only through my eyes.

PRINCE: And when she speaks?

KEAN: What do you expect them to hear? They will wait until I answer her. Besides, Juliet's part isn't a good one. It has long tedious speeches. I have had the whole play cut and considerably lightened.

PRINCE: All the same, she must speak if we are to notice her existence.

KEAN: I shall observe the audience. If they watch her too closely, I will cut in on her lines.

PRINCE: I see. Why do you look at your watch?

KEAN: To see if it is time to take my goat's milk. I drink it to clear my voice.

PRINCE: Indeed? An hour and a half before the performance? And for your nerves?

KEAN: I beg your pardon?

PRINCE: What do you take for your nerves? You seem very agitated this evening.

KEAN: It is the unexpected pleasure of your visit.

PRINCE: Come now, Kean, we all know the cause of your impatience—everyone knows your secret.

KEAN: I have never had a secret from Your Royal Highness.

PRINCE: That was true—until yesterday.

KEAN: Yesterday?

PRINCE: The letter you showed Madam de Koefeld.

KEAN: Ah, sir, that contained Miss Danby's secret.

PRINCE: I thought I recognized your handwriting. And I wondered if the secret you were confiding to the lady were not your incorrigible heart. [He repeats] "I have often wondered how a woman who loved me truly . . ."

KEAN: Sir!

PRINCE [*continuing*]: ". . . could grant me the favor of an hour without compromising herself. . . ."

KEAN: Sir, sir—who told you?

PRINCE: Ah, indeed? Who could possibly know? . . . [*Pause.*] What is the matter, Mr. Kean?

KEAN [*white with passion*]: Merely a touch of fury, sir. [*He sits down.*]

PRINCE: Mr. Kean! Did I ask you to sit down?

KEAN [*laughing, with an effort*]: I, sitting down? Before Your Royal Highness—never. I have merely sunk into a chair.

PRINCE: You stammer—you can hardly speak!

KEAN [*bitterly*]: Yes, indeed. Can you imagine that on a stage? I am Othello—I learn that Desdemona is false, and I sink into a chair. I can hear the hisses from here. The public expects us to give more nobility and amplitude to the expression of our feelings. Sir— I have all the gifts; the trouble is they are imaginary. Let a sham prince steal my sham mistress, you would see if I knew how to lament. But when a real prince tells me to my face: "You trusted a woman and last night she and I made a fool of you," anger turns my limbs to water, and I am incapable of speech. I have always said that Nature was a very inferior copy of Art. [*He has recovered.*] So, Sir, Madam de Koefeld told you everything?

PRINCE: You confess? You confess you asked her to meet you tonight at the theater, and you are waiting for her now? Very well, I shall be generous—since I have your confession, I will put an end to your torment. She told me nothing. [KEAN *is silent.*] Nothing —not a word. I was joking. [*Pause.*] Come, Kean, must I give you my word?

KEAN: I believe in Your Royal Highness's word as I believe in Holy Writ—except when it is question of a woman. Sir, we have lied together to too many husbands.

PRINCE: Husbands, yes. But not to you, my friend!

KEAN: To me? Oh, sir! What about Jenny? And May? And Laura? [*Another pause.*] Someone must have read you that letter, otherwise how would you have known?

PRINCE: How? But, my poor fool, you yourself have read it to me a thousand times! Firstly, three years ago—before you sent it to Lady Blyton; secondly, last year, before you slipped it into Countess Potocha's hand . . . Thirdly . . . No, the third time I took the liberty of learning it by heart, and sent it on my own account to Lady Portarlington.

KEAN [*laughing*]: So that's the way of it.

PRINCE [*laughing*]: Yes, indeed! Nothing else.

KEAN [*laughing*]: I read it to you myself! And you knew nothing at all?

PRINCE: Nothing! I took a chance. [*Reproachfully*] Oh, Kean! The selfsame letter! Have you no shame?

KEAN [*raising his head—ironically*]: Am I not the selfsame man? Besides, this time everything is changed.

PRINCE: How changed? You wrote the same letter.

KEAN: I wrote it, yes. But I didn't show it to you.

PRINCE: Then you really love her?

KEAN: She is my life!

PRINCE [*laughing*]: Romeo!

KEAN: No, no, I am no Romeo. Romeo loved to the death. I tell you I love her with my life. In an hour, I shall make my entrance and enact an imaginary love story; but what I feel now is real. It cannot be acted, nor sung, nor spoken. It makes me stammer—it bewilders me.

PRINCE: Very well—cure yourself.

KEAN: If I could!

PRINCE: And you cannot?

KEAN: Sir, this time, I am not in love for my pleasure.

PRINCE: Kean, if I asked you to give up this woman?

KEAN [*strongly*]: So that was why you came tonight? [*He rises.*]

PRINCE [*coldly*]: That was why. . . .

KEAN: Then you, too . . .

PRINCE: Am in the same case? [*Laughing*] God, no. I have already enshrined three women in my heart— what should I do with a fourth? What I have to say is for your own sake. You are cutting a very poor figure in all this. Last night you behaved like a lunatic. These mad passions are not fitted to your years, Kean —they deprive you of reason, you have said it yourself, and England cannot afford to lose her finest actor.

KEAN: If England wishes to keep me, she must leave me my private affairs. I have to experience them all to act them better. Until now, I have only known the joys of love—at present I am enduring the horrors, and you shall see the profit I have drawn if you come tomorrow night to see me play Othello.

PRINCE [*without moving, firmly*]: Kean, give up this woman.

KEAN: I beg Your Royal Highness to pardon me.

PRINCE: If not from good sense, then at least from obedience.

KEAN: Oh, forgive me, sir. I believed I was addressing the gay gallant I have often followed in his nocturnal adventures—and more than once brought home on my shoulders. But I realize my fault; I am speaking to the Prince of Wales. Obey? It is the first of my duties. But if Your Royal Highness insists that I submit to his commands, then at least he must excuse me from sharing his pleasures. It makes it difficult for me to—respect him.

PRINCE [*sharply*]: Kean! [*Pause.*] Let us say I am speaking in the name of the King.

KEAN: Of the King? Does His Majesty concern himself with my love affairs?

PRINCE [*sharply and very quicky*]: His Majesty desires you not to meddle with his ambassadors. Count de Koefeld is an important diplomat who serves the in-

terests of his country while at the same time helping
ours. Suppose it were discovered . . . Come, Kean,
you know that he would be recalled immediately.
And who would they send in his place? Do you know
we have important commercial treaties with Denmark?

KEAN: Cheese.

PRINCE: I beg your pardon?

KEAN: I say that these important treaties are reduced
to the purchase of cheese in Copenhagen. What a
strange bargain. Sir! In one scale you place a cheese,
and in the other you weigh my heart.

PRINCE: If I were to add gold?

KEAN: On the side of my heart?

PRINCE: No—on the side of the cheese. You have
debts. . . .

KEAN: Who should know better than you, sir? We in-
curred them together.

PRINCE: If you agree, the King will see them paid.
Come, Kean, I know your heart, and you cannot make
me believe it is worth more than six thousand pounds.
There! [*He holds out a paper.*]

KEAN [*approaching*]: What is it?

PRINCE: A written renunciation.

KEAN [*reading*]: "In consideration of the sum of six
thousand pounds, I agree to renounce the pursuit
of . . ." Pooh! Six thousand pounds! Sir, I have no
doubt you are valuing my love at its correct level, but
I should have believed you attached more value to
my word! It is not enough for you that I sell my soul
to the devil—you want me to sign a contract as well.

PRINCE [*laughing. Still seated, he folds the paper and
holds it in his hand*]: Kean—on any other occasion,
your word would have been enough. But would you
expect me to trust it when it is a question of a
woman? How many times have we lied to their
husbands? How many times have you betrayed me
with my own mistresses? With this letter in my pos-

session, I can be at peace. If you tried to see Elena, I should have it sent to her immediately. Come, sign, and the money will be brought to you this evening. [*Pause.*] Well?

KEAN: If His Majesty is concerned with the money-lenders of his kingdom, he should begin by settling your own debts. Your creditors have been waiting longer than mine, sir.

PRINCE [*calm, but furious*]: Mr. Kean, is this a way to address me?

KEAN: Sir, is this a way to treat me?

PRINCE: There, there—I own I was wrong. But I am not used to seeing you take your love affairs seriously. Lady Blyton herself—I believe you would have preferred six thousand pounds. And Lady Montague . . .

KEAN: Lady Blyton, sir, wished to feel Othello's hand laid on her fair shoulders, and Romeo's mouth pressed to her fair lips. I sometimes wonder if she had ever heard the name of Kean. As for Lady Montague, I never meant anything to her. At the beginning of our affair, I would not have left her for six thousand pounds, but that was because she had offered me seven thousand to stay.

PRINCE: Kean! Cynicism does not become you.

KEAN: What's this, sir? You have the bad grace to reproach me for selling myself at the very moment you endeavor to buy me? What am I, if not the man you have made of me?

PRINCE: I?

KEAN: You, and all the others. We believe that men need illusion—that one can live and die for something other than cheese. What have you done? You took a child, and you turned him into an actor—an illusion, a fantasy—that is what you have made of Kean. He is sham prince, sham minister, sham general, sham king. Apart from that, nothing. Oh, yes, a national glory. But on condition that he makes

no attempt to live a real life. In an hour from now, I
shall take an old whore in my arms, and all London
will cry "Vivat!" But if I kiss the hands of the woman
I love, I shall find myself torn in pieces. Do you understand that I want to weigh with my real weight
in the world? That I have had enough of being a
shadow in a magic lantern? For twenty years I have
been acting a part to amuse you all. Can't you understand that I want to live my own life?

PRINCE: Who can prevent you?

KEAN: What rights have I left? We players have been
declared outside the law. Can I be a member of Par-
liament? Buy a commission? Fight a duel? Act as
witness in a court of law? More than that—I cannot
even get a license to sell cheese. You have debarred
me from every profession—except the practice of love.
I can only be a man in your wives' beds—it is only
there that I can become your equal. Very well—but
let no one disturb me there!

PRINCE: Listen to me, you lunatic. We are not thinking
of you, but of her reputation. Your encounters are
the talk of London. Did you see how Lady Gosville's
eyes sparkled last night? That serpent guessed your
game, and Lord knows how many times she has re-
peated the story this morning.

KEAN: Every ambassador's wife has a lover and no one
complains!

PRINCE: Lovers, yes. But . . .

KEAN: But not Kean! As long as their lovers have titles,
even if they are dishonored, or fortunes, even if they
are Shylocks, everyone bows before them. But if one
of them glances at an actor—even the greatest in the
land—let her look to herself! She would be more
easily pardoned if she had slept with a stable boy!
[Pause.] I don't give a damn for the scandal.

PRINCE: Are you mad? She would be . . .

KEAN: Repudiated? Driven from court? Pointed at by
the mob? All the better, she would have no one in

the world but me. Do you think I cannot replace
the world?

PRINCE: You want her happiness, and yet you are ready
to harm her?

KEAN: You said I wanted her happiness?

PRINCE: You love her!

KEAN: I love her and I want to destroy her. That is how
we actors behave. Do you not think I have dreamed
of heaping honors on the woman I love? But since
that is denied me, I accept the risk of dishonor for
her. If I must destroy myself and her with me, I
accept; at least, I shall have marked her for life.

PRINCE: Kean, you hate her!

KEAN: I? I would give everything . . .

PRINCE: To destroy her reputation? What good does
it do you? To cure your sick pride, a woman would
have to renounce her pride of her own free will; to
save you, she would have to desire her own shame;
you will never feel you are a man like us until she has
preferred the dishonor you bring her to the honors
we could give her: you will never be revenged on the
world until the woman who loves you destroys the
nobility in herself to follow you. In pursuing Elena,
it is we, the real men, you are attacking. [*He laughs.*]
It is we you would like to overcome.

KEAN: And supposing it has happened?

PRINCE: But, Kean, she would have to love you!

KEAN: Well?

PRINCE: Poor Kean! [*Pause.*] Do you believe that?

KEAN: I believe it so firmly, sir, [*glancing at his watch*]
that I must implore Your Royal Highness . . .

PRINCE: To leave you? [*He laughs.*] I will lay you a
wager she never comes.

KEAN: I say she will. She has already started. . . .

PRINCE: Do you accept the bet?

KEAN: I accept.

PRINCE: What stakes?

KEAN: If she does come, you will satisfy my creditors.

PRINCE: Agreed. And if she does not come . . .

KEAN: I sign your paper.

PRINCE: I see—in either case I pay your debts. [*Pause.*]
She will not come: there is a ball tonight at Marlborough House and I sent her an invitation myself
this morning. She is dressing this very moment. . . .

KEAN: Can you believe she would prefer a dance? . . .

PRINCE: To your dressing room? Yes, I do believe it.
Kean, do you think OUR wives would prefer YOU forever?

KEAN: To convince you, Your Royal Highness need only
remain with me until you hear a knock at this door.

PRINCE: I will stay with you till you are called down
for your first scene.

[*Knock.* KEAN *turns to the secret door.*]

Ah, no, Master Kean. It was that door. [*He points
to the other door.*]

KEAN: Come in!

SOLOMON: A note, sir.

KEAN [*taking the note and reading*]: Very well, sir, you
have won your bet. The salon of Lady Marlborough
has more attraction for the Danish Ambassador's wife
than the dressing room of a humble actor. Laugh if
you will! No, there is no need. I know I am nothing
beside her husband—although he is almost senile.
But why can I be nothing? I must be a fool, for I cannot understand why all England places me at once so
high and so low. [*Crying out*] You are tearing me
apart! Between your admiration and your scorn, you
are destroying me. Am I king or buffoon? Tell me!
. . . Ah, I must be made with pride—it is impossible
for me not to believe I am a king . . . Come, sir,
you need not be afraid. It is only Kean the actor,
acting the part of Kean the man. I am the man who
makes himself disappear, night after night. And you,
who are you? You are playing the part of the Prince of
Wales? Very well, we shall see which of us wins the
greater applause. And the Countess? I would say, of

we three, she is by far the best actress. [*He laughs.*]
What shall we call the play? *As You Like It*, no
doubt. Or *Much Ado about Nothing*? Wait, we must
make sure of a happy ending. The prince and the
countess must have plenty of children, and the old
count must receive a great many decorations. As for
the buffoon—ah well, his debts will be repaid. Give
me your paper, sir!

PRINCE [*gently*]: No.

KEAN: No? But surely you want me to sign.

[*There is a knock at the door.* KEAN *opens, but there
is no one there; then he begins to laugh.*]

What . . . again?

[*Confronted with emptiness, he stands for a moment,
then closes the door.*]

This seems to be a night of deceptions.

[*Another knock.* KEAN *smiles, a hand on his heart.*]

I fear our conversation has lost its purpose.

[*The secret door opens slowly.*]

PRINCE: I fear it too.

[*A veiled woman appears.*]

KEAN [*rushing forward*]: Elena!

PRINCE [*bowing*]: Good night, Mr. Kean. Good evening, madam. [*He goes.*]

[KEAN *pulls the beard of one of the masks hanging on
the wall, and the door closes.*]

KEAN: I knew you would come; your letter convinced
only reason; my heart refused to believe your words.
I had despaired of seeing you, but I still hoped. Thank
you, Elena, thank you for justifying my faith. [*He
drops on one knee and kisses her hands.*]

ANNA [*pulling away her hand*]: How beautiful! But
alas, I . . . I am not Elena.

KEAN [*abruptly*]: Then who are you who dared . . . ?
[*He draws back her veil.*] You are Miss Danby.

ANNA [*sadly*]: Yes, but for your sake I wish I were
Elena.

KEAN: Who allowed you to use this door?

ANNA: I should never . . . I see you are displeased. [*Quickly*] It wasn't entirely my fault; I was told at your house that you had gone to the theater, so I came here, and found all the doors closed except one by the main entrance. I pretended I wanted to buy a ticket, and asked the man if I could see you.

KEAN: You were veiled?

ANNA: I have to be. My guardian and Lord Neville are looking for me.

KEAN: Then it was a misunderstanding, that's all. [*He laughs.*] And my lady is dressing to go to her ball. She will find it hard to convince the Prince of her innocence. Today is indeed a day of deceptions.

ANNA: Then you are not angry with me?

KEAN: On the contrary. You have won my bet and saved me a humiliation.

ANNA: I?

KEAN: Yes. Are you surprised?

ANNA: No. I bring luck to my friends—you will notice it more when we know each other better. So I can stay . . . [*She sits down, very much at ease, smoothing her dress.*]

KEAN: You . . . er . . . Yes, indeed, why not stay? I like company. What do you want of me?

ANNA [*as if reciting*]: Sir, a moment ago . . . I no longer knew if I could ask your help, or if I should have to go for refuge to the convent in Mayfair.

KEAN: To a nunnery, go! And quickly too . . . [*He laughs.*] Are you a Catholic?

ANNA: Yes.

KEAN: Irish, perhaps?

ANNA: Yes.

KEAN: I like the Irish: they never drown their whisky. Would you like a drink?

ANNA: No thank you.

KEAN: In that case, allow me to drink alone. [*He*

drinks.] To the Emerald Isle! [*He drinks.*] To the state of Denmark! You see, I am making free with you. Have you heard I am a great drunkard?

ANNA: I have been told so.

KEAN [*refilling his glass*]: It wasn't true these last few weeks. But I feel I am about to return to my wicked habits. You will have the honor of seeing the great Kean in a state of stupefaction.

ANNA: Mr. Kean! You . . . you should not drink at all this evening. . . .

KEAN: Because you are in my room? You come in by mistake, and on top of that, you expect me to change my habits. You will lose nothing: wine makes me more gallant. [*He advances on her, glass in hand.*]

ANNA: I wasn't thinking of myself, but . . . you have to appear tonight.

KEAN: If I am not mistaken, madam, you came here to ask my advice—not burden me with a lecture. [*He drinks.*] Besides, don't be afraid. There is no better actor than a drunkard. The public is so stupid they see nothing but the general effect. You yourself, I have seen you cheering me a hundred times. How your eyes sparkled.

ANNA: Did you really notice me?

KEAN: Yes, and you made me laugh, because I was drunk—my little Irish nun—drunk as an Irish lord. [*He laughs and goes to the table, laying down his glass. Then he goes behind the screen where he changes his clothes for his Romeo costume.*]

ANNA: I know.

KEAN [*behind the screen*]: Pooh!

ANNA [*bringing a diary from her reticule and consulting the pages*]: You were drunk on December 15th. You staggered when you bowed to the queen, and you called her Polonius. [*Turning the pages*] You were drunk again on December 18th, and you spoke the Fortinbras soliloquy so beautifully you had the whole house in tears.

KEAN: You see!

ANNA: Yes. Only that night, the play was *Lear*.

KEAN: What did the audience do?

ANNA: Well, King Lear is supposed to be mad, so it wasn't surprising he should take himself for Hamlet. December 22nd . . .

KEAN [*furiously*]: Enough, enough! So you knew I was drunk, and you applauded all the same?

ANNA: I wanted to encourage you.

KEAN: Encourage me? Me!

ANNA [*concealing her laughter, teasing him*]: Each word cost you such an effort, and besides, you looked so frail. I was afraid all the time you would forget your part and stand there lost in the middle of a sentence with all those people watching you. Ah, it was then I appreciated your technique. On a night like that, I am cold with fear. Fortunately, you have an excellent prompter.

KEAN: In other words, you applauded the prompter?

ANNA: And you too. There is nothing so moving as a man fighting his tongue. Besides, I knew you must be unhappy.

KEAN [*annoyed*]: Unhappy! [*He appears wearing his Romeo wig.*] I, Kean, unhappy! It is the first time that has ever been said to me. Normally, I am envied far more than I am pitied. That man who left just now, he envies my success, my talents, even the women who love me. Do you know who it was? The Prince of Wales.

ANNA: Then Romeo isn't unhappy?

KEAN: "Are you unhappy? Are you in love?" Every woman asks the same questions. To be or not to be. I am nothing, my child. I play at being what I am. From time to time, Kean himself plays a scene for Kean. Why should I not have my private audience too? [*He drinks.*] You are lucky tonight! You are going to see a private performance. You will see the whole gamut, from the sublime to the obscene. [*He laughs. Then, changing his tone*] I am suffering the tortures of the damned!

ANNA: Kean!

KEAN [*experiencing with three different intonations*]: The tortures of the damned! The tortures of the damned! The tortures of the damned! Which intonation do you prefer? Dear Miss Danby, I torture myself in my spare time in order to experience everything. [*He drinks.*] Leave me alone. . . .

ANNA [*rising, slowly afraid*]: Why?

KEAN [*glass in hand*]: I feel I am going to make you hate me.

ANNA: You will find that very hard to do. [*She smiles.*] I shall stay.

KEAN: You have been warned! You won't be startled if Romeo changes into Falstaff. I think you would have done better to go to your nunnery in the first place. [*Pause.*] Do I frighten you?

ANNA: No.

KEAN: No? You are right. Kean is a pistol charged with blanks. He makes a noise, but he doesn't do any harm. He can be mocked and insulted—insulted, do you hear?—and what happens? Nothing at all. He sinks into a chair and stammers! [*He laughs.*] Words, words, words! Remember! [*He drinks.*] You may be making a great mistake, my little nun. You are making the acquaintance of the actor Kean at a very bad moment. Tonight the great Kean loves very few of the genus woman, and if one should come into his clutches . . . Beauty . . . nobility . . . they are out of my reach. [*He goes to her.*] Do you know my secret ambition? To have a beautiful woman between these four walls and humiliate her. [*Sharply, as she makes no move.*] Fly from me! Why don't you fly from me?

ANNA [*sitting down again and spreading her skirts*]: Because I feel perfectly safe.

KEAN [*on his knees beside her*]: Will you sleep in my bed?

ANNA [*calmly*]: No.

KEAN: I should treat you like a sister. [*Quoting*] "Lady, shall I lie in your lap?"

ANNA: "No, my lord." That's Ophelia's line. I know the whole part by heart.

KEAN: Indeed. [*He rises and looks at her carefully.*] What do you want?

ANNA [*rising*]: To be an actress.

KEAN [*bursts out laughing*]: Forgive me—it's ridiculous: the cheesemonger's daughter wants to be an actress! Your father would turn in his grave, Miss Danby! You an actress! But it's the lowest profession of all! What a strange idea. Who put it into your head?

ANNA: You.

KEAN: I?

ANNA: Your example proved that it can be glorious and honorable.

KEAN [*during the following scene he finishes getting into his Romeo costume*]: Honorable! [*He drinks and rises, swaying a little.*] Do I look honorable? My poor child, you were born honorable; it is the privilege of purveyors of cheese. Famous, yes, I am famous. And then? If the gossips of your village stain your good name, that is dishonor: but if all England knows you are a whore, that is fame. If I had time, I should offer you my arm, and we should take a walk through the streets of London. You would hear the murmurs as we pass: "Is that really Kean? I thought him much better-looking. How much stouter he's grown! And doesn't he think a lot of himself! How old he looks! Have you seen his hair? He must be wearing a wig. I should like to find out if it's real!" In the old days, when a man had committed some terrible crime, every loyal citizen had the right to shoot him at sight, like a mad dog. That is fame. Go home, Miss Danby, there is no place for you here.

ANNA [*smiling*]: Mr. Kean, I ran away from home last night; that is quite enough to ruin a woman's reputation.

KEAN: Wasn't it enough?

ANNA: Since I have begun, I might as well go on to the end.

KEAN: You asked my advice, and I gave it to you.

ANNA: That was not what I asked you. I wanted to know if you thought I could become an actress.

KEAN: I should have to hear you first.

ANNA: I know every woman's part in the whole of Shakespeare.

KEAN: Indeed. [*Pause.*] Who taught you?

ANNA: You.

KEAN: I again? [*He begins to put on his make-up.*]

ANNA: I played the parts with you. I have heard you so often, and then I imagined the criticism you would give me.

KEAN: Let us see the results. What will you try?

ANNA: Desdemona, Juliet, Ophelia—whatever you please.

KEAN: Ophelia will do.]

[*As she recites, he drinks.*]

ANNA: "There's rosemary, that's for remembrance: pray you, love, remember: there's pansies, that's for thoughts . . . There's fennel for you, and columbines: there's rue for you: and here's some for me: we may call it herb of grace o' Sundays: O, you must wear your rue with a difference."

KEAN: You want the truth.

ANNA: Yes.

KEAN: The whole truth.

ANNA: Yes. [*Frightened by his tone.*] Very nearly the whole truth.

KEAN: Get thee to a nunnery!

ANNA [*gazing at him*]: Is there—no hope?

KEAN: Not the slightest.

ANNA: Was I . . . very bad?

KEAN [*scornfully*]: Worse than bad. Very good.

ANNA [*her eyes still on him*]: Then . . . then . . . if
I work hard . . . I know how to work, you know—
and I'm very strong-minded. I always get what I want.

KEAN: You have to be strong-minded to grow rich
among cheese: and the daughters of cheesemongers
inherit their strength of will from their fathers. You
will try and acquire your talent in driblets, as your
father amassed his pennies. How hard you're going to
work! It makes me tired merely to think of how hard
you're going to work. And you will make progress—
you will make such progress. You will never stop
making progress. It will begin by being bad, then
not too bad, then really not bad, then good, very
good, better still, perfect, better than perfect. And
then? [*Imitating her*] "I always get what I want."
[*In his own voice*] With determination, my child, you
can even get the moon which, after all, is only made
of green cheese. But you cannot BECOME an actress.
Do you think you have to act WELL? Do I act well?
Do I look as though I could work hard? You are born
an actor as you are born a prince. And determination
and hard work have nothing to do with that fact.

ANNA: Mr. Kean, I HAVE to become an actress.

KEAN: What for?

ANNA: To earn my living.

KEAN: Have you no money?

ANNA: I left everything when I ran away.

KEAN [*bursting out laughing*]: Left everything! So
you've come to the gutter to make an honest living!
We'll save our pennies like papa! Hard work and
economy: what an edifying picture! Shakespeare, Mar-
lowe, Ben Jonson, d'you hear? You cannot act to
earn your living. You act to lie, to deceive, to deceive
yourself; to be what you cannot be, and because you
have had enough of being what you are. You act
because you want to forget yourself. You act the hero
because you are a coward at heart, and you play the

saint because you are a devil by nature. You act a
murderer because you long to poison your best friend.
You act because you are a born liar and totally unable to speak the truth. You act because you would
go mad if you didn't act. Act! Do I know myself
when I am acting? Is there ever a moment when I
cease to act? Look at me; do I hate all women, or
am I acting at hating them? Am I acting to make
you afraid, or do I very truly desire to make you pay
me for your whole sex? Get thee to a nunnery, and
give your virtues to God. Go home to your golden
guineas, and leave us in peace with our cardboard
coins!

ANNA [*gently*]: Mr. Kean, could you try to act at being
kind?

KEAN [*startled*]: Kind? After all, why not? It isn't a part
in my repertoire, but I don't mind improvising. . . .
[*Pause.*] If I were kind . . . if I were kind . . . [*Acting*] You have seen the gilded surface of our life, and
it has dazzled you; now I must show you the reverse
of this brilliant medal—it has two crowns; one of
flowers and one of thorns.

ANNA [*laughing*]: You are funny when you are kind.

KEAN [*imperturbably*]: There are many things difficult
for a man of my years to say, difficult for a child of
your age to understand.

ANNA [*acting*]: Edmund Kean would never utter a word
that was unfit to be heard by Anna Danby.

KEAN [*in a changed voice*]: Are you prepared to sell
yourself?

ANNA [*as herself*]: Is it absolutely necessary?

KEAN: Indispensable. You must go to bed with . . .
Let me see . . . [*He counts on his fingers.*] The
director, the leading actor, the author . . . not
counting the understudies . . .

ANNA: To start with the author—that's easy, Shakespeare is dead. As for the director, he does as the
leading actor tells him.

KEAN: Now for the leading actor. Supposing you come to see our national hero, the great Kean . . . Let us play the scene. We shall see if you can improvise. I am Kean, you are yourself. You have just arrived. Go out. Pretend to go out.
[*She runs to the door and turns to face him.*]
Now come in.
[*She comes forward.*]
Don't we knock?

ANNA: Oh, forgive me. [*She goes back to the door and knocks.*]

KEAN: Come in. [*She comes forward.*] Shut the door. [*For a moment she is at a loss, then makes as if shutting a door.*]

CALL BOY [*off*]: Five minutes, please.

KEAN: Good. Now come in. No, no, don't raise your veil. There, that's perfect. [*He acts*] What do you want, my child?

ANNA [*sincerely, but very much the ingénue*]: Mr. Kean, I want to act.

KEAN: No, no, no. Not like that. You are throwing away your chances. This is a vain creature. You must flatter him. Begin again. Invent—create.

ANNA: I don't know how.

KEAN: Speak as you feel.

ANNA [*improvising*]: Here I am in his very room . . . Should I have the courage to tell him what has brought me here? . . . Ah, dear God—give me strength, for I feel my courage failing.

KEAN [*acting*]: What do you want of me?

ANNA [*in ecstasy*]: Ah, it is his voice! [*To* KEAN] Forgive me, sir, however modest you may be, you must understand that your reputation—your talent—your genius . . .

KEAN: Very good—very good indeed . . .

ANNA: . . . disturb me far more than your kind reception reassures me. Yet they say you are as good as you are great.

KEAN: I am not good.

[*He walks up to her, looking her up and down, touching her chin, her arms.*]

Not bad—not bad at all.

ANNA: Are you really saying that, or is it in your part?

KEAN [*vicious*]: I don't know. What does that prove? That you could drive a man to distraction? How am I to know that you can make an audience happy? Show me your legs.

ANNA [*acting*]: Oh, sir!

KEAN: What? Does that embarrass you?

ANNA [*spoken*]: I? Not in the least! [*She lifts her skirts.*]

KEAN: Are you mad? You should have refused! [*He beats her dress down.*]

ANNA: Why? I want to be an actress.

KEAN: It's out of character. Say: Horror!

ANNA: Horror! [*She giggles.*]

KEAN: Better than that.

ANNA [*trying to get it right*]: Horror! Horror . . . horror!

KEAN: Good. Now walk. Better than that. Like a queen. Not bad for a cheesemonger's daughter. Now be ashamed.

ANNA: Why?

KEAN: Because I have humiliated you. Good God, I told you! I detest all women. I touch your shoulder. . . .

ANNA: Ah! . . .

KEAN: I bend over you. . . . I shall break your pride. Perhaps take revenge on you for a woman I hate. Are you a virgin?

ANNA [*after a pause*]: No.

KEAN: Of course you're a virgin. Say, yes.

ANNA: Yes.

KEAN: Better than that.

ANNA: Yes.

KEAN [*annoyed*]: Make up your mind—are you or aren't you?

ANNA: Whatever you like.

KEAN: You are a virgin and you're afraid of me.

ANNA: Oh, no, Mr. Kean.

KEAN [*pushing her into a chair and leaning over her*]:
Little fool, you wanted to cheat me, eh? You planned
your comedy well; the brutal fiancé, the midnight
flight, the secret stair, the fortunate coincidences.
You wanted to have your game without paying. To
earn the right to make a fool of me, you have to be
at least a countess. You will pay your shot. You are
proud, aren't you? Stubborn and proud. You are all
proud, you devilish regiment of women. Well, you
shall never set foot on a stage unless you do all I
ask. Choose.

ANNA [*rising*]: I have made my choice; I will do anything you ask.

KEAN: Incapable of improvising.

ANNA: I speak how I feel. I will do anything you
ask. . . .

KEAN [*quickly*]: You can work with me, and if you have
the smallest talent, I will engage you in my company.
Don't be afraid; unconditionally.

ANNA: Without asking—anything?

KEAN: No, no, of course not! I was only acting.

ANNA [*disappointed*]: I see.

KEAN: I told you!

ANNA: One never knows with you.

KEAN: Nor with you either, little nuisance! Run along.
You've won.

ANNA [*amazed*]: Are you acting at being kind?

KEAN: I don't know. I'm drunk—that's all I know. Take
advantage of it.

ANNA: I will. [*She kisses* KEAN *on both cheeks and runs
away lightly.*] I'll be here in the morning! [*She has
gone.*]

KEAN [*left alone, continues to dress, singing to himself.
Suddenly he realizes he is singing, stops himself with
a scandalized "Oh!" Then*] Elena . . . Elena . . .

[*Annoyed.*] No! [*More somberly*] Ah, Elena, you hurt me very much tonight. . . .

CALL BOY: Beginners, please.

KEAN [*with a sidelong glance in the mirror*]: Elena, you hurt me very much. . . . [*Articulating*] Hurt me ve-ry much . . . Ele-na, you hurt me ve-ry much. [*He puts on his stage shoes, takes his hat and cape.*] Elena . . . [*He looks at himself in the mirror.*] Juliet . . . Juliet . . . [*He recites.*] "It was the lark, the herald of the morn, No nightingale."

[SOLOMON *enters.*]

SOLOMON: Your call, sir.

KEAN [*a glance at the mirror*]: Solomon, how old am I?

SOLOMON [*promptly*]: Eighteen, sir.

KEAN [*reciting*]:

> "Night's candles are burnt out, and jocund day
> Stands tiptoe on the misty mountain tops:
> I must be gone and live, or stay and die."

Stay and die! Ridiculous! Anyone in front, tonight?

SOLOMON: Full house.

KEAN: Idiots! They have come to see a Romeo of forty-five whose Juliet has furnished him with a pair of horns! [*He laughs.*] I'll give them Romeo. I'll give them Romeo. [*Before he goes, he turns to the audience and cries*] The public are all fools!

[SOLOMON *throws open the door.* KEAN *disappears toward the stage* (off). *We hear the National Anthem in the distance, the rustle of the audience, then silence as the people rise. We see the theater in reverse, with the lighted stage, and the actors preparing to begin the play.*]

CURTAIN

ACT III

*At the **Black** Horse.*

The members of Old Bob's troupe of acrobats, among
them FANNY, DAISY, KITTY, *and* PIP *are practicing a*
number. PETER POTT, *the landlord, is watching them.*
There are various customers in the background.

KEAN *enters, dressed as a sailor. He settles at a table, and*
calls loudly:

KEAN: Wine!

PETER POTT [*who is watching the dance*]: All in good
time, sir!

KEAN [*furious*]: What's this? Bring me a drink, you
villain, or I'll burn the place down over your ears.

PETER POTT [*joyfully*]: Oh, it's you, sir!

KEAN: No.

PETER POTT: What?

KEAN: No, it isn't I!

PETER POTT: Mr. Kean!

KEAN: Gone away till the end of the month.

PETER POTT: But I know you!

KEAN: Have you ever seen me like this? [*He does look*
very depressed, almost mad.]

PETER POTT: Oh no, fortunately!

KEAN: Then you can swear this isn't I. Go and fetch
me a bottle, and bring me a harlot to share it.

PETER POTT: Well, sir . . .

KEAN: What is it?

PETER POTT: These people are waiting for you—you
told them to meet you here.

KEAN [*looking at them dully, without recognizing*
them]: The devil! Give me a drink.

[PETER POTT *goes, nodding to one of the girls to go*
to KEAN.]

THE GIRL: Here I am!

KEAN: What's your name?

FANNY: Fanny.

KEAN: Fanny—foolish Fanny. Do you make love on credit?

[PETER POTT *has returned with champagne. He signs to the girl to say yes.*]

FANNY: Yes, sir.

KEAN: Call me Romeo. [*He pours out the wine. The acrobats have crowded round him and stare at him in silence.*] Who are you? What do you want?

[*Disappointed, the acrobats murmur among themselves.*]

Why, it's you! [*He rises and goes to them.*] My poor friends—my brothers—forgive me—I am drunk. There's a child to be christened?

[*One of the acrobats*—PIP—*replies, still very depressed.*]

PIP: A christening party—yes. You invited us, then you forgot us. . . .

KEAN: I? Forget my companions in misfortune? Kiss me—all of you. I love you from the bottom of my heart. [*To* PETER POTT] Have you a meal for us?

PETER POTT: Of course!

KEAN: Then lead us to it! [*To the acrobats*] Where is the lucky father?

PIP: Oh, sir—poor old Bob—he's had an accident. . . .

KEAN: You don't mean . . .

PIP: No—but he has broken his leg and the doctor says he must stay in bed for six weeks.

KEAN: Well, that'll be six weeks of rest. God, I envy him.

PIP: Still, during that time . . .

KEAN: Well?

PIP: The whole company could die of hunger!

KEAN: Can't you do the act without him?

PIP: You know we can't.

KEAN: You'd starve while you had the chance of a good

meal, and you'd have gone away with your empty
bellies because you thought I didn't recognize you.
Ah, I know the pride of you tumblers—my own pride
of the old days. Wait . . . [*He fumbles for his purse,
then remembers it has gone. Furiously*] The devil!
. . . I have no money . . . [*He picks up a jug of
water and holds it out to* FANNY.] Juliet, pour that
over my head. [*She hesitates.*] Pour, I tell you—I
must clear my brain. [*She pours the water over him
—he shakes his head.*] Now—get back to your paying
customers. [*He looks at her more closely.*] No, you're
as thin as a rail, you'd better dine with us too. . . .
A week without food . . . that happened to me, you
know, sixteen years ago. It seems like three weeks
. . . Peter—Peter Pott! Pen, ink and paper . . .
[PETER *goes out, and comes back immediately with
paper and writing materials.*]

KITTY: What is he doing? [*They all huddle in a corner.*]

KEAN [*writing*]: Carry this to the director of Drury
Lane. Tell him tomorrow I will play the last act of
Othello for the benefit of one of my friends who has
had an accident.

PIP: Ah, what a true friend.

KITTY: In good times as well as bad.

PETER [*calling*]: Tom! [*A sailor comes forward.* KEAN
gives him the letter.]

KEAN: Take this—wait for a reply. Now—are you all
ready? I want my dinner!

ALL: Ready!

KEAN: Then let's go!

DAISY: We mustn't keep the Vicar waiting.

KEAN: The Vicar is patient . . . but a good supper
should never be kept waiting. [*To* PIP] We'll give
your little brother a splendid christening.

PIP: It's a sister!

KEAN: Never mind! We'll take good care of her all the
same.

PETER: I'll see if the spit is turning.

KEAN [*on his way to the dining room*]: Wine! Wine!

JOE [*appearing*]: Here, sir.

PETER: Not a drop of water in the wine you give Mr. Kean!

JOE [*who wears an apron*]: And the others?

PETER: Use your own discretion.

JOE: I understand.

[*They have all gone into the other room where the music now begins.* ANNA *appears.*]

PETER [*seeing her, comes forward respectfully, wiping his hands*]: Miss?

ANNA: Can you give me a room?

PETER [*mysteriously*]: It's quite ready.

ANNA [*surprised*]: Indeed?

PETER: I was told to prepare my best room for a lady who would be coming tonight. I presume it is you?

ANNA [*aside, smiling*]: He thinks of everything. [*Aloud*] Take me to my room, please. I am so afraid someone may see me.

[PETER *shows her toward the stairs.*]

PETER [*calling*]: Dolly: show the lady up to Number One.

[DOLLY *appears, very dignified, and precedes* ANNA *up the stairs.*]

Can I send you up anything, Miss?

ANNA: No, thank you, nothing. [*She disappears.*]

[SOLOMON *appears.*]

PETER: Good evening, Mr. Solomon.

SOLOMON: Has Mr. Kean gone?

PETER: Not yet. He's having supper with the acrobats.

SOLOMON: Tell him I am waiting and must speak to him at once.

PETER [*to* JOE]: Joe, d'you hear? Fetch Mr. Kean.

[JOE *goes out to the other room. The music swells as he opens the door.*]

[*To* SOLOMON] You're too late for supper and too early for breakfast—what can I give you?

SOLOMON [*bad-temperedly*]: Nothing. I couldn't swallow a drop.

[KEAN *enters with his napkin round his neck, glass in hand.*]

KEAN: Well? What's the matter?

SOLOMON: Oh, sir, a disaster.

KEAN: Oh, is that all? What else did you expect?

SOLOMON: It's the jeweler—that devilish jeweler. He has taken out a warrant for your arrest, and the sheriff and bailiffs have gone to your house.

KEAN: What the devil do I care since I'm not there myself?

SOLOMON: They say they'll wait till you come back.

KEAN: Splendid! In that case, I won't go home.

SOLOMON: Sir!

KEAN: Come along, Solomon, join us at supper.

SOLOMON: I'm not hungry!

[ANNA *runs gaily down the stairs.*]

ANNA: Here I am!

KEAN: Eh?

ANNA: I said: here I am! [*The music stops.*]

KEAN: By the lord, so I see. What the devil are you doing here?

ANNA: I was in my room and I heard your voice.

KEAN: In *your* room? D'you have a room in this brothel?

ANNA [*amused*]: Is it a brothel?

KEAN: Er . . . very nearly.

ANNA: The room you took for me is very clean.

KEAN: I? Take a room for you? [*To* SOLOMON] Go in to supper. I'll follow. [SOLOMON *goes.*] What's all this about? Why do I find you wherever I go?

ANNA [*showing him a letter*]: If you didn't want to see me, why did you send me a letter?

KEAN [*exasperated*]: Ah—ah! I never wrote you a letter.

ANNA [*reading*]: "You have been followed: your retreat is discovered. Meet me tonight at the docks. Ask for the Black Horse. Someone will meet you to bring you to me. Fear nothing and trust me. I respect you as much as I love you. Kean."

KEAN [*repeating the last words*]: As much as I love you. [*He shrugs.*]

ANNA [*obstinately*]: As much as I love you. Your very words.

KEAN: If I had wanted to see you, I would never have taken these precautions.

ANNA: You added a postscript: "I have been followed. That is why I cannot come myself, and why the man who will fetch you will probably be masked."

KEAN: Masked. [*He begins to laugh.*] It seems I am out of luck. I leave the theater to plunge headlong into melodrama. I've had enough of the theater, of swords and mysteries and masked conspirators. Do you know why I'm here? To eat and drink! That is life! I have the right to live, haven't I? [*Furiously*] I respect you as much as I love you! A masked man! [*Harshly*] Look at me. You wrote that letter yourself!

ANNA: No.

KEAN: Bah! You're quite capable of it!

ANNA: I am quite capable of it, but I didn't.

KEAN: Show me. [*He looks at the letter.*] It's a man's hand. You've fallen straight into their laps.

ANNA: I?

KEAN: It's obviously a trick of your guardian, or your betrothed.

ANNA: Not my guardian—he's no imagination.

KEAN: Lord Neville has enough for two. It's quite clear: they've made you come here, and they'll pluck you like a flower.

ANNA: No.

KEAN: Why not?

ANNA: Because you will save me.

KEAN: Obviously. But will you please tell me why I can't take two steps without running into you? Why all London last night whispered that I had eloped

with you? Why this evening you come to my room
through my secret door, and why, now, I find you in
this thieves' den, where apparently I am going to
have to grapple with a gang of masked men?

ANNA: They may not be masked.

KEAN: Why do you have to bring tragedy—and when
I say tragedy, I mean tragical-comical into the cross-
roads of my life? Is there so much of the romantic in
this head? [*He taps her forehead.*]

ANNA: Romantic? Kean, you're wrong! I'm not romantic
at all.

KEAN: No?

ANNA: I'm not romantic, but I've been horribly bored.
[*Sweetly*] And this evening I'm not bored at all. [*At
ease*] Won't you sit down? Can I have some champagne?

KEAN [*sitting down unwillingly*]: My guests are waiting.

ANNA: I know. [*Pause.*] I was so bored with my guardian
that I actually fell ill.

KEAN: You aren't going to tell me the story of your life?

ANNA: Would you rather tell me the story of yours?

KEAN: No.

ANNA: I haven't a glass. . . .

KEAN: Then you don't have to drink.

[ANNA *takes the bottle and wipes the top with her
muff.*]

ANNA: Let me explain. I was bored and I pined away.
I fell into a decline. Do you know what that means?

KEAN: Yes. You needed a husband.

ANNA: I needed amusement. That's what the doctors
said. They said: she will die. She needs dances,
parties, theaters . . . Dances! . . . Do you like dancing?

KEAN: I never dance.

ANNA: Neither do I. So, I . . . slipped. Oh, merely
from boredom. So, after that, I was only allowed
the theater because they could keep an eye on me
there.

KEAN [*furiously*]: You were a fool.

ANNA: Why?

KEAN: A fool to . . . to slip. It . . . it doesn't suit you in the least. Who with?

ANNA: Bah! it was so long ago . . . besides, it was so boring I became a virgin again immediately afterward. So, I went to the theater. To Drury Lane. The first evening, it was Romeo! The evening went by in a dream. I never spoke, I never breathed, I never even applauded at the end of the play.

KEAN: A pity; actors need encouragement. Who played Romeo?

ANNA: Next evening, I was taken to the Moor of Venice. Ah, what a magnificent creature! And how delightfully jealous! I should adore to be stifled with a pillow: I think that shows great delicacy of feeling. To die among feathers—how agreeable. I liked him better than Romeo because I have always preferred older men.

KEAN: H'm! And who played Othello?

ANNA: Next time, it was Hamlet. A poor young man who soliloquized too much. But so prettily. How unfortunate that he was in love with that goose. I should have answered him: "I like men who have plenty to say for themselves." Anyway, she died. Good riddance. But the poor boy died too. And so stupidly. That evening I cried: oh, how I cried. But don't be afraid. I applauded too.

KEAN: And who was Hamlet?

ANNA: Kemble!

KEAN [*startled*]: What?

ANNA [*laughing*]: No, no, Kean, no. It was you, of course. And Romeo was you. Othello was you. Hamlet was still you. But admit Kemble isn't bad?

KEAN: Don't be foolish. Kemble plays Hamlet like a carpet-seller.

ANNA: Yet the critics have given him great praise.

KEAN: Critics don't hurt us with their bad notices. They

destroy us with the good notices they give other
people.

ANNA: So I made enquiries, and I found you were a
drunkard, a libertine, crippled with debts, melancholy
and mad by turns, and I said to myself: "That man
needs a wife."

KEAN: Indeed!

ANNA: A wife. A cheesemonger's daughter, willful and
stubborn, to bring a little order into his ways.

KEAN: Order! I see! And genius? What happens to that
while my life is being ordered?

ANNA: You don't understand. I shall supply the order,
and you will supply the genius. Oh, Kean, everything
will be tidy. Every night from nine to midnight you
will rage through your parts, and then you will come
home and find peace, luxury . . . [*Lowering her
lashes*] . . . and love . . .

KEAN: Come here, little sister. Do you know what I
think? You are even madder and more romantic than
I. [*He kisses her on the forehead.*]

ANNA: Don't you want me?

KEAN: No, of course not. With your method and my
madness, the house would blow up at the end of the
first week.

ANNA: You will accept in the end—I'm sure of that.
You are a very weak character, and everything I
want . . .

KEAN: . . . you get. I know.

[*The* SAILOR *runs in.*]
What is it?

SAILOR: A letter from the theater, Mr. Kean. The
answer to your note.

KEAN: Let me see. [*He glances at the letter.*] Very good.
[*To the* SAILOR] Go back to the theater. Tell them
to put the posters out tomorrow morning. I will find
someone else to play myself. [*The* SAILOR *goes.*] You
who always get what you want—do you *want* to play
Desdemona?

ANNA: Desdemona?

KEAN: Tomorrow night I am giving a benefit for one of my friends: I only decided this evening, and now they tell me there is no time to get Miss MacLeish who has gone to the country until Friday. Do you want to take her place?

ANNA: But I have never . . .

KEAN: Come to the theater at noon tomorrow, and I'll work with you until the performance.

ANNA: You mean . . . I should play . . . with you?

KEAN: Naturally. Who else?

ANNA: You see—you see! It's proof positive I'm going to marry you.

KEAN: Yes, yes, of course. In the meantime I'll have to get you out of this hornet's nest.

ANNA: What hornet's nest? Oh, I had forgotten. How amusing it all is! What are you going to do?

KEAN [*calling*]: Peter! Fetch the constable.

[*A* CONSTABLE *enters.*]

KEAN: Ah, here he is. Constable, this is Miss Danby, one of the richest heiresses in London. Her guardian is trying to force her into a marriage against her will. I put her into your care. . . .

CONSTABLE: And who are you, sir, to give me orders with such authority?

KEAN: What matter WHO demands the law's protection, since in the eyes of the law all men are equal? If you wish to know, I am the actor . . . [*He rises to his full height.*] Kean!

CONSTABLE: Oh, sir! Why didn't I recognize you? I've seen you play a hundred times, sir—I'm one of your greatest admirers. . . . This lady requires protection? Naturally, sir, naturally—everything to serve your interests. May I know how . . .

KEAN: Anna, take this officer upstairs, and tell him the story. I must stay here—I am expecting a guest.

ANNA: I do hope you knock him down.

KEAN: Why not? Particularly if he is the one I hope he is.

ANNA: Then I want to stay here—to see.

KEAN: Will you kindly go up to your room?

ANNA [*with a cry*]: Ah!

KEAN: What's the matter?

ANNA: You said that exactly as if I were your wife.

[*She runs upstairs, followed by the* CONSTABLE. *It is very dark. We see* LORD NEVILLE *enter masked—he speaks in a low voice to two masked men, disguised in long capes. All three of them hide.* KEAN *has not seen them.*]

KEAN: Masked? Why should he be masked? A man who makes a bet has no need to mask himself. . . . Good heavens! But it must be the bridegroom in person—Lord Neville himself. Caught red-handed in the act of rape and forgery. But . . . but . . . I have the right to strike him! I can beat him as much as I like! Prince—to take revenge on your noblemen, Kean has no need to strike through a woman. Since I cannot touch the shoulders of that lady, I can lay a noble lord on his back in the dust. A lord in the dust—I am a new man. I can beat a lord like a dog, with the law on my side. Oh, God, hear me—make him come—make him come! Here he is . . .

[LORD NEVILLE *appears alone.*]

NEVILLE: Stand aside, friend—I wish to pass.

KEAN: Stand back, friend—you cannot pass here.

NEVILLE: What does this mean?

KEAN: That I dislike masks.

NEVILLE: Indeed?

KEAN: Indeed. Masks went out of fashion with Queen Anne.

NEVILLE: A man may have good reason for hiding his face.

KEAN: Is yours so ugly? Disfigured perhaps by the small-pox? Covered with pimples? Strawberry marks over

your cheeks? Someone has cut off your nose and ears?
I'd regret that—nothing for me to do.

NEVILLE: Will you stand aside?

KEAN: No, my fine sir.

NEVILLE: What do you want? Money?

KEAN: I want to see the cut of your jib. And if you
won't take off your mask, I shall have to do it for
you.

NEVILLE: Insolence!

KEAN: Well? Which is it to be? You have a free hand
—use it. For if I have to raise mine, you may hear
it sing about your ears. You won't? Very good! Come
in all of you and bring some light. I've caught a fly-
by-night and I want to take a good look.

NEVILLE: Kean!

KEAN: Why, it's my lord Neville! What a surprise—I
make my excuses. I took you for a sneak-thief, and
I was about to chastise you. I have mistaken Polonius
for a rat so many times, it has become a kind of occu-
pational disease.

NEVILLE: This is a trap!

KEAN: Be assured, sir, it is one you cannot get out of.

NEVILLE: What do you want?

KEAN: You insulted me by using my name as a cloak
for your infamies, you must answer to me for that,
here and now.

NEVILLE: There is only one inconvenience, sir. A peer of
England cannot fight an actor.

KEAN [*dropping the stool he has raised*]: But of course,
what was I thinking of? You're a lord and I'm an
actor. How can we cross swords? You are descended
from the Plantagenets, in line direct—I might even
say you slid down. I am descended from no one—I
am the rising star. You inherited an immense fortune,
which you squandered in ten years; I have earned as
much money as you have spent, and if I choose, I can
rival the luxury of the Prince of Wales. You would
not deign to appear on a stage, even before an audi-

ence of kings, but you stoop to playing the cutthroat
in the lowest tavern in town. With me, there's this
difference—from eight to midnight I play anything
I choose, even the traitor Iago, but if after midnight
I had to play the part of Lord Neville, I should hold
myself dishonored. You sit in the House of Lords;
you make and unmake laws; the doors of the King's
palace open at the very sound of your name. But when
you wish to play tricks, you borrow mine. Not for
all the gold in the world would I borrow yours; my
name belongs to me—it was not given me, my lord,
it's my own creation.

[*He points to himself, then to* LORD NEVILLE, *and
shakes his finger, meaning that they will not fight.*]
You're right. We cannot cross swords. You have
fallen too low, mine would pierce the air above your
head—I have mounted too high—yours would hardly
touch the heel of my boot. [*Pause.*] My lord, in all
this, you have only forgotten two things: that I
might denounce your attempt to the police, and put
you into their hands: secondly, that you are in my
power. We will not fight: agreed. But what would
you say if I were to knock you down? Eh? Do you
know that actors have strong hands? I could crush
you as I crush this glass . . . [*He laughs.*] . . . if
I did not prefer to use it to propose a toast. Wine,
Peter. [PETER *fills his glass.*] To the health of Miss
Anna Danby, to her free choice of a husband . . .
and may that husband bring her all the happiness she
deserves. My lord, you are free to go.

NEVILLE: Mountebank!

ALL: Long live Kean!

[KEAN *glances up toward* ANNA'S *room. His eye falls
on one of her gloves, which he picks up. As he does
so, one of the assassins, holding a blackjack, prepares
to strike* KEAN, *who has thrown the glove aside. At
this moment,* KEAN *bends to pick it up, the blackjack strikes the table. One of the drinkers, who has*

been asleep at the table, wakes up at the sound. KEAN *has risen, and kicks the cutthroat in the stomach. The man falls, his arms spread wide. During this, the other cutthroat brings out a dagger and prepares to strike* KEAN. *The drinker,* JOHN, *springs at him, sends a blow crashing into his face, and sends him reeling to the foot of the stairs.* KEAN *falls back, saying:*]

KEAN: Well done, lad. What a magnificent ending to the act!

And

THE CURTAIN FALLS

ACT IV

KEAN's *dressing room.*
ANNA and SOLOMON *are rehearsing* Othello.

SOLOMON: "No; heaven forfend! I would not kill thy soul."

ANNA: "Talk you of killing?"

SOLOMON: "Ay, I do."

ANNA: "Then heaven have mercy on me!" What's the time?

SOLOMON: What—again?

ANNA: Again?

SOLOMON: You asked me the time, and I said "again"! That's the seventh time. It's half-past six.

ANNA [*crying*]: Solomon, he won't come!

SOLOMON [*hiding his anxiety*]: He will. He has to play tonight.

ANNA: And if he has decided not to?

SOLOMON: Oh, that! Of course he has decided not to.

ANNA: You see!

SOLOMON [*fetching the Othello breastplate*]: Every time he gets really drunk, he swears he will never set foot on a stage again; that he will go back to being a tumbler. It always happens!

ANNA: This time he may really mean it.

SOLOMON [*putting the breastplate behind the screen*]: How could he? He has promised this benefit to his old friends; he always keeps his word to them.

ANNA: Supposing there has been an accident?

SOLOMON: An accident—to him? He is luck personified. His only accidents are his successes in love.

ANNA: You say that to reassure me—I can see you are as anxious as I am.

SOLOMON: Not at all. Start again. "I would not kill thy soul."

ANNA: What can he be doing?

SOLOMON: What do you expect? He's sleeping off his wine.

ANNA: But where? He didn't go home last night.

SOLOMON: How should I know? Once we found him in a ditch on the road to Cambridge, ten miles away. No one ever knew how he got there. He was sleeping like a child: when we woke him up, he demanded his tea.

ANNA: What are you doing?

SOLOMON [*nervous*]: Just looking at the time.

ANNA: You see—you are worried.

SOLOMON: I told you to go over your part.

ANNA: You love him, don't you?

SOLOMON: Who?

ANNA: Him.

SOLOMON: Far more than any of his women.

ANNA: Then I promise you nothing will be changed. You can live with us.

SOLOMON: With you? When?

ANNA: When we are married. "That death's unnatural that kills for loving."

SOLOMON [*criticising*]: Not like that. You're putting too much fire into it.

ANNA: It's what I've got.

SOLOMON: It's not right for Desdemona. She was only a breath—a whisper.

ANNA: A breath? How could she be? She had to have courage to make her general marry her.

SOLOMON: She was an innocent victim—a martyr.

ANNA: Have you ever seen a beautiful woman being a martyr? Martyrdom is for the plain—we must allow them some compensation.

SOLOMON: That's ridiculous.

ANNA: How do you know? What do you know about women?

SOLOMON: Considering the numbers that have passed through this room, it would be very surprising if I didn't understand them.

ANNA: And Shakespeare—do you understand him too?

SOLOMON: I have held the book for more than forty years.

ANNA: That's a fine reason!

SOLOMON: And Mistress MacLeish—doesn't she understand? She always plays Desdemona with great gentleness. As soon as the curtain rises, you can see she is already dead.

ANNA: She has to play it that way because she's afraid of collapsing altogether. I am young—I have blood in my veins. I shall play it as I please.

"Alas, why gnaw you so your nether lip?
Some bloody passion shakes your very frame!"

There, now you've put me off. Why isn't he here? He's the only one who knows. He said: "Come to my room at twelve o'clock. Be on time."

SOLOMON: He was drunk.

ANNA: Of course he was drunk. But he said it again when he was sober.

SOLOMON: He never drew a sober breath all night.

ANNA: At six o'clock this morning he was sober. You didn't see him. It was in his carriage—he was taking me home to my aunt. The sun was shining, it was a lovely day—he took my hands and called me his heart's darling.

SOLOMON: If all the women he has called his heart's darling were entitled to a pension, the Treasury would go bankrupt.

ANNA: Mr. Solomon, you are a fool. And "little sister"? Are there many he has called "little sister"?

SOLOMON: Ah, that, no. Sisters aren't exactly in his line.

ANNA [proudly]: He called me little sister.

SOLOMON: It's nothing to be proud of.

ANNA: Solomon—I told him I had—slipped. Was I right?

SOLOMON: And naturally you have never—er—slipped?

ANNA: Of course not.

SOLOMON: People can tell, you know!

ANNA [*discontented*]: Oh?

SOLOMON: Yes. But it isn't important. He isn't concerned with that with you.
[KEAN's *voice is heard off—shouting:* "Do you call that a wig! Miss Cook—my shirt cuffs are torn again."]
Here he is.

ANNA: At last!

KEAN [*off*]: "What's that? My fault? I make too many gestures? I shall insist on Venetian lace—this stuff isn't good enough for the Moor . . . No . . . I don't need anyone to help me dress. . . ."

SOLOMON: Take my advice—slip out by the secret door. [*He pulls aside the curtain of costumes which conceals the door.*]

ANNA: Why?

SOLOMON: You heard him. He's in a black temper.

ANNA: But he needs me: I'm going to play tonight.

SOLOMON: Needs you! He's very far from thinking of you. He'll burst in here, calling for a carpet. . . .

ANNA: A carpet? . . .
[KEAN *erupts into the room. He is still dressed as a sailor, and is somewhat unsteady on his feet. He opens both doors wide, a cape thrown over one shoulder.* ANNA *remains seated, very calm, arranging the folds of her dress.*]

KEAN: Solomon! A carpet!

SOLOMON: What!

KEAN: A carpet—a lion skin—anything . . . [*He sees* ANNA.] It's you again!

ANNA: You told me . . .

KEAN: What? What did I tell you?

ANNA: That I should play Desdemona tonight.

KEAN: Did I indeed? I must have been infernally drunk!

Well then, madam, you will not play Desdemona, that's all.

ANNA [*disappointed*]: Oh! Why not?

KEAN: Because there will be no performance tonight. You hear, Solomon; I will never act again!

SOLOMON: Very good, Guv'nor.

KEAN: Not tonight, or ever again!

SOLOMON [*with a wink at* ANNA]: Yes, Guv'nor.

KEAN: You don't seem very upset?

SOLOMON: I'm heartbroken.

KEAN: Where's my carpet?

ANNA: What in the world do you want with a carpet?

KEAN: To practice my handsprings. That's the way I started and that's the way I shall end. Proclaim from the housetops that Kean, the acrobat, will do his tricks in Regent Street and St. James—on condition that he is paid eight guineas per window. I shall make a fortune within a week; while here, in this accursed theater, I have to slave for years to earn enough to retire with a slice of salt beef and a pot of ale to sustain my old age. Fame! Genius! Art! This time, Solomon, I have made up my mind. Do you know what I am? The victim of Shakespeare! I work my guts out for that grinning vampire!

ANNA: Give up your art! How could you!

KEAN: My art! Ha! Ha! It's easy to see you are accustomed to sell cheese. Cheesemongering is a peaceful profession—gentle and nourishing. But art is a cannibal; can't you see it is devouring me alive? I tell you, I have behaved like a fool—pulling chestnuts out of the fire for Shakespeare. To the devil with Shakespeare: he wrote the plays, why doesn't he act them!

ANNA [*gently*]: Kean! What's the matter?

KEAN: The matter is that my house is surrounded and my very bedroom crawling with bailiffs. I had to spend the night in a tavern and the whole day in a carriage. My spine is bent in two, and my skull split

open by hammer blows! The matter is that I am
going to be clapped in prison—and all for a miserable
four hundred pounds!

ANNA: I told you! If you would only put a little order
into your life, my love.

KEAN: Order! [*He laughs.*] This is the moment to discuss order! I want to create disorder! To whip a great
lady and betray her to a royal prince. And if that isn't
enough, I shall set fire to the theater. Order in a
desert, that's what I want. Set fire to the theater
and Kean will perish in the flames. What an exit!
God in heaven—what a head. [*Sharply*] Since when
have I become your love?

ANNA: Since yesterday.

KEAN: Yesterday? [*Worried*] What happened yesterday?

ANNA: A great many things.

KEAN [*more and more worried*]: Oh?

ANNA: You took my hands. . . .

KEAN: Your hands? And . . . ?

ANNA: That's all.

KEAN: Your hands! You see, Solomon, I am growing
old. It's time for me to retire.

SOLOMON: And you called her little sister.

ANNA: Yes.

KEAN: Did I? I see. . . . So I took your hands and
asked you to play Desdemona?

ANNA: Yes.

KEAN: Very well. You shall.

ANNA: I thought you were never going to act again?

KEAN [*grumbling*]: Oh, well—I shall have to go on
. . . because of poor Bob! But this is the last time!

SOLOMON: Yes, sir.

KEAN: The very last time, d'you hear?

SOLOMON: Yes, sir. [*Pause.*] Guv'nor, if you are appearing tonight, couldn't you . . . out of the takings . . .

KEAN: Eh?

SOLOMON: Keep back four hundred pounds?

KEAN: But the takings don't belong to me! Do you expect me to be paid for giving my services?

SOLOMON: You can pay it back . . . in a week . . . give me time to look round.

KEAN: What's this you say? That Kean should borrow money from a mountebank. Think of some other way.

SOLOMON [sulking]: Oh—if you won't help.

KEAN: Come here, you, and begin. What are we playing?

ANNA: The last scene of *Othello*.

KEAN: Charming! To have to roar with this head! Lie down and let me stifle you.

ANNA: Send Solomon away first!

KEAN: You don't want to die in front of him, eh? Solomon, behold her womanly modesty. It's true, there's nothing more naked than a corpse. [*To* SOLOMON] Get out!

SOLOMON [going]: I wouldn't mind. . . .

[ANNA *crosses slowly to the divan, but* KEAN *catches her by the arm.*]

KEAN [*at the table*]: Look at me. You would make a very lovely corpse. Aie!

ANNA: What is it?

KEAN: My head—my head.

[ANNA *takes a cloth out of the basin where it is lying ready and wrings it out.*]

I wish it were false, like Richard's hump. I could take it off.

ANNA: Does it ache very much?

KEAN: I'm paying for last night. You see what a fool I am. If I had made love to you, instead of getting drunk, I should be as proud as a peacock now, without an ache in my bones.

ANNA: Let me do this. [*She ties the napkin round his head, like a nightcap.*] That should be better.

KEAN: It's cool and refreshing. I must look a sight?

ANNA: You look splendid. Just like a pirate.

KEAN [*pleasantly surprised*]: A pirate? Why not? That's what I should have been!

ANNA: I could have gone to sea with you.

KEAN: Dressed as a boy. You would have been Kean's favorite cabin boy—Kean, the king of the Tortoise-shell Islands.

ANNA [*tenderly*]: And we could have been hanged together. . . .

KEAN: What a beautiful end: between heaven and earth—face to face, sticking our tongues out at each other. It's symbolic of all love stories. [*Pause.*] Good. Well—lie down and let me explain how you die. Give me the pillow. [*She lies down on the divan. He takes the pillow.*]

"She wakes."

ANNA: "Who's there? Othello?"

KEAN: "Ay, Desdemona."

ANNA: "Will you come to bed, my lord?"

[*The secret door opens suddenly.* ELENA *appears, and bursts out laughing.*]

ELENA: Kean in a nightcap with a pillow in his arms! Am I disturbing you?

[KEAN *snatches the napkin off in a rage.*]

I came to congratulate you. This morning, all London believes you married to this lady. But it appears the ceremony took place a long time ago; a real Darby and Joan already.

KEAN [*with dignity*]: Elena, I am rehearsing the last scene of *Othello*.

ELENA: Ah? And Mrs. Kean plays Desdemona? It's delightful—a real household of talent. Aren't you afraid of making your debut on top of an orgy, madam? Not too fatigued, I hope. If I can believe all I hear, last night, you were . . .

ANNA [*nods*]: In a very low haunt, yes, indeed.

ELENA: Kean, your wife is delightful, but her wit smacks of her father's shop. I have no taste for disputes, and

I will withdraw, happy to have been witness of your felicity.

KEAN: Madam, stay—and you, child, go to your room.

ANNA: I have no room.

KEAN: Solomon will find you one. Solomon! [SOLOMON enters.] Find a room for the child.

ANNA [rising]: I don't want to leave you alone with her!

KEAN: If you don't go immediately, you will certainly not appear tonight.

ANNA [very dignified, crosses past them and goes out. Then she puts her head round the door and adds]: If you want her to play instead of me, you'd better change the scene to the Taming of the Shrew. [She goes.]

KEAN: She has gone!

ELENA: So I see. Thank you, Kean; I was almost prepared to commit the greatest folly of my life, and you have prevented me. . . .

KEAN [in agitation—on his knees beside her]: If you had come last night, if only you had come . . .

ELENA: Ah, scold me! I betray my husband's trust—I cast aside morality and modesty—I come to you at the risk of a thousand dangers, and I find your dressing room transformed into a boudoir—a woman lying on your divan and you, Kean, wearing a nightcap! But I am the accused—I am the one who has to defend herself.

KEAN: Elena, there is nothing between Miss Danby and myself. [She does not reply.] I swear it. [She is silent.] Elena, do you believe me?

ELENA: Alas, I am fool enough to believe you. [She smiles. Pause.] But if you appear with her tonight, I will never see you again.

KEAN [rising]: It's too late to find someone else.

ELENA: I see. She is allowed to insult me, and in a few moments, I shall see her in your arms. How could I endure it?

KEAN [*imploringly*]: Elena, we are playing *Othello*. The final scene. I have to kill her. Kill her—d'you hear? With a pillow! I don't even have to touch her. If . . . that young lady has been unfortunate enough to displease you, surely you should be glad to see her stifled. Ah—none of this would have happened if you had only come to me last night!

ELENA [*rising*]: Why must you always come back to that! Do you know what you deserve? That I should not say a word! That I should not even answer your unjust reproaches. But I am not like you; your anxiety affects me, and I want you to be calm. Kean, I didn't come last night, because I was prevented.

KEAN [*harshly*]: Indeed! Is it a duty to attend a ball?

ELENA: For an ambassador's wife, yes, it is an official duty. Kean, I went to the ball because my husband ordered me to attend. There—

KEAN [*turning to look at her*]: Ordered you?

ELENA: Yes, ordered me. He had been instructed to pay his respects to the Prince of Wales.

KEAN: That's true—I had forgotten the Prince of Wales. So—the Count couldn't go to the ball alone? Couldn't you find an excuse?

ELENA: A headache? The vapors? Those are actors' tricks. You don't know my husband—he can be terrible.

KEAN: Indeed! I would never have thought it.

ELENA: What good would it be to be a diplomat, if one didn't know how to hide one's feelings? You force me to confess what I intended to hide. My husband is suspicious.

KEAN: Suspicious? Of us?

ELENA: Yes—of us. I was right not to want to tell you: you are upset. Do you see now why I couldn't disobey him? If I had refused to go to the ball, he would have pretended to go without me, and then come back later, hoping to surprise us. Ah—good heavens —supposing he hadn't found me at home! Kean, is

this the way you love me: do you want him to hurl
me into the gutter? To kill me?

KEAN [*desolate*]: Madam . . .

ELENA: He would do it. . . .

KEAN [*kissing her hand*]: Elena, forgive me.

ELENA: That is how you all are, you men—unjust, cruel,
and ungenerous. It isn't enough to entrust you with
our honor—we must still risk losing it for love of
you. Very well, Kean—go on to the very end—set
the limit on your unkindness—to your cruelty—to the
pain you are causing me. Say it—say it—that I must
be dishonored before you can love me.

KEAN: Elena! [*He falls on his knees.*] If you knew how
I have suffered!

ELENA: Yet they say you spent the night laughing and
singing!

KEAN: Laughing? Elena, I was drunker than I have
ever been in the worst moments of my life. I was
involved in a street fight—I insulted a lord. . . . I
would have killed him if it would have helped me
escape from these terrible sufferings. . . .

ELENA: Madman! For a mere mishap . . .

KEAN: You call that a mishap?

ELENA: What else?

KEAN: I am jealous, Elena. I have vitriol in my veins.

ELENA: Jealous? You?

KEAN [*seizing her in his arms*]: Jealous—tortured—ob-
sessed—humiliated—degraded.

ELENA: Jealous—good heavens, of whom?

KEAN: You know very well.

ELENA: No, indeed, I swear it.

KEAN: Swear nothing—I don't believe your vows.
Women have an instinct that tells them we love
them—long before we tell them ourselves.

ELENA: But so many young men pay their court to me.

KEAN: I'm not talking of them. Elena, was the Prince
of Wales at the ball?

ELENA: Yes, naturally.

KEAN: Did he speak to you?

ELENA: Yes, for some time.

KEAN: What about?

ELENA: What do you think? Nothing.

KEAN: Ah—that's as I feared!

ELENA: Very well—everything, if you prefer it.

KEAN: Nothing—everything—it's all the same. While lips speak and say nothing, eyes can make themselves understood without words.

ELENA: He always looks at me.

KEAN: And . . . how did he behave?

ELENA: What a question! As always; he was ironic, amusing, charming.

KEAN: Charming!

ELENA: Isn't he always charming?

KEAN: Alas!

ELENA: You are intolerable! Did I come here to discuss the Prince of Wales?

KEAN: Madam, he is in love with you!

ELENA [*genuinely surprised*]: He? But, Kean, you are confusing me. The Prince of Wales! He doesn't even notice me.

KEAN [*reproachfully*]: Elena!

ELENA: Well . . . if I must tell you . . . I did think . . . once . . . when he gave me this fan . . . And then, I never considered it again . . . I never thought of anyone but you!

KEAN [*taking the fan*]: The Prince of Wales came to this room yesterday and asked me to give you up. [*He tosses the fan onto his dressing table.*]

ELENA [*joyfully*]: The Prince of Wales? Is it possible? What did he say? Quickly, quickly—tell me everything.

KEAN: Alas, madam—you see!

ELENA: What do I see?

KEAN: Your voice—your manner—everything shows that this news delights you.

ELENA: Kean, have you gone mad? How could the

Prince of Wales know that I . . . that I wish you
well? Oh, Kean—was it you who told him?

KEAN: He guessed I loved you.

ELENA: Ah well—poor prince—supposing he does love
me; of course, I am only supposing it to please you.
What do you expect me to do?

KEAN [*very close to her*]: I couldn't see him at your side
without going mad.

ELENA: My Othello! But what can we do? It is too late
to cancel our plans. . . .

KEAN: Cancel what plans?

ELENA: He did us the honor of asking for a seat in our
box.

KEAN: Tonight?

ELENA: Yes.

KEAN: You mean he will be in your box while I play
tonight?

ELENA: Yes—while you hold that . . . creature in your
arms.

KEAN: Ah, madam, for me it is only a sham, like everything else in my life. Merely another piece of acting.

ELENA: You mean that I . . .

KEAN: I am going to make you a request, which I implore you not to refuse: all the time I am on stage,
do not speak to him, do not smile at him, do not
listen to him. Madam, never take your eyes off me.
If I surprise a trace of understanding between you,
I should no longer be master of myself.

ELENA: And what would happen?

KEAN: I don't know. Listen, supposing I lost my
memory, that I stood glued to the middle of the
stage, unable to speak? Supposing I were to break
down and weep? [*She laughs.*] Don't laugh! I should
be ruined!

ELENA: Do you realize you are asking me to insult the
King's brother? Kean, if he is offended it is Denmark
that will suffer.

KEAN [*rising, furiously*]: Denmark! Denmark! Always

Denmark and its milch cows. Madam! it is I who have been offended! Yes, I. Last night I was told that you didn't love me. That for you I was only a caprice, that you had glanced at an actor for lack of employment. For you, I was only a game, or at most a distraction.

ELENA: Madman!

KEAN: My love demands that you prove your own.

ELENA [*furious*]: Your love? No, your pride. You don't want me to prove it to you—you want me to prove it to the Prince. He humiliated you yesterday, by pretending that I didn't love you, and now you expect me to undeceive him. My love? Ah, you care little for me at this moment: what counts, in your eyes, is the opinion of the Prince.

KEAN: Elena—that proof will be understood by me alone—it will be valued by me alone. You are a great lady, and I am only actor, but I honor you, madam, when I count on you alone to prove to the actor that he can be loved like a prince.

ELENA: Very well. But service for service.

KEAN: Ask me anything!

ELENA: Send the little Danby home, and play the scene with Miss MacLeish.

KEAN [*in despair*]: Elena! Miss MacLeish is in the country—there is no time to fetch her.

ELENA: What do I care? It's up to you. Play the part with the prompter.

KEAN: The prompter! How on earth am I to do that?

ELENA: If you really have genius, you ought to make the audience believe him the most beautiful of Desdemonas.

KEAN [*groaning*]: I'm not a magician—I'm an actor.

ELENA: Very well, Mr. Kean. Your demands increase from day to day, and when, in return, one dares ask for the simplest and most legitimate favor, you refuse point blank. Very well, I tell you plainly. If that girl appears on the stage at your side, I will turn to the

Prince and smile at him till the end of the act. I will
make you pay for this. I . . .
[*There is a knock at the door.*]
[*Frightened*] Heavens!

KEAN: The door is locked. [*Calling*] Who is it?

PRINCE [*off*]: It is I.

ELENA [*in a low voice*]: The Prince of Wales!
[*During the following scene, she endeavors to open
the secret door.*]

KEAN [*aloud*]: Who?

PRINCE [*off*]: The Prince of Wales, of course.

COUNT [*off*]: And the Count de Koefeld.

ELENA [*low*]: My husband! I am lost! How can I open
this door?

KEAN [*low*]: Pull the beard!

ELENA: Which beard?

KEAN [*pointing to a bearded mask on the side of the
wardrobe*]: That one, and go, quickly. . . .
[ELENA *pulls the beard, and the door opens, squeaking.*
KEAN *coughs, to cover the sound, imitating the
squeaks.*]

KEAN [*aloud*]: Forgive me, sir . . . But for the moment I have the misfortune . . . [*In a low voice, to*
ELENA] Hurry, hurry! [*Aloud*] To have at my heels
certain gentlemen who pursue me for a matter of
£400 . . .

PRINCE: I understand!
[ELENA *is entangled in the costumes—the door has
stuck—she beats on it, but cannot get through.*]

KEAN [*aloud*]: And they would not hesitate to make
use of your Royal Highness's name . . .
[*He leans against the door to prevent anyone from
opening.*]

PRINCE: And so?

COUNT: And so?

ELENA [*clasping her hands*]: Oh! . . . Santa Maria! . . .

KEAN [*aloud*]: Be good enough to send me a note signed
by your own hand, sir.

[ELENA *pulls the beard on the mask so hard that it comes off, but the door opens with a great clatter.*]

PRINCE: What on earth are you doing?

KEAN [*aloud*]: I am fetching the key. [*Low to* ELENA *as she goes*] Farewell, Elena—I adore you—will you grant my prayer?

ELENA [*low*]: Will you grant me mine?

KEAN [*low*]: I . . .

ELENA: Service for service. I shall not go back on my word.

[*She disappears, the door closes abruptly.* KEAN *puts the costumes back in place. Through the keyhole of the other door comes a little roll of paper.*]

KEAN [*taking the note*]: A note of hand for £400 . . . a truly royal card. Come in, sir, it must indeed be you. [*He opens the door. The* PRINCE *and the* COUNT *enter.* SOLOMON *enters behind them and disappears behind the screen.*]

PRINCE: A debt of honor I owed you.

KEAN: Owed me?

PRINCE: Since yesterday.

KEAN: Ah, sir—the stakes were very much higher than that.

PRINCE: I know, Kean. This is only a beginning. [*To the* COUNT] We are talking of a wager we made, and I do not yet know if I have won or lost.

COUNT: In that case, sir, why do you pay?

PRINCE: Because the result makes no difference. Win or lose, Mr. Kean has arranged for me to pay.

KEAN: Then I accept. Solomon, you know what to do with this money.

SOLOMON: Yes, indeed . . . [*He goes.*]

[KEAN *goes behind the screen and begins to change.*]

COUNT [*low to the* PRINCE]: Are you sure he was with a woman?

PRINCE: Certain.

COUNT: Miss Danby, perhaps?

PRINCE: It's hard to tell. . . .

[*The* COUNT *sees the forgotten fan on the table and picks it up, slipping it into his pocket, without the* PRINCE *having seen.*]

COUNT: I shall find out—I promise you.

PRINCE: How?

COUNT: That is a diplomatic secret.

KEAN [*dressing behind the screen, an arm or a leg protruding from time to time*]: Well, sir? What's the news?

PRINCE: Nothing of great importance—I hear an insolent fellow insulted and threatened Neville last night.

COUNT [*shocked*]: Insulted Lord Neville? . . . Why?

KEAN: A lord can never be insulted—even with words.

COUNT [*to the* PRINCE]: I am not familiar with your English habits, sir, but when we Danes believe ourselves insulted, we fight the whole world.

KEAN: Long live Copenhagen! One day I shall go there to get myself killed.

COUNT [*sharply*]: You would be welcome. Until then, I thank you for allowing me to penetrate the Holy of Holies . . . and I bow before you—the High Priest. [*He goes to the door.*]

KEAN [*aside to the* PRINCE]: Your Royal Highness—I must speak to you . . .

PRINCE [*to the* COUNT]: I will rejoin you, Count.

COUNT: Your Highness will come to our box?

PRINCE [*aside to the* COUNT]: You will tell me everything?

COUNT [*aside to the* PRINCE]: I give you my word. [*He goes.*]

PRINCE [*watching* KEAN *making up as Othello*]: Now— you scoundrel—have I won or lost? Answer me!

KEAN: Sir, you know the result as well as I do. You saw Madam de Koefeld at the ball?

PRINCE: She did appear, certainly. But very late. That veiled lady . . .

KEAN: That veiled lady . . . was a cousin of mine.

PRINCE: Then I have won? [KEAN *does not answer.*] You will not say? Did I lose?

KEAN: In either case, sir, I beg your permission to keep silent; if you have lost, to protect the honor of a lady; if you have won, to protect my own pride.

PRINCE: Very well—I shall make my enquiries and finally learn the truth. What did you want with me?

KEAN: Sir, what am I to you? A protégé or a friend?

PRINCE: But . . . Devil take it! How can I answer? My purse is yours—my place is open to you day and night—when you require my influence, it is yours to command. Isn't that enough?

KEAN: All those favors are given by the prince to the subject. Supposing I asked you for one of the sacrifices granted between equals. . . .

PRINCE: Well?

KEAN: Would the goodwill of the patron stretch as far as the devotion of a friend?

PRINCE: Let us try.

KEAN: Sir . . . do not go to her box.

PRINCE: Her box? [*Understanding.*] Ah . . .

KEAN: You are young—handsome—and a prince. To amuse you, distract you, love you, you have London, the whole kingdom. Pay your court to the others. . . .

PRINCE [*imitating him*]: "But leave me Elena." Is that it? [KEAN *bows.*] Then I see, she did come. You confess.

KEAN: No!

PRINCE: If I leave her, another will take my place. . . .

KEAN: What do I care for the others! The others are so many sheep. . . . [*Pause.*] Do not go to her box, sir. Do not go to her tonight.

PRINCE: So this is the sacrifice?

KEAN: Yes.

PRINCE: Very well—I will not go. [*He takes a paper from his pocket.*] On condition that you sign this.

KEAN: What is it?

PRINCE: The receipt for your debts you were to have signed yesterday.

KEAN: Swearing I would never see her again?

PRINCE: Yes. Against six thousand pounds.

KEAN [*quickly*]: But I do not wish to sign.

PRINCE: You have betrayed yourself, Kean! If you do not wish to sign, then you have seen her again!

KEAN: No, sir, no, but . . . if you wish to avoid a scandal . . . that I shall regret . . .

PRINCE: Confess you are her lover?

KEAN: I cannot confess what isn't true!

PRINCE: Then sign.

KEAN: No, sir, I cannot sign.

PRINCE: Good-by, Kean.

KEAN: Sir . . . where are you going?

PRINCE: To applaud you.

KEAN: From your own box?

PRINCE: No half-confidences, Mr. Kean, or I will only give you a half-promise.

KEAN [*bowing*]: Do as you please, sir.

PRINCE: Thank you, Mr. Kean. [*He goes out angrily, banging the door.*]

[SOLOMON *appears, carrying the* Othello *belt and dagger.*]

SOLOMON: Sir! Sir . . . We must hurry. . . .

KEAN: I'm ready.

[*There is a knock at the secret door.*]

Solomon—someone knocked at the secret door. See who it is.

[SOLOMON *opens the door, and* GIDSA, ELENA'S *maid, enters.*]

KEAN [*making up*]: You, Gidsa? What has happened?

GIDSA: My mistress left her fan behind. I have come to fetch it.

KEAN: Her fan? Have you seen it, Solomon?

SOLOMON: No, sir.

KEAN: See if you can find it.

GIDSA [*searching*]: Oh, how could she have lost it? My

mistress is devoted to it. It was a present from the
Prince of Wales.

KEAN: Indeed! I had forgotten. Look carefully, Gidsa,
look carefully. The gift of a prince should not go
astray in the dressing room of an actor. [*Pause.*] Look
in the carriage. She may have dropped it there.

GIDSA: You're right. . . . I will see. [*She turns as she
is about to go through the secret door, seeing the
royal costumes.*] Oh—what lovely clothes!
[*She disappears, and the door closes.*]

KEAN [*bitterly, as he continues to make up*]: A royal
fan! . . . That must look very fine. [*He imitates
ELENA with her fan. Shouting*] Darius! [*To SOLOMON*]
Fetch that ridiculous girl!

SOLOMON [*opening the door*]: Darius!
[*We hear the voice of the STAGE MANAGER calling
"Beginners, please." There are impatient sounds from
the invisible audience.*]

KEAN: Where is he?

SOLOMON: Just coming, sir.

DARIUS [*off*]: Just coming . . . just coming . . . Othel-
lo's wig . . . all quite ready . . .
[*He enters, mincing, with the wig and comb.*]
Curled to perfection, sir—you'll be delighted.

KEAN [*imitating him*]: Hair style number one. I know,
I know. . . .

DARIUS: No, no, it's number three. Much more suitable
for a general.

KEAN: Come—put it on!

DARIUS [*to SOLOMON*]: Why is he so nervous today?
He'll have another triumph, you'll see. Ah, we're in
a bad mood. [*He helps KEAN to put on the wig.*]

STAGE MANAGER [*opening the door*]: May we ring the
curtain bell, sir?

KEAN: Yes. I'm ready.

S.M.: Thank you, sir. [*He bows and goes.*]

KEAN: Solomon—see who's in the theater, then come
back and tell me who is in Count de Koefeld's box.

[SOLOMON *goes.* ANNA *enters dressed as Desdemona, so
badly made up that she looks like a painted doll.*
KEAN *roars with laughter.*]

ANNA [*entirely at ease*]: Here I am.

KEAN: What on earth do you look like! Who made you
up?

ANNA: I did.

KEAN: You'd make a cat laugh. Come here. Kneel down
—I'll try and fix you up.

[*He alters her make-up and combs her hair while*
DARIUS *continues to arrange his own wig.*]

Are you nervous?

ANNA: No.

KEAN: Amateur—I'm not surprised. Don't worry. If
you hesitate, I will cut in. If you don't know where
to move, I'll take your arm. If you forget your words,
you need only say: "I love you." In a love scene, that
always fits in. [*Pause.*] I have no one to take my arm
or whisper me my lines. That's why I'm always nervous. You, you have me, but I am alone. Darius—
give me that bottle.

DARIUS [*aside, fetching the hidden bottle*]: He's off!

KEAN [*drinking*]: This is the finest cure for nerves. [*He
drinks.*] I'm exhausted.

[SOLOMON *returns.*]

Well?

SOLOMON: The theater is full, with a queue as far as the
river.

KEAN: What do I care. Is Madam de Koefeld in her
box?

SOLOMON: Not yet, but the Count is there with the
Prince of Wales and another lady.

KEAN: The Prince of Wales! I was sure! [*To* ANNA] If
I asked you not to appear tonight, would you be very
upset?

ANNA: Very.

KEAN: But if I asked you—for my sake?

ANNA: I would do anything.

KEAN: Thank you. [*He kisses her forehead. To* DARIUS]
Go and ask Miss Gish if she knows the part. She must
still be in the theater. If not—ask Miss Pritchett.
Hurry. [DARIUS *runs out.*]

DARIUS: I fly, sir.

ANNA: She doesn't want me to appear, does she?

KEAN [*gently*]: No.

ANNA: And it makes you happy to sacrifice me to her?

KEAN: Not particularly.

ANNA: That's what I thought: you don't look very
pleased.

S.M. [*at the door*]: Your call, Mr. Kean.

KEAN: I'm not ready.

S.M.: You told me we could begin!

KEAN: Go to the devil!

S.M. [*shouting*]: Hold the curtain! Hold the curtain!
[*The invisible audience becomes more vociferous.*]

DARIUS [*running in*]: Miss Gish doesn't know the part.
She says she can do Cordelia—would that help?

KEAN: No, it would not. What about Miss Pritchett?

DARIUS: Miss Gish reminds you that Miss Pritchett has
been ill since last Thursday.

KEAN: Very well—then I won't appear. [*But he continues to make up and get ready.*]

SOLOMON [*coming from behind the screen*]: Sir—sir—
what are you saying?

KEAN [*firmly*]: That I won't appear—that's what I'm
saying.

[*Through the open door, the* STAGE MANAGER *appears.*]

S.M.: Sir—you will be compelled!

KEAN: By whom—if you please?

S.M. [*in uncertain tones, recoiling slightly*]: The constable.

KEAN: Send for him—he is my best friend.

SOLOMON: In the name of heaven—you'll be thrown
into prison!

[STAGE HANDS *and* ACTORS *begin to cluster in the
doorway.*]

KEAN: In prison—in prison—there, at least I shall be free! I shan't have to act!

SOLOMON [*imploringly*]: Can nothing make you change your mind?

KEAN: Nothing.

S.M.: The house is sold out!

KEAN: Give back the money!

FIREMAN [*appearing from behind the* STAGE MANAGER, *with a* STAGE CARPENTER]: Mr. Kean . . . to please us!

CARPENTER: It's our favorite part!

KEAN: I refuse. . . . I refuse. . . . I refuse. . . .

[ANNA *kneels beside him.* SOLOMON *drops back, signing to the others that everything will be all right.* DARIUS, *frightened, has taken refuge behind the screen. Prolonged whistles and cat-calls from the invisible audience.*]

ANNA [*gently, beside* KEAN]: Kean, what about Bob? It isn't his fault if you are unhappy. You aren't happy now, but if you don't play tonight, you will be even less happy. You gave them your word, you know. It will be the first time you've broken a promise.

KEAN [*after a pause, smiles and kisses her hand*]: Where is Darius?

DARIUS [*popping his head out from behind the screen*]: Here I am!

KEAN [*rising*]: My cloak!

DARIUS [*holding it out*]: I pressed it myself!

KEAN: My belt!

SOLOMON [*holding it out*]: Here it is! Here it is!

S.M. [*who has been standing in the doorway with the others, all smiles*]: Thank you, thank you, Mr. Kean!

KEAN: My dagger! [*Everyone hurries round.*]

DARIUS: His dagger! His dagger! Here it is—no, over there. . . . [*The* STAGE MANAGER *holds out the dagger.*]

KEAN: Well—what are you standing there for? Go and tell them I am going on.

[*The* CARPENTER, *the* FIREMAN *and the* STAGE MAN
AGER *rush off to the stage, crying:* "He's going on—
he's going on—he's going on."

[*Going to the door and calling after them.*] Make an
announcement. Say I am ill—nervous—anything you
like . . .

S.M.: Yes, yes—Guv'nor—leave it to me. . . .

KEAN [*surveying himself in the mirror*]: Well—you
great cart horse—harnessed and ready—go and
plough through your Shakespeare!

[*The noise of the audience increases.* KEAN *goes to the
door and exits.* ANNA, *knowing she is going to play,
picks up the book and reads through her part. She
follows* KEAN *with great dignity. The noise from the
audience diminishes.*]

LIGHTS OUT

ACT IV

SCENE II

The curtain of the theater rises on the curtain of Drury Lane. The gas jets of the footlights appear, as well as the prompter's box in the center of the stage. The whole scene is lit entirely from below. In the stage theater the COUNT DE KOEFELD *is half asleep in the stage box on the dress circle level. The audience continues to show impatience. A theater* ATTENDANT *walks up and down, trying to quiet them down. A* DRESSER *runs across to the* ATTENDANT, *crying:* "He's going to appear." *The* ATTENDANT *shouts up at the gallery:* "Quiet—quiet! He's going to appear."

ATTENDANT [*catching up with the* DRESSER, *pointing to* LORD NEVILLE *who has come into the stage box left, followed by a* DANDY]: Keep your eye on that one! He's the man Kean insulted last night. . . .

DRESSER: He doesn't look as if he means to make trouble!

ATTENDANT: Keep your eye on him all the same. . . . The Prince of Wales will be here tonight. . . .
[*The* STAGE MANAGER *appears in front of the curtain and bows. The* ATTENDANT *and* DRESSER *say:* "Sh! Sh!"]

DRESSER: What's he going to say?

ATTENDANT: Maybe the Guv'nor won't play after all. . . . [*He taps his forehead significantly.*]

S.M.: Quiet . . . quiet, please . . . My lords, ladies and gentlemen . . . Mr. Kean is very tired and fearing not to be worthy of your kind attentions, asks me to request your indulgence.
[*Applause from the audience and cries of* "Bravo!"]

Mr. Kean will not be playing in his own scenery, since
that has been lent to Mr. Macready for a Provincial
tour.

[*"Oh!" of disappointment from the gallery.*]

But we have done our best . . . Lastly, the part of
Desdemona will be taken by a young lady making her
first appearance on any stage.

[*"Ah!" of satisfaction from the audience. The* STAGE
MANAGER *goes, as the* PRINCE *of* WALES *enters the box
with* ELENA *and* AMY. *He nods to* LORD NEVILLE, *who
bows. The orchestra plays the National Anthem.
LORD NEVILLE, *the* DANDY, ELENA, AMY, *and the* COUNT
rise. The house lights go down. SOLOMON *enters and
takes his place in the prompter's box.*]

PRINCE [*to* ELENA]: Who is playing Desdemona?

ELENA [*drily*]: I hope it is Miss MacLeish.

PRINCE: Why?

ELENA [*recovering herself*]: Because he is used to her.
With anyone else, he would be quite ridiculous.

AMY [*very excited*]: Did you see?

ELENA: Who?

AMY: Over there, in the box opposite. It's Lord Neville.
There's sure to be trouble. Kean struck him last night,
apparently because of some girl.

ELENA: That story must be greatly exaggerated.

[*The* COUNT *has gone to sleep.*]

PRINCE: Madam, I am full of admiration for your
husband. How can he sleep in this din?

ELENA [*furiously, shaking her husband*]: Sir!

COUNT [*waking with a start*]: Eh?

ELENA: Sir, we have his Royal Highness with us tonight, and you promised me not to go to sleep.

PRINCE [*amicably*]: Please, madam. The Count is not
asleep—he is practicing diplomatic impenetrability.

[*The* COUNT *smiles and drops off to sleep again.*]

[*The curtain of the inner stage rises.* ANNA, *as Desdemona, is asleep in bed.*]

ELENA [*between her teeth*]: He shall pay for this!

AMY: What was that, dear?

ELENA: Nothing.

[*Desdemona sleeps on. There is a torch burning on either side of the bed.* KEAN, *as Othello, enters.*]

KEAN: "It is the cause, it is the cause, my soul:
Let me not name it to you, you chaste stars!
It is the cause. Yet I'll not shed her blood,
Nor scar that whiter skin of hers than snow
And smooth as monumental alabaster.
Yet she must die, else she'll betray more men.
Put out the light, and then put out the light:
If I quench thee, thou flaming minister,
I can again thy former light restore,
Should I repent me: but once put out thy light,
Thou cunning'st pattern of excelling nature,
I know not where is that Promethean heat
That can thy light relume. When I have pluck'd the
    rose,
I cannot give it vital growth again,
It must needs wither: I'll smell it on the tree.
[*Kissing her.*]
Ah, balmy breath, that dost almost persuade
Justice to break her sword! One more, one more:
Be thus when thou art dead, and I will kill thee,
And love thee after: one more, and this the last:
So sweet was ne'er so fatal. I must weep,
But they are cruel tears: this sorrow's heavenly;
It strikes where it doth love. She wakes."
[*Applause.*]

PRINCE [*to* AMY]: Well, what do you think?

AMY: I prefer Kemble!

[*Applause continues.*]

ANNA [*as Desdemona*]: "Who's there?"

KEAN [*spoken*]: Be quiet—let them applaud till the end. [*He bows.*]

ANNA [*after a suitable pause*]: "Who's there, Othello?"

KEAN: "Ay, Desdemona."

ANNA: "Will you come to bed, my lord?"

KEAN: "Have you pray'd tonight, Desdemona?"

ANNA: "Ay, my lord."

KEAN: "If you bethink yourself of any crime
Unreconciled as yet to heaven and grace,
Solicit for it straight."

ANNA: "Alas, my lord, what may you mean by that?"

KEAN: "Well, do it and be brief: I will walk by."
[*She prays. He walks round the bed.*]

PRINCE: Who is the girl?

ELENA: How should I know?
[KEAN *stops and stares at them. They are quiet.*]

KEAN: "I would not kill thy unprepared spirit;
No, heaven forfend! I would not kill thy soul."

ANNA: "Talk you of killing?"

KEAN: "Ay, I do."

ANNA: "Then . . ." [*She hesitates.*] "Then . . ."

SOLOMON [*prompting*]: "Heaven have mercy on me."
[*She doesn't understand. He repeats*]
"Then heaven have mercy on me!"

ANNA [*desperately, as Desdemona*]: I love you.

SOLOMON [*prompting*]: "Then heaven have mercy on
me. . . ."

ANNA [*losing her head*]: I love you, I love you, I love
you.

KEAN [*improvising*]: You love me not, and the hour
is unfit for your lies. You should pray, at this fatal
moment, saying: "Then heaven have mercy on
me."

ANNA [*getting it*]: Oh, yes. Thank you. "Then heaven
have mercy on me."

KEAN: "Amen, with all my heart."

ELENA [*to the* PRINCE]: On top of everything, she
doesn't know her lines.

COUNT [*waking with a start*]: Who doesn't know her
lines?

ELENA: That girl.

COUNT: Which one? Ophelia?

ELENA: Yes, that's right. Go to sleep.

[*The* COUNT *goes to sleep.* KEAN *has deliberately turned toward the box.*]

ANNA: "If you say so, I hope you will not kill me."

KEAN [*absently*]: Yes, yes, in a minute.

NEVILLE: He's in trouble. [*He brings a whistle from his pocket and blows it.* KEAN *shivers, and turns back to* ANNA.]

KEAN: "Think on thy sins."

ANNA: "They are loves I bear to you."

KEAN: "Ay, and for that thou diest."

ANNA: "That death's unnatural that kills for loving.
Alas, why gnaw you so your nether lip? . . .
Why gnaw you so your nether lip?"

SOLOMON: "Some bloody passion . . ."

ANNA: "Some bloody passion frames your shake. . . ."
[*Murmur of surprise from the audience.*]

KEAN [*spoken*]: Idiot—get on with it.

ANNA [*spoken*]: I can't!

KEAN [*spoken*]: Very well. [*As Othello, superbly carry-it off.*] And why should I not shake, since thou hast shaken my soul? The courage that has never quailed, thou has blasted with inconstancy. Sorceress, 'tis thou who hast transformed Othello!
[*Applause,* KEAN *bows.*]

AMY [*to the* PRINCE]: Is that Shakespeare?

PRINCE [*indifferently*]: Probably.

KEAN [*to* ANNA]: Quickly—carry on.

ANNA: How can I, when you're making it up!

KEAN [*to* SOLOMON]: Give her the line!

SOLOMON: I can't find the place.

ANNA [*making up her mind suddenly, hurling herself half out of bed and clinging to* KEAN]: I love you! I love you!
[*He tries to free himself. They struggle, she crying: "I love you," until he finally manages to throw her back on the bed.*]

KEAN: "That handkerchief which I so loved and gave thee

Thou gavest to Cassio."

ANNA: "No, by my life and soul!
Send for the man and ask him."

KEAN: "Sweet soul, take heed,
Take heed of perjury, thou art on thy death-bed."

ANNA: "Ay, but not yet to die."

KEAN: "Yes, presently."

ANNA: "Then Lord have mercy on me!"

KEAN: "I say amen."

ANNA: "O, banish me, my lord, but kill me not!"

KEAN: "Down, strumpet!"

ANNA: "Kill me tomorrow; let me live tonight!"

KEAN: "Nay, if you strive . . ."

ANNA: "But half an hour!"

ELENA: Good heavens! Why on earth doesn't he kill her? Have you ever seen such a bad performance?

[*The* PRINCE *laughs.* AMY *and* ELENA *laugh with him.* KEAN *turns to the box and folds his arms.*]

PRINCE: Everything is possible, madam, except that anyone could be as beautiful as you.

KEAN [*in a voice of thunder*]: Silence!

[*The* PRINCE, *momentarily startled, recovers.*]

PRINCE [*to* ELENA]: Good heavens. I believe he's speaking to me.

ELENA: Sir, sir, I implore you—watch the stage and don't look at me again.

KEAN: May I ask Your Royal Highness to be quiet.

PRINCE [*slightly raising his voice*]: Madam . . .

ELENA [*speaking without looking at him*]: Not another word, if you love me. If there is a scandal, I shall be the first victim.

PRINCE [*scowling at* KEAN]: Very well, let us hear Mr. Kean. I am curious to know just how far he will go.

KEAN: Where do you think you are? At court? In a boudoir? Everywhere else you are a prince, but here I am king, and I ask you to be quiet, or we will stop the performance. We are working, sir, and if there is one thing the idle should respect, it is the labor of others.

PRINCE [*between his teeth*]: Mr. Kean! You are ruining yourself.

KEAN: And if I want to be ruined?

PRINCE [*shrugging his shoulders*]: Fool!

KEAN [*threateningly*]: What did you say?

[*The audience begins to murmur—he turns on them.*] Are you still there? I had forgotten you. You paid to see blood and now you demand blood. Isn't that so? But only stage blood, of course. [*Pause. The* PRINCE *laughs again.*] What would you say if I showed you real blood?

[*He comes down to the stage box and tries to draw his sword. The hilt comes away in his hand with a short piece of the broken blade. The* PRINCE *bursts out laughing. The audience laughs and jeers. We hear:* "Throw him in jail! Arrest him!" *etc.*

The CONSTABLE *appears and begins to make his way toward the stage. The* PRINCE *sees him.* KEAN *remains motionless, his head hanging, overcome.*]

PRINCE: Officer! [*The* CONSTABLE *looks up.*] Where are you going?

CONSTABLE: To arrest him, sir.

PRINCE: Go back to your place, and wait for your orders.

[*The* CONSTABLE *retires.* ANNA, *meanwhile, has picked up a cushion and tries to make* KEAN *go on with the scene.*]

ANNA: Othello . . .

[*He doesn't reply.*]

Othello!

KEAN [*shivering*]: Who calls me Othello? Who thinks I am Othello? [*Pointing to himself*] Is this Othello? He was a killer. . . . I—I am nothing but a fool. Ah, God, make me Othello—give me his strength and passion—for a moment—a single moment. I have played the part so often, it should be possible. Only for a moment—the time to pull down the pillars of the theater. [*He makes a violent effort, as if he were trying to transform himself into Othello.*] What do I lack? I wear the Moor's garments—I stand here in his shoes—I am a character who has found himself in the wrong part. Ah, Prince, Prince, you are in luck's way. If it were real, you would not escape me this time.

[*Cries and "oh's" of shocked surprise.*]

Ladies and gentlemen—there will be no execution tonight. We are pardoning all the guilty. [ANNA *comes to him, pillow in hand.*] Get out of here—you don't know your part. [*He takes the pillow.*] Give me that.

[SOLOMON *catches* ANNA *by the arm and drags her off stage.*]

KEAN [*turning to* ELENA]: You, madam—why not play Desdemona? I should stifle you with this very lovingly. [*He raises the pillow above his head.*] Ladies and gentlemen—the instrument of the crime. See how I treat it. [*He hurls the cushion into the box at* ELENA'S *feet.*] To the loveliest in the land. That cushion was my heart—my coward's heart—for her to rest her feet upon. [*Beating his breast*] This man isn't dangerous. You were wrong to take Othello for a tragic cuckold. He . . . I . . . am a co-co-comic cuckold.

[*Laughter, followed by cries of "Oh!"*]

[*To the* PRINCE OF WALES, *familiarly.*] You see, sir, I was right. Now I am in a real rage, I can only stammer.

[*The cat-calls redouble. "Down with Kean! Down with the actor Kean!" He takes a step toward the audience and stares at them. The whistles stop.*]

All against me? All? What an honor! But why! Ladies and gentlemen, will you allow me a question? What have I done to you? I know you all—but this is the first time I see you with murderous faces. Are these your real aspects? You come here each night and throw bouquets at my feet, crying bravo. I thought you really loved me. . . . But who were you applauding? Eh? Othello? Impossible—he was a sanguinary villain. It must have been Kean. "Our great Kean—our dear Kean—our national idol." "Well, here he is—your beloved Kean. [*He drags his hands over his face, smearing the make-up.*] Behold the man. Look at him. Why don't you applaud? Isn't it strange. You only care for illusion.

NEVILLE [*from his box*]: Mountebank!

KEAN: Who is that? Why, it's Lord Neville. [*He crosses to the other box.*] I hesitated a moment ago because I am afraid of princes, but I warn you that black beetles cannot frighten me. If you don't keep your mouth shut, I will take you between two fingers and crush you. Like that. [NEVILLE *is silent. The audience waits.*] Good night, ladies—good night, sweet ladies. Romeo, Lear, and Macbeth make you their adieus. I must rejoin them, and give them your regards. I return to the imaginary world where my real fury awaits me. Tonight, kind ladies, I shall be Othello, in my own home, sold out, house full, and commit my murders in my own fashion. Of course, if you had really loved me . . . But we must not ask too much, must we. By the way, I was wrong just now to mention Kean. Kean the actor, died very young. [*Laughter.*] Be quiet, murderers, it was you who killed him. It was you who took an infant and turned him into a monster. [*The audience is silent.*] That's right. Silence—a silence of death. Why were you booing just now? There was nobody on stage. No one. Or perhaps an actor playing the part of Kean playing the part of Othello. Listen—I am going to tell you something. I am not alive—I only pretend. Ladies and gentlemen—your humble servant. I . . . [*He hesitates, then shrugs.*] The rest is silence.

[*He turns, and marches upstage in silence, kicking over one of the canvas flats and disappearing into the back of the stage.*]

COUNT: It's over. Well, sir, what did you think of Kean?

PRINCE: He was magnificent.

[*The* PRINCE *rises, and the orchestra in the inner theater plays the National Anthem.*]

CURTAIN

ACT V

KEAN's *house. Ten o'clock next morning.* SOLOMON, *looking very glum, pours out and swallows two or three quick glasses of brandy. The* STAGE MANAGER *and* DARIUS *tiptoe in.*

SOLOMON: What do you want?

S.M.: To see him!

SOLOMON: He is in his room—with the doctor. Sign here . . . on this list.
[*He shows them a long list on the table. They both sign their names.*]

S.M.: How did he spend the night?

SOLOMON: On all fours—on top of the cupboard.

DARIUS: Is he really mad?

SOLOMON: Bedlam!

DARIUS: Is the doctor bleeding him?

SOLOMON: For the fourth time.

DARIUS: [*a little scream*]: Ah!

S.M.: What is his madness like?

SOLOMON: Very dangerous!

S.M.: What does he do?

SOLOMON: He strikes everyone.

S.M.: Everyone?

SOLOMON: Everyone, but preferably his friends.

DARIUS: He must have been bitten by a mad dog!

SOLOMON: I fear so. [*A pause. Pretending to listen*] Sh!

DARIUS [*frightened*]: Is it . . .

S.M.: Kean? [SOLOMON *nods.*]

BOTH [*hurrying for the door*]: Good-by. Good-by. Poor Solomon. [*They have gone.*]
[KEAN *enters, very preoccupied, without seeing* SOLOMON.]

SOLOMON: Guv'nor . . .

KEAN [*startled*]: What? [*He sees* SOLOMON.] I'm not the
Guv'nor any more. Call me Mr. Edmund. [*Pause.*]
Was someone here? I heard you talking.

SOLOMON: Actors, Guv'nor.

KEAN: Actors? Then there was no one. [*He laughs.*] No
one. What did you say to them?

SOLOMON: I tell everyone you are raving mad.

KEAN: That the great Kean is mad? Idiot, the opposite
has happened. Cry from the housetops that a shop-
keeper called Edmund has recovered his senses. [*He
takes him by the chin.*] Now I know: Shakespeare is
a cheese.

SOLOMON [*frightened*]: What . . . ?

KEAN: And I sell him by the pound. Why didn't you
tell me?

SOLOMON [*frightened*]: Why didn't I tell you what?

KEAN: That I was a cheesemonger. [*Calming down*] You
see I am in my right mind? Well—go and proclaim
it from the housetops.

SOLOMON: No.

KEAN [*springing at him*]: What's that?

SOLOMON: If I tell them you're in your right mind, they
will put you in prison.

KEAN: Prison? Because I'm in my right mind? What
a strange world! Very well—I shall go to prison.

SOLOMON: If you go to prison, you will never act again.

KEAN [*going to him*]: What a fate!

SOLOMON [*gently*]: Guv'nor, you mustn't let them.

KEAN: What do you want me to do?

SOLOMON: If you would only . . . just for a day or
two . . .

KEAN: What?

SOLOMON: Pretend . . .

KEAN [*tapping his forehead*]: To . . . ?

SOLOMON: Yes. [KEAN *starts to protest. Hurriedly*] You
were so magnificent in Lear.

KEAN [*slowly*]: Lear? [*To* SOLOMON, *affectionately*] My

dear fellow, even if I wanted to, it would be impossible. I can never act again.

SOLOMON [*startled*]: You can never . . . Since when?

KEAN: Since last night. I've been thinking. To act you must take yourself for someone else. I thought I was Kean, who thought he was Hamlet, who thought he was Fortinbras . . .

SOLOMON: But Hamlet . . .

KEAN: Yes. Hamlet does think he is Fortinbras. Sh! It's a secret. What a series of misunderstandings! [*Pause.*] Fortinbras doesn't think he is anyone. Fortinbras and Mr. Edmund are alike. They know who they are and they say only what is. You can ask them about the weather, the time of day, and the price of bread. But never try to make them act on a stage. You're an old fool—you understand nothing. What's the weather like?

SOLOMON: Can't you see? The sun is shining.

KEAN [*going to the window*]: Is that your sun? I shall have to grow accustomed to it. Kean's sun was painted on a stage canvas. Solomon, the London sky is a painted cloth; every morning, you drew the curtains, I opened my eyes, and I saw . . . Ah, I don't know what I saw. When the man himself is a sham, everything is a sham around him. Under a sham sun, the sham Kean cried the tale of his sham sufferings to his sham heart. Today, the star is real. How flat real light is. Truth should be blinding, dazzling. It's true —it's true I am a ruined man. I tell you, I can't believe it. There are moments when I believe I am going to understand, and then it eludes me. [*Pause. He brings a purse from his pocket.*] There are a hundred florins in this purse. Divide the rest between the servants and dismiss them all. I shall wait for the police here. [*He installs himself in a regal attitude.*]

SOLOMON: That is Richard III's chair.

KEAN [*sharply*]: In this very chair. When you go, leave the main door wide open. I want the police to have free access.

SOLOMON: Like the Gauls invading the Roman Senate?

KEAN: Who told you I was thinking of that?

SOLOMON: It was in Brenius—the new play you gave me to read.

KEAN: My God, you are right. I am making a gesture. D'you know, my whole life is made up of gestures: there is one for every hour, every season, every period of my entire life. I learned to walk, to breathe, to die. Now at last those gestures are dead. Like so many dead branches. I killed them all last night, at one blow. If I try and repeat one, it breaks in my hand. You never make gestures, do you? No, of course not. I will root them out, and if I cannot, I will cut off my arms. [*He laughs.*] D'you hear? D'you hear? Ah, mountebank—you're going to have a hard life. You must learn to be simple—perfectly simple. [*With sudden violence, addressing the chair*] Out of my sight! Out of my sight, or I will kill you. [*Calming*] No, stay. You do not incommode me. [*He sits down.*] No. [*He rises.*] You see: the man in the armchair wasn't me, it was Richard III. And that one is Shylock, the Jew of Venice. Oh well—it will have to happen by degrees. I will imitate the natural until it becomes second nature. [*Pause.*] Tell me—you saw me last night?

SOLOMON: Alas!

KEAN: Well—what did I do?

SOLOMON: You insulted the Prince of Wales, a peer of the realm, and seven hundred and eighty-two people.

KEAN: Yes, yes, I know. But what was it?

SOLOMON: They say it was a crime. Lese majesty.

KEAN: That's not what I asked you, fool. Was it a gesture or an act?

SOLOMON: I couldn't say.

KEAN: It was a gesture, d'you hear? The last. I took

myself for Othello, and that woman, laughing in her box—I took her for Desdemona. A meaningless gesture, for which I need account to no one. Sleepwalkers are innocent of their crimes.

SOLOMON: That's exactly what I said; you can't be guilty and that's why you must defend yourself.

KEAN [*loudly*]: You lie! It was an act. It was an act since it has ruined my life. Seven hundred and eighty-two people saw me commit a crime. A deliberate act. But I? Did I intend to commit that crime? Or did I dream it? It was only an imaginary suicide. But the pistol was loaded and the great Kean killed himself in earnest. [*He takes his head in his hands.*] If only I could put back the clock! Fool! If I could live my life again, it would be to do deliberately what I have done in spite of myself. If you must ruin your life, let it be in the sight of the world. Ah, Solomon—prison frightens me. [*Pause.*] You know the story of the frog who wished to be as big as the ox. The ox was the Prince of Wales. An ox? Say rather a bull. I was sick with pride. Pride is the opposite of shame. A bubble—it fills and fills, and then it bursts. Last night, I pricked the bubble myself. [*Pause.*] When I come out of jail, I shall sell cheese. How fortunate I am— the end of pride, the end of shame. At last I can become a nobody. [SOLOMON *has picked up the list and holds it carelessly.*] What's that?

SOLOMON: Nothing interesting. The list of fools who have called on the nobody this morning.

KEAN: Let me see. [*He reads.*] All the names—except the one I want. If she didn't come—it may be because she couldn't. Solomon, let no one enter, except . . .

SOLOMON: Except her. [*He laughs.*]

KEAN: Why do you laugh?

SOLOMON: Because you have come to yourself. Mr. Edmund isn't capable of passion.

KEAN: No, he is not. [*Pause.*] That is all that remains

of Kean, a mad and hopeless passion. If this fire dies
out in my heart, there will be nothing left but cinders.
It must burn. It must. Go, go . . . and if she comes,
bring her in immediately.

SOLOMON: Yes, Guv'nor. [*He goes.*]

KEAN [*alone*]: Ten o'clock and not a word from her.
Ah, you were more concerned for your fan than for
my safety, madam. [*Pause.*] Supposing it were the
Count who found the fan? But . . . but it's obvious!
Of course he did. He found it when he came to my
room. And when I think that at this moment she is
suspected, accused, humiliated, perhaps, and calling
to me for help . . . Solomon! Solomon!

SOLOMON [*appearing*]: Sir . . .

KEAN: Order the horses!

SOLOMON: Horses?

KEAN: Unless you want to pull my carriage yourself?

SOLOMON: Your carriage!

KEAN: Yes—I'm going out.

SOLOMON: Out?

KEAN: Can't you see I have a fever? That my head is
burning? Besides, I can lower the blinds—I will only
drive beneath her windows.

[*Knock at the door.*]

SOLOMON: Someone knocked. . . . Do you still want
the carriage?

KEAN: Go and see.

SOLOMON: At once . . .

[ANNA *enters timidly.*]

KEAN: Oh, good heavens! [*Aloud*] Solomon! I told you
not to admit anyone.

SOLOMON [*smiling*]: Do you call Miss Anna someone?
She will only stay for a moment . . . she wants to say
good-by.

KEAN [*going to* ANNA]: Good-by? You are going away?

ANNA: Yes.

[SOLOMON *smiles as he looks at them and goes out
discreetly.*]

KEAN: You are leaving London?

ANNA: And England.

KEAN: Oh . . . Oh, well, that's good. You're quite right, child. The rats must leave the sinking ship. Well, what are you waiting for? Can't you see my ship has struck?

ANNA: If you really had been mad, I would have stayed to nurse you.

KEAN: I wasn't lucky enough; I am merely a man dishonored, ruined—whose career is finished, and on top of everything, threatened with prison. There's nothing here to attract a woman.

ANNA: Oh, Kean—why did you do it?

KEAN: Do what?

ANNA: Last night.

KEAN: The improvisation at the end? Oh well, to amuse myself. Don't you ever want to break things?

ANNA: No. Why?

KEAN: I don't know why. To see what will happen. Supposing your life were only a dream—you pinch yourself, and you wake up. Last night, I pinched myself. A pretty suicide, wasn't it? Fame and fortune, that was all a game, but prison, you see, will be very real. Brr . . . how real it must be—particularly in winter. Where are you going?

ANNA: To America.

KEAN: America? What will you do there?

ANNA: A manager from a New York theater saw me last night. He thought I was very good.

KEAN: He had the effrontery to think you good while I was dying on the stage! The man has no heart.

ANNA: All the same, he has given me a contract.

KEAN: He's mad—completely mad. And you—you're a fool. You aren't ready yet! I would have made you work.

ANNA: You wouldn't have been able to—you would have been in prison.

KEAN: Good heavens, you're right. And your guardian —is he allowing you to go? He lacks authority.

ANNA: After last night, he only has one thought—to send me to the antipodes.

KEAN: In a sense, I understand. Oh, well, it's all over.

ANNA: All over.

KEAN: But why are you going?

ANNA [*surprised*]: Why? Because you don't love me.

KEAN: Oh, yes . . . I see.

ANNA: Have you forgotten?

KEAN: Today my head is hardly my own. In fact, your plan didn't succeed?

ANNA: No.

KEAN: I thought you always got what you wanted.

ANNA: I thought so, too.

KEAN: You see, it was only a bluff. I said to myself: "That child always gets what she wants: one of these days, I shall find myself madly in love with her." It promised to be very amusing. And then, no; it was only more theater. I'm afraid I'm disappointed in you. But you need have no regrets. I should have been a very bad husband.

ANNA: That was what I hoped.

KEAN: If I do marry, you can be sure it will be to have someone I can talk to about myself.

ANNA: I'm a very good listener.

KEAN: So much the better for you. You can listen to one of those Puritans in New Scotland. I think you would make a very good minister's wife. When do you go?

ANNA: In two hours' time.

KEAN [*startled*]: What?

ANNA: A cabin has been booked for me on the *Washington*.

KEAN [*furiously*]: I see. Good luck and good-by.

ANNA: Good luck.

KEAN: Will you write to me while I'm in prison?

ANNA: I'll send you some food parcels.

KEAN [*sarcastic*]: They'll be rotten before they arrive.
[*Pause.*] I could order you to stay. . . .

ANNA: Order me?

KEAN: Exactly. Don't be afraid; I shall do no such thing.
But it would be my right. [*He begins to be angry.*]
After all, it's your fault that all this happened. If you
hadn't appeared on the stage, Elena would never
have defied me, and I shouldn't have caused the
scandal. Yes, yes, all things considered you are the
only one responsible. And I know what a great many
men would say in my place. They would say that it is
too easy to enter a man's life, to ruin it, and fly
away with a flick of your wings. Yes, viewing events
clearly, that is exactly what they'd say. Without men-
tioning your scandalous devotion, you provoke a
scandal, break my heart and my career, get yourself
a contract in New York, and I have to be thrown
into prison. In brief, the good are punished and the
wicked get their reward. I don't mean I want to
keep you. You can imagine there is no room for you
in my life. But it is certain that if you had had a little
feeling—that is perhaps too much to ask—let us say
a little tact, or merely a touch of politeness, the idea
of deserting me would never have entered your head.
You really are deserting me. Abandoning me—betraying me . . .

ANNA: But since you don't love me . . .

KEAN: Fortunately! It would be charming if I were to
fall in love with an irresponsible child who destroys
a man's life as an evening's entertainment!

ANNA: You're talking nonsense: if you loved me, of
course I would stay.

KEAN: That's right—for you to deign to stay, I must fall
on my knees, put on a pair of white gloves, and ask
your guardian for your hand in marriage. Have you
ever seen a man of forty on his knees before a child?
Do you know what I should do if I weren't an
honorable man? [*He rises and marches on her.*] I

should give you a sound thrashing! Yes—a thrashing.
None of this would have happened if you had been
thrashed every time you deserved it.

SOLOMON [*running in*]: Sir—sir—she's here!

KEAN [*off balance—without thinking*]: Send her to the
devil! Eh? What? D'you mean . . .

ANNA [*moving to go*]: Is it Elena?

KEAN: Yes, but you needn't imagine I've finished with
you. Go in there—little fool—and to pass the time
think of the good hiding you are going to get from
me in a moment. [*He pushes her into his room. To*
SOLOMON] Ask her to come in.

[SOLOMON *goes.* ELENA *enters.*]

Ah, Elena! Is it you? You have come, in spite of the
risks. . . . If you knew how I have wanted you! Will
you forgive me?

ELENA: A woman must always pardon the follies committed for her sake.

KEAN: Let me look at you! How pale you are, and how
lovely. How happy I am! I cannot regret my madness,
even if it has ruined me, if I owe it the honor of
your visit.

ELENA [*sitting down*]: I hesitated for a long time. But
our common danger . . .

KEAN: Danger?

ELENA: A letter could be intercepted. . . . I feared that
you were already arrested.

KEAN: Ah! has it come to that?

ELENA: Alas! Kean, you must fly!

KEAN: Fly? I—leave England like a coward. You know
me very ill.

ELENA: If not for your sake, then for mine . . .

KEAN: On one condition, one only . . . Do you love
me, Elena?

ELENA [*lowering her eyes*]: Can you ask?

KEAN: Yes. The fan you left behind on my table . . .

ELENA: Well?

KEAN: Has been found?

ELENA: By whom?

KEAN: I fear it was your husband.

ELENA: Great heavens! [*Pause.*]

KEAN [*softly*]: Elena—must I fly alone?

ELENA: Kean—you are mad . . . no, no, it's impossible.

KEAN: My carriage is ready.

ELENA: Cruel! And my honor?

KEAN: What could be more honorable than to leave England with the king of London? Here you are only a countess—in exile you would be a queen.

ELENA [*a pause*]: And my husband?

KEAN: I bow before his future grief.

ELENA: It will kill him.

KEAN: It is he or I. We must save the younger man.

ELENA: Later, when we have recovered our senses, how shall we endure the guilt of his death?

KEAN: Very easily.

ELENA: And if he kills you first?

KEAN: Highly improbable.

ELENA: Ah! How do you know?

KEAN: Too short-sighted.

ELENA: Kean! And my children?

KEAN [*very surprised*]: Children? Surely, madam, you have none?

ELENA: I have sworn to have children.

KEAN: Sworn? To whom?

ELENA: To my husband—before God.

KEAN: Is that all? Before God, you shall have them— I'll see to that.

ELENA: You don't understand. I promised my husband to give him a son and heir.

KEAN: God has not taken note of your vows. He is only concerned with the preservation of the race, not of a particular family.

ELENA: But I adore him already—my unborn son! If

I go with you, I must strangle him in my bosom. Ah, Kean, I have loved you as far as adultery, do not drive me as far as infanticide!

KEAN: In a word, you refuse?

ELENA: Did I say that? Accept, refuse—whichever way, I choose despair. Ah, my friend, I can see it too clearly. If you want to ruin my life, you must make me mad.

KEAN [*tenderly*]: Elena, my love! [*He takes her in his arms.*]

ELENA [*freeing herself*]: Not like that! Talk to me— intoxicate me with your words: you must use your whole genius. I can feel that the fight will be terrible. I shall resist with my whole strength, and only give way on the edge of the precipice. Show me that I am the world to you, and that you will be the world to me. . . . [KEAN *does not reply. She repeats, astonished*] . . . and that you will be the world to me.

KEAN [*annoyed*]: Don't prompt me.

ELENA [*astounded*]: What?

KEAN [*startled*]: Don't . . . [*He stops.*]

ELENA: What did you say?

KEAN: You were standing there, repeating the last words of your speech. It reminded me . . . [*He begins to laugh.*] Madam, you were giving me my cue.

ELENA: How dare you . . . ? [*She rises.*]

KEAN: Oh, I dare nothing. I will never act again. Curtain!

ELENA: Look at me. I see.

KEAN: What?

ELENA: You are suffering the tortures of the damned.

KEAN: Not as much as that, I assure you.

ELENA: You are tortured by your love, and you are trying to debase it out of revenge. It's horrible, Kean, and very wonderful. Here, my dear, take my hand, press it to your lips. Well? How long must I wait? Kiss my hand.

KEAN [*without taking it*]: Elena—I told you it was

over. You aren't going to try and act the comedy
alone?

ELENA [*suddenly*]: Take me away!

KEAN: What?

ELENA: You told me your carriage was ready? Very
well, take me with you. You think I'm acting. You
can spend the rest of your life repaying me for that
word. I am full of passion, jealous, real, terrible—I
can be angel or tiger. For the man I loved, I should
lay modesty and reputation at his feet—I should go
with him everywhere, to the galleys, to the very
scaffold. [*She looks at him with sparkling eyes.*] Ha!

KEAN [*without moving*]: And it is I you love?

ELENA: You? I hate you. Well, what are you waiting
for? Abduct me! Carry me off. [*He does not move.
Long silence.*] So, I see. You were speaking the truth.
Your love was only another act. I confess; when you
made that . . . confession . . . just now, I gazed at
you with all my strength, but I couldn't believe you.
Now I have driven you into the open. I said: Take me
away, and you stand there like a fool, ashamed of your
lack of feeling, and too cowardly to have even a surge
of pride. A woman ready to ruin herself for you?
Good heavens, what have you to do with her? The
ones whose happiness you deign to make, others must
clothe, feed, and protect. You play the lover every
evening at Drury Lane, and sometimes in the afternoon in a lady's boudoir. Don't be afraid, sir, I give
you back your liberty. You will fly alone. But don't
believe I bear you any ill will; it is I who should ask
your forgiveness. I was fool enough to take you for
a man. It isn't your fault you are only an actor.

KEAN: Is an actor not a man?

ELENA: No, my friend. The Prince of Wales was quite
right. He is only a reflection.

KEAN: Oh, he said I was a reflection! [*He catches her up
in his arms.*] Very well, let us go!

ELENA [*frightened*]: What are you doing?

KEAN: Abducting you. [*He starts for the door, still carrying her in his arms.*]

ELENA: Wait! Wait!

KEAN: What for?

ELENA: I . . . I want to get my breath. Put me down. Please—just for a moment, and I will come with you gladly. [*He puts her down.*] So, we go together?

KEAN: Yes, together.

ELENA: Will you regret nothing?

KEAN: Nothing. And you?

ELENA: Nothing. Where are we going? Madrid? Rome? Paris?

KEAN: Amsterdam.

ELENA: Oh. [*Pause.*] I don't like Amsterdam.

KEAN: Neither do I. It can't be helped. [*He starts to pick her up again.*]

ELENA: One more word. [*He stops.*] How long will you give me to learn my parts?

KEAN: Which parts?

ELENA: All of them. Desdemona—Juliet—Ophelia . . .

KEAN: Oh! You expect to act?

ELENA: What else am I to do all day? Wait for you?

KEAN: You won't go on the stage, Elena. Neither will I. That's over. You are eloping with Mr. Edmund, the jeweler. I have some very fine jewels—the gifts of admirers. I am planning to start a business. Don't be afraid. You will have everything. Except perhaps friends. But we will be enough for each other. On working days, I will go to the shop, and you will lie on the sofa and read novels. Three times a week we will go to the theater to replenish our provision of love words. Come! [*He moves toward her, but she runs round the other side of the table.*]

ELENA: Let me go! Let me go! Help!

[KEAN *begins to laugh.*]

KEAN [*imitating her*]: To the galleys! To the scaffold! To the ends of the earth! [*He laughs.*] You see, you were only acting.

ELENA [*looks at him, disconcerted, then begins to laugh*]: That sounds a little severe: say rather, coquetting.

KEAN: Be frank. You came to ask me for your letters.

ELENA [*indignant*]: No!

KEAN: No? Very well, I will keep them.

ELENA [*weakly*]: I didn't want to ask for them . . . immediately.

KEAN: Not immediately, of course, you would have observed the conventions. Only time is short; they are coming to arrest me. [*He fetches the letters.*] Here they are. Count them.

ELENA: I trust you.

KEAN: No, you don't trust me at all. [*He counts.*] One, two, three, four, five, six, seven.

ELENA [*carelessly*]: There were eight.

KEAN: Don't you remember—I tore up the eighth in front of you. Here, take them. [*She doesn't move.*] What? Not yet? [*He lays them on the table.*] I leave them within reach; you can take them when you judge the time has come.

ELENA: Kean!

KEAN: What is it? Am I going too fast? I confess that in a modern play I should have refused to give them to you at first. But I have cut a few lines. Do you know where we went wrong; we started two or three tones too high. [*Smiling*] Why on earth did we both decide to be noble?

ELENA: Oh, Kean, it's so amusing to live above the level of your strength. [*Dreaming*] A real passion must be very wonderful.

KEAN [*doubtfully*]: Do you think so?

ELENA: With your genius, you could do anything. I haven't your powers, so I should rely on love. Love is the genius of the poor. [*She laughs. Without malice*] If I had gone away with you, you would have been finely caught.

KEAN: Not in the least. All I risked was that you would

have come as far as Dover.

ELENA: In other words, you were only attacking the ambassadress?

KEAN: Say rather the ambassador. I am a bastard. For a bastard, it's flattering to supplant an Excellency. And you? Was it the king of London you wanted to attract?

ELENA: I want to attract all men. Because I am ugly.

KEAN: You? Ugly?

ELENA: My poor friend, all women are ugly. Beauty is very hard work; if you knew how tiring it is to have to paint and perfume a long white animal every day!

KEAN [smiling]: So it has to be made worth while?

ELENA: Of course. [They both laugh.] Enough! Enough! Let us keep to the sentimental comedy; we women very rarely adventure on the terrain of farce. Come—talk to me—say anything. I dislike being left unprotected.

KEAN: Good luck, Elena.

ELENA [surprised]: Good luck?

KEAN: Yes. I'm not in the last act, and I won't stay for the calls. But you still have your best scenes to play.

ELENA: My best scenes?

KEAN: With the Prince of Wales.

ELENA: Ah, yes. Perhaps.

KEAN: So I wish you luck. That's all.

ELENA: Aren't you jealous any more? [KEAN shakes his head.] How strange.

KEAN: No. Not in the least. Do you know why? The Prince of Wales, was I. Listen—we are three victims. You, because you were born a woman—he, because he was too highly born, and I, because I was a bastard. The result is you enjoy your beauty through the eyes of others, and I discover my genius through their applause. As for him, he is a flower. For him to feel he is a prince, he has to be admired. Beauty, royalty, genius; a single and same mirage. We live all three on the love of others, and we are all three incapable of loving ourselves. You wanted my love—I yours, he, ours. What a mix-up. You were right. Three reflections, each of the three believing in the existence of the other two; that was the comedy. Jealous? Oh, no, it is you who will be jealous. The Prince only cares for me, my women, and my dressing gowns. Why do you laugh?

ELENA: Because I was thinking of Shakespeare.

KEAN: Is that amusing?

ELENA: Yes. Because if this were Shakespeare, we should all have been dead by now. You would have killed the prince in a duel.

KEAN: Your husband would have had me murdered.

ELENA: The king would have had his head cut off.

KEAN: And you would have stabbed yourself on our triple tomb.

ELENA [laughing]: What a massacre!

KEAN: Regret nothing. You managed brilliantly, and God knows the scene wasn't easy to play. Spite, passion, anger—you did them all, even sincerity. You are the one with genius. Good-by, Juliet—farewell, Desdemona—au revoir, Beatrice.

ELENA: Au revoir, Falstaff!

KEAN: That was unkind. Are you angry with me?

ELENA: No one can be angry with Mr. Edmund. As for the great Kean . . .

KEAN: Well?

ELENA: I shall never forget he killed himself for me.

KEAN: For you? Hm!

ELENA: Sh! Sh! Of course he killed himself for my sake. Besides, jeweler, how do you know? What do you know about love?

KEAN: He breathed his last in my arms.

ELENA: And what did he say before he died?

KEAN [softly]: That he was dying for your sake.

ELENA: You see!

KEAN: He also asked me to return your letters. [*He holds them out.*] Will you take them?

ELENA: Yes. To gratify the last wish of a dying man. Thank you. [*She slips them into her dress.*] What should I wish Mr. Edmund? A passionate love?

KEAN: A jeweler is incapable of inspiring passion. Wish rather that I may fall in love—it will be a change. [*He kisses her hand.*]

COUNT [*off*]: I tell you I shall go in.

SOLOMON [*off*]: And I say that you shan't.
　　[ELENA *and* KEAN *look at each other and begin to laugh.*]

ELENA [*laughing*]: Heavens—my husband! I am lost!

KEAN: Can you hear that? He isn't playing in the same production as we are. Listen to those intonations! Pure tragedy!

ELENA: He thinks he is still in Shakespeare.

KEAN: Nobody told him. [*Laughing*] He has come to kill me.

ELENA [*laughing*]: How horrible—I couldn't bear it. [*Going toward the room where* ANNA *is hiding.*] I shall wait in here until you have finished.

KEAN: No, not in there. [*He points to the other room.*] In here.

ELENA: Naturally, I forbid you to fight: the Count isn't a young man, and accidents happen so easily.

KEAN: Poor man! Don't be afraid. Yesterday I should have provoked him in a dream, killed him in a dream, and he would have been dead in good earnest. Good-by, Elena.

ELENA [*closing the door*]: Good-by.

COUNT [*off*]: I tell you I must see him.

KEAN [*opening the door*]: What's the matter, Solomon? Why didn't you show the Count in?

SOLOMON: But you told me . . .
　　[*The* COUNT *enters, followed by* SOLOMON.]

KEAN: That I could see no one? It's true—but I couldn't expect the honor of receiving the Danish Ambassador.

COUNT: Sir—you remember what I told you yesterday?

KEAN: Yes, indeed. What was it?

[SOLOMON *goes.*]

COUNT: I told you that if we Danes are insulted, we fight the whole world.

KEAN: Ah, yes, I remember. What a fine saying, and what pleasure it gave me.

COUNT: Thank you. I . . .

KEAN: What breadth of vision, especially. Ah, we English, we're unaccustomed to such language.

COUNT: Well—I have been insulted and I intend to fight.

KEAN: Insulted? You amaze me. A soul like yours cannot be offended. It must understand everything. Whoever the wretch may be who has had the temerity to displease you—I am sure at this moment he is more wretched than you.

COUNT: I tell you I want to fight.

KEAN: Very well. If nothing can make you change your mind—I should be delighted to be your second.

COUNT: My second! Sir—I came here to challenge you.

KEAN: Me? Oh, no, sir.

COUNT: What?

KEAN: I regret. It's impossible.

COUNT: Why not?

KEAN: Because I never fight. To begin with, I haven't insulted you.

COUNT: Yes. Mortally.

KEAN [*gentle reproach*]: Sir—surely I should know.

COUNT: I understand your delicacy, but it is only a further insult.

KEAN: I have offended you? After all—because you say so . . . Very well, I apologize.

COUNT: Apologize?

KEAN: Most abjectly.

COUNT: I won't accept.

KEAN: Allow me to insist. I swear to you it is offered
with all my heart. No? Well, you cannot leave here
without some gift—a snuffbox, some flowers. Since
I cannot make you amends by force of arms, I must
at least offer you some compensation.

COUNT: That's where you are mistaken, sir. You will
make me amends.

KEAN: Alas, no. No question. Since you have been insulted, I find it natural that you wish to fight. But for
the same reason, I hope you will find it just that I do
not wish to fight, since you have not insulted me.

COUNT: What's that got to do with it?

KEAN: What will you wager that it won't happen? I am
very good-natured, and I don't lose my temper easily.

COUNT: You are a liar, sir.

KEAN [beaming]: How true—of course, a professional
liar.

COUNT: A coward!

KEAN: Sincerely—I don't think so. I will search my
conscience.

COUNT: A dog!

KEAN: No, no, a dog is a quadruped. [Amicably] Come,
you don't believe a word you're saying.

COUNT: Sir, I have insulted you irreparably. My intention was to sting you to the quick.

KEAN: But sir, since you say so, how could I be angry
with you?

COUNT [raising his hand]: Coward!

KEAN [catching his hand]: Fear nothing, sir—I have
already forgotten this moment of madness. [He
bows.] No, definitely, sir, it's no good, I cannot fight
you. It is only children who fight. Children and lords.
You see—last night I realized I wasn't the one any
longer and I could never be the other. Yes, I have
given a few sword-thrusts in my time—but I was still
living in my comedy. I risked death because of my
lack of breeding. Besides, I hated all lords. Because

their blood didn't flow in my veins, I wanted to let it out of their own. That is all over—Mr. Edmund never fights. Sir, isn't it enough to have had the misfortune to wound you—must I go so far as to kill you?

COUNT: Very well—I cannot force your hand. But I must spend my rage.

KEAN: Spend it—spend it—my carpets are thick. They will soak up your fury.

COUNT: Remember, if not on you, it will fall on your accomplice.

KEAN [*interested*]: Have I an accomplice?

COUNT: You know quite well. You are afraid of my vengeance, and you have taken refuge behind a woman.

KEAN: Is there a woman in this affair? Do I know her? Let me guess. Is she young or old?

COUNT: I will show you. Do you know this fan?

KEAN: A fan?

COUNT: It belongs to the Countess.

KEAN: Indeed!

COUNT [*losing his temper again*]: Well, sir—I found that fan last night. . . .

[SOLOMON *enters precipitately.*]

SOLOMON: An urgent note from the Prince of Wales.

KEAN: Later.

SOLOMON: No, at once.

KEAN [*to the* COUNT]: Will you excuse me?

COUNT [*sneering*]: Read it—but I shall not move a step.

KEAN [*he reads the note rapidly*]: Count—do you know the Prince of Wales's handwriting?

COUNT: I don't see what . . .

COUNT [*reading*]: "Er . . . er . . . er . . . Will you please search your room. I believe I left the Countess's fan there last night. I had borrowed it in order to have it copied for a friend. . . . I shall come and ask you this afternoon for an explanation of the stupid quarrel you tried to fasten on me at the theater last night because of the little ballet dancer. I should never have believed a friendship of such long standing . . . er . . . er Your affectionate George." Perfect. Well—this is a very convenient letter, Mr. Kean.

KEAN: Can you deny it is the Prince's writing?

COUNT: I deny nothing. That is why I only half believe you.

KEAN: What must I do to reassure you?

COUNT: Only one thing—allow me to see the veiled lady who came in here a little while ago.

KEAN: No lady has been here this morning.

COUNT [*furiously*]: You are lying. [*Calming down*] Come, Mr. Kean—don't spoil the effect of this letter. I am half convinced—persuade me altogether.

KEAN: There is no lady here.

COUNT: I tell you I saw her come in with my own eyes.

KEAN: I . . .

[ANNA *enters.*]

ANNA: Well, Kean—what about my thrashing? Oh, forgive me, I didn't know you had a guest.

COUNT: Well, sir, you see?

KEAN: You said: "A lady." How could I think you meant this child?

COUNT: To me she is a lady—and a very lovely one. I am grateful. [*He bows, takes a step, then turns.*] Do not forget that consulates are inviolable, and that the Danish Embassy is a consular palace.

KEAN: Thank you, sir.

COUNT: Good-by. [*He bows.*] Madam.

ANNA: Oh, not yet, sir.

COUNT: You will be soon, young lady; I am quite sure. [*He goes.*]

KEAN: Thank you.

ANNA: Why didn't you fetch me in yourself?

KEAN: You were listening? Oh, well, I did think of it—but I didn't want to compromise you.

ANNA: Bah! I am already—a little more or less . . .

KEAN: In other words, you have made me a present of your reputation.

ANNA: It would seem so.

KEAN: Without even knowing if I would marry you? Do you know that yesterday that would have made me wild with joy?

ANNA: Why not today?

KEAN: Yesterday I wanted a woman—any woman—to ruin herself for my sake. . . .

ANNA: And today?

KEAN [*looking at her*]: I am conscious of more concrete advantages. [*Pause.*] Now we must deal with the other. [*He takes a step toward the other door.*] Go back to your room. No—stay. What does it matter now? Elena? [*He opens the door.*] Eh?

ANNA: What? [*He goes into the room and returns at once.*]

KEAN: Gone—flown away—disappeared. And the window's open. It's miraculous. [*He laughs.*]

ANNA: How can you laugh? That window overlooks the river. She may perhaps . . .

KEAN: Have killed herself? Don't worry. Women like Elena never kill themselves. But I should very much like to know . . .

SOLOMON [*entering*]: Two visitors are waiting downstairs. Which one shall I bring up first?

KEAN: Who are they?

SOLOMON: One is the constable—the other is the Prince of Wales.

KEAN: What does the constable want?

SOLOMON: To arrest you. He is in tears—he admires you so much.

ANNA: Oh!

KEAN: And the Prince? What does he want?

PRINCE [*entering*]: To stop you being arrested.

KEAN: Thank you, sir. And thank you for your letter. Unhappily, Elena . . . [*He waves toward the window.*]

PRINCE: Don't worry. She is safe.

KEAN: How?

PRINCE: A friend watches over you. Foreseeing your danger, he had a boat under your window, and carriage at your door.

KEAN: Where is she now?

PRINCE: At home, where I had her taken.

KEAN: Sir, you have saved me twice over. How can expiate my sins toward you?

PRINCE: By forgiving me those I committed against you. I have obtained from the King that your six months in prison shall be changed to a year of exile.

KEAN: Where is Your Royal Highness sending me?

PRINCE: Where you please. Provided you leave England Paris—Berlin—New York . . .

KEAN [*looking at* ANNA]: I choose New York.

ANNA [*going to him*]: What did you say?

KEAN: We leave in an hour. Have you chosen a boat?

PRINCE: Choose yourself.

KEAN: Then I settle for the *Washington*. [*He calls* Solomon, send someone to book me a berth.

ANNA: We shall need two.

KEAN: Why two?

ANNA: Because I need one as well!

KEAN: But I thought . . . So you lied?

ANNA: Yes.

KEAN: What for?

ANNA: To make you marry me.

PRINCE [*who has not been listening*]: I hope America suits you.

KEAN: I expect to marry there, sir. Miss Anna Danby looks unimportant, but she always gets what she wants.

ANNA: Your Royal Highness. [*Curtsy.*]

PRINCE [*surprised*]: What's this, Mr. Kean? Taking a lady with you?

KEAN: Unless His Majesty objects?

PRINCE [*serious*]: No, of course not; if your intentions are honorable . . .

KEAN: Your Royal Higness seems disappointed.

PRINCE: I? Not at all. At your age, it's high time to settle down. Only, you—you surprise me. I thought you had fire in your veins, passion in your soul—I attributed your taste for exaggeration to the profundity of your feelings. . . . And I'm afraid I may have been wrong. Tell me frankly: isn't your heart broken?

KEAN: Not at all.

PRINCE [*persisting*]: Just a little? Merely cracked?

KEAN: Not even cracked.

PRINCE: How strange. In your place I . . . and I who was feeling guilty; good heavens, what a fool I was. You don't love her any more?

KEAN: Who?

PRINCE: Elena, of course!

KEAN: Did I ever love her?

PRINCE [*furiously*]: Then allow me to tell you that I find you unpardonable. You rushed into the affair with your eyes closed, and naturally, I followed you. Now you tell me . . . [*He turns to* ANNA.] Particularly as she wasn't at all my type. And without my blind confidence in your fiancé's taste . . . I sometimes wondered what he saw in her? I believed she must have hidden charms. [*Turning to* KEAN, *furiously*] But if you don't love her, what am I to do with her? [*He looks at* ANNA.] You, at least, madam— one need only look at you to see that our great Kean has remained the most subtle of connoisseurs. [*To* KEAN] Fascinating, dear fellow. Fascinating!

KEAN: Sir, you say that of every woman I have the honor to present to you.

PRINCE: This time it's different. Your fiancée would have been fascinating even if I had met her alone. [*He crosses to* ANNA.]

KEAN: Sir, sir! I'm going to marry this one!

ANNA [*softly, to* KEAN]: Don't be afraid, darling. Prince
seduce shepherdesses, not the daughters of cheese
mongers.

PRINCE: So, young lady. You always get what yo
want.

ANNA: Yes, sir.

PRINCE: I can believe you. If you decided you wante
to seduce a royal prince, I am sure you would succeed

ANNA: So am I, sir. So sure I don't even want to try
[KEAN *begins to laugh, reassured.*]

PRINCE [*to* KEAN]: She's much too good for you. [*Stil
looking at her*] How bored I shall be without you two
I shouldn't have got the King to forgive you. If yo
had stayed here in prison, I could have gone to se
you. Miss Danby and I could have talked about you

KEAN: You can talk about me with Elena.

PRINCE [*sharply*]: Elena bores me. I shall arrange fo
the Count de Koefeld to be recalled to Denmark im
mediately. As for you, take care. I need only say on
word . . .

ANNA [*softly*]: Sir . . .

PRINCE: Well?

ANNA [*sadly*]: I would have wished Your Royal High
ness to spare me, but since we must tell you every
thing—Kean still loves her.

PRINCE: He loves Elena?

ANNA: Madly.

PRINCE [*reassured, but still incredulous*]: Why didn'
he say so?

ANNA: Can't you see he was trying to save his face

KEAN [*furious*]: Really!

ANNA [*pinching him to make him keep quiet*]: An
because he didn't want to cause me pain.

PRINCE: But he is marrying you.

ANNA: Exactly. Does one marry the woman one loves
Just as you came in, d'you know what he was saying
He said: "You will be my little nurse."

KEAN [*furious*]: I never . . .

PRINCE: Kean, is that true?

KEAN: I . . . [ANNA *kicks him. Crossly*] Yes, yes, if you like.

PRINCE [*relaxing*]: My dear Kean, you are yourself again! I knew your heart was as wide as the sea. You love her! Then you find her . . .

ANNA [*quickly*]: Fascinating!

PRINCE: Fascinating, that's right. She has . . .

ANNA: Something. Those were his very words.

PRINCE: "She has something." Perfect! Perfect! Kean, I wounded you, didn't I? Forgive me, please. If you knew how penitent I shall be. [*Gay and carefree, to* ANNA] You must look after him, you know. England is entrusting you with her most precious treasure. [*To* KEAN] You aren't angry with me?

KEAN [*exasperated*]: Don't let's discuss it. [*Crying out*] Solomon? What are you doing? Go and book us two berths on the *Washington*.

SOLOMON [*entering with his luggage*]: Three.

KEAN: Why three?

SOLOMON: If you are going to keep up the comedy, you will certainly need a prompter.

KEAN [*to* SOLOMON *and* ANNA, *linking arms with them both*]: My true, my only friends.

PRINCE [*at the door*]: Mr. Kean, you are an ungrateful wretch!

KEAN [*going to him*]: Ah, sir, what an exit. With your permission, let it be the last word of our play.

[*The two men embrace, while* SOLOMON *kisses* ANNA *on the forehead.*]

CURTAIN

NEKRASSOV

A Farce in Eight Scenes

TRANSLATED FROM THE FRENCH
BY SYLVIA AND GEORGE LEESON

Nekrassov *was presented for the first time at the Théâtre Antoine, Paris, in June 1955.*

CHARACTERS

ROBERT ⎫
⎬ *Two bums*
IRMA ⎭

GEORGES DE VALÉRA

INSPECTOR GOBLET

FIRST POLICEMAN

SECOND POLICEMAN

JULES PALOTIN—*Editor of* Soir à Paris

SECRETARY

SIBILOT

TAVERNIER

PERIGORD

MAYOR OF TRAVAJA

INTERPRETER

MOUTON—*Chairman of* Soir à Paris

VERONIQUE

LERMINIER ⎫
⎪
CHARIVET ⎪ *Directors*
⎬ *of* Soir
NERCIAT ⎪ à Paris
⎪
BERGERAT ⎭

MESSENGER

FIRST BODYGUARD

SECOND BODYGUARD

MADAME CASTAGNIÉ

INSPECTOR BAUDOUIN

INSPECTOR CHAPUIS

MADAME BOUNOUMI

PERDRIÈRE

DEMIDOFF

PHOTOGRAPHERS, SERVANTS, GUESTS, TWO MALE NURSES

SCENE I

*The bank of the Seine, near a bridge. It is moonlight.
Two bums, a man and a woman, are huddled on the
bank. He is asleep. She is sitting and dreaming.*

IRMA: Oh!

ROBERT [*only half awake*]: Eh?

IRMA: Isn't it pretty?

ROBERT: What?

IRMA: The moon.

ROBERT: The moon's not pretty, you see it every day.

IRMA: It's pretty because it's round.

ROBERT: In any case it's for the rich. And so are the
stars. [*He settles down again and goes to sleep.*]

IRMA: Look! Look! [*She shakes him.*]

ROBERT: Can't you leave me in peace?

IRMA [*very excited*]: Over there! There! There!

ROBERT [*rubbing his eyes*]: Where?

IRMA: On the bridge near the lamp. It's one of them!

ROBERT: Nothing extraordinary in that. It's the season
now.

IRMA: He is looking at the moon. That tickles me because just now I too was looking at the moon. He is
taking off his jacket. He's folding it up. He's not
bad looking.

ROBERT: Anyway, he's a weak character.

IRMA: Why?

ROBERT: Because he wants to drown himself.

IRMA: Still, that would be in my line, drowning. But
not to dive in. I would lie on my back, let myself
go, and the water would come in everywhere like a
little lover.

ROBERT: That's because you're a woman. A real man
has to make a splash when he leaves this world. That

fellow there, it wouldn't surprise me if he was a bit of a woman. [*He lies down again.*]

IRMA: Aren't you going to wait to see him jump?

ROBERT: Plenty of time. You can wake me up when he's decided. [*Goes to sleep.*]

IRMA [*to herself*]: This is the moment I like best! Just before the plunge. They look so sweet. He is bending down. He is looking at the moon in the water. The water flows on but the moon stands still. [*Shaking* ROBERT] There he goes! There he goes! Lovely dive.

ROBERT: Bah! [*He gets up.*]

IRMA: Where are you going?

ROBERT: His jacket! It's up there.

IRMA: You're not going to leave me alone with him!

ROBERT: You've nothing to be afraid of. He's at the bottom. [*He starts to go out.*] Blast it, he's not dead.

IRMA: Eh?

ROBERT: It's nothing. His head has come up, just the head. That's usual. [*He sits down again.*] Only I'd better wait a little. While he's alive, I don't touch the jacket. That would be stealing. [*He clicks his tongue in disapproval.*]

IRMA: What's happened?

ROBERT: I don't like it.

IRMA: What?

ROBERT: He's swimming.

IRMA: Oh, you're never satisfied.

ROBERT: I don't like frauds!

IRMA: Fraud or not, he'll do it.

ROBERT: All the same, he's a fraud! Besides, the jacket is lost. At least I'm waiting for him to die. But I bet you the first person who crosses the bridge won't have my delicacy. [*He goes up to a mooring post and unwinds the rope around it.*]

IRMA: Robert, what are you doing?

ROBERT [*unwinding the rope*]: I'm unfastening this rope.

IRMA: What for?

ROBERT [*same action*]: To throw it to him.

IRMA: But why do you want to throw it to him?

ROBERT: For him to catch it.

IRMA: Stop, you old fool! Leave that to those who get paid to do it. We bums should stick together like flowers in a garden. If you stick your neck out, you'll get into trouble.

ROBERT: You talk like a book, old girl.

IRMA: Then don't throw him the rope.

ROBERT: I have to throw it to him.

IRMA: Why?

ROBERT: Because he's swimming.

IRMA [*going to the edge of the quay*]: Stop, there! Stop! You see, it's too late. He's gone under. Good riddance!

ROBERT [*having a look himself*]: What a life! [*He lies down again.*]

IRMA: The jacket? Aren't you going to look for it?

ROBERT: I've no heart for the job now. There's a man dead for want of help. Well, it makes me think of myself. If someone had helped me in my life . . . [*He yawns.*]

IRMA: Quick, Robert, quick!

ROBERT: Let me sleep.

IRMA: Quick, I tell you! The rope! He's coming to the surface. [*She pulls* ROBERT *up.*] You dirty dog! You'd leave a man in trouble.

ROBERT [*he gets up, yawning*]: You've changed your mind, then?

IRMA: Yes.

ROBERT [*having unwound the rope*]: Why?

IRMA: Because he's come to the surface again.

ROBERT: Women! I give up! [*Throws the rope.*]

IRMA: Good shot! [*Indignant*] Would you believe it! He's not taking it!

ROBERT [*pulling in the rope*]: You're all the same! There's a man who's just thrown himself into the water and you expect him to let himself be pulled out without protesting! Don't you know the meaning of honor? [*Throws the rope in again.*]

IRMA: He's caught it! He's caught it!

ROBERT [*disappointed*]: Well, he didn't make much fuss about it. I told you he's a bit of a woman.

IRMA: He's pulled himself up. Saved! Aren't you proud of yourself? I feel proud. It's as if you'd given me a child.

ROBERT: You see! There are not only bad people in life. If only I'd met someone like me to pull me out of the gutter. [GEORGES *appears, the water running from him.*]

GEORGES [*furious*]: You scum . . .

IRMA [*sadly*]: There you are!

ROBERT: That's man's ingratitude for you!

GEORGES [*taking hold of* ROBERT *and shaking him*]: Why did you interfere, you fleabag? Do you think you're Providence?

ROBERT: We thought . . .

GEORGES: Nothing of the kind! It's as bright as day and you could not mistake my intentions. I wanted to kill myself, do you hear? Have you fallen so low that you no longer respect the last wish of a dying man?

ROBERT: You were not a dying man.

GEORGES: Yes I was, since I was going to die.

ROBERT: But you were not going to die, since you are not dead.

GEORGES: I am not dead because you have violated my last wish.

ROBERT: What was it?

GEORGES: The wish to die.

ROBERT: That wasn't your last wish.

GEORGES: It was.

ROBERT: It wasn't, you were swimming.

GEORGES: A fine thing! I was swimming just a little while waiting to go under. If you hadn't thrown the rope . . .

ROBERT: Eh! If you hadn't taken it . . .

GEORGES: I took it because I was forced to . . .

ROBERT: Forced by what?

GEORGES: By human nature, of course. Suicide is against nature!

ROBERT: You see!

GEORGES: What do I see? So you're a nature-lover? I knew quite well that my nature would protest but I had arranged for it to protest too late—the cold was to have numbed me and the water was to choke me. I foresaw everything, everything, except that an old dotard would speculate on my baser instincts!

ROBERT: We meant no harm.

GEORGES: That's just what I blame you for! Everybody means harm—couldn't you have done the same as everybody? If you had meant harm, you would have waited quietly for me to sink, you would have crept up onto the bridge to pick up the jacket I left there, and you would have made three people happy—I, who would be dead, and you two, who would have gained three thousand francs.

ROBERT: The jacket is worth three thousand francs! [*He tries to slip away, but* GEORGES *catches him.*]

GEORGES: Three thousand at least! Perhaps four. [ROBERT *tries to escape but* GEORGES *hangs on to him.*] Stay here! As long as I live, my clothes belong to me.

ROBERT: Alas!

GEORGES: A fine jacket, brand new, very warm, in the latest style, silk-lined, with inside pockets! It'll slip from under your nose, I'll die with it on. Do you understand, idiot? It was in your interest for me to die.

ROBERT: I knew it, sir. I thought only of you.

GEORGES [*violently*]: What did you say? Liar!

ROBERT: I wanted to do you a service.

GEORGES: You lie! [ROBERT *tries to protest.*] Not a word or I'll clout you.

ROBERT: Clout me as much as you like. I'm telling the truth.

GEORGES: I have lived thirty-five years. I have experienced every kind of meanness and I thought I knew the heart of man. But I had to wait for my last day to hear a human being dare to say to my face [*pointing to the river*] and beside my deathbed, that he wanted to do me a service! No one, do you hear, no one has ever done anyone a service. Fortunately. Do you know that I should be under an obligation to you? Me, under obligation to you? You see, it makes me laugh. I choose to laugh at it. [*Seized with suspicion*] Tell me—do you imagine, by any chance, that I owe my life to you? [*Shaking him*] Answer!

ROBERT: No, sir, no.

GEORGES: Who does my life belong to?

ROBERT: It is yours, entirely yours.

GEORGES [*releasing* ROBERT]: Yes, it's mine. I owe it to no one, not even to my parents who were the victims of a miscalculation. Who fed me, brought me up? Who consoled my first sorrows? Who protected me from the dangers of the world? I, and I alone. I owe account to no one but myself. I am a self-made man. [*Seizing* ROBERT *by the scruff of the neck*] Tell me the real reason that drove you! I want to know before I die. Money, eh? You thought I would give you money?

ROBERT: When people kill themselves, sir, it is because they haven't any.

GEORGES: Then it must be something else. [*Struck with an idea.*] Why, of course! It's because you're monsters of vanity.

ROBERT [*stunned*]: Us?

GEORGES: You said to yourselves: "There's a man of quality, well-dressed, well set up, whose features without being regularly handsome, nevertheless are marked with intelligence and energy. Surely this gentleman knows what he wants. If he has decided to put an end to his days it must be for excellent reasons. But I, the sewer rat, the wood louse, the stinking mole with the rotten brain, I see more clearly than that man. I know his interests better than he does, and I decide for him that he shall live!" Isn't that vanity?

ROBERT: Goodness . . .

GEORGES: Nero snatched slaves from their wives to throw them to the fish. And you, more cruel than he, you snatch me from the fish to throw me to Man. Did you even stop to think what Man wanted to do with me? No, you only followed your own whim. Poor France, what is going to become of you if your bums give themselves the pleasures of a Roman emperor!

ROBERT [frightened]: Sir . . .

GEORGES: Of a Roman emperor! Your supreme pleasure is to make those who have failed in life, fail to achieve death. Huddled in the shadows, you lie in wait for those who have lost all hope so that you can pull their strings.

ROBERT: What strings?

GEORGES: Don't play the innocent, Caligula! We all have strings, and we dance when someone knows how to pull them. I've learned that to my cost. I've played that game for ten years. Only I, unlike you, would not attack deprived children, girls who have gone astray, and unemployed fathers of large families. I went to the rich, in their homes, at the height of their power, and I sold them the wind. Ah! Life is a game of poker in which the pair of sevens beats the royal flush, since a Caligula of the bums can make me dance by moonlight. I who juggled with the great ones of the earth. [Pause.] Well, I am going to drown myself. Good night.

ROBERT and IRMA: Good night.

GEORGES [coming back to them]: Just one thing—you're not going to do it again?

ROBERT: Do it again?

GEORGES: Yes! The rope, you're not going to . . .

ROBERT: Oh, that! No. I swear to you, you won't catch us at that again.

GEORGES: Even if I struggle?

IRMA: We shall wash our hands of it.

GEORGES: If I call for help?

IRMA: We shall sing to drown your voice.

GEORGES: Splendid. That's splendid! [*He does not move.*]

ROBERT: Good night.

GEORGES: What a waste of time! I should have been dead ten minutes ago.

ROBERT [*timidly*]: Oh, sir, what's ten minutes?

IRMA: When you have all Eternity before you?

GEORGES: I'd like to see you there! Eternity was right there just in front of me, that's a fact. But I let it slip away because of you, and I don't know how to recapture it.

ROBERT: It can't be far away.

GEORGES [*pointing to the river*]: No need to look for it! It is there. The question is how to get back to it. Understand me, I had the rare opportunity of crossing a bridge and of being desperate at the same time. Such coincidences don't often recur. Proof is that I am no longer on the bridge. And I hope, I say HOPE, that I am still desperate. Ah! There they are!

ROBERT [*starting involuntarily*]: Who?

GEORGES: My reasons for dying. [*He counts on his fingers.*] They are all there.

ROBERT [*quickly*]: We don't want to keep you, sir, but since you've found them again . . .

IRMA [*quickly*]: If we're not being indiscreet . . .

ROBERT [*quickly*]: We would be interested to know them.

IRMA [*quickly*]: We see a great many suicides at this time of year.

ROBERT [*quickly*]: But it isn't every day that one has the chance to speak to one.

GEORGES: Hide your faces, O stars! Withdraw thy moon,

O sky! It needs a double sun to light up the depth of human stupidity. [*To the bums*] Do you dare to ask me my reasons for dying? It is I, poor unfortunates, who should ask you your reasons for living!

ROBERT: Our reasons . . . [*To* IRMA] Do you know them?

IRMA: No.

ROBERT: We live . . . that's how it is. . . .

IRMA: Since we've begun, we'll go on. . . .

ROBERT: We'll get there, anyway, so why get off on the way?

GEORGES: You will get there, yes, but in what condition? You'll be carrion before you're corpses. Take the chance that I offer you. Give me your hands and let us jump. As a threesome, death becomes a picnic.

IRMA: But why die?

GEORGES: Because you have fallen. Life is like a panic in a theater on fire. Everyone is looking for the exit, no one finds it, and everyone knocks everyone else down. Tough luck to those who fall. They are immediately trampled on. Can't you feel the weight of forty million Frenchmen treading on your face? They're not going to tread on mine. I have trampled on all my neighbors. Today I am on the ground. Oh, well, good night! I'd rather eat dandelions than old boots. Do you know that for a long time I carried poison in the setting of a ring? What a joke! I was dead already. I soared above human enterprise and viewed it with the detachment of an artist. And what pride! I shall myself have brought about both my death and my birth. A self-made man, I destroy my own creator. Let us jump, friends. The only difference between man and beast is that man can put an end to his life and the beast cannot. [*He tries to pull the bum with him.*]

ROBERT: You jump first, sir. I want to think about it.

GEORGES: Haven't I convinced you then?

ROBERT: Not quite.

GEORGES: It's high time that I did away with myself. I'm slipping. Previously, I only had to talk to convince. [*To* IRMA] And you?

IRMA: No!

GEORGES: No?

IRMA: Not for anything.

GEORGES: Come on! You will die in the arms of an artist. [*He tries to drag her.*]

ROBERT: My old woman, for God's sake, my old woman. She is mine. She is my wife. Help! Help!

GEORGES [*releasing the old woman*]: Shut up there. They'll hear you. [*Lights on the bridge and in the distance. Whistles.*]

ROBERT [*seeing the electric torches*]: The cops!

GEORGES: They're looking for me.

ROBERT: Are you a burglar?

GEORGES [*hurt*]: Do I look like a burglar, my good man? I am a swindler. [*Whistles off stage.*] [*Thoughtfully*] Death or five years in prison? That is the question.

ROBERT [*looking over to the bridge*]: They look as if they're coming down.

IRMA: What did I tell you, Robert? They'll take us for his accomplices and beat us till we're half dead. [*To* GEORGES] I beg you, sir, if you still intend to kill yourself, don't let us stop you. We would be very grateful to you if you'd make up your mind before the cops are on top of us. Please do us this favor, sir.

GEORGES: I have never done anyone a favor and I'm not going to begin on the day of my death. [*The two look at each other and then throw themselves on* GEORGES, *trying to push him into the water.*] Hey there, what are you doing?

IRMA: We're giving you a hand, sir.

ROBERT: As it's only the first step which comes hard . . .

IRMA: We want to make it easier for you.

GEORGES: Will you let me go!

ROBERT [*pushing*]: Don't forget that you are on the ground, sir.

IRMA: Fallen, finished, a washout!

ROBERT: And they're going to tread on your face!

GEORGES: Are you going to drown your own child?

IRMA: Our child?

GEORGES: I am your child. You said it yourself just now. [*He pushes them over backward.*] I have rights over you, infanticides! It's your job to protect the son you have brought into the world against his will. [*Looking to the right and left.*] Have I time to escape?

ROBERT: They are coming from both sides.

GEORGES: If they take me, they will beat you up, therefore my interests are yours. That's what I like. In saving me you will be saving yourselves and I shall owe you nothing. Not even thanks. What's that? [*He points to something dark on the quayside.*]

ROBERT: It's my spare suit.

GEORGES: Give it to me. [ROBERT *gives it to him.*] Splendid! [*He takes off his trousers and puts on* ROBERT's *suit.*] What filth! It's full of lice. [*He throws his trousers into the Seine.*] Scratch me!

ROBERT: We're not your servants.

GEORGES: You are my father and mother. Scratch me, or I'll hit you. [*They scratch him.*] Here they come! I'm going to lie down and go to sleep. Say that I'm your son. [*He lies down.*]

ROBERT: They won't believe us.

GEORGES: They will believe you if you let your heart speak.

[*Enter* INSPECTOR GOBLET *and* TWO POLICEMEN.]

INSPECTOR: Good day, my beauties.

ROBERT [*grunting indistinctly*]: Huh!

INSPECTOR: Who shouted?

IRMA: When?

INSPECTOR: Just now.

IRMA [*pointing to her husband*]: It was him.

INSPECTOR: Why did he shout?

IRMA: I was beating him.

INSPECTOR: Is it true, what she says? Answer! [*He shakes him.*]

ROBERT: Don't touch me! This is a free country and I have the right to shout when my wife beats me.

INSPECTOR: Tut, tut. Keep calm, take it easy; I'm a police officer.

ROBERT: I'm not afraid of the police.

INSPECTOR: That's a bad thing.

ROBERT: Why? I haven't done anything wrong.

INSPECTOR: Prove it.

ROBERT: It's up to you to prove that I am guilty.

INSPECTOR: That would suit me fine, but the police force is poor. We prefer confessions which cost nothing to proofs which cost a fortune.

ROBERT: I have not made a confession.

INSPECTOR: Be calm, you will. Everything will be done legally. [*To the* TWO POLICEMEN.] Take them away.

FIRST POLICEMAN: What do we make them confess, chief?

INSPECTOR: Well, the Pontoise murder and the Charenton burglary. [*They are taking the bums away.*] Stop! [*He goes toward them. Gently*] Couldn't we come to a friendly arrangement, we three? I should hate anything to happen to you.

IRMA: That would suit us, Inspector.

INSPECTOR: I am looking for a man. Thirty-five years of age, five foot ten, black hair, gray eyes, tweed suit, very smart. Have you seen him?

ROBERT: When?

INSPECTOR: Tonight.

ROBERT: Goodness, no. [*To* IRMA] Have you?

IRMA: Oh no! Such a fine man, you can be sure I would have noticed him! [GEORGES *sneezes.*]

INSPECTOR: Who's that?

IRMA: It's our big son.

INSPECTOR: Why are his teeth chattering?

IRMA: Because he's sleeping.

ROBERT: His teeth always chatter when he sleeps. Ever since he was a baby.

INSPECTOR [to POLICEMEN]: Shake him. [*They shake* GEORGES *who gets up rubbing his eyes.*]

GEORGES: People with mugs like yours shouldn't be allowed to wake people up suddenly.

INSPECTOR [*introducing himself*]: Inspector Goblet. Be civil.

GEORGES: Civil? I've done nothing; too honest to be civil. [*To the bums*] I was dreaming, mum.

INSPECTOR: Didn't your father's shouting wake you?

GEORGES: Did he shout?

INSPECTOR: Like a stuck pig.

GEORGES: He's always shouting. I'm used to it.

INSPECTOR: Always? Why?

GEORGES: Because mum's always beating him.

INSPECTOR: She beats him and you don't stop her? Why?

GEORGES: Because I'm on mum's side.

INSPECTOR: Have you seen a tall, dark man with gray eyes in a tweed suit?

GEORGES: Did I see him, the swine! He's the one who wanted to push me into the water.

INSPECTOR: When? Where?

GEORGES: In my dream.

INSPECTOR: Idiot! [*A* POLICEMAN *comes running in.*]

SECOND POLICEMAN: We've found his jacket on the bridge.

INSPECTOR: There! He's jumped in, or wants us to think he did. [*To the bums*] You heard nothing?

IRMA: No.

INSPECTOR [*to* POLICEMAN]: Do *you* believe he's drowned himself?

FIRST POLICEMAN: I'd be surprised.

INSPECTOR: Me too. He's a lion, that fellow. He'll fight to his last breath. [*He sits down by the edge of the water.*] Sit down, lads. Yes, go on, sit down. We are

all equal in the face of defeat. [*The* POLICEMEN *sit
down.*] Let us draw comfort from the sights of nature.
What a moon! Do you see the Great Bear? Oh, and
the little one! On such a wonderful night a man
hunt should be a pleasure.

FIRST POLICEMAN: Alas!

INSPECTOR: I told the chief, you know. I said to him:
"Chief, I might as well tell you that I shan't catch
him." I'm second-rate and I'm not ashamed of it.
The second-rate are the salt of the earth. Give me
a second-rate murderer and I'll pick him up in no
time. We second-raters understand each other and
know what to expect. But that man, well, I just don't
sense him. He is the crook of the century, the man
without a face, a hundred and two swindles and not
one conviction. What can I do? Genius makes me
uneasy. I don't know what to expect. [*To the* POLICE-
MEN] Where is he? What is he doing? What are his
reactions? How do you expect me to know? Such
men are not made like us. [*He bends over.*] Here,
what's this? [*He picks up the trousers.*] His trousers!

FIRST POLICEMAN: He must have taken them off to
swim.

INSPECTOR: Impossible: I found them on the third
step, above the water. [GEORGES *crawls out left and
disappears.*] Wait a bit . . . he got undressed
here. He must have found clothes to change into.
And those clothes . . . why, of course! [*He turns
toward the place* GEORGES *has left.*] Stop him! Stop
him! [*The* POLICE *start running.*]

ROBERT: Irma?

IRMA: Robert?

ROBERT: You understand?

IRMA: I understand. Give me your hand.

ROBERT: Good-by, Irma.

IRMA: Robert, good-by.

INSPECTOR [*turning to them*]: As for you, you dirty
tramps . . .

[*The two bums jump into the water holding each other by the hand.*] Pull them out! Pull them out! Stop them! Stop them! [*The* TWO POLICEMEN *run up and throw themselves into the water. The* INSPECTOR *wipes his forehead.*] Well, didn't I say I wouldn't catch him!

CURTAIN

SCENE II

The office of the Editor of Soir à Paris. *A large desk for* PALOTIN. *A small one for his* SECRETARY. *Chairs, telephone, etc.* Soir à Paris *posters. A mirror.*

JULES [*looking at photos of himself*]: They're a good likeness of me. What do you think?

SECRETARY: I like that one best.

JULES: Get some thumb tacks. We'll put them on the wall. [*He pins the photos on the wall while speaking.*]

SECRETARY: The Board of Directors has met.

JULES: When?

SECRETARY: Yesterday.

JULES: Without letting me know? That's not so good. What did they say?

SECRETARY: Lucien tried to listen in but they spoke too softly. On his way out, the Chairman said he would come and see you today.

JULES: That stinks, Fifi! That stinks! The old miser wants my scalp. [*Telephone.*]

SECRETARY: Hello, yes. Very good, sir. [*To* JULES] What did I tell you? It's him. He asks if you can see him in an hour.

JULES: Of course, since I can't stop him.

SECRETARY: Yes, sir. Very good, sir. [*She hangs up.*]

JULES: Miser! Skinflint! Screw! [*There is a knock at the door.*] What is it? [*The door opens and* SIBILOT *appears.*] Oh, it's you, Sibilot. Come in. What do you want? I can spare you three minutes. [SIBILOT *enters.*] Sit down. [JULES *never sits down. He walks up and down the room.*] Well? Speak!

SIBILOT: Seven years ago, chief, you decided to devote page five to the fight against Communist propaganda and you did me the honor of confiding it entirely to me. Since then, I have worn myself out on the job. I count as nothing the fact that I have lost my health, my hair, my good humor, and if, to serve you, it were necessary to become even sadder and more crotchety, I wouldn't hesitate for a moment. But there is one thing I cannot renounce without making the paper suffer and that is material security. The fight against the separatists demands invention, tact, and sensibility. To make an impact on people's minds, I'll even go so far as to say it is necessary to be a bit of a visionary. These qualities have not been denied me, but how shall I retain them, if I am tormented by external cares? How can I find the avenging epigram, the vitriolic remark, the damning word? How can I paint the apocalypse which threatens us, and prophesy the end of the world, if my shoes let in water and I cannot afford to have them resoled?

JULES: How much do you earn?

SIBILOT [*pointing to the typist*]: Ask her to go out. [JULES *looks at him with surprise.*] Please, just for a moment.

JULES [*to the* SECRETARY]: Go and get the front-page proof. [*She goes out.*] What stops you speaking in front of her?

SIBILOT: I'm ashamed to admit what I earn.

JULES: Is it too much?

SIBILOT: Too little.

JULES: Let's have it.

SIBILOT: Seventy thousand.

JULES: A year?

SIBILOT: A month.

JULES: But that's a very fair salary and I don't see what you're ashamed of.

SIBILOT: I tell everybody that I get a hundred thousand.

JULES: Well go on telling them. Wait, I'll allow you to go up to a hundred and twenty. People will then believe you get ninety.

SIBILOT: Thank you, chief. . . . [*Pause.*] You couldn't actually give it to me?

JULES [*stunned*]: The hundred and twenty?

SIBILOT: Oh no! the ninety. For the last five years my wife has been in a clinic and I can no longer afford to pay for her upkeep.

JULES [*touching his forehead*]: She is . . . [SIBILOT *nods.*] Incurable? [*Another nod.*] Poor old chap . . . [*Pause.*] What about your daughter? I thought she helped you.

SIBILOT: She does what she can but she's not rich. And she hasn't the same ideas as I have.

JULES: Money has no ideas.

SIBILOT: The fact is . . . she is progressive.

JULES: Oh, that's nothing. She'll grow out of it.

SIBILOT: In the meantime I bolster up my budget with Moscow gold. For a professional anti-communist it's embarrassing.

JULES: On the contrary, you are doing your duty. While that gold is in our hands, it can do no harm.

SIBILOT: Even with Moscow gold, the end of the month is a nightmare!

JULES [*with suspicion*]: Look at me, Sibilot. In the eye. Right in the eye. Do you love your work?

SIBILOT: Yes, chief.

JULES: Hm! And me, my boy, do you love me?

SIBILOT: Yes, chief.

JULES: Well, say it!

SIBILOT: Chief, I love you.

JULES: Say it better than that.

SIBILOT: I love you.

JULES: Flabby, flabby, flabby! Sibilot, our paper is an act of love, the link between the classes, and I want my colleagues to work here for love. I would not keep you on another minute if I suspected you of doing your work for what you can get out of it.

SIBILOT: You know, chief, love, on page five. I don't often have the chance. . . .

JULES: What a mistake, Sibilot! On page five love is between the lines. You are fighting for the sake of love against the scoundrels who want to impede fraternization of the classes by preventing the bourgeoisie from integrating its proletariat. It's a splendid task, I know some who would consider it a duty to do it for nothing. And you, you, who are lucky enough to serve the noblest of causes and to be paid for it into the bargain, you dare to ask me for a raise? [*The* SECRETARY *returns with the newspaper.*] Leave us now. I shall give your case my benevolent consideration.

SIBILOT: Thank you, chief.

JULES: I promise you nothing.

SIBILOT: Thank you, chief.

JULES: I shall call you when I have come to a decision. Good-by, my friend.

SIBILOT: Good-by, chief. And thank you. [*He goes out.*]

JULES [*to* SECRETARY]: He earns seventy thousand a month and he wants me to give him a raise. What do you say to that?

SECRETARY [*indignant*]: Oh!

JULES: See that he doesn't set foot in here again. [*He takes the newspaper and looks it over.*] Oh! Oh! Oh! [*He opens the door of his office.*] Tavernier! Perigord! Front Page Conference! [*Enter* TAVERNIER *and* PERI-GORD. *The* SECRETARY *goes out.*]

JULES: What's wrong, boys? Cares of the heart? Health worries?

TAVERNIER [*astonished*]: Goodness, no . . .

PERIGORD [astonished]: I don't think . . .

JULES: Then you don't love me any more?

TAVERNIER: Oh, Jules!

PERIGORD: You know very well that everyone adores you.

JULES: No, you do not adore me. You love me a little, because I am lovable, but you do not adore me. It isn't zeal you lack, but ardor. That's my greatest misfortune. I have fire in my veins and I am surrounded by lukewarm people!

TAVERNIER: What have we done, Jules?

JULES: You have botched up the front page for me by giving it headlines that would make the South Sea Islanders laugh.

PERIGORD: What should we have put, chief?

JULES: I am asking you, boys. Suggest something! [Silence.] Think hard, I want a stirring headline, an atomic headline! For the past week we've been stagnating.

TAVERNIER: There's Morocco, of course.

JULES: How many deaths?

PERIGORD: Seventeen.

JULES: There! Two more than yesterday. Put it on page two. And you'll headline: "Marrakesh: moving demonstrations of loyalty." Subheading: "Healthy elements of population reject troublemakers." Have we a photo of the ex-Sultan bowling?

TAVERNIER: It's in the library.

JULES: Front page. Middle. Caption: "Ex-Sultan of Morocco settles down in his new residence."

PERIGORD: All that doesn't make the big headline.

JULES: Exactly. [He thinks.] Adenauer?

TAVERNIER: He blew up at us yesterday.

JULES: Ignore it, not a word. The war? How is it today? Cold? Hot?

PERIGORD: Good.

JULES: Lukewarm, in fact. It's like you. [PERIGORD raises his finger.] You have a headline?

PERIGORD: "War danger recedes."

JULES: No, boys, no. Let war recede as much as it likes but not on the front page. On the front page the danger of war increases. What about Washington? No one spilt anything? Ike? Dulles?

PERIGORD: Not a word.

JULES: What are they up to? [TAVERNIER *raises his finger.*] Go on.

TAVERNIER: "America's Disturbing Silence."

JULES: No.

TAVERNIER: But . . .

JULES: America does not disturb; she reassures.

PERIGORD: "America's Reassuring Silence."

JULES: *Reassuring!* My dear fellow, I am not alone. I have my duties to the shareholders. You think I am going to amuse myself by splashing "reassuring" in big type so that people can see it from a distance. If they are reassured in advance, why should they buy my newspaper?

TAVERNIER [*raising a finger*]: "Disturbing Silence of USSR."

JULES: Disturbing? The USSR disturbs you, now? And what about the H Bomb? What is it? Chickweed for the birds?

PERIGORD: I propose a lead-in: "America is not worried by the" and underneath: "Disturbing Silence of the USSR."

JULES: You're teasing America, son. Finding fleas.

PERIGORD: Me?

JULES: Of course! If this silence is disturbing, America is wrong not to be disturbed by it.

PERIGORD: "Washington is neither worried nor unconcerned about the DISTURBING SILENCE OF THE USSR."

JULES: Now what do you call that? A newspaper headline or a charge of wild elephants? Rhythm, good God, rhythm. It has to go quickly, quickly, quickly! A newspaper is not written, it has to dance. Do you know how the Yanks would write your headline?

"USSR: SILENCE; USA: SMILES." It has swing! Oh! If only I had Americans working with me! [SECRETARY *enters.*] What is it?

SECRETARY: The Mayor of Travaja.

JULES [*to* PERIGORD]: Are the photographers here?

PERIGORD: No.

JULES: What! You haven't called the photographers?

PERIGORD: But I didn't know . . .

JULES: Keep him waiting and get hold of all the photographers in the building. [*To* PERIGORD] How many times have I told you that I want a human newspaper. [*The* SECRETARY *goes out.*] We are much too far away from our readers. *Soir à Paris* must be associated in everybody's mind with a familiar, smiling and compassionate face. Whose face, Tavernier?

TAVERNIER: Yours, Jules.

JULES [*to* PERIGORD]: Travaja has been destroyed by an avalanche, and its mayor is coming to receive the proceeds of the collection we organized. How is it you didn't understand, Perigord, that this was an occasion for me to appear for the first time to our readers and to be the reflection of their own generosity? [*The* SECRETARY *enters.*]

SECRETARY: The photographers are here.

JULES: Bring the Mayor in. [*She goes out.*] Where is Travaja? Quick!

PERIGORD: Peru.

JULES: Are you sure? I thought it was in Chile.

PERIGORD: You should know better than I do.

JULES: And you? What do you think?

TAVERNIER: I would have leaned toward Peru but you must be right; it's . . .

JULES: No soft soap! I'm not ashamed of being self-taught! Bring the map of the world! [*They bring it.* JULES *kneels in front of it.*] I can't find Peru.

TAVERNIER: Near the top on the left. Not so high. There!

JULES: Why, it's a pocket handkerchief. Where's Travaja?

TAVERNIER: It's the black dot on the right.

JULES [*dryly*]: You see better than I do, Tavernier.

TAVERNIER: I beg your pardon, Jules. [THE MAYOR *of Travaja and his* INTERPRETER *enter, followed by* PHOTOGRAPHERS *and* SECRETARY.]

JULES: Good God, where's the check? [*He goes through his pockets.*]

TAVERNIER: In your jacket.

JULES: But where is my jacket?

THE MAYOR [*as if to commence an oration*]: Na . . .

JULES [*hurriedly*]: Good day, sir! Sit down here! [*To the* PHOTOGRAPHERS] He's all yours. Keep him busy.

THE MAYOR: Na . . . [*The* PHOTOGRAPHERS *surround him. Flash bulbs.*]

JULES: Tavernier, Perigord! Help me. [*On hands and knees under the desks.*]

THE MAYOR: Na . . . [*Photos.*] Na . . . [*Photos.*]

JULES [*pulling his jacket from under a table and drawing out the check. Cry of victory*]: I've got it!

THE MAYOR: Na . . . [*Photos.*] Ouj ja! . . . [*He bursts into tears.*]

JULES [*to* PHOTOGRAPHERS]: Take it! For God's sake, take it! [*To* SECRETARY] Take the caption: "Mayor of Travaja weeps with gratitude before our editor." [*The* PHOTOGRAPHERS *have taken their photos. THE* MAYOR *is still weeping. To* INTERPRETER.] Tell him to stop. The photos have been taken.

INTERPRETER: O ca ri.

THE MAYOR: Ou pe ca mi neu.

INTERPRETER: He prepared a speech on the plane. He is crying because he's been prevented from giving it.

JULES: You'll translate it and we'll publish it in full.

INTERPRETER: Ra ca cha pou!

THE MAYOR: Paim pon!

INTERPRETER: He insists on making it. Permit me to

observe that the city of Travaja is situated 12,380
feet above sea level and the air is rarefied. Because
they easily become breathless, speakers have learned
to be concise.

JULES: Quick, then. Quick!

THE MAYOR [*slowly*]: Na vo ki. No vo ka. Kay ko ray.

INTERPRETER: The children of Travaja will never forget the generosity of the French people. [*Pause.*]

JULES: Go on.

INTERPRETER: That is all.

JULES [*giving the signal for applause*]: Marvellous
speech! [*To* PERIGORD] All the same it will be just as
well to pad it out. [*To* THE MAYOR] Just we two,
Travaja. [*He hands him the check.* THE MAYOR *takes
it.*] Take it back from him, quick! It's for the photographers. [*The check is taken from* THE MAYOR.]

A PHOTOGRAPHER [*placing a telephone directory on the
floor*]: Julot.

JULES: Eh?

PHOTOGRAPHER: If you'd be so good as to stand on the
directory.

JULES: Why?

PHOTOGRAPHER: Generosity comes from above.

JULES: Then give me two directories. [*He stands on
the directories and hands the check over.* THE MAYOR
takes the check. Flash.*]

PHOTOGRAPHER: Again! [*He takes the check from* THE
MAYOR *and hands it back to* JULES. *Same action.*]
Again! [*Same action.* THE MAYOR *begins to cry.*]

JULES: Enough, for God's sake, enough! [*He puts the
check into* THE MAYOR's *hand. To* INTERPRETER] How
do you say good-by?

INTERPRETER: La pi da.

JULES [*to* THE MAYOR]: Lapida!

MAYOR: La pi da. [*They kiss.*]

JULES [*taking* THE MAYOR *in his arms*]: Boys, I believe
I am crying. Picture, quick!

[*Photos.* JULES *wipes a tear and smilingly shows his wet fingers to* THE MAYOR, THE MAYOR *does likewise and touches* JULES'S *finger with his own. Photo.*]

JULES [*to* PHOTOGRAPHERS]: Show him around. Sacre-Coeur, the Unknown Soldier, the Folies-Bergères. [*To* THE MAYOR] Lapida!

THE MAYOR [*goes out backward, bowing*]: La pi da, la pi da. [PHOTOGRAPHERS *and* INTERPRETER *go out.*]

JULES: Boys, is there any greater pleasure than doing good? [*Abruptly*] Oh! Oh! Oh!

PERIGORD [*worried*]: Jules . . .

JULES: Silence, boys. I feel an idea coming.

PERIGORD [*to typist*]: Stop, Fifi, stop. Here's the Idea! Silence. [JULES *paces up and down.*]

JULES: What day is it today?

PERIGORD: Tuesday.

JULES: Splendid. I want a weekly day of kindness. It will be Wednesday. I am counting on you, Roger. On Fridays, find refugees, escapees, survivors, ragged orphans. On Saturdays you open the fund and on Wednesdays, you announce the results. Understand, son? What are you going to prepare for us for next Wednesday?

PERIGORD: Well, I . . . Why not the homeless?

JULES: Homeless? Excellent. Where do they live, your homeless? In Caracas? Puerto-Rico?

PERIGORD: I was thinking of those in France.

JULES: You're crazy! The objects of our compassion must be victims of strictly natural catastrophes. Otherwise you'll sully love with sordid stories of social injustice. Do you remember our campaign: "Everyone is happy"? We didn't quite convince everybody at the time. Well, this year we shall launch a new campaign: "Everyone is good," and you'll see everybody'll believe us. That's what I call the best propaganda against communism. The headline, boys, the headline! What did you propose?

TAVERNIER: Nothing was proposed, Jules. We were in the soup.

PERIGORD: Apart from the seventeen dead Moroccans . . .

TAVERNIER [*taking him up*]: . . . two suicides, a miracle at Trouville, exchanges of diplomatic notes, a jewel robbery . . .

PERIGORD [*taking him up*]: four road accidents and two frontier incidents . . .

TAVERNIER [*taking him up*]: . . . nothing at all has happened.

JULES: Nothing new! And you complain? What do you want? The storming of the Bastille? The 1879 Oath of the Tennis Court? Boys, I am a government newspaper, and it isn't up to me to write history since the government refuses to make it and the public doesn't want it. Everyone to his trade. Let historians write history, and daily papers, everyday news. And everyday news is anything but new. It is what has been going on every day since the beginning of the world. Homicides, robberies, abduction of minors, fine exploits, and the reward of virtue. [*Telephone.*] What is it?

SECRETARY [*who has lifted the receiver*]: It is Lancelot, chief.

JULES: Hello. Oh! Ah! At what time? Good, good, good. [*He hangs up.*] Your headline is found, boys. Georges de Valéra has just escaped.

PERIGORD: The crook?

TAVERNIER: The fifty million man?

JULES: That's the one. The genius of the century. You will put his photo on the front page beside mine.

TAVERNIER: The good and evil, chief.

JULES: Compassion and indignation are sentiments which aid digestion. Don't forget our paper comes out in the afternoon. [*Telephone.*] What? What? What? No! No! No details? Oh! Oh! Oh! Good! [*He hangs up.*] Oh, God, oh God, oh God!

TAVERNIER: Have they caught him?

JULES: No, but headlines never come singly. A little while ago I had none, now I have one too many.

TAVERNIER: What's happened?

JULES: The Soviet Minister of the Interior has disappeared.

PERIGORD: Nekrassov? Is he in jail?

JULES: Even better, he's chosen freedom.

PERIGORD: What do we know about it?

JULES: Practically nothing. That's what gets me. He didn't appear at the Opera last Tuesday and no one has seen him since.

TAVERNIER: Where does the news come from?

JULES: From Reuter and A.F.P.

TAVERNIER: What about Tass?

JULES: Not a word.

TAVERNIER: Hm!

JULES: Yes. Hm!

TAVERNIER: Well? What's it to be? Nekrassov or Valéra?

JULES: Nekrassov. We'll put "NEKRASSOV DISAPPEARS," and as subheading "Soviet Minister of the Interior chooses freedom." Have you a photo?

PERIGORD: You know it, Jules. Looks like a pirate. He wears a patch over his right eye.

JULES: You'll put it next to mine to keep the contrast between Good and Evil.

PERIGORD: And Valéra's?

JULES: On page four. [*Telephone.*] If this is another headline, I'll shoot somebody!

SECRETARY: Hello. Yes. Yes, sir. [*To* JULES] It's the Chairman of the Board of Directors.

JULES: Tell him to come up, the skinflint!

SECRETARY [*in telephone*]: Yes, sir. Right away, sir. [*She hangs up.*]

JULES [*to* TAVERNIER *and* PERIGORD]: Disappear, boys. So long. [PERIGORD *and* TAVERNIER *go out.* JULES *re gards his jacket with perplexity then, after an instant's hesitation, puts it on.*] [*Enter* MOUTON.]

JULES: Good day, Mr. Chairman.

MOUTON: Good day, my dear Palotin. [*He sits down.*] Sit down.

JULES: If you don't mind, I'd rather stand.

MOUTON: I do mind. How do you expect me to talk to you if I have constantly to look all around the office for you?

JULES: As you wish. [*Sits down.*]

MOUTON: I have brought you some excellent news. The Minister of the Interior phoned me yesterday and he gave me to understand that he was thinking of granting us the exclusive rights to advertise Public Appointments.

JULES: Public   Appointments?   It's . . . it's   unexpected! . . .

MOUTON: Isn't it? Following that telephone conversation I took it upon myself to call a meeting of the Board and all our friends agree that this decision is of the utmost importance. We could improve the quality of the paper while reducing costs.

JULES: We shall appear in twenty pages. We'll knock out *Paris-Presse* and *France-Soir!*

MOUTON: We shall be the first daily to publish color photos!

JULES: And what does the Minister ask in return?

MOUTON: Nothing, my dear chap. Nothing. Nothing at all. We accept favors when they are a recognition of merit and we reject them when they are an attempt to buy our consciences. The Minister is young, go-ahead, a sportsman. He wants to galvanize his colleagues, to make the government really modern. And as *Soir à Paris* is a government paper, it is being given the means to modernize itself. The Minister even coined this charming phrase: "Let the daily rag become the daily flag."

JULES [*bursts out laughing, then suddenly becomes serious*]: He called my paper a rag?

MOUTON: It was a joke. But I must tell you that some of my colleagues have pointed out to me that *Soir à Paris* is tending to go to sleep. The general layout of the paper is perfect, but we no longer find in it that bite, that style which caught the public imagination.

JULES: We must take into consideration the relaxation of international tension. Perigord was just telling me quite correctly that nothing is happening.

MOUTON: Of course, of course! You know that I always defend you. But I understand the Minister. "Virulence," he said to me, "will be the New Look of French politics." He will do more for us than for our colleagues when we have shown our mettle. And now, the occasion arises for us to show that we have the requisite "virulence." In substance, this is what the Minister told me. A by-election is going to take place in Seine-et-Marne. It's the constituency the Communists have chosen for a trial of strength. The Cabinet accepts the challenge; the election will be fought on the question of for or against German rearmament. You know Mme Bounoumi; she's the government candidate. This Christian housewife mother of twelve children, knows how to reach the hearts of the French masses. Her simple and touching propaganda could serve as an example to our politicians and to the editors of our big daily papers. Look at this poster! [*He takes out a poster from his brief case and unrolls it. It reads:* "BROTHERHOOD THROUGH REARMAMENT" *and lower down:* "TO PRESERVE PEACE, ALL MEANS ARE GOOD, EVEN WAR."] How direct it is! I would like to see it on your wall.

JULES [*to* SECRETARY]: Fifi! Thumb tacks! [SECRETARY *puts the poster on the wall.*]

MOUTON: If merit were rewarded, Mme Bounoumi would easily win. Unfortunately, the situation is not

very bright. To start with we can only count on three
hundred thousand votes. The Communists have as
many, perhaps a little more. A good half of the elec-
tors will abstain as usual. There remain about another
hundred thousand votes which are bound to go to
the Radical deputy, Perdrière. That means there will
be a second ballot with the risk that the Communist
will get in the second time.

JULES [*who doesn't understand*]: Ah! Ah!

MOUTON: The Minister sees only one way to avoid
what he doesn't hesitate to call a disaster, that is, to
get Perdrière to stand down in favor of Mme Bounoumi. Only—Perdrière won't stand down.

JULES: Perdrière? But I know him. He's an avowed
enemy of the Soviets. We've dined together.

MOUTON: I know him even better. He is my neighbor in
the country.

JULES: He said some very sensible things.

MOUTON: You mean he condemned the policy of the
USSR?

JULES: Exactly.

MOUTON: There's a man for you! He detests the Communists and doesn't want to rearm Germany.

JULES: Astonishing contradiction!

MOUTON: His attitude is purely sentimental. Do you
know what's at the bottom of it? The Germans
plundered his estate in 1940, and deported him in
1944.

JULES: So?

MOUTON: That's all. He won't learn anything and he
won't forget anything.

JULES: Oh!

MOUTON: And mark you, it was nothing much. He was
only deported for eight or ten months.

JULES: Proof of that is that he returned.

MOUTON [*shrugging his shoulders*]: Well, there you are.
He obstinately sticks to his memories. He has Ger-
manophobia. What is even more absurd is that his-

tory does not repeat itself. In the next war, it will be Russia that the Germans will plunder and Russians whom they will deport.

JULES: Why, of course!

MOUTON: You can be sure he knows all that!

JULES: And that doesn't shake his convictions?

MOUTON: On the contrary! He maintains he would not allow Russians to be put into Buchenwald. [*Light smile.*] There's no mistake about it, when you talk to him about the Germans, he sees red. [*Polite laugh from* JULES.] Well, there you are! You know it all. Perdrière fears the Germans more than the Russians. He will stand down if you make him fear the Russians more than the Germans.

JULES: If YOU make him . . . Who is that YOU?

MOUTON: You.

JULES: Me? How do you expect me to set about it? I have no influence over him.

MOUTON: You'll have to acquire it.

JULES: By what means?

MOUTON: His hundred thousand voters read *Soir à Paris.*

JULES: Well?

MOUTON: Be virulent. Create fear.

JULES: Fear? But that's all I do. My entire fifth page is devoted to the red peril.

MOUTON: Exactly. [*Short silence.*] My dear Palotin, the Board directed me to tell you that your fifth page is no longer worth anything. [JULES *gets up.*] My dear chap, I beg you to remain seated. [*Urging*] Do me the favor. [JULES *sits down again.*] We used to gain something from reading page five. I remember your fine series "War Tomorrow." People trembled with fear. And your photo montages: Stalin on horseback entering Notre Dame in flames! Real masterpieces. But for more than a year I've noted a suspicious slackening off, criminal oversights. You used to speak of famine in the USSR and you don't mention it any more. Why? Do you claim the Russians have enough to eat?

JULES: Me? I'd watch it.

MOUTON: The other day, I saw your photo: "Soviet housewives queueing in front of a food store," and I was stunned to note that some of those women were smiling and that all of them were wearing shoes. Shoes in Moscow! It was obviously a Soviet propaganda photo that you took for an A.F.P. photo by mistake. Shoes! For the love of God, you might at least have cut off their feet. Smiles! In the USSR! Smiles!

JULES: I couldn't cut off their heads.

MOUTON: Why not? Shall I tell you something? I began to wonder whether you hadn't changed your opinions.

JULES [*proudly*]: My paper is an objective one, a government paper, and my opinions don't change unless the government changes its opinions.

MOUTON: Good. Very good. And you're not worried?

JULES: Why should I be?

MOUTON: Because people are beginning to feel reassured.

JULES: To be reassured? My dear Mr. Chairman, don't you think you're exaggerating?

MOUTON: I never exaggerate. Two years ago, there was an open-air dance in Rocamodour. Lightning struck suddenly a hundred yards away. Panic. A hundred deaths. The survivors declared at the inquest that they had thought they were being bombed by a Soviet plane. There's your proof that the objective press did its work well. Good. Yesterday, the Institute of French Public Opinion published the results of its latest gallup poll. Do you know what they are?

JULES: Not yet.

MOUTON: The investigators interrogated ten thousand persons from all walks and conditions of life. To the question: "Where will you die?" ten per cent replied that they hadn't any idea, and the others—

that is, almost all—that they would die in their beds.

JULES: In their beds?

MOUTON: In their beds. And those were average Frenchmen, readers of our paper. Ah! How far away Rocamodour is, and what a setback in two years!

JULES: There wasn't a single one of them who replied that he would die burned to ashes, pulverized, or dissolved into vapor?

MOUTON: In their beds.

JULES: What? Not one who mentioned the H bomb, the deathray, radioactive clouds, death ash, or poisoned rains?

MOUTON: In their beds. In the middle of the twentieth century, with the astounding advances in technique, they believe they will die in their beds. As in the Middle Ages! Ah! my dear Palotin, let me tell you in all friendliness that you are very guilty.

JULES [*getting up*]: But I had nothing to do with it!

MOUTON [*also getting up*]: Your paper's flabby! Lukewarm! Insipid! Maudlin! Yesterday again, you spoke of peace. [*He advances on* JULES.]

JULES [*retreating*]: No.

MOUTON [*advancing*]: Yes. On the front page!

JULES [*still retreating*]: It wasn't me. It was Molotov. I only printed his speech.

MOUTON [*advancing*]: You printed it in full. You should have given extracts.

JULES: The requirements of a news service . . .

MOUTON: Does that count when the Universe is in danger? The Western Powers are united by terror. If you restore their feeling of security, where will they find the strength to prepare for war?

JULES [*cornered against the desk*]: War? What war?

MOUTON: The next one.

JULES: But I don't want war.

MOUTON: You don't want it? But tell me, Palotin, where do you think you will die?

JULES: In my . . .

MOUTON: In your . . .

JULES: In a . . . How do I know?

MOUTON: You are a neutralist who won't face facts, a shameless pacifist, a merchant of illusions.

JULES [*jumping up on the directories and shouting*]: Leave me alone. Peace! Peace! Peace! Peace!

MOUTON: Peace! You see, that's what you want. [*Pause. JULES jumps down.*] Come, let us sit down again and keep calm. [*JULES sits down again.*] Nothing prevents me recognizing your great qualities. I was telling the Board again yesterday: "You are the Napoleon of objective news." But will you be the Napoleon of virulence?

JULES: I will be that as well.

MOUTON: Prove it.

JULES: How?

MOUTON: Get Perdrière to stand down. Launch a terrible, a gigantic campaign. Shatter the morbid dreams of your readers. Show that the material survival of France depends on the German army and American supremacy. Make yourself fear life more than you fear death.

JULES: I . . . I will do it.

MOUTON: If the task frightens you, there is still time to withdraw.

JULES: It doesn't frighten me. [*To* SECRETARY] Get Sibilot right away.

SECRETARY [*on telephone*]: Send Sibilot.

JULES: Ah! The poor sods, the poor sods!

MOUTON: Who?

JULES: The readers! They are quietly fishing, playing cards every evening, and making love twice a week expecting to die in their beds, and I am going to spoil their pleasure.

MOUTON: Don't weaken, my friend. Think of the dangerous situation you are in, and of how I continually defend you. Think above all of the country! Tomorrow at ten o'clock, the Board of Directors will be meeting. It would be very desirable if you could submit your new plans to us. No, no, remain seated. Don't bother to see me out.

[MOUTON *goes out.* JULES *jumps to his feet and paces the room almost at a run.*]

JULES: Oh God, oh God, oh God! [*Enter* SIBILOT.]

JULES: Come here!

SIBILOT: I thank you, chief.

JULES: Don't thank me, Sibilot, don't thank me yet.

SIBILOT: Ah! I want to do it in advance no matter what your decision. I didn't think you would call me so quickly.

JULES: You were mistaken.

SIBILOT: I was mistaken. I was mistaken through my want of love. Through denouncing Evil, I had come to see it everywhere and I no longer believed in human generosity. To be quite frank, chief, I had become suspicious of Man, of Man himself.

JULES: And you are reassured?

SIBILOT: Completely. From this moment I love Man and I believe in him.

JULES: You are lucky. [*He paces the room.*] My friend, our conversation has opened my eyes. Didn't you tell me that your work required invention?

SIBILOT: Yes, it does.

JULES: Sensibility, tact, and even poetry?

SIBILOT: Absolutely!

JULES: In fact—don't let us be afraid of words—a kind of genius?

SIBILOT: I wouldn't have dared. . . .

JULES: Don't be shy!

SIBILOT: Well, in a certain way. . . .

JULES: Splendid. [*Pause.*] That proves that you are not at all the man I need. [SIBILOT *gets up, disconcerted.*] Sit still! I'm the boss here. I'm the one that does the walking around here. And I shall walk until tomorrow if I want to.

SIBILOT: Didn't you say? . . .

JULES: Sit down! [SIBILOT *sits down again.*] I said that
you are an incompetent, a muddlehead, and a sabo-
teur. Tact? Finesse? You? You allow photos through,
which show Soviet women in fur coats, shod like
queens, and smiling from ear to ear! The truth is,
Sibilot, that you have found a haven, a job, a retreat
for your old age! You take page five of *Soir à Paris*
for an old folks' home. And from the height of your
seventy thousands you despise your comrades who are
killing themselves at the job. [*To* SECRETARY] For he
earns . . .

SIBILOT [*with a heartrending cry*]: Chief, don't say it!

JULES [*pitiless*]: Seventy thousand a month in order to
boost up Soviet Russia in my paper!

SIBILOT: It's not true!

JULES: I sometimes wonder whether you aren't an
undercover man!

SIBILOT: I swear . . .

JULES: An undercover man, a crypto, a fellow traveler!

SIBILOT: Stop, chief! I think I am going mad!

JULES: Didn't you yourself confess to me that you
received Moscow gold?

SIBILOT: But it's my daughter. . . .

JULES: Oh, yes, it's your daughter! So? Someone has
to give it to you. [SIBILOT *tries to get up.*] Sit down!
And choose: either you've sold out or you're an incompetent!

SIBILOT: I give you my word that I am neither one nor
the other!

JULES: Prove it!

SIBILOT: But how?

JULES: Tomorrow I am launching a campaign against
the Communist Party. I want to have them on their
knees in a fortnight from now. I need a first-class
demolition man, a bruiser, a woodcutter. Will it be
you?

SIBILOT: Yes, chief.

JULES: I'll believe you if you give me an idea right away!

SIBILOT: An idea . . . for the campaign . . .

JULES: You have thirty seconds.

SIBILOT: Thirty seconds for an idea?

JULES: You have only fifteen left. Ah! We shall see if you have genius.

SIBILOT: I . . . the life of Stalin in pictures!

JULES: The life of Stalin in pictures? Why not Mohammed? Sibilot, the thirty seconds are up, you are fired!

SIBILOT: Chief, I beg of you, you can't do . . . [*Pause.*] I have a wife, I have a daughter.

JULES: A daughter! Why, of course, it's she who keeps you.

SIBILOT: Listen to me, chief. If you sack me, I shall go home and gas myself.

JULES: Wouldn't be much of a loss! [*Pause.*] I'll give you until tomorrow. But unless you come into my office tomorrow morning at ten 'clock with a shattering idea, you can pack your bags.

SIBILOT: Tomorrow morning? . . .

JULES: You have the whole night before you. Get going!

SIBILOT: You shall have your idea, chief. But I should like to tell you that I no longer believe in Man.

JULES: For the job you have to do, that will be an advantage. [SIBILOT *goes out, crushed.*]

CURTAIN

SCENE III

A room—night.
GEORGES *enters through the window, almost knocks over
    a vase, but catches it in time. Whistles blow off stage.
    He flattens himself against the wall. A* POLICEMAN
    *puts his head through the open window and shines
    his torch into the room.* GEORGES *holds his breath.
    The* POLICEMAN *disappears.* GEORGES *breathes again.
    He is seen to be fighting against a desire to sneeze.
    He holds his nose, opens his mouth, and ends up by
    sneezing noisily.*

VERONIQUE [*off stage*]: What's that?
    [GEORGES *sneezes again. He rushes to the window and
    puts his leg over the sill. Whistles quite close. He
    hurriedly climbs back into the room. At that mo-
    ment* VERONIQUE *enters and puts on the light.*
    GEORGES *draws back and stands against the wall.*]
GEORGES [*with his hands up*]: It's all up!
VERONIQUE: What's all up? [*She looks at* GEORGES.]
    Well! A thief?
GEORGES: A thief? Where?
VERONIQUE: Aren't you a thief?
GEORGES: Not in the least. I'm paying you a visit.
VERONIQUE: At this time of night?
GEORGES: Yes.
VERONIQUE: And why have you got your hands up?
GEORGES: Because it is nighttime. A nocturnal visitor
    puts his hands up when he's surprised. It's customary.
VERONIQUE: Well, you've done the polite thing; now
    put them down.
GEORGES: It wouldn't be wise.
VERONIQUE: In that case, keep them well up. Make

yourself at home. [*She sits down.*] Take a seat. You
can put your elbows on the arm rest. It's more comfortable. [*He sits down with his hands up. She
watches him.*] You're right. I ought never to have
taken you for a thief.

GEORGES: Thank you.

VERONIQUE: Not at all.

GEORGES: Still, appearances are against me, and I'm
glad that you've been good enough to believe me.

VERONIQUE: I believe your hands. Look how ghastly
they are. You've never done anything with your
hands.

GEORGES [*under his breath*]: I work with my tongue.

VERONIQUE [*continuing*]: Whereas a thief's hands are
quick, lively, sensitive. . . .

GEORGES [*annoyed*]: What do you know about it?

VERONIQUE: I've covered the courts.

GEORGES: You've covered them? That's nothing to boast
about.

VERONIQUE: I covered them for two years. Now I'm on
foreign affairs.

GEORGES: A journalist?

VERONIQUE: That's right. And you?

GEORGES: An artistic career is more in my line.

VERONIQUE: What do you do?

GEORGES: For my living? I talk.

VERONIQUE: And what are you doing in this room?

GEORGES: Just that.

VERONIQUE: Good. Then talk.

GEORGES: What about?

VERONIQUE: You should know. Say what you have to
say.

GEORGES: To you? Oh, no. Call your husband.

VERONIQUE: I am divorced.

GEORGES [*pointing to a pipe on the table*]: Is it you who
smokes the pipe?

VERONIQUE: It's my father's.

GEORGES: You live with him?

VERONIQUE: I share his flat.

GEORGES: Call him.

VERONIQUE: He's at his paper.

GEORGES: Ah, so you're both journalists?

VERONIQUE: Yes, but on different papers.

GEORGES: That means we're alone in this flat.

VERONIQUE: Does that shock you?

GEORGES: It's a bad situation; compromising for you, and unpleasant for me.

VERONIQUE: I don't find it compromising.

GEORGES: All the more reason why I find it unpleasant.

VERONIQUE: Good night, then. You can come back when my father is home.

GEORGES: Good night, good night. [*He gets up slowly. Whistles sound outside. He sits down again.*] If you don't mind, I prefer to wait for him here.

VERONIQUE: I don't mind, but I was just going out. I'm quite willing to leave you alone in the flat, but I'd still like to know why you came here.

GEORGES: That's fair enough. [*Pause.*] There! [*Pause.*]

VERONIQUE: Well? [GEORGES *sneezes and stamps his feet.*]

GEORGES: A cold. A cold. The one ridiculous remnant of a flop. I wanted to cool off, and I've caught a cold.

VERONIQUE [*giving him a handkerchief*]: Blow your nose.

GEORGES [*still with his hands up*]: Impossible.

VERONIQUE: Why?

GEORGES: I can't lower my hands.

VERONIQUE: Stand up. [*He stands up. She pulls at his arms, but cannot pull them down.*] Are you paralyzed?

GEORGES: It's the effect of distrust.

VERONIQUE: Do you distrust me?

GEORGES: I distrust women.

VERONIQUE [*dryly*]: Very well. [*She takes the handkerchief from him.*] Blow! Harder! There you are. [*She folds the handkerchief, and puts it in his pocket.*]

GEORGES [*furious*]: How unpleasant! God, how unpleasant!

VERONIQUE: Relax.

GEORGES: Easy to say.

VERONIQUE: Throw your head back, close your eyes, and count up to a thousand.

GEORGES: And what will you do while my eyes are closed? You'll slip out to call the police or you'll go and get a pistol. . . .

VERONIQUE: Do you want me to put my hands up? [*She raises her hands and* GEORGES *slowly lowers his.*] At last. Do you feel better?

GEORGES: Yes. More comfortable.

VERONIQUE: Then you'll be able to tell me.

GEORGES: Naturally. What?

VERONIQUE: For the past hour I've been asking you what you're doing here.

GEORGES: What I'm doing here? Nothing simpler. But put your hands down. I can't stand it. I can't talk to you while you have your hands above your head. [VERONIQUE *lowers her hands.*] Good.

VERONIQUE: I'm listening.

GEORGES: How I wish your father were here! I like women; I adore covering them with jewels and caresses. I'd gladly give them anything—except explanations.

VERONIQUE: How curious. Why?

GEORGES: Because they don't understand them, madam. Let us suppose, just by way of example, of course, that I were to say to you: "I am a crook, the police were chasing me, your window was open, I came in." That would appear simple and clear. Well, what does that suggest to you?

VERONIQUE: What does it suggest to me? I don't know. . . .

GEORGES: There, you see. You don't even know.

VERONIQUE: It suggests to me that you were a crook. . . .

GEORGES: Is that all?

VERONIQUE: Isn't that the main point? [*A brief silence.*]
I think it's a pity.

GEORGES: You prefer thieves?

VERONIQUE: Yes, because they work with their hands.

GEORGES: All for the workers, eh? [*Pause.*] In any case,
the experiment has succeeded. You've got everything
wrong.

VERONIQUE: Then you're not a crook.

GEORGES: No. That's not the point. The point is that
I have the cops at my tail. A man wouldn't fail to
understand. [*Shouting suddenly.*] I've got the cops
on my tail, don't you understand?

VERONIQUE: All right. Don't shout. [*Pause.*]

GEORGES: Well? What are you going to do with me?

VERONIQUE: Draw the curtains. [*She goes to the window
and draws the curtains.*]

GEORGES: And what about me?

VERONIQUE: You? What can I do? Are you a guitar that
I should pluck you, a mandoline that I should strum
you, or a nail that I should bang you on the head?

GEORGES: Well, then?

VERONIQUE: Then nothing. I've nothing to do with you.

GEORGES: Nothing is the most imprecise reply. Nothing can mean anything. Anything can happen. You
could burst into tears, or poke my eyes out with your
hatpin. Oh, how I wish I had met your father. Do
you know what he would have said?

VERONIQUE: I'm going to hand you over to the police.

GEORGES [*with a start*]: You're going to hand me over
to the police?

VERONIQUE: No. I'm telling you what my father would
have said.

GEORGES: Quite right. There's a man for you.

VERONIQUE: Perhaps so, but if he'd been here you would
already be in handcuffs.

GEORGES: Oh, no.

VERONIQUE: No?

GEORGES: No. I know how to persuade men. They have

logical minds. I control their thoughts by logic. But you, madam, where's your logic? Where's your common sense? If I've understood you, you DON'T intend to hand me over.

VERONIQUE: You've understood rightly.

GEORGES: And that's just why you will hand me over. Don't protest. You're like all women; impulsive and hysterical. You will smile at me, cajole me, and then you will take fright at my ears or at a hair sticking out of my nose and you'll start screaming.

VERONIQUE: Did I scream when I discovered you?

GEORGES: Of course not. But you will. I know women. Whenever they feel like screaming, they let you have it. You're still holding yours in. But just let the police knock at the door, and you'll enjoy yourself by letting it go. What a pity you're not a man. You might have been my luck. As a woman, by your very nature you're my fate.

VERONIQUE: I'm your fate?

GEORGES: What else? A door which shuts, a noose which tightens, an ax which falls—that's woman.

VERONIQUE [*irritated*]: You've come to the wrong floor. For fate call on the lady on the second floor, who has ruined two family men. As for me, I leave all doors open, and I . . . [*She stops and bursts into laughter.*] You nearly made me . . .

GEORGES: I beg your pardon.

VERONIQUE: You have two strings to your bow: logic for men and challenge for women. You pretend to think that we are all alike, while really believing that each of us wishes to be unique. "You are a woman, therefore you'll hand me over." You thought to lead me on so that I would have to prove to you that I'm not like anyone else. My poor chap, you've wasted your time, for I've no desire to be unique. I'm like all women, and I am content to be like them.

[*There is a ring at the doorbell.*]

GEORGES: Is it? . . .

VERONIQUE: I'm afraid it is. [*He raises his hands.*]

GEORGES: Are you going to give me up?

VERONIQUE: What do you think? [*She sees his raised hands.*] Put your hands down. You'll make me lose my head. [*He lowers his hands and puts them in his pockets.*]

GEORGES: What are you going to do?

VERONIQUE: What any woman would do in my place. [*Pause.*] What would they do?

GEORGES: I don't know.

VERONIQUE: Don't you think they'd scream?

GEORGES: I tell you, I've no idea.

VERONIQUE: You were more confident just now. [*Another ring at the door.*] You've only to say one word, and I'll become impulsive, hysterical.

GEORGES: Have I fallen so low that my fate is in a woman's hands?

VERONIQUE: Give the sign, and I'll put it back into the hands of men.

[*There is a knock at the door, and someone says "Police."*]

GEORGES [*making his decision*]: It's understood that I'm under no obligation to you.

VERONIQUE: Understood.

GEORGES: That you won't expect any gratitude from me . . .

VERONIQUE: I'm not so foolish.

GEORGES: And that I'll repay evil for good.

VERONIQUE: Of course.

GEORGES: Then hide me. [*Suddenly nervous.*] Quick! What are you waiting for?

VERONIQUE: Go in there.

[*He disappears. She opens the door, and the IN-SPECTOR pokes his head through the doorway.*]

INSPECTOR: Naturally, madam, you haven't seen a dark man about five feet ten in height. . . .

VERONIQUE [*quickly*]: Naturally, I haven't.

INSPECTOR: I was sure of it. [*He bows and disappears. She closes the door.*]

VERONIQUE: You can come back.

[GEORGES *comes in, wrapped in a red blanket. She laughs.*]

GEORGES [*with dignity*]: There's nothing to laugh at. I'm trying to warm myself up. [*He sits down.*] You lied.

VERONIQUE: Well I never!

GEORGES: That's rich!

VERONIQUE: I lied for you.

GEORGES: That won't solve anything.

VERONIQUE: This is too much! Perhaps you don't tell lies?

GEORGES: It's different with me. I'm dishonest. But if all honest people behaved like you . . .

VERONIQUE: Well?

GEORGES: What would happen to the social order?

VERONIQUE: Bah!

GEORGES: Bah what? What do you mean, bah?

VERONIQUE: This social order of yours . . .

GEORGES: Do you know a better one?

VERONIQUE: Yes.

GEORGES: Which one? Where is it?

VERONIQUE: Take too long to explain. Let's just say that I lied to the cops because I don't like them.

GEORGES: What are you? A pickpocket, a kleptomaniac?

VERONIQUE: I've told you that I'm a journalist, and I'm honest.

GEORGES: Then you like them. Honest people like the cops. That goes without saying.

VERONIQUE: Why should I like them?

GEORGES: Because they protect you.

VERONIQUE: They protect me so much that they set on me last week. [*Pulling up her sleeves*] Look at these bruises.

GEORGES: Oh!

VERONIQUE: That's what they did.

GEORGES [*surprised*]: Was it a mistake?

VERONIQUE: No.

GEORGES: You were guilty, then?

VERONIQUE: We were demonstrating.

GEORGES: Who's we?

VERONIQUE: I—and other demonstrators.

GEORGES: What were you demonstrating?

VERONIQUE: Our discontent.

GEORGES: Incredible! Look at yourself and look at me,
and tell me which of us has the right to be discontented. Well, I'm not discontented. Not at all. I've
never complained. I've never demonstrated in all my
life. On the threshold of prison, on the brink of
death, I accept the world. You're twenty, you're free,
and you reject it. [*Suspicious*] In fact, you're a red.

VERONIQUE: Pink.

GEORGES: This is getting interesting. What about your
father? What does he say to all this?

VERONIQUE: It worries him to death, poor man.

GEORGES: Is he on the other side?

VERONIQUE: He writes for *Soir à Paris*.

GEORGES: You thrill me. That's my paper. A great and
honest man, your father, with only one weakness—
you . . . [*He shivers, sneezes, and wraps himself
more tightly in his blanket.*] Delightful evening! I
owe my life to a bum with a taste for doing unnecessary favors and my freedom to a revolutionary who
makes a cult of mankind. It must be kindness week.
[*Pause.*] You ought to be happy; you've sown disorder,
betrayed your class, lied to your natural protectors,
humiliated a man. . . .

VERONIQUE: Humiliated!

GEORGES: Of course! You have made me into a mere
object—the unfortunate object of your philanthropy.

VERONIQUE: Would you be any less an object in the
Black Maria?

GEORGES: No, but I'd be able to hate you and seek

refuge in my own soul. Ah, you've done me a bad turn.

VERONIQUE: I?

GEORGES [*vigorously*]: A very bad turn. You see no further than the end of your nose. But I think about things. I think of the future. It's dark, a very dark future. Saving people is not everything, my girl. You must give them the means to live. Have you asked yourself what's to become of me?

VERONIQUE: You'll become a crook again, I suppose.

GEORGES: That's just it—I shan't.

VERONIQUE: What? Are you going to become an honest man?

GEORGES: I don't say that. I say that I no longer have the means to be dishonest. One needs a certain amount of capital to be a crook: a certain outlay, two suits, a dinner suit, a dress suit if possible, twelve shirts, six pairs of underpants, six pairs of socks, three pairs of shoes, a range of ties, a gold tie pin, a leather brief case, and a pair of horn-rimmed glasses. All I possess are these rags and I haven't a cent. How do you expect me to manage? Can I present myself to the manager of the Bank of France in this get-up? I've been brought very low. Much too low for me to be able to climb up again; and it's all your fault. You've saved me from jail only to plunge me into destitution. In prison I could save my face. As a bum I lose face. I, a bum? I've nothing to thank you for, madam.

VERONIQUE: Suppose I were to get you a job?

GEORGES: A job? Thirty thousand francs a month, work, and an employer? Keep it. I'm not selling myself.

VERONIQUE: How much would you need to build up your wardrobe?

GEORGES: I've no idea.

VERONIQUE: I have a little money on me.

GEORGES: Don't say any more. Money is sacred. I never accept money: I take it.

VERONIQUE: Then take it.

GEORGES: I can't take it from you, since you're giving it
   to me. [*Suddenly*] I'll make you a proposal. It's an
   honest one of course, but then I have no right to
   make things difficult. I'll give you an interview, with
   exclusive world rights.

VERONIQUE: You give me an interview?

GEORGES: Aren't you a journalist? Ask me some questions.

VERONIQUE: What about?

GEORGES: About my art.

VERONIQUE: I've told you, I'm on foreign affairs. Besides, my paper is not interested in crooks.

GEORGES: Of course. A progressive paper! What a bore
   it must be. [*Pause.*] I am Georges de Valéra.

VERONIQUE [*unable to restrain her interest*]: The . . .

GEORGES: Yes, the great Valéra.

VERONIQUE [*hesitantly*]: Well, of course . . .

GEORGES: I imagine your rag is poor.

VERONIQUE: Yes, fairly poor.

GEORGES: All I ask is two suits, a dozen shirts, three
   ties and a pair of shoes. You can pay me in kind.
   [*He stands up.*] In 1917 a blue baby was born in
   Moscow of a Black Guard and a White Russian.

VERONIQUE: No.

GEORGES: Doesn't that interest you?

VERONIQUE: I haven't the time. I told you I was going
   out.

GEORGES: What about later?

VERONIQUE: Frankly, no. Crooks, you know, pleasant or
   otherwise . . .

GEORGES: Go to the devil. [*The door to the flat is heard
   to open and close.*] What's that?

VERONIQUE: Good heavens! My father!

GEORGES: I'm going . . .

VERONIQUE: If he sees you, he'll give you up. Go in
   there for the moment. I'll get round him.
   [GEORGES *disappears at the moment that the door
   opens.* SIBILOT *enters.*]

SIBILOT: You still here?

VERONIQUE: I was just going. I didn't think you'd be home so soon.

SIBILOT [*bitterly*]: Nor did I.

VERONIQUE: Listen, Dad, there's something I have to tell you.

SIBILOT: The swine!

VERONIQUE: Who?

SIBILOT: Everybody. I'm ashamed to be a man. Give me a drink.

VERONIQUE [*pouring him a drink*]: Now, just imagine . . .

SIBILOT: Ungrateful wretches, liars, rogues, and scoundrels, that's what we are. The sole justification for the human species is the protection of animals.

VERONIQUE: Just now I had . . .

SIBILOT: I'd like to be a dog. They show us an example of love and fidelity. But no, canines are the dupes of man. They are stupid enough to love us. I'd like to be a cat. A cat? No. All mammals are alike. Oh, to be a shark to follow in the wake of ships and devour the sailors.

VERONIQUE: Poor old Dad, what have they done to you now?

SIBILOT: They've kicked me out, my child.

VERONIQUE: They kick you out once a fortnight.

SIBILOT: This time it's the works. Veronique, you're my witness that I've been feeding on Communists for nearly ten years. It's indigestible and monotonous food. How many times have I wanted to change my diet; to feed on priests, for example, or freemasons, millionaires or women. In vain. The menu is fixed for ever. Have I ever jibbed at it? I'd no sooner finished digesting Malenkov when I had to start on Khrushchev. Did I complain? Every day I invented a new sauce. Whose idea was the sabotage of the cruiser *Dixmude*? And who thought up the business of the

conspiracy against the nation? And the story about
the carrier pigeons? I did. They were all mine. For
ten years I've defended Europe, from Berlin to
Saigon. I've fed on Viet-Minh, I've fed on the Chi-
nese, I've fed on the Soviet Army, with its planes
and tanks. Now, my girl, see the extent of human
ingratitude. The first time my stomach turns, the boss
throws me out.

VERONIQUE: Have you really been thrown out?

SIBILOT: Like a dishrag. Unless I find an idea by tomorrow.

VERONIQUE [*without any sympathy*]: You'll find it, don't
worry.

SIBILOT: No; not this time. What do you expect? I'm
not a titan. I'm a very ordinary man who has worn
out his gray matter for seventy thousand francs a
month. It's true that for ten years I shone. I was
Pegasus, I had wings. The wings have caught fire, and
what's left? An old nag, fit for the boneyard. [*He
walks up and down.*] Ten years of loyal service. You'd
expect a human word, a gesture of gratitude. Nothing. Reprimands and threats, that's all. I shall end up
by hating your Communists. [*Timidly*] My dear
girl? . . .

VERONIQUE: Yes, Dad?

SIBILOT: You wouldn't have any . . . now I'm saying
it just in the air—you wouldn't have an idea? You
don't know anything against them?

VERONIQUE: Oh, Dad!

SIBILOT: Listen, my dear, I've never objected to the
company you keep, even though it has been awkward
for me, and might perhaps be the reason for my bad
luck. I've always left you free, ever since your poor
mother's illness, only asking that you save me from
the worst when your friends take power. Won't you
reward my tolerance? Are you going to leave your
poor old father in the lurch? I'm asking you to make

a little effort, my child, just a little one. You see the Communists at close quarters. You must have a lot on your mind.

VERONIQUE: No, Dad.

SIBILOT: Come on!

VERONIQUE: They're my friends.

SIBILOT: All the more reason. Who are the people whose seamy side you know, if not your friends? The only friends I have are at the paper, and, I tell you, if I wanted to speak out. . . . Here! I'll make an exchange with you. You tell me what you know about Duclos, and I'll give you the lowdown on "Braces" Julot. You'll have a terrific story. Will you do it?

VERONIQUE: No, Dad.

SIBILOT: I'm Job. My own daughter abandons me on the dungheap. Go, then.

VERONIQUE: I'm going. I'm going. But I wanted to tell you . . .

SIBILOT: Veronique, do you know who is dying? Man. Work, Family, Fatherland. All finished. There, that's a story. The Twilight of Man. What do you say to that?

VERONIQUE: You can read that every month in *Preuves*.

SIBILOT: You're right. To hell with him.

VERONIQUE: Who?

SIBILOT: Man. I'm a fool to wear myself out for seventy thousand francs a month. After all, the Communists haven't done me any harm. For seventy thousand francs a month, it would even be justifiable for me to be on their side.

VERONIQUE: I didn't make you say that.

SIBILOT: No, my girl, no. You won't tempt me. I'm an old-fashioned man. I love freedom too much. I have too much respect for human dignity. [*He pulls himself together.*] Respect for human dignity is proper, beautiful. Thrown out like a dishrag. An old employee, a family man. Thrown into the street with a month's wages and no pension. Here! That's an idea perhaps. Old workers get no pensions in the USSR. [*He looks at himself in the mirror.*] There'd have to be something about their gray hairs.

VERONIQUE: They have pensions, Dad.

SIBILOT: Be quiet. Let me think. [*Pause.*] It's no good. The readers would be right in saying "Maybe the Russian workers don't have pensions, but that's no reason for rearming Germany." [*Pause.*] Veronique, Germany MUST be rearmed. But why, eh? For what reason?

VERONIQUE: There's no reason.

SIBILOT: Yes, my girl, there is one; and this is it. All my life I've been as furious as any Russian about it, and I've had enough. Let the others get worked up about it for a change. And they will, if Germany rearms, I tell you. Rearm, then! Rearm Germany! Rearm Japan! Set fire to the four corners of the globe! Seventy thousand francs to defend Man. Think of that. At that price Man can damned well go under.

VERONIQUE: You'll go under as well.

SIBILOT: So much the better. My life has been one long funeral, and no mourners following the coffin. But my death will make some stir. What an apotheosis! I'd like to go out like a rocket, if only I could see old Julot spinning above my head. Seventy thousand francs a month. Seventy thousand kicks in the pants daily. We'll all go under together, and long live war! [*He sputters and coughs.*]

VERONIQUE: Here, have a drink. [*He does so.*]

SIBILOT: Ooh!

VERONIQUE: There's a bum in my room.

SIBILOT: Is he a Communist?

VERONIQUE: Not at all.

SIBILOT: Well, what am I supposed to do about it?

VERONIQUE: The police are after him.

SIBILOT: Then phone the police station and ask them to come and get him.

VERONIQUE: But, Dad, I want to save him.

SIBILOT: What's he done, this pal of yours? If he has stolen, he must be punished.

VERONIQUE: He hasn't stolen. Be a sport. Don't worry about him. Go on quietly looking for your idea. In the morning he will go without making any noise, and we shan't see him again.

SIBILOT: Very well. If he keeps perfectly quiet I'll close my eyes to his presence. But if the police come, don't bank on my telling lies.

VERONIQUE [*half-opening the door of her room*]: I'm going. You can stay the night here, but don't leave my room. Good-by. [*She closes the door.*] See you tomorrow, Dad. And don't worry about your idea. Your people use the same idea every time, and you'll just have to dig it up again.

SIBILOT: Go to the devil! [*She goes out.*] The same idea. Of course it's the same idea. And what next? I've got to have something good if I have to dress it up again every time. [*He puts his head between his hands.*] The life of Stalin in pictures. They don't want that, the idiots. I wonder why. [GEORGES *sneezes.* SIBILOT *listens, then returns to his meditations.*] Sabotage . . . conspiracy . . . treason . . . terror. [*At each word he thinks and shakes his head.*] Famine . . . famine, eh? [*Pause.*] No. Done to death. Used ever since 1918. [*He looks through his newspapers.*] What have these Russians done? [*Looking through the papers*] Nothing? Impossible. It is incredible that in a country of 200 million inhabitants a day should pass without an injustice or some foul crime being committed. I've got it! The Iron Curtain. [*He thinks awhile.*] Sabotage . . . conspiracy . . . [GEORGES *sneezes. Irritated*] If only I could work in peace. Treason . . . conspiracy . . . Let's start from the other end. Western culture. The mission of Europe. The right to think. [GEORGES *sneezes.*] Stop it! Stop it! [*He starts to dream again.*] The life of Stalin in pictures. [*Whistles sound in the street. He is in torment, and buries his head in his hands.*] Oh! The life of Stalin without pictures. [GEORGES *sneezes.*] I'll kill that fellow.

GEORGES [*off stage*]: Oh, my God! Oh, my God!

SIBILOT: God help me! God help me! [*He goes to the telephone and dials a number.*] Hello! Police? This is Rene Sibilot, journalist, 13 rue Goulden, ground floor, the door on the left. Someone has broken into my flat. It seems that the police are looking for him. That's right. Send someone over.

[*During the last few words, the door opens and* GEORGES *enters.*]

GEORGES: A healthy reaction at last. Sir, you are a normal man. Allow me to shake your hand. [*He comes forward with his hand held out.*]

SIBILOT [*jumping back*]: Help!

GEORGES [*throwing himself on* SIBILOT]: Ssh! [*He puts a hand over* SIBILOT'*s mouth.*] Do I look like a murderer? What a misunderstanding! I admire you, and you think that I want to cut your throat. Yes, I admire you. Your phone call was sublime. It should serve as an example to all good people who have been misled by a false liberalism into surrendering their rights. Don't be afraid that I may escape. I want to contribute to your glory. Tomorrow the papers will report that I was arrested at your place. You believe me, don't you? Do you believe me? [SIBILOT, *still gagged, signs assent.*] Good. [*He releases* SIBILOT *and steps back a pace.*] Let me look at the honest man in his full and splendid majesty. [*Pause.*] Suppose I were to tell you that I tried to kill myself just now in order to escape my pursuers?

SIBILOT: Don't try to get round me.

GEORGES: Splendid. And suppose I were to take a box of pills from my rags, swallow them and fall dead at your feet?

SIBILOT: Well?

GEORGES: What would you say?

SIBILOT: I'd say "The rogue has saved the law a job."

GEORGES: The quiet certitude of an irreproachable conscience. It is easy to see, sir, that you have never entertained any doubts about what is right. . . .

SIBILOT: Of course!

GEORGES: . . . and that you don't listen to these subversive doctrines which make the criminal a product of society.

SIBILOT: A criminal is a criminal.

GEORGES: Splendid! A criminal is a criminal. That's well said. Ah, there's no danger that I'd touch your heart by telling the story of my unfortunate childhood.

SIBILOT: It would do you no good. I had a tough childhood myself.

GEORGES: And little you'd care that I'm a victim of the first World War, the Russian Revolution, and the capitalist system?

SIBILOT: There are others who are victims of all that—me, for example—and who don't stoop to thieving.

GEORGES: You have an answer for everything. Nothing saps your convictions. Ah, sir, with that bronze forehead, those enamel eyes, and that heart of stone, you must be an anti-Semite.

SIBILOT: I should have known it. Are you a Jew?

GEORGES: No, sir, no. And I'll admit to you that I share your anti-Semitism. [*At a gesture from* SIBILOT] Don't be offended. Share is going too far, let's say that I pick up the crumbs. Not having the good fortune to be honest, I don't enjoy your assurance. I have doubts, sir, I have doubts. That is the prerogative of troubled souls. I am, if you like, a probabilist anti-Semite. [*Confidentially*] What about the Arabs? You hate them, don't you?

SIBILOT: That's enough. I have neither the time nor the inclination to listen to your nonsense. I ask you to go back into that room immediately and to wait there quietly until the police arrive.

GEORGES: I'll go. I'll go back into the other room. But just tell me that you hate the Arabs.

SIBILOT: Er, yes.

GEORGES: Say it better than that, just to please me, and I swear to you it's my last question.

SIBILOT: They should stay where they belong.

GEORGES: Wonderful. Allow me, sir, to take off my hat to you. You are honest to the point of ferocity. After this brief tour of the horizon, our identity of views is plain, which doesn't surprise me. What honest people we scoundrels would be if your police would give us the chance.

SIBILOT: Are you going to clear out?

GEORGES: Just one word more, sir, just one, and then I'll go. What! You, a Frenchman, son and grandson of French peasants, and I, a man without a country, provisional guest of France—you honesty itself, and I the criminal—we can shake hands disregarding all vices and virtues, both condemning the Jews, the Communists, and subversive ideas? Our agreement is of deep significance. I know its significance, sir, and I'll tell you what it is: we both respect private property.

SIBILOT: You respect property?

GEORGES: I? But I live on it, sir. Why shouldn't I respect it? Come, sir, your daughter wanted to save me. You have given me away, but I feel closer to you than to her. The practical conclusion that I draw from all this is that we have the duty, you and I, to work together.

SIBILOT: Work together? Who? We? You're mad.

GEORGES: I can do you a great service.

SIBILOT: You amaze me.

GEORGES: Just now I had my ear to the door, and I heard everything you said to your daughter. You were looking for an idea, I believe. Well, I'm in a position to give you that idea.

SIBILOT: An idea? About Communism?

GEORGES: Yes.

SIBILOT: You . . . you know the subject?

GEORGES: A crook has to know everything.

SIBILOT: All right, give me your idea quickly, and I'll ask the court to be lenient with you.

GEORGES: Impossible.

SIBILOT: Why?

GEORGES: I can only help you if my hands are free.

SIBILOT: The police . . .

GEORGES: Yes, the police. They're coming. They'll be here in a couple of minutes. That just gives me time to introduce myself: an orphan, driven since childhood to choose between dying of starvation or using my wits. There's no credit in my having chosen to use my wits. I have an excess of genius, sir, as you have an excess of honesty. Have you ever thought what an alliance of genius and honesty could do, of inspiration and obstinacy, of light and blindness? We should be masters of the world. I have ideas. I produce dozens every minute. Unfortunately, they convince no one. I don't pursue them enough. You, you have none, but ideas hold you in their grip, they furrow your brow, and you are blinded by them, and that is just why they convince others. They are dreams of stone; they fascinate all who have a nostalgia for petrification. Suppose that now a new thought emanated from me and took possession of you. It would quickly take on your manner, poor thing; it would become so gross and true that it would capture the Universe.

[*A ring at the doorbell.* SIBILOT, *who has been listening fascinated, starts with surprise.*]

SIBILOT: It's the . . .

GEORGES: Yes. You must decide. If you hand me over, you'll have a sleepless night and you'll be sacked tomorrow. [*The bell rings again.*] If you save me, my genius will make you rich and famous.

SIBILOT [*tempted*]: What proof have I of your genius?

GEORGES [*going into the other room*]: Ask the inspector.
[*He disappears while* SIBILOT *goes to the open door
to admit the* INSPECTOR.]

INSPECTOR: M. Sibilot?

SIBILOT: Yes.

INSPECTOR: Where is he?

SIBILOT: Who?

INSPECTOR: Georges de Valéra.

SIBILOT [*impressed*]: You're looking for Georges de
Valéra?

INSPECTOR: Yes. Oh, no hope, of course. He's as slippery
as an eel. Do you mind if I sit down? [*He does so.*]
I see that you haven't a grand piano. I congratulate
you.

SIBILOT: Don't you like grand pianos?

INSPECTOR: I've seen too many.

SIBILOT: Where?

INSPECTOR: Among the rich. [*He introduces himself.*]
Inspector Goblet.

SIBILOT: Delighted.

INSPECTOR: I like your place. I'll be sorry to leave it.

SIBILOT: Make yourself at home.

INSPECTOR: You don't know how much at home I am.
Your living room is the exact replica of mine. Nineteen twenty-five?

SIBILOT: Eh?

INSPECTOR [*with a sweep of his hand*]: The furniture:
nineteen twenty-five?

SIBILOT: Ah, 1925? Oh, yes.

INSPECTOR: The Decorative Arts Exhibition, our
youth . . .

SIBILOT: The year of my wedding.

INSPECTOR: And mine. Our wives chose the furniture
with their mothers; we weren't even consulted. The
in-laws lent the money. Do you like those 1925
chairs?

SIBILOT: You know, in the end one no longer sees them.

[*Shaking his head*] To me, it was a temporary arrangement. . . .

INSPECTOR: Naturally. What isn't temporary? And then, one fine day, twenty years later . . .

SIBILOT: We are aware that we shall soon die, and that the temporary has become permanent.

INSPECTOR: We shall die as we have lived, in 1925. [*He gets up quickly.*] What have you there? An original?

SIBILOT: No, it's a reproduction.

INSPECTOR: So much the better. I hate original paintings and private carriages, because the rich collect them and we're forced to know all the hallmarks.

SIBILOT: Who is?

INSPECTOR: We of the Society Branch.

SIBILOT: What for?

INSPECTOR: So that we can keep up a conversation. [*Going to the picture*] This is a Constable. I wouldn't have thought that you liked Constables.

SIBILOT: I prefer them to the mildew.

INSPECTOR [*looking behind the picture*]: Ah, because BEHIND the Constable . . .

SIBILOT: That's right.

INSPECTOR: The damp, eh?

SIBILOT: It's being near the Seine.

INSPECTOR: Don't tell me. I live at Gennevilliers. [GEORGES *sneezes several times and starts to swear.*] What's that?

SIBILOT: The neighbor. He can't stand the damp. It gives him colds.

INSPECTOR: You're lucky it's the neighbor. At Gennevilliers I'm the one who catches cold. [*He sits down again.*] Man is a strange animal, my dear sir. I'm enraptured by your flat because it reminds me of my own, which gives me the horrors.

SIBILOT: How do you explain that?

INSPECTOR: Well, it's because my job takes me into the fashionable quarters. I was in the Society Branch, and now they've put me on to J.3; murders and swindles,

which again leads me to places like Passy. I carry out
my investigations above my station, my dear chap,
and they make me feel it. I have to go in through the
servants' entry, wait between a piano and a big green
plant, smile at women in tight-fitting dresses and
perfumed men who treat me like a servant. Meanwhile, as they put mirrors everywhere, I see my ugly
mug on all the walls.

SIBILOT: Can't you put them in their places?

INSPECTOR: In their places? But that's where they are.
I'm the one who isn't in my place. But you must know
all about that in your game.

SIBILOT: I? If I were to tell you that I have to kiss my
editor's backside every day.

INSPECTOR: It's not possible. Do they make you?

SIBILOT: Figuratively speaking.

INSPECTOR: I know what you mean, and I can tell you
that I've kissed the Director of the Sûreté's backside
over a thousand times. You know, what I like about
your place is the feeling of discomfort and proud
humility. At last I'm doing my investigating among
equals; at home, so to speak. I'm free. If I felt like
taking you inside and giving you the once-over, no
one would protest.

SIBILOT: Surely you're not thinking of that?

INSPECTOR: Good God, no. You have far too nice a face.
A face like mine. A sixty-thousand-francs-a-month
face.

SIBILOT: Seventy.

INSPECTOR: Sixty, seventy, it's all the same. It's at a
hundred that you start to change. [*Moves.*] My poor
Sibilot.

SIBILOT: My poor Inspector. [*They shake hands.*]

INSPECTOR: Only we can appreciate our poverty and our
greatness. Give me a drink.

SIBILOT: Gladly. [*He fills two glasses.*]

INSPECTOR [*raising his glass*]: To the defenders of Western culture. [*He drinks.*]

SIBILOT: Victory to those who defend the rich without loving them. [*He drinks.*] By the way, you haven't got an idea, have you?

INSPECTOR: Against whom?

SIBILOT: Against the Communists.

INSPECTOR: Ah, you're on propaganda. Well, you won't find your idea; it's much too tricky for you. No more than I'll find my Valéra.

SIBILOT: Is he so smart?

INSPECTOR: He? If I weren't afraid of using fancy words, I'd say he's a genius. By the way, didn't you tell me that he had taken refuge in your flat?

SIBILOT: I . . . I said that someone . . .

INSPECTOR: It's he, without the slightest doubt. If he was here a few minutes ago, he should still be here. All the windows of the building are being watched. I have men in the corridor and on the stairs. Good. Well, that proves the esteem I have for him. I shan't search this room. I shan't even look in the other rooms. Do you know why? Because I know that he has managed to make himself unrecognizable or to get away from the neighborhood. Who knows where he is? And in what disguise? Perhaps you are he.

SIBILOT: I?

INSPECTOR: Keep calm. Mediocrity can't be counterfeited. Let's close the matter, my dear chap. Give me a couple of lines for my report. You saw him, you rushed to the phone to inform us, and he took advantage of the few minutes your back was turned to disappear. Is that it?

SIBILOT: I . . .

INSPECTOR: Splendid. [*Pause.*] Now I must leave, taking with me the pleasant memory of these brief moments. We shall have to meet again.

SIBILOT: Nothing would please me more.

INSPECTOR: I'll phone you some time. When we're both free, we'll go to the cinema together, like a couple of lads. Don't bother to see me out. [*He goes out.*]

SIBILOT [*opening the door of the other room*]: Give me your idea and clear out.

GEORGES: No.

SIBILOT: Why?

GEORGES: My ideas wither without me. We're inseparable.

SIBILOT: Under those conditions I'll manage without you. Get out!

GEORGES: Didn't you hear what the Inspector said? I'm a genius, Dad.

SIBILOT [*with resignation*]: Well? What do you want?

GEORGES: Very little. I want you to keep me here till the police have evacuated the building.

SIBILOT: And then what? No money?

GEORGES: No, but you can slip me one of your old suits.

SIBILOT: All right. Stay. [*Pause.*] Now, your idea.

GEORGES [*sits down, pours himself a glass of wine and unhurriedly lights one of* SIBILOT'S *pipes*]: Well, here it is . . .

CURTAIN

SCENE IV

JULES PALOTIN's *office.* JULES, TAVERNIER, PERIGORD, *and the* SECRETARY *are present.*

JULES: What's the time?

TAVERNIER: Two minutes to ten.

JULES: And no Sibilot?

TAVERNIER: No.

JULES: He's always been early.

PERIGORD: He's not late yet.

JULES: No, but he's no longer early. He's letting me down. [*The telephone rings and the* SECRETARY *answers it.*]

SECRETARY: Hello? Yes. Yes, sir. [*To* JULES] The Board is about to meet and the Chairman asks if there's anything new.

JULES: Anything new? He can go to hell. Say I've gone out.

SECRETARY [*into telephone*]: No, sir, he must have gone to the Composing Room. [*To* JULES] He doesn't seem very pleased.

JULES: Tell him I've got a pleasant surprise for him.

SECRETARY [*into telephone*]: As he left the office he said that he had a pleasant surprise for you. Very good.

JULES: What did he say?

SECRETARY: The Board are expecting you to phone them.

JULES: The old miser. Bandit. I'll give him surprises. [*To* SECRETARY] Ask Sibilot to come right away.

SECRETARY [*into telephone*]: Send Sibilot up to the chief. [*To* JULES] He hasn't come yet.

JULES: What's the time?

SECRETARY: Five past ten.

JULES [*to the others*]: I told you. He begins by not being early, and ends up by being late. [*Pause.*] Well, well, well. We'll wait. [*He sits down and takes up a restful attitude.*] We'll wait calmly. [*He strikes another restful attitude.*] In complete calm. [*To* TAVERNIER *and* PERIGORD] Relax. [*The* SECRETARY *starts to type. He shouts*] I said calmly. [*He jumps suddenly to his feet.*] I'm not made for waiting. Someone is being killed.

TAVERNIER: Where, chief?

JULES: How should I know? In Cairo, Hamburg, Valparaiso, Paris. A jet plane explodes over Bordeaux. A peasant discovers the footprint of a Martian in his

field. I am news, my boys. News doesn't wait. [*The
telephone rings.*] Is it Sibilot?

SECRETARY [*into telephone*]: Hello. Yes. Yes, sir. [*To
JULES*] It's the Minister of the Interior. He asks if
there's anything new.

JULES: I'm not here.

SECRETARY: No, sir, the editor isn't here. [*To JULES*]
He's furious.

JULES: Say that I've got a surprise for him.

SECRETARY: The editor said just a while ago that he has
a surprise for you. Very good, sir. [*She hangs up.*]
He'll ring back in an hour.

JULES: An hour! An hour to find that surprise . . .

PERIGORD: You'll find it, Jules.

JULES: I? I'd be the first one to be surprised. [*He stops
walking.*] Let's calm down again. Let's try to think
of something else. [*Pause.*] Well?

TAVERNIER [*surprised*]: Well?

JULES: Think.

PERIGORD: Yes, chief. What about?

JULES: I've just told you; of something else.

PERIGORD: We're doing so.

JULES: Think out loud.

PERIGORD [*thinking*]: I wonder if the landlord is going
to repair the roof. My lawyer advises me to take him
to court. He says I'd win, but I'm not so sure. . . .

TAVERNIER [*thinking*]: Now where did I put that book
of Metro tickets? I've looked in all my pockets. Yet
I can remember standing at the booking office this
morning. I took out my money with my right hand,
and with my left hand . . .

JULES: Thieves!

TAVERNIER [*coming to with a start*]: What's that?

JULES: At last I have seen into your hearts. And what
do I find? Roofs and Metro tickets. Your thoughts
belong to me. I pay for them, and you steal them
from me. [*To the SECRETARY*] I want Sibilot. Phone
his home.

SECRETARY: Very good, Jules. [*She dials a number and waits.* JULES *stops walking about and waits.*] No reply.

JULES: I'll throw him out. I won't hear a word from him. I'll throw him out. Whom shall I put in his place?

TAVERNIER: Thierry Maulnier?

JULES: No.

TAVERNIER: He has a noble mind, and a great fear of Communism.

JULES: Yes, but he can't put his fear across to others, and I know of two people who, as a result of reading his articles, rushed straight out and joined the C.P. [*Quickly*] Any news of Nekrassov?

PERIGORD: He's reported in Rome.

JULES: In Rome? That's done it. The Christian Democrats will grab him.

TAVERNIER: Tass has issued a denial, saying he's been in the Crimea for the past fortnight.

JULES: Why not? Let's give him a miss for the moment. Await confirmation, and above all say nothing about him being in Rome. With the crisis in the French hotel industry, this isn't the time to give a boost to the Italian tourist trade. Come, boys, let's take the bull by the horns. Ready?

TAVERNIER } Ready, Jules.
PERIGORD }

JULES: What do we need to launch a campaign?

PERIGORD: Headline type.

JULES: We have it. What else?

TAVERNIER: A victim.

JULES: We have that too. What else?

PERIGORD: A theme.

JULES: A theme, that's it. A theme.

TAVERNIER: A striking theme.

PERIGORD: Shattering.

TAVERNIER: Terror and sex appeal.

PERIGORD: Corpses and legs.

JULES: Ah, I see the theme, I see it.

TAVERNIER: So do we, chief, we see it. . . .

JULES: I've got it.

PERIGORD: We've got it. We've got it.

JULES: You've got it too?

TAVERNIER: Of course.

JULES: Well, tell me what it is.

PERIGORD: Well, it's, it's a general view. . . .

TAVERNIER: An overall picture that it's difficult to . . .

PERIGORD: I think we'll have to find someone for the . . .

TAVERNIER: And then, for the . . .

JULES: So! [*He sits down weakly, then speaks sharply.*] Are you laughing, boys?

TAVERNIER [*indignant*]: Us, Jules, how could you think that?

JULES: You'd better not laugh. If I go under, you go with me.

[*The phone rings and the* SECRETARY *answers it.*]

SECRETARY: Yes? Send him right up. [JULES] It's Sibilot.

JULES: At last.

[JULES *packs* TAVERNIER, PERIGORD, *and the* SECRETARY *off as* SIBILOT *enters with* GEORGES.]

JULES: My dear Sibilot. Do you know I'd almost given you up?

SIBILOT: You must excuse me, chief.

JULES: Oh, forget it. Who's this chap?

SIBILOT: A man.

JULES: I can see that.

SIBILOT: I'll tell you about him in a moment.

JULES: Good morning, sir. [GEORGES *does not reply.*] Is he deaf?

SIBILOT: He doesn't understand French.

JULES [*to* GEORGES, *showing him a chair*] Sit down. [*He makes a gesture to indicate sitting, but* GEORGES *remains standing.*] Doesn't he understand signs, either?

SIBILOT: Not when you make them in French.

[GEORGES *walks away and takes from the desk a news-paper which carries the large headline "Nekrassov Disappears."*]

JULES: Does he read?

SIBILOT: No, no, no, he's looking at the pictures.

JULES [*placing his hands on* SIBILOT'S *shoulders*]: Well, old chap?

SIBILOT [*not understanding*]: Well?

JULES: Your idea?

SIBILOT: Ah, my idea. [*Pause.*] Chief, I'm so sorry. . . .

JULES [*angrily*]: Haven't you an idea?

SIBILOT: I mean . . . [GEORGES, *behind* JULES, *signs to him to speak.*] Oh, yes, chief, of course I have.

JULES: You don't seem very proud of it.

SIBILOT: No. [*Sign from* GEORGES.] But I . . . I am a modest man.

JULES: Is it good at least? [*Sign from* GEORGES.]

SIBILOT [*mutters*]: Ah, too good.

JULES: And you complain? Sibilot, you're a card. [*Pause.*] Let's hear it. [*Silence.*] Aren't you going to tell me? [*Silent exhortations from* GEORGES. SIBILOT *remains silent.*] I see what it is. You want your raise. Listen, old chap, you shall have it, I promise. You'll have it if your idea pleases me.

SIBILOT: Oh, no! No, no.

JULES: What's the matter?

SIBILOT: I don't want a raise.

JULES: Very well, I won't give you a raise. There. Are you satisfied? [*Exasperated*] Are you going to talk? [SIBILOT *points to* GEORGES.] Well?

SIBILOT: That's it.

JULES: What do you mean . . . it?

SIBILOT: Him.

JULES [*not understanding*]: He is it?

SIBILOT: He's the idea.

JULES: Your idea is him?

SIBILOT: It's not MY idea. No, no, it's not MY idea.

JULES: Is it his then? [GEORGES *signifies "No."*]

SIBILOT [*obeying* GEORGES]: No.

JULES [*pointing to* GEORGES]: Then, who is he?

SIBILOT: A . . . a foreigner.

JULES: What nationality?

SIBILOT: Er . . . [*Closing his eyes*] Soviet.

JULES [*disappointed*]: I see.

SIBILOT [*taking heart*]: A Soviet official who has broken through the Iron Curtain.

JULES: A high official? [GEORGES *signs to* SIBILOT *to say yes.*]

SIBILOT: Yes . . . [*Becomes terrified again.*] That is, no. Just ordinary. Very ordinary. Quite a small official.

JULES: In short, a nobody.

SIBILOT: That's it. [*Furious gestures from* GEORGES.]

JULES: And what do you expect me to do with your Soviet official?

SIBILOT: Nothing, chief, absolutely nothing.

JULES: What do you mean, nothing? Why have you brought him?

SIBILOT [*recovering*]: I thought he could supply us with . . .

JULES: What?

SIBILOT: Some information.

JULES: Information! On what? Soviet typewriters? Desk lamps and ventilators? Sibilot, I instruct you to launch a campaign on a grand scale, and you offer me tittle-tattle that *Paix et Liberté* wouldn't touch. Do you know how many Soviet officials choosing freedom I've had through this office since Kravchenko? A hundred and twenty-two, my friend, genuine and fake. We have had Embassy chauffeurs, children's nurses, a plumber, and seventeen hairdressers, and I've got into the habit of sending them to my colleague Robinet of *Figaro*, who doesn't turn his nose up at small stuff. Result—a general slump in Kravchenkos. The latest one, Demidoff, a great administrator, a distinguished economist, hardly ran to four issues and even Bidault no longer invites

him to dinner. [*He goes toward* GEORGES.] Ah, sir, so
you've broken through the Iron Curtain. You've
chosen freedom! Good, give him a bowl of soup and
send him to the Salvation Army.

SIBILOT: Bravo, chief.

JULES: Eh?

SIBILOT: You don't know how pleased I am. [*Revenge-
fully, to* GEORGES] To the Salvation Army, to the
Salvation Army.

JULES: Is that all? Have you no other idea?

SIBILOT [*rubbing his hands*]: None, absolutely none.

JULES: Idiot! You're fired.

SIBILOT: Yes, chief, thank you, chief. Good-by, chief.
[*He is about to go out, but* GEORGES *stops him and
brings him back to the middle of the room.*]

GEORGES: Allow me.

JULES: So you speak French?

GEORGES: My mother was French.

JULES [*to* SIBILOT]: So you lied as well. Clear out!

GEORGES [*holding* SIBILOT]: I kept it from him as a precaution.

JULES: I congratulate you, sir, on your good command
of our beautiful language, but in French, as in
Russian, you're wasting my time, and I'd be pleased
if you'd leave my office at once.

GEORGES: That's what I intend to do. [*To* SIBILOT.] To
France-Soir, quickly.

JULES: To *France-Soir*? Why?

GEORGES [*making to go out*]: Your time is too precious.
I shan't bother you any more.

JULES [*standing in front of him*]: I know my colleague
Lazareff well and I can assure you he'll do nothing
for you.

GEORGES: I don't doubt that. I don't expect anything
from anyone, and no one can help me, but I can do
plenty for his paper and for your country.

JULES: You?

GEORGES: Yes.

JULES: Well, what can you do?

GEORGES: You'll be wasting your time.

SIBILOT: Yes, chief, yes. You'll be wasting your time. [*To* GEORGES] Let's go.

JULES: Sibilot, keep your place! [*To* GEORGES] I have five minutes to spare after all, and it shan't be said that I sent anyone away without giving him a hearing.

GEORGES: Are you asking me to stay?

JULES: Yes, I'm asking you to stay.

GEORGES: Very well. [*He dives under the table and crawls on hands and knees.*]

JULES: What are you doing?

GEORGES: No hidden tape recorders? No microphones? Good. [*He stands up.*] Have you courage?

JULES: I think so.

GEORGES: If I speak your life will be in danger.

JULES: My life in danger? Don't speak. Yes, speak. Speak up.

GEORGES: Look at me. Closer. [*Pause.*] Well?

JULES: Well, what?

GEORGES: You published my photo on your front page.

JULES: Oh, you know how it is with photos. [*Looking at him*] I don't see anything.

GEORGES [*putting a black patch over his right eye*]: And like this?

JULES: Nekrassov!

GEORGES: Don't shout, or you're lost. There are seven armed Communists in your offices.

JULES: Their names.

GEORGES: Later. There's no immediate danger.

JULES: Nekrassov! [*To* SIBILOT] And you didn't tell me!

SIBILOT: I swear I didn't know, chief. I swear it.

JULES: Nekrassov. My dear Sibilot, you're a genius.

SIBILOT: Oh no, chief, that's going too far.

JULES: Nekrassov. Well, I adore you. [*He embraces* SIBILOT.]

SIBILOT [*slumping into an armchair*]: It's all up. [*He faints.*]

GEORGES [*looking at him with contempt*]: Alone at last. [*To* JULES) Let's talk.

JULES: I wouldn't want to hurt your feelings, but . . .

GEORGES: You couldn't, even if you wanted to.

JULES: What proof have I that you're Nekrassov?

GEORGES [*laughing*]: None.

JULES: None?

GEORGES: None at all. Search me.

JULES: I don't . . .

GEORGES [*violently*]: I tell you to search me!

JULES: All right! All right! [*He searches him.*]

GEORGES: What have you found?

JULES: Nothing.

GEORGES: There, that's conclusive proof! What would an impostor do? He would show you his passport, a family allowance book, a Soviet identity card. Now you, Palotin, if you were Nekrassov and if you decided to break through the Iron Curtain, would you be stupid enough to keep your papers on you?

JULES: Good heavens, no!

GEORGES: That's what I had to prove to you.

JULES: I hadn't thought of that! [*Thoughtfully*] But in that case anybody could . . .

GEORGES: Do I look like anybody?

JULES: You've already been reported in Italy. . . .

GEORGES: Of course! And tomorrow I'll be reported in Greece, in Spain, and in Western Germany. Bring those impostors here. Bring them all here, and the truth will stagger you. The real Nekrassov has lived for thirty-five years in the Red Hell. He has the eyes of a man who has been at death's door. Look at my eyes! The real Nekrassov has killed 118 people with his own hands. Look at my hands! The real Nekrassov has carried on a ten-year reign of terror. Bring here all the impostors who have stolen my name, and you will see which of us is the most terrible. [*Abruptly*] Are you afraid?

JULES: I . . . [*He retreats, and almost knocks the attaché case over.*]

GEORGES: Don't touch the case!

JULES: Oh! [*Looking at the attaché case.*] What's inside?

GEORGES: You'll know later. Keep away. [JULES *recoils.*] You see. You're afraid, already. Ah, I'll make you die of fright, all of you. You'll see whether I'm Nekrassov.

JULES: I'm afraid; and yet I hesitate. What if you were deceiving me!

GEORGES: Well?

JULES: The paper would be sunk. [*The telephone rings.*] Hello? Good morning, my dear Minister. Yes, yes. Of course. Nothing is more important to me than this campaign. Yes, yes. No, I'm not in the least unwilling. I ask you to give me a few hours. Just a few hours. Yes, something new. I can't explain over the phone, but I beg you not to worry. . . . He's hung up. [*He puts the receiver back.*]

GEORGES [*ironically*]: You badly need me to be Nekrassov.

JULES: Unfortunately.

GEORGES: Then, I am.

JULES: I beg your pardon.

GEORGES: Have you forgotten your catechism? The proof of God is man's need of Him.

JULES: You know the catechism?

GEORGES: We know everything. Come on, Jules, you heard the Minister. If I'm not Nekrassov, then you're no longer Palotin, the Napoleon of the press. Are you Palotin?

JULES: Yes.

GEORGES: Do you want to remain so?

JULES: Yes.

GEORGES: Then I'm Nekrassov.

SIBILOT [*coming to*]: He's lying, chief; he's lying.

JULES [*throwing himself on* SIBILOT]: Idiot! Blunderer!

Fool! Who asked you to butt in? This man is Nekrassov, and he's just proved it to me.

SIBILOT: He's proved it to you?

JULES: Conclusively.

SIBILOT: But I swear to you . . .

JULES: Clear out; this moment!

GEORGES: Go, Sibilot, old chap. Wait for me outside.
[*They push* SIBILOT *out.*]

SIBILOT [*going out*]: I'm not responsible for anything.
I wash my hands of the whole affair. [*The door
closes behind him.*]

GEORGES: To work.

JULES: You do know everything, don't you?

GEORGES: About what?

JULES: About the Soviet Union?

GEORGES: Of course.

JULES: And it's . . . terrible?

GEORGES [*earnestly*]: Ah!

JULES: Could you tell me. . . .

GEORGES: Nothing. Call your Board of Directors, I want
to put forward certain conditions.

JULES: You could make them to me. . . .

GEORGES: Nothing, I tell you. Call the Board.

JULES [*taking up the telephone*]: Hello. My dear chairman, the surprise is here. It's waiting for you. Yes,
yes, yes. Oh, yes. You see that I always keep my
promises. [*He hangs up.*] He's furious, the old skunk.

GEORGES: Why?

JULES: He was hoping to have my scalp.

GEORGES: What's his name?

JULES: Mouton.

GEORGES: I'll remember that name. [*Pause.*]

JULES: Still, while we're waiting, I would have
liked . . .

GEORGES: A sample of what I know. Good. Well, I can
reveal the details of the famous Plan C for the occupation of France in the event of world war.

JULES: There's a Plan C for the occupation of France?

GEORGES: You mentioned it in your paper last year.

JULES: Did we? Oh, yes, but I was awaiting confirmation.

GEORGES: Didn't you write at that time that Plan C contained the list of people to be shot? Well, you were right.

JULES: They're going to shoot Frenchmen?

GEORGES: A hundred thousand.

JULES: A hundred thousand!

GEORGES: Did you write that? Yes or no.

JULES: You know, one writes without thinking. Have you the list?

GEORGES: I have learned the first twenty thousand names off by heart.

JULES: Let me have some. Who'll be shot? Herriot?

GEORGES: Of course.

JULES: So he's among them; he who has always been so friendly to you. I find that very funny. Who else? All the Ministers, I suppose?

GEORGES: And all former Ministers.

JULES: That is, one out of every four deputies.

GEORGES: Excuse me! One deputy out of four will be shot as a former Minister, but the other three will be executed for other reasons.

JULES: I see, all the Assembly will be shot, except the Communists.

GEORGES: Except the Communists? Why?

JULES: Well, because the Communists, after all . . .

GEORGES: Huh!

JULES: But . . .

GEORGES: You're not yet sufficiently hardened to bear the truth. I shall make my revelations gradually.

JULES: Do you know Perdrière?

GEORGES: Perdrière?

JULES: We'd like him to be on the list.

GEORGES: Oh! Why!

JULES: Oh, nothing. Give him something to think about. If he isn't, it's just too bad.

GEORGES: I know of two Perdrières. One is called René. . . .

JULES: That's not the one.

GEORGES: Good, for he's not on the list.

JULES: Ours is called Henri. A Radical-Socialist.

GEORGES: Henri, that's it. That's the one I know. A deputy?

JULES: No, he was, but he isn't any longer. He's a candidate in the Seine-et-Marne by-election.

GEORGES: That's the one. You may be sure he won't be spared. As a matter of fact, he's in the first batch.

JULES: You give me great pleasure. And who among the journalists?

GEORGES: Plenty.

JULES: Who, for example?

GEORGES: You!

JULES: Me? [*He rushes to the telephone.*] Perigord, six-column-spread headline: "Nekrassov in Paris. Our editor on the black list." Funny, eh? Yes, very funny. [*He hangs up. Suddenly*] Me? Shot? It's impermissible.

GEORGES: Huh!

JULES: But I'm a Government paper. There'll still be a government when the Soviets occupy Paris.

GEORGES: No doubt.

JULES: Well?

GEORGES: They'll keep *Soir à Paris*, but liquidate the staff.

JULES: Shot. The funniest thing is that it isn't entirely unpleasing to me. It gives me standing, stature. I'm growing. [*He stands before the mirror.*] Shot. Shot. That man [*pointing to himself in the glass*] will be shot. Heh, I see myself with different eyes. Do you know what it reminds me of? The day I received the Legion of Honor. [*Turning to* GEORGES] What about the Board of Directors?

GEORGES: You have only to name them, and I'll tell you what their fate will be.

JULES: Here they are. [*The members of the Board enter.*]

MOUTON: My dear Palotin.

JULES: Gentlemen, here is my surprise.

ALL: Nekrassov.

JULES: Yes, Nekrassov. Nekrassov, who has supplied me with conclusive proofs of his identity, who speaks French, and who is ready to make stupendous revelations. Among other things, he knows by heart the names of twenty thousand people whom the Soviet command is going to shoot when the Russian troops occupy France.

[*Murmurs from the Board—"Names," "Are we on the list?", "Am I?".*]

GEORGES: I would like to know these gentlemen by name.

JULES: Naturally. [*Pointing to the nearest one*] M. Lerminier.

LERMINIER: Delighted.

GEORGES: Executed.

JULES: M. Charivet.

CHARIVET: Delighted.

GEORGES: Executed.

JULES: M. Nerciat.

NERCIAT: Delighted.

GEORGES: Executed.

NERCIAT: I am honored, sir.

JULES: M. Bergerat.

BERGERAT: Delighted.

GEORGES: Executed.

BERGERAT: Which proves, sir, that I am a good Frenchman.

JULES: And this is our chairman, M. Mouton.

GEORGES: Mouton?

JULES: Mouton.

GEORGES: Ah.

MOUTON [*coming forward*]: Delighted.

GEORGES: Delighted.

MOUTON: I beg your pardon.

GEORGES: I said delighted.

MOUTON [*laughing*]: You've made a slip?

GEORGES: No.

MOUTON: You meant to say executed.

GEORGES: I meant to say what I said.

MOUTON: Mouton, m o u t o n.

JULES: M for Mary, O for Oswald . . .

GEORGES: It's no use. M. Mouton is not on the list.

MOUTON: You must have forgotten me.

GEORGES: I forget nothing.

MOUTON: And why, if you please, do they not deign to
execute me?

GEORGES: I don't know.

MOUTON: Ah, no, that's not good enough. I don't know
you, yet you dishonor me, and refuse to give an
explanation. I demand . . .

GEORGES: The press black list was supplied to us by
the Ministry of Information without comment.

NERCIAT: My dear Mouton.

MOUTON: It's a joke, gentlemen, merely a joke.

GEORGES: A Soviet Minister never jokes.

MOUTON: This is extremely unpleasant. Friends, tell
M. Nekrassov that my position makes me the declared
victim of the Soviet Government. Ex-soldier of the
1914 war, Croix de Guerre, chairman of four boards
of directors, and I . . . [*He pauses.*] Well, say something! [*Embarrassed silence.*] Palotin, you don't intend to publish this list?

JULES: I shall do what you decide, gentlemen.

BERGERAT: Naturally, it must be published.

MOUTON: Well, see that you put my name in. The
public wouldn't understand it if I were left out. You
would have protests.

[GEORGES *takes up his hat as if to go.*]

JULES: Where are you going?

GEORGES: To *France-Soir*.

NERCIAT: To *France-Soir*? But . . .

GEORGES: I never lie, that's my strong point. You will
publish my statements without altering them, or I
shall go elsewhere.

MOUTON: Go to the devil! We'll manage without you.

NERCIAT: You're mad, my dear chap.

CHARIVET: Completely mad.

BERGERAT [to GEORGES]: Please excuse us, sir.

LERMINIER: Our chairman is rather upset . . .

CHARIVET: And you can understand how he feels.

NERCIAT: But we want the Truth.

BERGERAT: The whole Truth.

LERMINIER: And nothing but the Truth.

JULES: And we shall print whatever you wish.

MOUTON: I tell you this man is an impostor. [Murmurs
of disapproval.]

GEORGES: If I were you, sir, I wouldn't talk of impostors,
for it is you who are not on the black list, not I.

MOUTON [to the members of the Board]: Are you going
to allow your chairman to be insulted? [Silence.] The
heart of man is a shell filled with rottenness. You have
known me for twenty years, but what does that matter
to you? It is enough for an unknown to utter one
word, and you turn on me. On me, your friend.

CHARIVET: My dear Mouton.

MOUTON: Away! Your soul is poisoned by greed. You
hope to thrill old women with sensational and un-
founded revelations. You hope to double the circulation. You sacrifice twenty years of friendship for a
golden calf. Well, gentlemen, publish your revelations. I shall leave you, and I am going to find proof
that this man is a liar, an impostor, a crook. Pray
God that I find it before the whole world laughs at
your stupidity. Good-by. When we meet again you
will be in sackcloth and ashes, and you will beat your
breasts, begging my forgiveness. [He goes out.]

NERCIAT: Well.

CHARIVET: Well, well.

LERMINIER: Well, well, well.

BERGERAT: Well, well, well, well.

GEORGES: Ah, gentlemen, you'll see plenty more like that.

NERCIAT: That will suit us.

BERGERAT: Speak! Quickly!

GEORGES: One moment, gentlemen. I have some explanations to give you, and some conditions to make.

LERMINIER: We're listening.

GEORGES: To avoid any misunderstandings, I must first tell you that I despise you.

NERCIAT: Of course, that goes without saying.

BERGERAT: And we would not expect it to be otherwise.

GEORGES: To me, you are the abject props of capitalism.

CHARIVET: Bravo!

GEORGES: I left my country when I saw that the masters of the Kremlin were betraying the principles of the revolution; but don't deceive yourselves, I remain a Communist, OUT AND OUT!

LERMINIER: That does you credit.

NERCIAT: And we respect your candor.

GEORGES: In providing you with the means to overthrow the Soviet régime, I am not unaware of the fact that I am prolonging bourgeois society for a century.

ALL: Bravo! Very good! Very good!

GEORGES: I resign myself to it with sorrow because my main objective is to purify the revolutionary movement. Let it die, if it must. In a hundred years' time it will rise again from its ashes. Then we shall resume our march forward, and then, I am pleased to tell you, we shall win.

NERCIAT: That's right. In a hundred years' time!

CHARIVET: In a hundred years' time, the deluge.

NERCIAT: For my part I've always said that we're going toward Socialism. The thing is to go slowly.

BERGERAT: Till then, let's have only one aim: down with the Soviet Union!

CHARIVET: Bravo! Down with the Soviet Union!

LERMINIER: Down with the Soviet Union! Down with the Soviet Union! Smash the French Communist Party!

[*The* SECRETARY *brings in glasses of champagne on a tray.*]

NERCIAT [*raising his glass*]: To the health of our dear enemy.

GEORGES: Your health. [*They clink glasses and drink.*] Here are my conditions. I want nothing for myself.

LERMINIER: Nothing?

GEORGES: Nothing. A flat in the Avenue Georges V, two bodyguards, decent clothes, and pocket money.

NERCIAT: Agreed.

GEORGES: I shall dictate my memoirs and revelations to a reliable journalist.

JULES: Would you like Cartier?

GEORGES: I want Sibilot.

JULES: Splendid.

GEORGES: I understand that he's getting a raise. What does he earn?

JULES: Er . . . seventy thousand a month.

GEORGES: You bloodsucker. You'll treble it.

JULES: It's a promise.

GEORGES: To work, then.

JULES: What about the seven Communists?

GEORGES: Which Communists?

JULES: The armed ones in my offices.

GEORGES: Ah . . . er . . .

NERCIAT: There are Communists on *Soir à Paris*?

JULES [*to* GEORGES]: Seven. Isn't that right?

GEORGES: Yes, yes, yes, that's the figure I gave you?

NERCIAT: Unbelievable. How did they slip in?

GEORGES [*laughing*]: You are naïve.

LERMINIER: Armed? What arms?

GEORGES: The usual armament: Grenades, plastic bombs, revolvers. And there are probably a few tommy guns under the floor.

NERCIAT: But it's highly dangerous.

GEORGES: No, not for the moment. Let's get back to our subject.

BERGERAT: But that is our subject.

NERCIAT: Allow me to tell you that your first task must be to prevent the massacre of the Board of Directors.

GEORGES: They are not thinking of massacring you.

NERCIAT: Then why these arms?

GEORGES: Pah!

NERCIAT [*astonished*]: Pah?

GEORGES: You'll know everything in its turn.

JULES: In any case, we must clean up the staff. M. Nekrassov will give us these seven names.

LERMINIER [*laughing*]: Of course he'll give them to us. He will be pleased to do so.

BERGERAT: The swine. The swine. The swine. The swine.

LERMINIER: You'll throw them out this very morning.

JULES: And what if they shoot at me?

BERGERAT: Phone the police and get a carload of inspectors.

NERCIAT: Handcuffs on at the first move.

CHARIVET: You can bet they won't dare do a thing.

LERMINIER: In any event, it would be good to give their addresses to the Ministry of the Interior. We mustn't neglect the usual official channels.

NERCIAT: I should think not. Palotin, you'll telephone all our morning and evening colleagues to give them the list. Those scoundrels must be black-listed out of the profession.

LERMINIER: Away with them!

CHARIVET: Let them starve, the pirates.

BERGERAT: Unfortunately, their Party will feed them.

CHARIVET: Their Party? They'll drop them as soon as it's known that they've been found out.

NERCIAT: You don't think they'll throw bombs in revenge?

CHARIVET: The building will be guarded by Security
   Guards.
LERMINIER: By the troops if necessary.
CHARIVET: For six months.
LERMINIER: For a year. For two years.
BERGERAT: Ah, they are looking for trouble, those
   rogues. Well, they'll get it, I assure you.
NERCIAT [*turning to* GEORGES]: We're listening, my
   dear sir.
GEORGES: I'm afraid I can't remember all the names.
JULES [*to the* SECRETARY]: Fifi, get the staff list. [FIFI
   brings the list. He takes it and speaks to GEORGES.]
   This will refresh your memory. You have only to
   point them out.
   [*He puts the list on his desk and signs to* GEORGES
   to sit. GEORGES *sits at the desk. Long silence.*]
BERGERAT: Well?
GEORGES [*unable to restrain himself*]: I'm not a stool
   pigeon.
LERMINIER [*surprised*]: Pardon?
GEORGES [*aware of his slip*]: I meant to say . . .
BERGERAT [*suspicious*]: You refuse to give the names?
GEORGES [*recovering himself*]: You shall have names by
   the thousand. But you are children. In order to un-
   cover a handful of enemies you are going to give the
   alarm to all the others. The situation is much more
   serious than you think. Do you know that the whole
   world has been tricked, that you have been living in
   a fool's paradise, and that if fate had not put me on
   your track you would have died in ignorance?
BERGERAT: In ignorance of what?
GEORGES: Ah, how can I make myself understood? The
   minds of men are not ready to receive the truth, and
   I cannot reveal everything at once. [*Suddenly.*] Look
   at this case. [*He takes the attaché case and puts it on*
   JULES'S *desk.*] Is there anything remarkable about it?
JULES: Nothing.

GEORGES: Pardon me, what is remarkable about it is that it is like all such cases.

NERCIAT: You would swear it was made in France.

GEORGES: It was *not* made in France. But you can get one like it at the Hotel de Ville market for three thousand five hundred francs.

LERMINIER [*amazed*]: Oh.

BERGERAT: Well I never!

GEORGES: Is there anything so terrible about this harmless object, *without any distinguishing mark?* It looks so ordinary that it becomes suspect for that very reason. Shielded from investigations and descriptions by its insignificance, its appearance instantly strikes one with horror, but one immediately forgets its form and even its color. [*Pause.*] Do you know what they put in it? Fifteen pounds of radioactive powder. In each of your large towns a Communist is stationed with an attaché case just like this one. It may be a churchwarden, an inspector of finances, a teacher of dancing and deportment, or it may be an old maid who lives with her cats and her birds. The case lies in the attic, underneath other cases, amid trunks, old stoves, and wicker baskets. Who would think of looking for it there? But on the appointed day the same code message will be delivered in every French town, and all the cases will be opened at the same time. You can guess the result—a hundred thousand deaths a day.

ALL [*in terror*]: Ah!

GEORGES: You see. [*He goes to open the case.*]

BERGERAT [*cries out*]: Don't open it.

GEORGES: Don't be afraid. It's empty. [*He opens it.*] Come closer. Look at the trade-mark, see the handles, touch the leather. . . .[*The members of the Board come nearer, one by one, and timidly touch the case.*]

BERGERAT [*touching it*]: It's true. It's true, by heavens.

LERMINIER [*also touching it*]: What a nightmare!

CHARIVET: The scoundrels!

NERCIAT: The scoundrels, the scoundrels, the scoundrels.

BERGERAT: Ah, how I hate them.

LERMINIER: All the same, we're not going to die like
rats. What shall we do?

GEORGES: Have detection instruments made. We still
have a few months. [*Pause.*] Do you understand? Are
you convinced that it will be hard going, and that
you risk losing all by punishing a few unimportant
underlings?

CHARIVET: Give us their names, just the same.

LERMINIER: We promise you that their suspicions won't
be aroused.

BERGERAT: But we want to know with whom we have
to deal . . .

NERCIAT: And face the danger. . . .

GEORGES: Very well. But you must follow my instruc-
tions to the letter. I have just thought of a way of
rendering them harmless.

BERGERAT: What is it?

GEORGES: Raise their wages. [*Murmurs.*] Announce that
you are delighted with their services, and that you are
giving them a substantial rise.

BERGERAT: You think we can corrupt them?

GEORGES: No, not that. But you will bring them into
disrepute in the eyes of their leaders. This inexplica-
ble favor will make it appear that they have turned
traitor.

LERMINIER: Are you sure?

GEORGES: It's obvious. Then you won't have to worry
about them any more. The hand of Moscow will see
that they are liquidated. [*He goes to the desk, sits
down, and points to seven names on the list.*]

NERCIAT: No, no, no. I won't give these scoundrels a
raise.

LERMINIER: Take it easy, Nerciat.

BERGERAT: You've been told that it's in order to get
rid of them more easily.

CHARIVET: We embrace them to strangle them.

NERCIAT: Very well, do as you please.

[GEORGES *rises and holds out the list.*]

JULES [*reading*]: Samivel? It's not possible.

BERGERAT: Madame Castagnié? Who would have thought it?

GEORGES [*interrupting them with a gesture*]: This is nothing. I shall raise the curtain a little at a time, and you will see the world as it is. When you mistrust your own son, your wife, your father, when you look in the mirror and ask yourself whether you aren't a Communist without knowing it, then you are beginning to get a glimpse of the truth. [*He sits down at* JULES's *desk and invites them to be seated.*] Be seated, gentlemen, and let's get to work. We haven't much time if we wish to save France.

CURTAIN

SCENE V

The drawing room of a flat in the Avenue Georges V. Curtains and shutters closed. Three doors. One on the left leads to the bedroom, the second, at the back, to the bathroom, and the third, on the right, to the hall. Enormous bunches of flowers are heaped up in vases against the wall. Roses predominate.

A messenger enters carrying a bouquet of roses in a basket, followed by the two BODYGUARDS *who have their revolvers thrust into his back. He puts the basket down and hurries out backward through the door on the right with his hands in the air. The door on the left opens, and* GEORGES *comes in, wearing his dressing gown and yawning.*

GEORGES: What is it?

FIRST BODYGUARD: Flowers.

GEORGES [*yawning and coming over to the flowers*]:
More roses. Open the window.

FIRST BODYGUARD: No.

GEORGES: No?

FIRST BODYGUARD: Dangerous.

GEORGES: Aren't you aware that these roses stink?

FIRST BODYGUARD: No.

GEORGES: You're lucky. [*He takes the envelope and
opens it.*] "With the passionate admiration of a
group of French women." They admire me, eh?

FIRST BODYGUARD: Yes.

GEORGES: They love me?

FIRST BODYGUARD: Yes.

GEORGES: A little, a lot, passionately?

FIRST BODYGUARD: Passionately.

GEORGES: To love so much, they must hate like hell.

FIRST BODYGUARD: Hate whom?

GEORGES: The others. [*He bends over the flowers.*] Let
us breathe the perfume of hate. [*He inhales.*] It is
powerful, vague, and foul. [*Pointing to the flowers.*]
There's the danger. [*The guards draw their revolvers
and aim at the flowers.*] Don't shoot. It's a thousand-
headed hydra. A thousand red angry little heads
which throw out their odor and yell themselves hoarse
before they die. These roses exhale poison.

SECOND BODYGUARD: Poison?

FIRST BODYGUARD [*to* SECOND BODYGUARD]: Toxicology
laboratory, Gutenberg 66–21.

[SECOND BODYGUARD *goes toward the telephone.*]

GEORGES: Too late. Everything is poisoned here because
I work in hatred.

FIRST BODYGUARD [*not understanding*]: Hatred?

GEORGES: Ah! It's an evil-smelling passion. But if you
want to pull strings, you must pick them up wherever
they may be, even from the dungheap. I have them
all in my hands. It is my day of glory, and long live

hatred, since it is to hatred that I owe my power.
Don't look at me like that. I am a poet. Are you employed to understand me or to protect me?

FIRST BODYGUARD: Protect.

GEORGES: Well then, protect, protect. What time is it?

FIRST BODYGUARD [*with a quick look at his wrist watch*]:
Half-past five.

GEORGES: What's the weather like?

SECOND BODYGUARD [*goes to consult the barometer near
the window*]: Set fair.

GEORGES: Temperature.

FIRST BODYGUARD [*goes to consult a thermometer, hanging on the wall*]: Seventy.

GEORGES: A fine spring afternoon. A clear sky, the sun
flashing on the window panes. A peaceful crowd,
dressed in light clothes, is walking up and down the
Champ-Elysées, the afternoon sunlight softening
their faces. Oh well, I'm glad to know it. [*He yawns.*]
What's the timetable?

FIRST BODYGUARD [*consulting a list*]: Five-forty, Sibilot,
for memoirs.

GEORGES: Next?

FIRST BODYGUARD: Six-thirty, a woman journalist from
Figaro.

GEORGES: Search her carefully. You never know. Next?

FIRST BODYGUARD: A dance.

GEORGES: Where?

FIRST BODYGUARD: At Madame Bounoumi's.

GEORGES: *She's* giving a dance?

FIRST BODYGUARD: To celebrate the withdrawal of her
rival, M. Perdrière.

GEORGES: I'll celebrate it. It's my doing. Away you go!
[*They go out.* GEORGES *closes the door and yawns.*]

GEORGES [*goes to the mirror, looks at himself, and puts
out his tongue*]: Disturbed sleep, coated tongue, loss
of appetite—too many official banquets. And I'm
hardly ever out of doors. [*He yawns.*] A touch of
boredom. It's quite natural. One is always alone at

the height of one's power. Little transparent men,
I see into your hearts, but you can't see into mine.
[*Telephone rings.*] Hello? Speaking. I'm a rat? Ah,
it's you, my dear sir; the man who thinks I'm a rat.
This is the thirty-seventh time you've been good
enough to tell me. Please understand that I'm now
fully aware of your sentiments, and don't bother to
tell me again. He's hung up. [*He starts to walk
about.*] A rat. A traitor to the Party. It's easily said.
Who is a rat? Not I, Georges de Valéra, who has
never been a Communist, and never betrayed anyone.
Not Nekrassov, who is on a cure in the Crimea,
thinking no evil. My unknown caller is thus talking
rot. [*He goes toward the mirror.*] Oh, for my childhood! Oh, the pretty painted wooden sledge. My
father would sit me on it. Off we go. Bells ringing,
whips cracking, the snow . . . [SIBILOT *has entered
during this speech.*]

SIBILOT: What are you doing there?

GEORGES: Practicing my scales.

SIBILOT: What scales?

GEORGES: I'm lying to myself.

SIBILOT: To yourself as well?

GEORGES: To myself first. I am much too cynical, and
therefore it is absolutely necessary that I fool myself
first. Sibilot, I'm dying. You find me in my death
throes.

SIBILOT: Eh?

GEORGES: I die Valéra to be reborn Nekrassov.

SIBILOT: You are not Nekrassov!

GEORGES: I am he from head to toe, from maturity back
to childhood.

SIBILOT: From head to toe you are a miserable crook,
who is heading for disaster and will drag me down
with him unless I put things right.

GEORGES: Ho! Ho! [*Looking at him.*] So you're cook-
ing up some stupid gesture of honesty which will
finish us. Well, speak! What do you want to do?

SIBILOT: Confess the truth!

GEORGES: Idiot! Everything was going so well.

SIBILOT: I made up my mind a little while ago, and I have come to warn you. Tomorrow morning at eleven o'clock I shall throw myself at Jules's feet and confess everything. You have seventeen hours in which to prepare your escape.

GEORGES: Are you mad? Perdrière stands down, *Soir à Paris* has doubled its circulation, you get 210,000 francs a month, and you want to give yourself up?

SIBILOT: Yes!

GEORGES: Think of me, you wretch! I have supreme power, I am the giddy peak of the Atlantic Pact, I hold war and peace in my hands, I am writing history. Sibilot, I am writing history and you choose this moment to throw a banana skin in my path! Do you know that I have dreamed of this moment all my life? Take advantage of my power. You will be my Faust. Do you want money? Beauty? Youth? . . .

SIBILOT [*shrugging his shoulders*]: Youth . . .

GEORGES: Why not? It's a question of money. [SIBILOT *goes to leave.*] Where are you going?

SIBILOT: To give myself up.

GEORGES: You'll give yourself up, don't fear; you'll give yourself up. But there is no hurry. We have time for a chat. [*He brings* SIBILOT *back to the center of the room.*] You're scared to death, my friend. What's wrong?

SIBILOT: Mouton will have your scalp, and mine too. He's joined up with Demidoff, a real Kravchenko, confirmed by Tass Agency, and he's looking for you. If they find you—and they're bound to—Demidoff will denounce you as a fraud. We'll be done for.

GEORGES: Is that all? Let them bring your Demidoff. I'll take care of him. I'll take them all on—industrialists and bankers, magistrates and ministers, American colonists, Soviet refugees, and I'll make them dance. Is that all?

SIBILOT: Oh, no! There's much worse!

GEORGES: So much the better. I shall enjoy myself.

SIBILOT: Nekrassov has just made a statement on the radio.

GEORGES: I have? I swear to you that I have done nothing of the kind.

SIBILOT: It's not a question of you. I said Nekrassov.

GEORGES: I'm Nekrassov.

SIBILOT: I am talking of the one in the Crimea.

GEORGES: Now why do you want to meddle? You are French, Sibilot. Keep your own doorstep clean, and don't concern yourself with what is happening in the Crimea.

SIBILOT: He claims he is cured, and that he will be back in Moscow toward the end of this week.

GEORGES: So?

SIBILOT: So! We're done for.

GEORGES: Done for? Because a Bolshevik spouts nonsense over the microphone? You, Sibilot, you, the champion of anticommunism, you put trust in those people? Really, I'm disappointed in you.

SIBILOT: You'll be less disappointed on Friday, when all the ambassadors and foreign journalists, invited to the Opera House in Moscow, see Nekrassov in person, in the government box.

GEORGES: On Friday . . .

SIBILOT: Yes.

GEORGES: It's been announced?

SIBILOT: Yes.

GEORGES: Well, they'll be seeing my double. For I have a double over there just like the other ministers. We're so afraid of attempts on our lives that we have doubles to take our places at official ceremonies. Now take that down. It's to be published tomorrow. Wait. I must give it just that amusing little touch of authenticity. I must invent the anecdote that couldn't be invented. Here it is. My double resembled me so much that we couldn't be told apart at ten paces.

Unfortunately, when they brought him to me I noticed that he had a glass eye. Imagine my embarrassment! I had to spread the rumor that an incurable disease had destroyed my right eye. That's the origin of this patch. You will caption it, "Nekrassov wears an eye patch because his double had a glass eye." Have you taken it down?

SIBILOT: What good will that do?

GEORGES [*with authority*]: Write! [SIBILOT *shrugs his shoulders, takes out his pencil, and writes some notes.*] You'll conclude with this challenge. When the alleged Nekrassov takes his place in the government box, let him take off his eye patch if he dares. I shall take mine off at the same time in front of oculists and doctors. They will all see that I have two perfectly good eyes. As for the other, if he has only one eye, we have the conclusive proof that this man is not me. Are you writing?

SIBILOT: I am writing, but it will do no good.

GEORGES: Why?

SIBILOT: Because I want to give myself up. I am honest, do you understand. Honest! honest! honest!

GEORGES: Who's said anything to the contrary?

SIBILOT: I have. I! I!

GEORGES: You?

SIBILOT: I, who tell myself a hundred times a day that I am a dishonest man! I lie, Georges, I lie as I breathe. I lie to my readers, to my own daughter, and to my boss.

GEORGES: Didn't you lie, then, before you knew me?

SIBILOT: I lied, but I had the approval of my superiors. I manufactured lies that were controlled, that bore the official stamp, big news lies, lies in the public interest.

GEORGES: And aren't your present lies in the public interest? They're no different.

SIBILOT: Perhaps not, but I make them without Government guarantee. I am the only one on earth who

knows who you are. That's what is suffocating me.
My crime is not that I lie but that I'm alone in it.

GEORGES: Well, go on, then! What are you waiting for?
Run and give yourself up! [SIBILOT *takes a step.*] One
simple question, one only, and I'll let you go. What
are you going to tell Jules?

SIBILOT: All.

GEORGES: All what?

SIBILOT: You know very well.

GEORGES: But I don't. . . .

SIBILOT: Well, I shall tell him that I have lied and
that you are not *really* Nekrassov.

GEORGES: I don't understand.

SIBILOT: It's quite clear.

GEORGES: What do you mean, *really?* [SIBILOT *shrugs
his shoulders.*] Are you *really* Sibilot?

SIBILOT: Yes, I am Sibilot, yes. I am that unfortunate
father whom you have corrupted, you wretch, and
who is bringing shame upon his gray hairs.

GEORGES: Prove it.

SIBILOT: I have papers.

GEORGES: So have I.

SIBILOT: Mine are genuine.

GEORGES: So are mine. Do you want to see the alien's
permit issued to me by the Prefecture of Police?

SIBILOT: It's worthless.

GEORGES: Why, if you please?

SIBILOT: Because you're not Nekrassov.

GEORGES: And are your papers valid?

SIBILOT: Yes.

GEORGES: Why?

SIBILOT: Because I am Sibilot.

GEORGES: You see. It's not the papers that prove identity.

SIBILOT: Well, no, it's not the papers.

GEORGES: Well, then? Prove to me that you are Sibilot.

SIBILOT: Everybody will tell you.

GEORGES: Everybody means how many people?

SIBILOT: A hundred, two hundred, I don't know, a thousand . . .

GEORGES: A thousand people take you for Sibilot; you would like me to accept their word for it; and yet you challenge the evidence of two million readers who take me for Nekrassov?

SIBILOT: It's not the same. . . .

GEORGES: Are you trying to silence this tremendous clamor which makes me the hero of freedom and the champion of the West? Do you set your miserable individual conviction against the collective faith which is stirring those good citizens? It's you whose identity is not even established. It is you who are heedlessly going to drive two million men and women to despair. Courage! Ruin your boss! Go even further! Bring about the downfall of the government. I know who'll get the biggest laugh out of it.

SIBILOT: Who?

GEORGES: The Communists, of course. Would you work for them?

SIBILOT [*anxiously*]: Look here, Georges!

GEORGES: You would not be the first one they've paid to demoralize public opinion.

SIBILOT: I swear to you.

GEORGES: How do you expect me to believe you; you who have just confessed your profound dishonesty?

SIBILOT [*in a panic*]: You must believe me. I am a dishonest honest man, but I am not a dishonest man.

GEORGES: Agreed. But then . . . then . . . Ho, ho! What's happening to you? My poor friend, I wonder if I will be able to get you out of this.

SIBILOT: What is it now?

GEORGES: How can I make you understand? Listen? Put on one side forty million Frenchmen, our contemporaries, sure that they are living right in the middle of the twentieth century, and on the other side one individual, a single one, who obstinately declares that he is the Emperor Charles the Fifth. What would you call that man?

SIBILOT: A lunatic.

GEORGES: And that is exactly what you are; you who are trying to deny the truths founded on universal assent.

SIBILOT: Georges!

GEORGES: Do you know what Jules will do to you when he sees his oldest employee throw himself on his knees and beg him to bury his newspaper with his own hands?

SIBILOT: He'll fire me.

GEORGES: Will he? Nothing of the kind. He'll have you locked up.

SIBILOT [*utterly crushed*]: Oh!

GEORGES: Here, read this telegram. It's from McCarthy, offering me an engagement as a permanent witness. Here are congratulations from Franco, from the Fruit Company, a cordial word from Adenauer, a letter signed by Senator Borgeaud. In New York my revelations have sent shares up on the Stock Exchange. There is a boom everywhere in the war industries. There are great interests at stake. Nekassov is no longer only me. It is a generic term for the dividends drawn by the shareholders in armament factories. That's objectivity, old chap. There's reality for you. But it will crush you if you try to stop it. Good-by, my poor chap. I was very fond of you. [SIBILOT *does not budge.*] What are you waiting for?

SIBILOT [*in a choked voice*]: Can I be cured?

GEORGES: Of your madness?

SIBILOT: Yes.

GEORGES: I hope it's not too late.

SIBILOT: But if you were to undertake to cure me, Georges? If you'd be good enough to do it?

GEORGES: Eh! I am not a psychiatrist. [*Pause.*] It's true, it is mainly a question of re-education. Do you wish me to re-educate you?

SIBILOT: Please.

GEORGES: Let us begin. Assume an attitude of honesty.

SIBILOT: I don't know how.

GEORGES: Sink down deeply into this armchair. Put your feet on this pouf. Put this rose in your buttonhole. Take this cigar. [*He hands a mirror to* SIBILOT.]

SIBILOT [*looking at himself*]: Well?

GEORGES: Do you feel more honest now?

SIBILOT: Perhaps a little more.

GEORGES: Good. Leave aside your personal convictions, and tell yourself that they are false because no one shares them. They exile you. Rejoin the flock. Remember that you are a good Frenchman. Look at me with the countless eyes of the Frenchmen who read us. Whom do you see?

SIBILOT: Nekrassov.

GEORGES: Now I shall go out and come in again. Put yourself in a state of sincerity. Collective sincerity, of course. When I open the door, you will say to me: "Good afternoon, Nikita. . . ." [*He goes out.* SIBILOT *settles down, drinks and smokes.* GEORGES *returns.*]

SIBILOT: Good afternoon, Nikita.

GEORGES: Good afternoon, Sibilot.

SIBILOT: Did I say it well?

GEORGES: Not too bad. [*He walks round* SIBILOT'S *armchair, suddenly bends over him, and puts his hands over* SIBILOT'S *eyes.*] Cuckoo!

SIBILOT: Leave me alone . . . Nikita!

GEORGES: You're improving. Get up. [SIBILOT *gets up with his back to* GEORGES. GEORGES *tickles him.*]

SIBILOT [*wriggling and laughing in spite of himself*] Stop it . . . Nikita.

GEORGES: I'll cure you all right. [*Pause.*] Enough for today. To work. Chapter eight: "Tragic Interview with Stalin."

SIBILOT [*writing*]: "Tragic Interview with Stalin." [*The telephone rings.*]

GEORGES [*lifting the receiver*]: Hallo! Yes? Madame Castagnié? Just a moment. [*Turning to* SIBILOT] I seem to know that name.

SIBILOT: She's a typist at *Soir à Paris.*

GEORGES: Ah! One of the seven they wanted to sack and that I got a raise for? What does she want with me?

SIBILOT: Jules must have sent her!

GEORGES [*into the telephone*]: Send her up. [*Turning to* SIBILOT *after putting the receiver down.*] "Tragic Interview with Stalin." Subheading: "I escape from the Kremlin in a sedan chair."

SIBILOT: Nikita! Is that possible?

GEORGES: Nothing more natural. I am being chased. I hide in one of the rooms of the museum where carriages are kept. In a corner is a sedan chair. . . .

A BODYGUARD: Madame Castagnié.

GEORGES: Show her in. And don't frighten her with your revolvers. [*Enter* MME CASTAGNIÉ.]

SIBILOT [*going toward her*]: Good afternoon, Mme Castagnié.

MME CASTAGNIÉ: Good afternoon, M. Sibilot. I didn't expect to find you here. [*Pointing to* GEORGES] Is he Nekrassov?

SIBILOT: That's him. That's our Nikita.

GEORGES: My compliments, madam.

MME CASTAGNIÉ: I would like to know why you had me dismissed?

GEORGES: What?

SIBILOT: You've been dismissed?

MME CASTAGNIÉ [*to* GEORGES]: You know very well I have, sir. Don't pretend to be surprised.

GEORGES: I swear to you . . .

MME CASTAGNIÉ: M. Palotin sent for me just now. The directors were there, and they didn't look at all pleased.

GEORGES: What happened?

MME CASTAGNIÉ: What happened? They dismissed me.

GEORGES: But why? For what reason?

MME CASTAGNIÉ: When I asked them their reason, I thought they would jump down my throat. They all shouted in my face. "Ask Nekrassov! Nekrassov will tell you."

GEORGES: Swine! The swine!

MME CASTAGNIÉ: I don't wish to be rude, but if you have given them bad reports about me, you are an even bigger swine than they are.

GEORGES: But I haven't said anything! I haven't done anything! I don't even know you.

MME CASTAGNIÉ: They told me to ask you so you must know something.

GEORGES: Madam, have you ever seen me before today?

MME CASTAGNIÉ: Never.

GEORGES: There you are, then.

MME CASTAGNIÉ: What does that prove? Perhaps you wanted my job.

GEORGES: What would I do with it? That's a joke, madam, and a joke in bad taste.

MME CASTAGNIÉ: I am a widow with a sick daughter. If I lose my job we shall be unable to live. That is nothing to joke about.

GEORGES: You are right. [*Turning to* SIBILOT] The swine!

MME CASTAGNIÉ: What have you got against me?

GEORGES: Nothing. On the contrary, Sibilot is my witness that I wanted to get you a raise.

MME CASTAGNIÉ: Get me a raise?

GEORGES: Yes.

MME CASTAGNIÉ: You're a liar. Just now you said you didn't know me!

GEORGES: I know you slightly. I know the loyal service you've given for more than twenty years. . . .

MME CASTAGNIÉ: I've only been there for five years.

GEORGES: I'll admit everything to you. Important political reasons . . .

MME CASTAGNIÉ: I've never meddled in politics. And my poor husband wouldn't even hear of it. I'm not well educated, sir, but I'm not a complete fool, and I'm not taken in by your fancy talk.

GEORGES [*lifting up the receiver*]: Give me *Soir à Paris*. [*To* MME CASTAGNIÉ.] It's a misunderstanding! Just a misunderstanding! [*Into the telephone*] Hullo, *Soir à Paris*? I want to talk to the editor. Yes. Nekrassov speaking. [*To* MME CASTAGNIÉ] You'll get your job back. I'll see to that. And with apologies.

MME CASTAGNIÉ: I don't want apologies. I want my job back.

GEORGES: Hello? He's not in his office? Is he in the building? Where? Right. Tell him to call me as soon as he gets back. [*He puts the receiver down.*] Everything will be all right, madam, everything will be all right. In the meantime, will you allow me. . . . [*Taking out his wallet.*]

MME CASTAGNIÉ: I don't want charity.

GEORGES: What do you mean? It's not a question of charity, but a friendly gift. . . .

MME CASTAGNIÉ: You're no friend of mine.

GEORGES: Not now. But I shall be when you've got your job back. You'll see! You'll see! [*Suddenly remembering.*] Oh! [*Pause.*] What about the others?

MME CASTAGNIÉ: The others?

GEORGES: Do you know if anyone else has been dismissed?

MME CASTAGNIÉ: So I heard.

GEORGES: Who? How many?

MME CASTAGNIÉ: I don't know. They gave me my notice. I took things and left.

GEORGES [*turning to* SIBILOT]: You'll see, they'll have sacked them too. The dirty swine! The bunglers! I thought I had frightened them. Well, Sibilot, old chap, there's a lesson for you. Fear is less powerful than hate. [*He picks up his hat.*] I must put an end

to this nonsense. Come with us, madam. As if I
would attack the poor! It would be the first time in
my life. I'm going to take Jules by the throat. . . .
[*He opens the door.* A BODYGUARD *appears.*]

THE BODYGUARD: No!

GEORGES: What do you mean, no? I want to go out.

BODYGUARD: Impossible! It's dangerous!

GEORGES: All right, you come with us.

BODYGUARD: Not allowed.

GEORGES: And suppose I try to get out?

BODYGUARD [*with a short derisive laugh*]: Ha!

GEORGES: Oh! go away. I shan't go out. [*To* SIBILOT]
Go with Mme Castagnié, find Jules and tell him that
I think this is beyond a joke. Unless all those who
have been dismissed are reinstated within twenty-four
hours, I shall give the rest of my memoirs to *Figaro*.
Please go, madam, I may have wronged you, but it
was unintentional, and I give you my word that you
will be compensated for it. [SIBILOT *and* MME CASTAG-
NIÉ *go out.*] Aren't you going to say good-by to me,
Sibilot?

SIBILOT: Good-by.

GEORGES: Good-by, whom?

SIBILOT: Good-by, Nikita.

GEORGES: Call me as soon as you've seen Jules.

Sacked . . . [*He starts walking up and down.*] It's
not my fault. Hatred is an emotion which is completely foreign to me. I am obliged to play with
terrible forces, of which I know little. But I'll adapt
myself, I'll . . . Sacked! . . . And they only had
their wages to live on. They may have saved twenty
thousand francs. . . . I'll shower them with gold.
The Board of Directors will meet them at the door
with roses, with armfuls of roses. . . .

A BODYGUARD [*entering*]: The woman journalist from
Figaro.

GEORGES: Show her in! Wait, is she pretty?

BODYGUARD: Not bad.

[GEORGES *goes over to the mirror, puts on his black patch, looks at himself for a moment, takes it off, and puts it in his pocket.*]

GEORGES: Tell her to come in. [VERONIQUE *comes in.*]

GEORGES [*seeing* VERONIQUE]: Ah! [*He puts up his hands.*]

VERONIQUE: I see you recognize me.

GEORGES [*lowering his hands*]: Yes. Are you on *Figaro* now?

VERONIQUE: Yes.

GEORGES: I thought you were with the Communists.

VERONIQUE: Things change. Where's Nekrassov?

GEORGES: He's . . . he's gone out.

VERONIQUE: I'll wait for him. [*She sits down.*] Are you waiting for him, too?

GEORGES: Me? No.

VERONIQUE: What are you doing here?

GEORGES: Oh, you know, I never do very much. [*Pause.*] [*He gets up.*] I'm beginning to think Nekrassov won't come back this evening. You would do better to call again tomorrow.

VERONIQUE: All right. [GEORGES *seems relieved. She pulls a notebook out of her bag.*] But while I have you here, you can tell me what you know about him.

GEORGES: I don't know anything.

VERONIQUE: Go on with you! You must be a close friend of his, or his bodyguards wouldn't leave you in his room while he's out.

GEORGES [*disconcerted*]: A close friend of his? Of course, it's . . . it's quite natural. [*Pause.*] I'm his cousin.

VERONIQUE: Ah, ah!

GEORGES: My mother's sister remained in Russia. Nekrassov is her son. The other morning I found a newspaper on a bench. I picked it up and saw that my cousin had just arrived. . . .

VERONIQUE: You managed to contact him, you talked to him about the family, he welcomed you with open arms. . . .

GEORGES: And took me on as his secretary.

VERONIQUE: Secretary! Pah!

GEORGES: Wait a minute. I became his secretary for a lark. Within a fortnight I'll make off with the cash.

VERONIQUE: In the meantime you are helping him with his filthy work.

GEORGES: Filthy work! Look here, sister, you don't come from *Figaro*.

VERONIQUE: Of course not!

GEORGES: You've lied again.

VERONIQUE: Yes.

GEORGES: Did your progressive paper send you?

VERONIQUE: No. I came on my own. [*Pause.*] Well, tell me about him. What does he do when you're together.

GEORGES: He drinks.

VERONIQUE: What does he say?

GEORGES: He says nothing.

VERONIQUE: Nothing?

GEORGES: Nothing.

VERONIQUE: Does he never talk about his wife? Or the three sons he left over there?

GEORGES: Leave me alone! [*Pause.*] He took me into his confidence, and I don't want to betray him.

VERONIQUE: You don't want to betray him, and yet you're going to rob him.

GEORGES: I'm going to rob him, but that doesn't prevent me from having my feelings. I've always had a liking for my victims. My profession demands it. How can I rob people without being pleasant, and how can I be pleasant to them unless I like them? All my affairs have started off with my victim and I taking a sudden fancy to each other.

VERONIQUE: And you took a sudden fancy to Nekrassov?

GEORGES: Oh, only a very small one.

VERONIQUE: To that skunk?

GEORGES: I forbid you to . . .

VERONIQUE: Are you defending him?

GEORGES: I am not defending him. I am shocked to hear
  you say such a word.

VERONIQUE: Isn't he a skunk?

GEORGES: Perhaps he is. But you have no right to condemn a man you don't even know.

VERONIQUE: I know him very well.

GEORGES: You know him?

VERONIQUE [*quietly*]: Naturally! Since it's you.

GEORGES [*repeating, without understanding*]: Ah! Since
  it's me. [*Jumping to his feet*] It's not me! It's not me!
  It's not me! [*She looks at him, smiling.*] Where did
  you get that idea?

VERONIQUE: My father . . .

GEORGES: He told you?

VERONIQUE: No.

GEORGES: Well?

VERONIQUE: Like all those whose speciality is lying in
  public, he lies very badly in private.

GEORGES: Your father's in his dotage! [*He walks across
  the room.*] Well! Suppose for a moment, just to
  please you, that I were Nekrassov.

VERONIQUE: Thank you.

GEORGES: What would you do if I were? Give me away
  to the cops?

VERONIQUE: Did I give you away the other evening?

GEORGES: Would you publish my real name in your rag?

VERONIQUE: That would be a blunder at this stage. We
  lack proof, and no one would believe us.

GEORGES [*reassured*]: In fact, I have rendered my enemies powerless?

VERONIQUE: For the moment, yes, we are powerless.

GEORGES [*laughing*]: Left, right, center, I have you all
  in my hands. You must be bursting with anger, my
  beauty! Secret for secret. Yes, I am Nekrassov. Do
  you remember the miserable bum you took into your
  room? What a long way I have come since! What a
  dizzy leap! [*He stops, and looks at her.*] Come, now,
  what are you really doing here?

VERONIQUE: I came here to tell you that you're a skunk.

GEORGES: Drop the fine words; I am proof against them. Every morning *l'Humanité* calls me a slimy rat.

VERONIQUE: They are wrong.

GEORGES: I'm glad to hear you say so.

VERONIQUE: You're not a slimy rat. You're a skunk.

GEORGES: Oh, you get on my nerves. [*He takes a few steps and comes back to* VERONIQUE.] Now, if a high Soviet official were to come to Paris with the express purpose of giving weapons to the enemies of his people and his Party, then I agree that he would be a skunk. I would go even further; he'd be a dirty louse. But I've never been a Minister nor a member of the CP. I was six months old when I left the Soviet Union, and my father was a White Russian. I am under no obligation to anyone. When you knew me, I was a smart crook, working alone; a self-made man. Well, I still am. Yesterday I was selling bogus properties and bogus titles, and today I am selling bogus secrets on Russia. Where's the difference? [*She doesn't reply.*] You're not particularly fond of the rich. Is it such a great crime to cheat them?

VERONIQUE: Do you really think you are cheating the rich?

GEORGES: Who's paying my tailor and my hotel bills? Who paid for my Jaguar?

VERONIQUE: Why are they paying?

GEORGES: Because I sell them my concoctions.

VERONIQUE: Why are they buying them?

GEORGES: Because . . . Damn it all! That's their business. I don't know.

VERONIQUE: They're buying them in order to palm them off on the poor.

GEORGES: The poor? What have the poor got to do with it?

VERONIQUE: Do you think that the readers of *Soir à Paris* are millionaires? [*Taking a paper from her bag.*]

"Nekrassov states that the Russian worker is the most wretched on earth." Did you say that?

GEORGES: Yes. Yesterday.

VERONIQUE: For whom did you say it? For the poor or for the rich?

GEORGES: How should I know? For everybody. For nobody. It's a joke of no importance.

VERONIQUE: Here, yes, among the roses. In any case no one in the Avenue Georges V has ever seen any workers. But do you know what that will mean in Billancourt?

GEORGES: I . . .

VERONIQUE: "Leave capitalism alone, or you will relapse into barbarism. The bourgeois world has its defects but it is the best of all possible worlds. Whatever your poverty, try to make the best of it, for you can be sure you'll never see anything better, and thank heaven that you weren't born in the Soviet Union."

GEORGES: Don't tell me they think that. They're not so stupid.

VERONIQUE: Luckily they aren't, or they would have no alternative but to drink themselves to death or put their heads in the gas oven. But even if one in a thousand swallowed your claptrap, you would be a murderer. You've been well taken in, my poor Georges.

GEORGES: Me?

VERONIQUE: Of course. You thought you were stealing money from the rich, but you are earning it. With what disdain, the other night, you refused the job I offered you: "Me, work!" Well, you have employers now, and they're making you work hard.

GEORGES: It isn't true.

VERONIQUE: Come, come. You know very well you are being paid to drive the poor to despair.

GEORGES: Listen!

VERONIQUE [*taking no notice*]: You were an innocent

crook with no malice—half dandy, half poet. Do you
know what they've made of you? A muckraker! You
will either come to despise yourself or you will have
to become vicious.

GEORGES [*under his breath*]: The rotten swine!

VERONIQUE: Who is pulling the strings this time?

GEORGES: The strings?

VERONIQUE: Yes.

GEORGES: Well . . . [*Mastering himself*] I am, as usual.

VERONIQUE: So you are setting out deliberately to drive
the poor to despair.

GEORGES: No.

VERONIQUE: Then, they're making use of you?

GEORGES: Nobody can make use of me—no one in the
world.

VERONIQUE: Nevertheless, you must make the choice;
you are either a dupe or a criminal.

GEORGES: The choice is quickly made. Long live crime!

VERONIQUE: Georges!

GEORGES: I drive the poor to despair? So what? Everybody for himself. Let them defend themselves. I
slander the Soviet Union? I do it on purpose. I want
to destroy Communism in the West. As for your
workers, whether they're in Billancourt or in Moscow,
I . . .

VERONIQUE: You see, Georges, you see, you're becoming vicious.

GEORGES: Vicious or good, I don't care. Good and evil,
I take it all upon myself. I am responsible for everything.

VERONIQUE [*showing him an article in* Soir à Paris]:
Even for this article?

GEORGES: Of course! What's it about? [*Reading*] "M.
Nekrassov states that he is well acquainted with
Robert Duval and Charles Maistre." I've never said
any such thing.

VERONIQUE: I thought not. As a matter of fact, that's
why I came to see you.

GEORGES: Robert Duval? Charles Maistre? Never heard the names.

VERONIQUE: They're journalists on our paper. They have written against German rearmament.

GEORGES: Well?

VERONIQUE: You are expected to say that the Soviet Union paid them.

GEORGES: And if I do?

VERONIQUE: They will be committed to a military court on a charge of treason.

GEORGES: Don't worry. They won't get a word out of me. Do you believe me?

VERONIQUE: I believe you, but take care. They are no longer satisfied with your lies. They're beginning to make them up for you.

GEORGES: You mean that paragraph? That's some over-zealous subordinate. I'll have him put in his place. I'm seeing Jules very shortly, and I'll order him to publish a denial.

VERONIQUE [without conviction]: Do what you can.

GEORGES: Is that all you have to tell me?

VERONIQUE: That's all.

GEORGES: Good night.

VERONIQUE: Good night. [With her hand on the door knob.] I hope you won't become too vicious. [She goes out.]

GEORGES [to himself]: That girl doesn't understand politics. A schoolkid, that's what she is! [Addressing the door] Did you think I'd fall into your trap? I always do the opposite of what I'm expected to do. [He crosses the room and goes to find his dinner jacket.] We'll drive Billancourt to despair! I'll think up some terrible slogans. [He goes to fetch a shirt and collar. He chants] Drive Billancourt to despair! Drive Billancourt to despair! [The telephone rings. He picks up the receiver.] Oh, it's you, Sibilot? Well? What? No, that's not possible. You've seen Jules himself? You told him that I insisted? Idiot! You didn't know how to speak to him. You're frightened of him. You ought to have browbeaten him. He's going to old Mother Bounoumi's tonight? Good. I'll speak to him myself. [*He hangs up.*] They refuse me something! Me? [*He sinks into an armchair, temporarily overwhelmed.*] I've had a bellyful of politics. A bellyful! [*He gets up suddenly.*] They're after me. They're after me. Well, I have the feeling they are going to meet up with me. I accept the challenge. Indeed, I welcome it. It's time I exerted my authority. [*Laughing.*] I'll send them scuttling underground. [*Telephone. He picks up the receiver.*] Hallo! You again! Excuse me, but who are you? Ah! Splendid! I was just thinking of you. A rat? Quite right, my dear sir. The lowest of rats. I go even further—a skunk. I get minor employees sacked. I hand journalists over to the cops. I drive the poor to despair, and that's only a beginning. My coming revelations will provoke a string of suicides. Now you, of course, you are an honest man. I can see that from here. Your clothes are worn, you take the Metro four times a day, you smell of poverty. The deserving are not rewarded. I have money, glory, women. If you meet me when I am in my Jaguar, look out! I purposely graze the sidewalk to splash honest people. [*He hangs up.*] This time I was the one who hung up first. [*He laughs.*] She was right, that girl, and I'm going to become vicious. [*Kicking the rose baskets over one by one.*] Vicious, vicious, vicious!

CURTAIN

SCENE VI

A small drawing room being used as a buffet, and open-
ing by means of double doors to a large room at the
back. To the left is a window half-open to the night.
Between the window and the doors there are tables
covered with white linen and laid with platters of
petits fours and sandwiches. Through the doors at
the back, guests can be seen passing backward and
forward. There is a crowd in the large room. Some
pass across the open doorway without entering the
small drawing room, while others come and help
themselves at the buffet bar. To the right is a closed
door. There is very little furniture apart from a few
armchairs and tables, the room having been cleared
so that the guests can circulate freely. BAUDOUIN *and*
CHAPUIS *enter and introduce themselves to* MME
BOUNOUMI.

BAUDOUIN [*stopping* MME BOUNOUMI *and introducing*
CHAPUIS *to her*]: Chapuis.
CHAPUIS [*introducing* BAUDOUIN]: Baudouin.
   [BAUDOUIN *and* CHAPUIS *take out their cards and*
   present them to her simultaneously.]
BAUDOUIN AND CHAPUIS: Inspectors from the Depart-
   ment of Defense of the State.
BAUDOUIN: Specially entrusted by the Government . . .
CHAPUIS: To protect Nekrassov.
BAUDOUIN: Has he arrived?
MME BOUNOUMI: Not yet.
CHAPUIS: It would be unwise to bring him in through
   the front door.
BAUDOUIN: And, if you will allow us, we will give
   orders . . .

CHAPUIS: That he should come in through the servants'
entrance . . .

BAUDOUIN [*pointing to the door on right*]: Which leads
directly here.

MME BOUNOUMI: Why all these precautions?

CHAPUIS [*confidentially*]: The possibility of an attack
cannot be ruled out.

MME BOUNOUMI [*taken aback*]: Ah!

BAUDOUIN: Don't be afraid, madam.

CHAPUIS: We are here!

BAUDOUIN: We are here!

[*They go out. Guests enter, among them* PERDRIÈRE,
JULES *and* NERCIAT.]

NERCIAT [*putting his arm around* PERDRIÈRE]: Here is
the prodigal son. I drink to Perdrière.

ALL: To Perdrière.

PERDRIÈRE: Ladies and gentlemen, I was an old fool.
I drink to the man sent by Providence to strip the
wool from my eyes.

JULES [*smiling*]: Thank you.

PERDRIÈRE [*not hearing him*]: To Nekrassov!

ALL: To Nekrassov!

JULES [*annoyed, to* NERCIAT]: Nekrassov! [*Shrugging
his shoulders.*] What would he be without me? [*He
moves away.*]

NERCIAT [*to* PERDRIÈRE]: Say something about Palotin.

PERDRIÈRE: I drink to Palotin who . . . who had the
courage to publish Nekrassov's revelations.

SOME OF THE GUESTS: To Palotin.

JULES [*annoyed*]: People don't understand the power
of the press.

PERDRIÈRE: I want to take this opportunity to ask you
all to forgive my obstinacy, my stupid blindness,
my . . . [*He starts to cry. They surround him.*]

MME BOUNOUMI: My good Perdrière.

PERDRIÈRE [*trying to gain control of himself*]: I ask you
to forgive me! I ask you to forgive me. . . .

MME BOUNOUMI: Let's forget the past. [*She embraces him.*]

JULES [*to the* PHOTOGRAPHERS]: Photos! [PERIGORD *is passing with a glass in his hand,* JULES *seizes him by the arm, spilling the contents of the glass.*] Here!

PERIGORD: The idea, chief?

JULES: Yes, the idea. Take down everything I say. [*To* ALL] Friends . . . [*They fall silent.*] You, I, Perdrière, all of us here, are future victims of the firing squad. I suggest that we transform this already memorable evening into a great moment in the tide of human affairs. Let us form the FFSV Club.

ALL: Bravo! Long live the FFSV.

JULES: During the evening we shall elect a provisional committee to draw up the constitution. I propose myself as president. [*Applause. To* PERIGORD] Front page tomorrow, with my picture. [*Enter* MOUTON *and* DEMIDOFF.] What's this? Mouton? [*He goes over to* NERCIAT *and* MME BOUNOUMI.] Did you see?

MME BOUNOUMI: Oh!

NERCIAT: Who invited him?

MME BOUNOUMI: I didn't. Who's that with him?

JULES: Demidoff.

NERCIAT: That Russian? They have a nerve.

MME BOUNOUMI: My God! The attack!

NERCIAT: What?

MME BOUNOUMI: The possibility of an attack cannot be ruled out.

NERCIAT: They've come to . . .

MME BOUNOUMI: I don't know, but I have two inspectors here, and I am going to warn them.

[*During this conversation,* MOUTON *has come forward among the guests. He smiles or holds out his hand to each in turn, but they all turn their backs on him. He bows to* MME BOUNOUMI.]

MOUTON: Madam . . .

MME BOUNOUMI: No, sir. No! We are all going to die.

We wish you a long life, but we do not acknowledge you.

THE GUESTS [*going out*]: Long live the FFSV! [*Turning to* MOUTON] Down with the future executioners! [*They go out.*]

[MOUTON *and* DEMIDOFF *are left alone.* DEMIDOFF *goes to the buffet and helps himself liberally.*]

MOUTON: Rather a chilly reception.

DEMIDOFF [*eating*]: I didn't notice.

MOUTON: You never notice anything.

DEMIDOFF: Never! I am here to expose the Soviet régime, and not to observe the customs of the West. [*He eats and drinks.*]

MOUTON: They take me for a Communist.

DEMIDOFF: That's strange.

MOUTON: No, it isn't strange. It's tragic, but it's not strange. You have to put yourself in their place. [*Suddenly*] Feodor Petrovitch!

DEMIDOFF: What?

MOUTON: That list is false, isn't it?

DEMIDOFF: What list?

MOUTON: The list of Future Firing Squad Victims . . .

DEMIDOFF: I know nothing about it.

MOUTON [*startled*]: What?

DEMIDOFF: I shall know when I've seen Nekrassov.

MOUTON: Then it could be true?

DEMIDOFF: Yes, if Nekrassov is really Nekrassov.

MOUTON: I should be lost. [DEMIDOFF *shrugs his shoulders.*] What a position! If the Russians spare me, it must be because I am useful to them.

DEMIDOFF: Obviously.

MOUTON: But that's absurd! Feodor Petrovitch, you can't possibly believe . . .

DEMIDOFF: I believe nothing.

MOUTON: My life speaks for me. I have done nothing but fight them.

DEMIDOFF: How do you know?

MOUTON [*shaken*]: Ah! How do I know? To be quite

frank, sometimes I feel I am being maneuvred. I can
recall some disturbing things. [*Pause.*] My secretary
was a Communist. As soon as I found out, I dismissed him.

DEMIDOFF: Was there a scandal?

MOUTON: Yes.

DEMIDOFF: You played their game.

MOUTON: Do you think so, too? I didn't dare admit it
to myself. [*Pause.*] During the last strikes, I was the
only one in my industry who granted nothing to the
strikers. Result: three months later, in the trade
union elections . . .

DEMIDOFF: All your workers voted for the CGT.

MOUTON: How do you know?

DEMIDOFF: It's the usual thing.

MOUTON: In fact, I gave them recruits. [DEMIDOFF *nods
in agreement.*] Alas! [*Pause.*] Feodor Petrovitch, look
at me! Have I the face of an honest man?

DEMIDOFF: Of an honest Westerner.

MOUTON: But a fine-looking old man?

DEMIDOFF: An old Westerner.

MOUTON: Could I be a Communist with a face like
this?

DEMIDOFF: Why not?

MOUTON: I built myself up with my own hands, by my
own work.

DEMIDOFF: By luck, also.

MOUTON [*smiling slightly at his memories*]: Yes, I have
had some luck.

DEMIDOFF: They were behind your luck.

MOUTON [*with a start*]: They?

DEMIDOFF: It is possible that they made your fortune
because you were their tool without knowing it. Perhaps they arranged everything in such a way that,
unknown to you, your every action produced the
effect desired by Moscow.

MOUTON: Does that mean that my whole life has been
nothing but a sham? [DEMIDOFF *nods agreement.*

Suddenly] Tell me frankly; if everyone takes me for a revolutionary, and if all my actions are those required by the Party, what distinguishes me from an active Party member?

DEMIDOFF: You? Nothing. You are an *objective* Communist.

MOUTON: Objective! Objective! [*He takes out his handkerchief and wipes his forehead.*] Ah! I am possessed! [*Suddenly looking at the handkerchief.*] What's this? The two of us are talking and I find myself waving a handkerchief. How did it get into my hand?

DEMIDOFF: You took it out of your pocket.

MOUTON [*distraught*]: I did? . . . Oh, it is worse than I thought. They have arranged for me to give the signal. What signal? To whom? To you, perhaps? How do I know that you aren't one of their agents? [DEMIDOFF *shrugs his shoulders.*] You see, I am going mad. Feodor Petrovitch, I beseech you, decommunize me!

DEMIDOFF: How?

MOUTON: Expose that blackguard!

DEMIDOFF: I will expose him if he is an impostor.

MOUTON [*seized with anxiety again*]: And suppose he really is Nekrassov?

DEMIDOFF: I shall brand him before everyone.

MOUTON [*with a start*]: Brand him . . .

DEMIDOFF: I contend that all those who left the Soviet Union after I did are accomplices of the régime. [GOBLET *appears in the background.*]

MOUTON: It would be best to treat him as an impostor, in any case.

DEMIDOFF: No. [*At a gesture from* MOUTON.] Say no more. I am incorruptible. [MOUTON *sighs.*] Well! What are you waiting for? Let's find him.

MOUTON: I have called in an inspector of the Sûreté. If the so-called Nekrassov is an impostor, he must be an international crook. I will have him imprisoned

for life. [*Seeing* GOBLET] Ah, Goblet! Come in.
[GOBLET *approaches*.] Look very carefully at the man
I shall point out to you. If he is an habitual criminal,
arrest him on the spot.

GOBLET: In front of everyone?

MOUTON: Naturally.

GOBLET: Is he handsome?

MOUTON: Not bad.

GOBLET [*sadly*]: People will again see the contrast.

MOUTON: What contrast?

GOBLET: Between his face and mine.

MOUTON: You refuse? . . .

GOBLET: I don't refuse at all. Only I prefer to arrest
them when they are ugly, that's all.
[BAUDOUIN *and* CHAPUIS *enter*.]

BAUDOUIN [*showing his card to* MOUTON]: Defense of
the State. Your papers?

MOUTON: I am Charles Mouton. . . .

CHAPUIS: Exactly! A suspect.
[MOUTON *shrugs his shoulders and shows his identity
card*.]

BAUDOUIN: Good. [*To* DEMIDOFF] We know you. Off
with you, and don't forget that you are a guest of
France.

CHAPUIS: Make yourselves scarce. We want to have a
word with Inspector Goblet.

MOUTON [*to* GOBLET]: We're going to have a look
around to see if our man has arrived. Wait for us
here.
[DEMIDOFF *and* MOUTON *go out*.]

BAUDOUIN [*barring* GOBLET's *exit*]: And what are *you*
up to here?

GOBLET: I'm a guest.

CHAPUIS: A guest? With a mug like yours?

GOBLET: If you're guests with your mugs, why shouldn't
I be with mine?

CHAPUIS: We're not guests. We're here on duty.

GOBLET: Well, so am I!

BAUDOUIN: Would you be looking for someone?

GOBLET: That's none of your business.

CHAPUIS: But look here, friend . . .

BAUDOUIN: Leave him alone; he's a close one. [*To* GOBLET] Look for anyone you like, but don't get in our way.

GOBLET [*bewildered*]: In your way?

CHAPUIS: Lay off Nekrassov!

GOBLET [*bewildered*]: Eh?

BAUDOUIN: Lay off him, pal, if you value your job.

GOBLET [*still trying to understand*]: Nekrassov?

CHAPUIS: Yes, Nekrassov. Don't touch him!

GOBLET: I don't take orders from you. I'm from the crime section, and I take my orders from my superiors.

CHAPUIS: That may be so, but your superiors take their orders from ours. Good night, pal.

BAUDOUIN [*smiling*]: Good night. Good night. [BAUDOUIN *and* CHAPUIS *go out.*]

GOBLET [*under his breath*]: Go to hell! [*Thinking*] Nekrassov! I've seen that name in the papers. . . . [*Enter* GEORGES, SIBILOT, *and the two* BODYGUARDS.]

GEORGES [*to the two* BODYGUARDS]: Go and play. [*He shuts the door on them. To* SIBILOT] Stand up straight! For God's sake look as if you're somebody! [*He ruffles his hair.*] Take it easy! There!

SIBILOT: Let's go in. [GEORGES *holds him back.*] What's the matter with you?

GEORGES: I feel dizzy. I shall go in. They will throw themselves at my feet. They will kiss my hands. It makes my head swim. How can one man be the object of so much love and so much hatred? Reassure me, Sibilot. It is not I whom they love, nor I whom they hate. I'm only a symbol, aren't I?

[MOUTIN *and* DEMIDOFF *pass across at the back.*]

SIBILOT: I . . . [*Seeing* MOUTON] Turn round!

GEORGES: What is it?

SIBILOT: Turn round, I tell you, or we shall be lost. [GEORGES *turns round, facing out front.*] Mouton has just passed by with Demidoff. They're looking for you.

GEORGES: To hell with Demidoff. It's Jules and Nerciat I'm concerned about. Those idiots think they can work me with strings.

SIBILOT: Listen, Nikita. . . .

GEORGES: Be quiet! I'll show them who's the master. Madame Castagnié will be back at her job tomorrow, or else . . . [*He stamps his foot with irritation.*] To hell with it!

SIBILOT: What's wrong now?

GEORGES: This evening I have to play the decisive round, and I don't feel in the mood for winning it. What's this? [A GUEST *staggers in. He leans against the buffet, picks up a glass, drinks, and holds the glass as if drinking a toast.*]

THE GUEST: Present! Fire! Long live France! (*He collapses.*]

GOBLET [*springing forward*]: Poor chap! [*He kneels beside him.*]

THE GUEST [*opening one eye*]: What an ugly mug! Give me the *coup de grâce*. [*He falls asleep.* GOBLET, *furious, pushes him under the buffet and pulls the tablecloth down over him.* GEORGES *sees him.*]

GEORGES [*to* SIBILOT]: Goblet! [*He turns his back quickly on* GOBLET.]

SIBILOT: Where?

GEORGES: Behind you. That's a bad start.

SIBILOT [*sure of himself*]: I'll take care of him.

GEORGES: You?

SIBILOT: He likes me. [*He goes toward the inspector, with open arms.*] Well, I *am* glad to see you.

GOBLET [*startled*]: I don't know you!

SIBILOT: Don't say that. Why, I'm Sibilot. Don't you remember me?

GOBLET [*still suspicious*]: Yes.

SIBILOT: Well then, let's shake hands.

GOBLET: No.

SIBILOT [*in a heartrending voice*]: Goblet!

GOBLET: You've changed.

SIBILOT: Go on with you!

GOBLET: You're dressed differently.

SIBILOT: Is that all? I was sent here by my editor and I borrowed these clothes so that I'd look smart.

GOBLET: You didn't borrow that face.

SIBILOT: What's wrong with my face?

GOBLET: It's a two-hundred-thousand-franc face.

SIBILOT: Are you mad? The face goes with the outfit. [*He takes* GOBLET *by the arm.*] I won't let you go. Are you thirsty?

GOBLET: Yes, but I can't swallow.

SIBILOT: Your throat, eh? Choked up? I know how it is. Ah! We're out of place here. Do you know what we ought to do? The pantry is light, airy, and spacious; plenty of nice-looking maids. Let's go down there and have a drink.

GOBLET: But I have to wait for . . .

SIBILOT: A drink, inspector, a drink. We'll feel at home. [*He pulls him out.*]

GEORGES [*alone*]: Ooh!

CHAPUIS [*appearing at a door*]: Psst!

BAUDOUIN [*at the other door*]: Psst!

GEORGES: Eh?

BAUDOUIN: We are Inspectors from the Defense of the State.

CHAPUIS: And we have come to welcome you. . . .

BAUDOUIN: To the State which we defend.

GEORGES: Thank you.

CHAPUIS: Don't you worry about anything. . . .

BAUDOUIN: Rely completely on us.

CHAPUIS: At the moment of danger, we shall be there.

GEORGES: The moment of danger? Is there any danger?

BAUDOUIN: The possibility of an attack cannot be ruled out. . . .

GEORGES: An attack on whom?

BAUDOUIN [*smiling*]: On you!

CHAPUIS [*laughing openly*]: On you!

GEORGES: Well, well! But tell me . . .

BAUDOUIN: Sh! Sh! We are on the lookout!

CHAPUIS: We are on the lookout!

[*They vanish as* MME BOUNOUMI *and her guests enter.*]

MME BOUNOUMI: Here is our savior!

ALL: Long live Nekrassov!

A MAN: Sir, you are a man!

GEORGES: Sir, you are another!

A WOMAN: How handsome you are!

GEORGES: For your pleasure, madam.

ANOTHER WOMAN: Sir, I would be proud to have a child by you.

GEORGES: Madam, we will consider the matter.

MME BOUNOUMI: Dear friend, will you say a few words?

GEORGES: Certainly. [*Raising his voice*] Ladies and Gentlemen, civilizations are mortal, Europe can no longer think in terms of liberty, but only in terms of destiny. The wonder of Greece is in danger. We must save it.

ALL: We shall die for the wonder of Greece! We shall die for the wonder of Greece!

[*Applause.* MME BOUNOUMI *pushes* PERDRIÈRE *toward* GEORGES.]

MME BOUNOUMI [*to* GEORGES]: Here is someone who admires you.

GEORGES: You admire me, sir? That is enough to make me love you. Who are you?

PERDRIÈRE: I am everlastingly obliged to you, sir.

GEORGES [*astonished*]: To me? I have obliged someone?

PERDRIÈRE: You have obliged me to step down.

GEORGES: Perdrière! [PERDRIÈRE *tries to kiss his hand. He prevents it.*] Well, I am delighted to meet you. [*They embrace.*]

MME BOUNOUMI: Photos! [*Flashes. She takes* GEORGES *by one arm,* PERDRIÈRE *takes his other arm.*] Now, the three of us. Take the group.

JULES [*quickly*]: Do you mind? [*He takes* PERDRIÈRE'S *arm.*]

GEORGES: No, my dear Jules, no. Later.

JULES: Why do you systematically refuse to be photographed with me?

GEORGES: Because you fidget. You'd spoil the film.

JULES: If you don't mind . . .

GEORGES: No, my dear chap, I have my public. People buy your rag in order to cut out my picture and they have the right . . .

JULES: You may have your public, but these are *my* photographers, and I consider it inadmissible that you should prevent them from photographing me.

GEORGES: Quickly, then. [*Flash.*] There, there. That's enough. Now I want a word with you.

[GEORGES *takes* JULES *by the arm and leads him downstage.*]

JULES: What do you want with me?

GEORGES: I want you to reinstate the seven employees whom you have dismissed.

JULES: What again! But that's none of your business, old man. It's strictly an internal affair.

GEORGES: Everything to do with the paper is my business.

JULES: Who is the editor? You or I?

GEORGES: You are. But you won't be for long if you play at that game. I'll ask the Board to get rid of you.

JULES: Very well, here is Nerciat, whom they elected as chairman on Thursday in place of Mouton. You have only to ask him.

GEORGES [*taking* NERCIAT *by the arm and leading him down to* JULES]: My dear Nerciat . . .

NERCIAT: My dear Nekrassov . . .

GEORGES: May I ask you a favor?

NERCIAT: It's granted before you ask it.

GEORGES: Do you remember that poor Madame Castagnié?

NERCIAT: Good gracious, no.

GEORGES: The secretary whom you dismissed.

NERCIAT: Ah, yes. She was a Communist.

GEORGES: She is a widow, my dear Nerciat.

NERCIAT: Yes. A Communist widow.

GEORGES: She has a sick daughter.

NERCIAT: Sick? A bad egg. A Communist brat.

GEORGES: She only had her wages to live on. Do you want her to put her head in the gas oven?

NERCIAT: That would be two Communists less. [*Pause.*] What do you want?

GEORGES: I want you to give her back her job.

NERCIAT: But, my dear Nekrassov, I cannot do anything by myself. [*Pause.*] Believe me, I will transmit your request to the Board. [GEORGES *is furious, but he contains himself.*] Is that all?

GEORGES: No. [*Taking* Soir à Paris *from his pocket.*] What's this?

NERCIAT [*reading*]: "Nekrassov states: I know the journalists Duval and Maistre personally." Well? That is a statement you made.

GEORGES: I did not.

NERCIAT: You didn't make it?

GEORGES: Certainly not.

NERCIAT: Ho, ho. [*To* JULES, *severely*] My dear Jules, you astonish me. You know the slogan of our paper —"The Naked Truth"!

JULES [*taking hold of* PERIGORD *as he is passing*]: Perigord, I am very surprised. Here is a statement attributed to Nekrassov, which he has never made.

PERIGORD [*taking the paper and reading it*]: Ah! It must have been little Tapinois!

JULES: Little Tapinois!

PERIGORD: She must have thought she was doing the right thing.

JULES: We can't have that on our paper, Perigord. "The Naked Truth." Sack Tapinois.

GEORGES: I am not asking for that!

JULES: Sack her, sack her.

GEORGES: No, Jules, please. We've had enough dismissals.

JULES: Well, give her a good telling off, and tell her that she has kept her job only through the personal intervention of Nekrassov.

GEORGES: That's right. [*Pause.*] As far as I'm concerned I shall be satisfied with a denial.

JULES [*taken aback*]: With a what?

GEORGES: A denial which you will publish tomorrow.

JULES: A denial?

NERCIAT: A denial?

PERIGORD: A denial?

[*They look at each other.*]

JULES: But, Nikita, that would be the worst blunder.

PERIGORD: They'd wonder what had come over us.

NERCIAT: Have you ever seen a paper deny its own statements, unless forced to do so by the courts?

JULES: We should immediately draw public attention to this unfortunate little paragraph.

PERIGORD: Which I am sure no one has read.

JULES [*to* NERCIAT]: Did you notice it, my dear chairman?

NERCIAT: I? Not at all. Though I read the paper from beginning to end.

JULES: If we start that little game, what will it lead to? Do we want to devote each issue to contradicting the previous one?

GEORGES: Very well. What do you propose doing?

NERCIAT: About what?

GEORGES: About this statement.

JULES: Just say no more about it. Bury it in the next day's news. That's always the best way. Do you think that our readers remember what they have read from one day to the next? My dear chap, if they had any memory we couldn't even publish the weather forecast!

NERCIAT [*rubbing his hands*]: Well, everything is settled.

GEORGES: No.

NERCIAT: No?

GEORGES: No! I insist that you publish a denial.

NERCIAT: You insist?

GEORGES: Yes, by virtue of the services which I have rendered you . . .

NERCIAT: We've paid you for them!

GEORGES: By virtue of the fame which I have acquired . . .

JULES: My poor Nikita, I didn't want to tell you, but your fame is on the downgrade. On Thursday we reached a top circulation of two million. But since then we've dropped to 1,700,000.

GEORGES: That is still well above your normal circulation.

JULES: Wait till next week.

GEORGES: Next week?

JULES: We'll drop back to 900,000, and then what will you be? A steep rise on our sales graph, a steep fall, and then nothing more—death.

GEORGES: Not so fast. I still have some sensational revelations!

JULES: Too late! It's shock tactics that count. The readers are saturated. If you were to tell them tomorrow that the Russians eat their children, it would no longer have any effect on them.

[*Enter* MOUTON *and* DEMIDOFF.]

MOUTON [*in a loud voice*]: Gentlemen! [*Everyone becomes silent and turns toward him.*] You have been betrayed.

[*Murmurs of surprise from the guests.*]

NERCIAT: Why have you come here, Mouton?

MOUTON: To expose a traitor. [*Pointing to* DEMIDOFF.] Here is Demidoff, the Soviet economist, who worked in the Kremlin for ten years. Listen to what he has

to tell us. [*To* DEMIDOFF, *pointing to* GEORGES] Have
a good look at that man who is passing himself off
as Nekrassov. Do you recognize him?

DEMIDOFF: I must change my glasses. [*He takes off his
glasses, puts on another pair, and looks around him.*]
Where is he?

GEORGES [*throwing himself upon him and embracing
him*]: At last! I have been looking for you for such
a long time.

[MOUTON *pulls him back.*]

MOUTON [*to* DEMIDOFF]: Do you recognize him?

GEORGES: Everyone leave the room; I have a secret
message for him.

MOUTON: We won't leave until this business is settled.
[*The Inspectors of the Defense of the State enter.*]

BAUDOUIN [*looming in front of* MOUTON]: Oh, yes, sir,
you'll go.

MOUTON: But I . . .

BAUDOUIN: Defense of the State. It's an order.

CHAPUIS [*to the others*]: You as well, gentlemen, if
you please. [*They usher all the guests out.* DEMIDOFF
and GEORGES *remain alone.*]

DEMIDOFF [*who has been examining* GEORGES, *and has
noticed nothing else*]: This man is not Nekrassov.

GEORGES: Save your energy—we are alone.

DEMIDOFF: You are not Nekrassov. Nekrassov is short,
and stocky, and has a slight limp.

GEORGES: He limps? I am sorry I didn't know that before. [*Pause.*] Demidoff, I've been wanting to speak
to you for a long time.

DEMIDOFF: I don't know you.

GEORGES: But I know you very well: I have found out a
great deal about you. You arrived in France in 1950.
At that time you were a Leninist-Bolshevik and you
felt very lonely. For a time you turned to the Trotsky-
ists and became a Trotskyist-Bolshevik. After the
failure of their group, you went over to Tito, and
called yourself a Titoist-Bolshevik. When the Soviet

Union became reconciled with Yugoslavia, you set your hopes on Mao Tse-tung, and called yourself a Tungist-Bolshevik. But China did not break with the Soviets, so then you called yourself a Bolshevik-Bolshevik. Is that right?

DEMIDOFF: It is correct.

GEORGES: All these great changes merely took place in your head and you have always been alone. At one time your articles were published in *Soir à Paris*, but now nobody wants them. You live in an attic with a goldfinch. Soon the goldfinch will die and the landlord will evict you, and you will have to sleep in a Salvation Army home.

DEMIDOFF: I'm not afraid of poverty. I have only one aim: to annihilate the Soviet bureaucracy.

GEORGES: Well, the game's up, old chap. The West has devoured you. You don't count any more.

DEMIDOFF [*catching him by the throat*]: You dirty snake!

GEORGES: Let go, Demidoff, let me go! I'm going to show you a way out.

DEMIDOFF [*letting him go*]: It's no use.

GEORGES: Why?

DEMIDOFF: You are not Nekrassov, and I have come here to say so.

GEORGES: Don't say it. You would be helping your enemies. Your hatred of the Soviets cannot be very strong if it has not silenced your love for the truth. Think! Mouton has brought you out of oblivion in order to bring about my downfall. When that's done, he'll drop you again. One day you will be found dead in a ditch, the victim of frustration and repressed hatred, and who will have the last laugh? All the bureaucrats in Russia!

DEMIDOFF: You are not Nekrassov. Nekrassov limps.

GEORGES: Yes, yes, I know. [*Pause.*] Demidoff, I want to join the Bolshevik-Bolshevik Party.

DEMIDOFF: You?

GEORGES: Yes. Do you realize the giant stride you have just taken? When a party has but one member, there is little chance that it will ever have two. But once it has two members, what is to prevent it from having a million? Do you accept?

DEMIDOFF [*stunned by the news*]: My party will have two members?

GEORGES: Yes, two.

DEMIDOFF [*suspicious*]: You know that we are based on the principle of centralization?

GEORGES: I know.

DEMIDOFF: And our rule is authoritarian democracy?

GEORGES: I know.

DEMIDOFF: I am the leader.

GEORGES: I will be the rank and file.

DEMIDOFF: The first sign of fraction work, and I'll expel you.

GEORGES: Don't worry, I'm devoted to you. But there's no time to lose. Today I am famous. Tomorrow, perhaps, I shall be forgotten. Seize the opportunity. My articles are being read all over the world. I shall write them at your dictation.

DEMIDOFF: Will you denounce the generation of technicians which has supplanted the old revolutionaries?

GEORGES: In every column.

DEMIDOFF: Will you say what I think of Orloff?

GEORGES: Who is Orloff?

DEMIDOFF: He was head of my department. A jackal!

GEORGES: Tomorrow he will be the laughingstock of Europe.

DEMIDOFF: Splendid! [*He holds out his hand.*] Put it there, Nekrassov. [GEORGES *shakes his hand. The guests appear hesitantly at the door.* MOUTON *and some guests come in.*]

MOUTON: Well, Demidoff, who is this man?

DEMIDOFF: Him? He is Nekrassov!

[*Applause.*]

MOUTON: You lie! What have you two concocted while
    you were alone?
GEORGES: I have been giving him news of the under-
    ground resistance which is being organized in the
    Soviet Union.
MOUTON: Impostor!
GEORGES [*to the guests*]: I call your attention to the
    fact that this individual is playing the game of the
    Communists!
GUESTS [*to* MOUTON]: Go back to Moscow! Go back to
    Moscow!
MOUTON: You are driving me to suicide, you scoundrel,
    but I'll take you to the grave with me. [*He pulls out
    a revolver and points it at* GEORGES.] You may thank
    me, gentlemen. I am ridding the earth of a black-
    guard and of an objective Communist!
MME BOUNOUMI: The attack! The attack!
    [BAUDOUIN *and* CHAPUIS *throw themselves upon*
    MOUTON, *and disarm him. The two* BODYGUARDS *enter
    at a run from the door on the right.*]
CHAPUIS [*to the two* BODYGUARDS, *pointing to* MOUTON]:
    Take the gentleman away.
MOUTON [*struggling*]: Leave me alone! Leave me alone!
THE GUESTS: Go back to Moscow! Go back to Moscow!
    [*The* BODYGUARDS *pick him up and carry him out by
    the door on the right.*]
BAUDOUIN [*to* THE GUESTS]: We have foiled the attack.
    Ladies and gentlemen, the danger is over. Please re-
    turn to the other rooms. We wish to be alone with
    M. Nekrassov for a few moments in order to discuss
    with him measures for ensuring his safety, but have
    no fear; we shall return him to you soon. [THE GUESTS
    leave.]
BAUDOUIN: You must admit, sir, that we are your
    guardian angels.
CHAPUIS: And that, without us, that scoundrel would
    have shot you dead.

GEORGES: I thank you, gentlemen.

BAUDOUIN: Don't mention it. We were only doing our duty.

CHAPUIS: And we are very happy to have rescued you. [GEORGES *bows slightly, and starts to go out.* BAUDOUIN *takes him by the arm.*]

GEORGES: But . . .

CHAPUIS: We have our difficulties, you know.

BAUDOUIN: And we would like you to give us a helping hand.

GEORGES [*sitting down*]: How can I be of service to you? [*The* INSPECTORS *sit down.*]

CHAPUIS: Well, we are working on a serious case affecting national morale.

GEORGES: Is the morale of France in danger?

CHAPUIS: Not yet, sir. We are keeping watch.

BAUDOUIN: But the fact is that attempts are being made to undermine morale.

GEORGES: Poor France! And who dares . . .

CHAPUIS: Two journalists.

GEORGES: Two out of forty million? This country must be easily demoralized.

BAUDOUIN: These two men are only symbols. And the government wants, through them, to strike at an obnoxious press which misleads its readers.

CHAPUIS: We must strike swiftly and hard.

BAUDOUIN: We plan to arrest them tomorrow. The day after at the latest.

CHAPUIS: But we've been told to obtain proof that the two accused have deliberately taken part in a plot against national morale. . . .

BAUDOUIN: Which we think is quite unnecessary . . .

CHAPUIS: But which the legal authorities consider it necessary to demand . . .

BAUDOUIN: But, for once, luck is on our side. . . .

CHAPUIS: We've got you.

GEORGES: You've got me?

BAUDOUIN: Don't you get it?

GEORGES: Indeed I do; or at least I think I do.

CHAPUIS: Well, you will be our witness.

BAUDOUIN: In your capacity as a Soviet Minister, you must have employed these journalists.

CHAPUIS: And you would do us a great favor by confirming it.

GEORGES: What are their names?

CHAPUIS: Robert Duval and Charles Maistre.

GEORGES: Maistre and Duval . . . Duval and Maistre. . . . No, I don't know them.

BAUDOUIN: Impossible!

GEORGES: Why?

CHAPUIS: You stated yesterday, in *Soir à Paris*, that you knew them very well.

GEORGES: They attributed words to me that I never used.

BAUDOUIN: That may be. But the article is there. And in any case, they are Communists. Duval is a leading member of the CP.

CHAPUIS: Come, come: Duval. You must know him.

GEORGES: In the Soviet Union each Minister has his own personal agents who are not known to the others. You need the Ministry of Propaganda, or Information, or perhaps Foreign Affairs. I, as you know, was Minister of the Interior.

BAUDOUIN: We appreciate your scruples . . .

CHAPUIS: . . . and in your place we should have the same scruples.

BAUDOUIN: But since Duval is a Communist . . .

CHAPUIS: It isn't necessary for you actually to have seen his name.

BAUDOUIN: And you can be morally certain that he is a Soviet agent.

CHAPUIS: You could therefore testify without any qualms that he was paid for his work.

GEORGES: I am sorry, but I shall not testify.

[*Pause.*]

BAUDOUIN: Very well.

CHAPUIS: Good.

BAUDOUIN: France is the land of liberty. Here everyone is free to speak or to be silent.

CHAPUIS: We bow to your wishes.

BAUDOUIN: And we hope that our chiefs will do so as well.

[*Pause.*]

BAUDOUIN [*to* CHAPUIS]: Will they?

CHAPUIS [*to* BAUDOUIN]: Who knows? The difficulty is that M. Nekrassov has many enemies.

BAUDOUIN [*to* GEORGES]: People who are annoyed by your fame . . .

CHAPUIS [*to* GEORGES]: And who claim that you were sent here by Moscow . . .

GEORGES: That's nonsense!

CHAPUIS: Of course.

[*They get up and stand on either side of him.*]

BAUDOUIN: But these slanders must be silenced.

CHAPUIS: By an act which definitely commits you.

BAUDOUIN: After all, only last month, you were the sworn enemy of our country . . .

CHAPUIS: . . . and there is nothing to prove that you aren't still. . . .

BAUDOUIN: We have been told many times that we are failing in our duty . . .

CHAPUIS: . . . and that we should take you straight back to the frontier.

BAUDOUIN: Imagine what would happen if we were to hand you over to the Soviet police!

CHAPUIS: You'd have a bad time, after the statements you've made.

GEORGES: You'd be heartless enough to throw me out? After I have put my trust in French hospitality?

CHAPUIS [*laughing*]: Ha, ha!

CHAPUIS [*to* BAUDOUIN]: Hospitality!

BAUDOUIN [*to* CHAPUIS]: Why not the right of asylum?

CHAPUIS: He thinks he's living in the Middle Ages!

BAUDOUIN: We are hospitable to English lords . . .

CHAPUIS: . . . German tourists . . .

BAUDOUIN: . . . American soldiers . . .

CHAPUIS: . . . and to those expelled from Belgium. . . .

BAUDOUIN: But frankly, you wouldn't want us to be hospitable to Soviet citizens!

GEORGES: It's blackmail, then?

CHAPUIS: No, sir, it's a dilemma.

BAUDOUIN: I would even say: an alternative. [*Pause.*]

GEORGES: Take me to the frontier. [*Pause.*]

BAUDOUIN [*changing his tone*]: My dear Georges, so you're going to be difficult?

CHAPUIS: You're going to play tough?

GEORGES [*jumping up*]: What?

BAUDOUIN: Sit down. [*They make him sit down.*]

CHAPUIS: You can't scare us, you know!

BAUDOUIN: We've seen real tough characters—men.

CHAPUIS: Everyone knows that swindlers are only sissies.

BAUDOUIN: Women.

CHAPUIS: Once you've had a little going over . . .

BAUDOUIN: You'll start talking. . . .

GEORGES: I don't understand what you mean.

CHAPUIS: Oh yes, you do.

BAUDOUIN: We mean that you are Georges de Valéra, the small-time crook, and that we could turn you over right away to Inspector Goblet, who is after you.

GEORGES [*trying to laugh*]: Georges de Valéra? It is a misunderstanding! I . . .

CHAPUIS: Take it easy. For the past week your bodyguards have been photographing you on the sly from every angle. They have even taken your fingerprints. We only had to compare the results with your police dossier. You've had it.

GEORGES: Hell! [*Pause.*]

BAUDOUIN: You know, we're not bad chaps.

CHAPUIS: And swindlers are not in our line.

BAUDOUIN: That's the business of the criminal branch, and our department doesn't think much of that lot.

CHAPUIS: We'll tell Inspector Goblet where to get off.

BAUDOUIN: We want those two journalists, that's all.

CHAPUIS: And if you give them over to us, you can be Nekrassov as much as you like.

BAUDOUIN: You will do us a few little favors.

CHAPUIS: We shall point people out to you from time to time.

BAUDOUIN: You will say that you know them. Just to please us.

CHAPUIS: And in exchange, we'll keep our mouths shut.

BAUDOUIN: We are the only ones who know, you see.

CHAPUIS: Of course, the Prime Minister has been told.

BAUDOUIN: But that doesn't matter. He doesn't know.

CHAPUIS: He said: "I don't want to know it."

BAUDOUIN: And he knows what he wants to know!

CHAPUIS: Get the idea, son?

BAUDOUIN: On Thursday we'll come for you and take you to the examining magistrate.

CHAPUIS: He will ask you if you know Duval . . .

BAUDOUIN: . . . and you will say, "Yes" because you can't do otherwise.

CHAPUIS: Good night, pal. At your service.

BAUDOUIN: See you Thursday, and don't forget. [*They go out.*] [GEORGES *is left alone.*]

GEORGES: Well! Well, well, well! . . . Well, well, well, well, well! [*He goes to the mirror.*] Farewell, great Russian steppe of my childhood, farewell, fame! Farewell, Nekrassov! Farewell, you dear great man! Farewell, traitor, skunk, farewell, rat! Long live Georges de Valéra! [*He looks through his pockets.*] Seven thousand francs. I have shaken the world, and it has brought me seven thousand francs. What a dog's game! [*To the mirror*] Georges, my good old Georges, you've no idea how glad I am to find you again. [*Recovering*] Ladies and gentlemen, Nekrassov is dead,

and Georges de Valéra is about to take French leave.
[*He thinks.*] The main door—impossible, the cops
are watching it. The servants' entrance . . . [*He
opens a door at the right.*] Hell! My two gunmen are
guarding the corridor. [*He crosses the room.*] The
window? [*He leans over.*] It's a forty-foot drop. I'd
crack my skull. No gutters? [*He climbs onto the
window sill.*] Too far away. My God, if I could find a
way of keeping my two gunmen busy . . . [DEMI-
DOFF *has come in, and seizes him round the waist,
pulling him off the window sill.*]

DEMIDOFF: Don't do that, member. I forbid it.

GEORGES: I . . .

DEMIDOFF: Suicide, yes, you think of it for the first three
months. Then you get over it, you'll see. I've been
through it. [*Confidentially*] I left the main room because I have had a little to drink. I mustn't get
drunk, member. See that I don't. I'm terrible when I
get drunk.

GEORGES [*very interested*]: Oh!

DEMIDOFF: Yes.

GEORGES: Really terrible?

DEMIDOFF: I smash everything. Sometimes I kill.

GEORGES: That's very interesting.

[MME BOUNOUMI *and* GUESTS *burst in.*]

MME BOUNOUMI [*to* GEORGES]: At last we can get together with you. You are not leaving, I hope? We're
going to begin the party games.

GEORGES: Games?

MME BOUNOUMI: Yes.

GEORGES: I know one that used to make everyone in
the Kremlin laugh till tears came to their eyes.

MME BOUNOUMI: You intrigue me. What is it?

GEORGES: At times when we were feeling good, we used
to make Demidoff drunk. You can't imagine the
wonderful ideas he has when he is drunk. He's a real
poet.

MME BOUNOUMI: How delightful! Shall we try?

GEORGES: Pass the word round, and I'll do the rest.

MME BOUNOUMI [*to a* GUEST]: We must make Demidoff drunk. It seems that he is very amusing when he has had a few drinks. [*The word gets round.*]

GEORGES [*to* DEMIDOFF]: Our friends want to drink a toast with you.

DEMIDOFF: Good. [*Looking at the glasses which a servant is bringing round*] What's this?

GEORGES: Dry Martini.

DEMIDOFF: No American drinks. Vodka!

MME BOUNOUMI [*to the* SERVANTS]: Vodka!

[SERVANT *brings glasses of vodka on a tray.*]

DEMIDOFF [*raising his glass*]: I drink to the destruction of the Soviet bureaucrats!

MME BOUNOUMI AND GUESTS: To the annihilation of the bureaucrats!

GEORGES [*taking a glass from the tray and giving it to* DEMIDOFF]: You are forgetting the technocrats.

DEMIDOFF: To the destruction of the technocrats! [*He drinks.*]

GEORGES [*handing him another glass*]: What about Orloff? [*To the* GUESTS] He was his boss.

DEMIDOFF [*drinking*]: To the hanging of Orloff!

GEORGES [*handing him a glass*]: This is the moment for a toast to the Bolshevik-Bolshevik Party.

DEMIDOFF: Do you think so?

GEORGES: Of course. It's your chance to make it known. Think of the publicity.

DEMIDOFF [*drinking*]: To the Bolshevik-Bolshevik Party!

GUESTS: To the Bolshevik-Bolshevik Party!

[*The majority are drunk by now. Paper hats, streamers, and toy trumpets appear. During the ensuing scene* DEMIDOFF'S *tirades are punctuated by the sounds of the toy trumpets.*]

DEMIDOFF [*to* GEORGES]: What shall I drink to now?

GEORGES [*holding out a glass*]: To your goldfinch!

DEMIDOFF: To my goldfinch!

GUEST: To his goldfinch!

[GEORGES *hands him another glass.*]

DEMIDOFF: And now?

GEORGES: I don't know. . . . What about France? That would be polite.

DEMIDOFF: No. [*Raising his glass*] I drink to the good little Russian people, who are kept in chains by bad shepherds.

GUESTS: To the Russian people!

DEMIDOFF: You will free them, won't you? My poor little people; you're going to free them?

ALL: We will free them! We will free them! [*Trumpets.*]

DEMIDOFF: Thank you. I drink to the deluge of fire and steel which will sweep down on my people.

ALL: To the deluge! To the deluge!

DEMIDOFF [*to* GEORGES]: What am I drinking?

GEORGES: Vodka.

DEMIDOFF: No.

GEORGES: Look!

[*He picks up the bottle and shows it to him.*]

DEMIDOFF: Stand clear, everyone! This is French vodka! I am a traitor!

GEORGES: Now, now, Demidoff.

DEMIDOFF: Silence, member! Any Russian who drinks French vodka is a traitor to his people. You must execute me. [*To* EVERYONE] Come on! What are you waiting for?

MME BOUNOUMI [*trying to calm him*]: My dear Demidoff, we wouldn't dream of such a thing.

DEMIDOFF [*pushing her away*]: Then liberate them, all of them, all of them, all the Russians! If a single survivor remains, he will point his finger at my breast and say to me: "Feodor Petrovitch, you drink French vodka." [*Replying to an imaginary questioner*] It's Orloff's fault, little father. I couldn't stand him any longer. [*He drinks.*] I drink to the liberating bomb!

[*A terrified silence. He turns threateningly to* PER-DRIÈRE.] Drink, you!

PERDRIÈRE: To the bomb!

DEMIDOFF [*threatening*]: To *which* bomb?

PERDRIÈRE: I . . . don't know. . . . To the H bomb.

DEMIDOFF: You skunk! You jackal! Do you think you can put a stop to history with a firecracker?

PERDRIÈRE: But I don't want to put a stop to it.

DEMIDOFF: And I want to put a stop to it at once. Because I know who is writing it. It is my little people with their bad shepherds. Do you understand? Orloff himself is writing history, but I have fallen out of it, as a little bird falls out of the nest. [*His eyes follow an invisible object flying across the room at great speed.*] How quickly it goes! Stop it! Stop it! [*Taking a glass.*] I drink to the Z bomb which will blow up the earth! [*To* PERDRIÈRE] Drink!

PERDRIÈRE [*in a choked voice*]: No.

DEMIDOFF: Don't you want the earth to blow up?

PERDRIÈRE: No.

DEMIDOFF: But how will you stop man's history unless you destroy the human race? [*At the window.*] Look! Look at the moon! Once upon a time it was a world. But the lunar capitalists had more sense than you. When they began to smell heresy there, they blew up the moon's atmosphere with cobalt bombs. That explains the silence of the heavens. Millions of moons are circling in space. Millions of clocks stopped at the same moment of history. There is only one left ticking around the sun, but if you have courage we can put an end to this disgraceful noise. I drink to the moon of the future! To the earth! [GEORGES *tries to slip away.*] Where are you going, member? Drink to the moon!

GEORGES: To the moon!

DEMIDOFF [*drinks and spits in disgust*]: Pah! [*To* GEORGES] Understand, member, I am on the future moon, and I am drinking French vodka. Ladies and gentlemen, I am a traitor. History will win. I am going to die, and my children will write my name in books: Demidoff, the traitor, drank French vodka at Madame Bounoumi's. I have done wrong, ladies and gentlemen. Wrong in the eyes of centuries to come. Raise your glasses; I feel lonely. [*To* PERDRIÈRE] You, you jackal, shout with me: Long live the historical process!

PERDRIÈRE [*terrified*]: Long live the historical process!

DEMIDOFF: Long live the historical process, which will crush me like a flea, and which will smash the old society as I am going to smash this table.

GEORGES [*opening the door at the right and letting in the two* BODYGUARDS]: He's gone mad! Get hold of him! [*The* BODYGUARDS *throw themselves on* DEMIDOFF *and try to control him.* GEORGES *gets ready to flee, but he finds himself face to face with* GOBLET, *who comes in by the door at right carrying* SIBILOT, *who is blind drunk, over his shoulders.*]

GOBLET [*putting* SIBILOT *down in an armchair*]: Lie down, old man. Wait while I get a cold compress for you.

SIBILOT: Good old Goblet; you're a mother to me. [*Bursts into tears.*] I have betrayed my mother. I dragged you into the kitchen to prevent you arresting a crook.

GOBLET [*drawing himself up*]: What crook?

SIBILOT: Georges de Valéra.
   [*During this time* GEORGES *makes a detour in order to reach the door at the right without passing in front of* SIBILOT *and* GOBLET.]

GOBLET: Georges de Valéra? Where is he?
   [GEORGES *has reached the door on the right.*]

SIBILOT [*pointing with his finger*]: There! There! There!

GOBLET: Good God!
   [*He pulls out his revolver and dashes off in pursuit of* GEORGES, *firing as he goes.*]

THE GUESTS [*terrified*]: The shooting's begun! **The**

shooting's begun!

DEMIDOFF [*in ecstasy*]: At last! At last! This is history! [BAUDOUIN *and* CHAPUIS *dash off in pursuit of* GOBLET DEMIDOFF *frees himself from the* BODYGUARDS *and dashes off in pursuit of the* INSPECTORS. *The* BODY-GUARDS *recover themselves and also dash off in pursuit.*]

CURTAIN

SCENE VII

SIBILOT'S 1925 *drawing-room.*

It is night. GEORGES *comes in by the window.* VERONIQUE *then comes in and puts the light on. She is wearing the same clothes as in Scene Three and is getting ready to go out.* GEORGES *comes behind her, hands raised and smiling.*

GEORGES: Good evening.

VERONIQUE [*turning round*]: Hello! Nekrassov!

GEORGES: He is dead. Call me Georges, and draw the curtains. [*He lowers his hands.*] You have never told me your name, girl.

VERONIQUE: Veronique.

GEORGES: Dear France! [*He drops into an armchair.*] I was sitting in this same armchair, you were getting ready to go out, and the cops were prowling around the house. We're back to where we started. How young I was! [*Listening*] Did you hear a whistle?

VERONIQUE: No. Are they after you?

GEORGES: They have been ever since I was twenty. [*Pause.*] I have just shaken them off. But not for long.

VERONIQUE: What if they come here?

GEORGES: They'll come. Goblet through habit, and the D.S. by following the scent. But not for another ten minutes.

VERONIQUE: You've got the D.S. after you?

GEORGES: Inspector Baudouin and Inspector Chapuis. Do you know them?

VERONIQUE: No. But I know the D.S. You are in danger.

GEORGES [ironically]: A little!

VERONIQUE: Don't stay here.

GEORGES: I must talk to you.

VERONIQUE: About yourself?

GEORGES: About your friends.

VERONIQUE: I'll see you tomorrow, wherever you like, and at whatever time you suggest. But, run!

GEORGES [shaking his head]: If I leave you now, you will never see me again. They'll get me. [At a gesture from VERONIQUE] Don't argue. You get to feel these things when you're in the profession. Besides, where do you expect me to go? I haven't a friend to hide me. At midnight, a man in a dinner jacket is not noticed, but wait till tomorrow in broad daylight. [Seized with an idea] Where are your father's old suits?

VERONIQUE: He gave them to the concierge.

GEORGES: And his new ones?

VERONIQUE: They aren't ready, except for what he's wearing.

GEORGES: You see. Luck has deserted me. Veronique, my star has fallen and my genius is fading. I'm finished. [He walks about.] They are going to arrest someone tonight, that's certain. But whom? Who is going to be arrested, can you tell me? Goblet is chasing Valéra and the D.S. is after Nekrassov. Whoever catches me first, I shall become what he wants me to be. What's your bet? The C.D. or the D.S.? Georges or Nikita?

VERONIQUE: I bet on the D.S.

GEORGES: Me too. [*Pause.*] Warn Maistre and Duval.

VERONIQUE: What do you want to warn them of?

GEORGES: Listen, my girl, and try to understand.
[*Patiently*] What will the Defense of the State
branch do with me? Put me in prison? They aren't
so stupid. Nekrassov is the guest of France. They've
probably rented a suburban villa for me, fairly isolated, with beautiful sunny rooms. They will install
me in the most beautiful of these rooms, and there
I'll keep to my bed night and day. Because Nekrassov
is very weak, poor chap. He has suffered so much.
That won't prevent your father from continuing
my sensational revelations. He has captured the style
and can manufacture them without me. [*Imitating
the cry of newsboys*] "Maistre and Duval went to
Moscow secretly. Nekrassov paid them in dollars!"
That's what I believe they call creating the psycho-
logical climate. When they have been thoroughly
dragged through the mud, the public will think it
quite natural that they should be charged with
treason.

VERONIQUE: The court won't take any notice of my
father's articles. They'll need witnesses.

GEORGES: How do you know I won't give evidence?

VERONIQUE: You?

GEORGES: Yes. On a stretcher. I don't like being beaten
up, and if they beat me every day I shall give way in
the end.

VERONIQUE: You think they'll beat you up.

GEORGES: They won't stand on ceremony. [*Pause.*] Oh!
you can despise me. I am too much of an artist to
have physical courage.

VERONIQUE: I don't despise you. And who said anything
about physical courage? It's enough to know what
you want.

GEORGES: If only I knew!

VERONIQUE: Do you want to become an informer?

GEORGES: No, but I don't want to have my face smashed in. So there's the choice.

VERONIQUE: You have far too much pride to talk.

GEORGES: Have I any pride left?

VERONIQUE: You are bursting with it.

GEORGES: Listen to that! Never mind. I'd be very relieved if Duval and Maistre were out of harm's way.

VERONIQUE: What difference would that make?

GEORGES: When I've had as much as I can stand, I could name them. At least I'd know they wouldn't go to jail.

VERONIQUE: But if you name them, they'll be convicted.

GEORGES: The conviction wouldn't matter, so long as they couldn't arrest them.

VERONIQUE [*disarmed*]: My poor Georges!

GEORGES [*not listening to her*]: You understand, kid. I shall disappear. You go and tell them to get away somewhere.

VERONIQUE: They won't run away.

GEORGES: With the cops after them and five years of jail hanging in front of them? You're crazy.

VERONIQUE: They won't run away because they are innocent.

GEORGES: And you were trying to get me to run away because I'm guilty? Fine logic! Follow your advice, and all the guilty in France would be quietly fishing for trout while the innocent were rotting in prison.

VERONIQUE: That's just about what does happen.

GEORGES: No smart talk, kid. The fact is you're letting them in for it.

VERONIQUE: Wait till they're arrested, then you'll see.

GEORGES: I see it all. You'll go and yell in the streets. Posters, meetings, processions. A regular circus. And where will your two friends be? In the cells. Of course, it's in your interest for them to be locked up as long as possible! [*He laughs.*] And I, poor fool, put my head in the lion's mouth to warn them. Warn them? You people don't care a rap about it. What a fool I

am! I don't blame you—every man for himself. But
I'm a bit disgusted with you, all the same, because
I shall be going to jail myself, and I have a feeling
of solidarity with these two poor chaps you're sac-
rificing. [VERONIQUE *dials a telephone number.*] What
are you doing?

VERONIQUE [*into the telephone*]: Is that you, Robert?
I'm putting you on to someone who wants to talk
to you. [*To* GEORGES] It's Duval.

GEORGES: The line may be tapped.

VERONIQUE: That doesn't matter. [*She gives him the
receiver.*]

GEORGES [*into the telephone*]: Hullo, Duval? Listen
carefully, old boy, you are going to be arrested tomorrow, or the day after at the latest, and most likely
convicted. You haven't even got time to pack a bag.
Make your getaway as soon as you put the receiver
down. Eh? Oh! Oh! [*Putting the receiver down*] Did
he let me have it!

VERONIQUE [*into the receiver*]: No, Robert, no, take it
easy; he's not a provocateur. Nothing of the sort. I'll
explain everything. [*To* GEORGES] Do you want me to
call Maistre?

GEORGES: It's not worth it. I understand. [*He bursts out
laughing.*] For the first time in my life I wanted to do
someone a good turn. It will certainly be the last.
[*Pause.*] There's nothing left for me but to go. Good
night. I'm sorry to have troubled you.

VERONIQUE: Good night.

GEORGES [*suddenly exploding*]: They are idiots, that's
what they are! Poor types with no imagination. They
have no idea what jail is like. But I have.

VERONIQUE: You haven't been locked up.

GEORGES: No, but I am a poet. Prison has been hanging
over me all evening and I feel it in my bones. Do
they know there's a five to two chance they'll come
out with tuberculosis?

VERONIQUE: Duval went to prison on October 17th,

1939, and came out on August 30th, 1944. He's tubercular.

GEORGES: Then, there's no excuse.

VERONIQUE: But, my dear Georges, he's doing exactly what you're doing—acting in his own interests.

GEORGES: His interests, or yours?

VERONIQUE: His, mine, ours. They are all one. You have nothing much except your own skin, and you want to save it. That's quite natural. Duval wants to save his skin, but he doesn't keep thinking about it. He has his Party, his work, and his readers. If he wants to save *all* that he is, then he must stay where he is. [*Pause.*]

GEORGES [*violently*]: Dirty egoists!

VERONIQUE: I beg your pardon.

GEORGES: Everyone will be happy. He will have his crown of thorns and you will have your circuses. But what about me, you rotten lot? What do I become? A traitor, a stool pigeon, an informer!

VERONIQUE: You've only to . . .

GEORGES: Oh, no! I'll be tied to a prison bed and the cops will beat me up three times a day. They'll stop for breath from time to time. Then they'll ask me: "Will you give evidence?" I'll be cornered. Bells will be ringing in my ears. My head will feel like a pumpkin, I'll think of those two martyrs, those two innocents who are playing a dirty trick on me by not running away, and I'll say to myself: "If you rat, they'll be in for five years." If I rat. Of course, you'll all be very pleased. There's no Christ without Judas, eh? Well, poor Judas. Here's a Judas with a heavy heart. I understand him, and I honor him. If I don't rat . . . Well! I'll still be getting the beatings because of you. And what will my reward be? To be spat upon. Your father will have filled *Soir à Paris* with my false statements, while your rags will celebrate the acquittal of Duval and the ignominious defeat of that slanderer Nekrassov. You will carry your friends in triumph and as they march, your joyful crowds will be treading on my face. Manipulated, just like a child! And by everybody.

There I was the instrument of hatred; here I am the instrument of history. [*Pause.*] Veronique! If you were to explain my position to your pals do you think they would be good enough to run away?

VERONIQUE: I'm afraid not.

GEORGES: The swine! I ought to kill myself, right here in front of you, and dirty your floor with my blood. You're lucky that I no longer have the courage to do it. [*He sits down again.*] I no longer understand anything about anything. I used to have my own little philosophy. It helped me to live. I've lost everything, even my principles. Ah! I ought never to have gone into politics!

VERONIQUE: Go, Georges. We ask nothing of you, and you don't owe anything to anyone. Please go.

GEORGES [*at the window, draws the curtains back a little*]: Night. The streets are deserted. I'll have to slink along by the walls until morning. After that . . . [*Pause.*] Shall I tell you the truth? I wanted them to catch me here. When you retire from the world, what counts is the last face you see. You remember it a long time. I wanted it to be yours. [VERONIQUE *smiles.*] You ought to smile more often. It makes you beautiful.

VERONIQUE: I smile at people whom I like.

GEORGES: There's nothing about me for you to like, and I don't like you. [*Pause.*] If I could prevent those fellows going to jail, what a good trick I'd be playing on all of you! [*He walks up and down.*] To the rescue, my genius! Show me you are still alive!

VERONIQUE: Genius, you know . . .

GEORGES: Quiet! [*He turns his back on* VERONIQUE *and bows.*] Thank you, thank you! [*Turning back to* VERONIQUE] I regret to inform you that your pals won't be arrested. Good-by to your circuses and your martyrs' crowns. Madame Castagnié will get her job back, and who knows if Perdrière's hundred thousand votes won't go to the Communist candidate on Sunday. I'll show you that no one can pull my strings as they like.

VERONIQUE [*shrugging her shoulders*]: You can't do anything.

GEORGES: Find someone to hide me. Come and see me tomorrow, and I'll give you an interview with exclusive world rights.

VERONIQUE: What, again!

GEORGES: Don't you want it?

VERONIQUE: No . . .

GEORGES: I had such a lovely title too: "How I Became Nekrassov," by Georges de Valéra.

VERONIQUE: Georges!

GEORGES: I'll stay with your friend for a fortnight. Photograph me from every angle, with and without the eye patch. I know them all: the Palotins, Nerciats, and Moutons. I'll give you revelations with chapter and verse.

VERONIQUE: As soon as the first article appears, they'll send the police to us. If we refuse to give you up, they'll publish everywhere that your statements are all lies.

GEORGES: Do you think they'll dare to arrest me once the first article is published? I know too much. And what if they do? If they want my address, you can give it to them. You make me sick, you and your martyrs. If you must have one, why not me?

VERONIQUE: You see, you're bursting with vanity.

GEORGES: Yes. [*Pause.*] Do you agree about the interview?

VERONIQUE: Yes. [*She kisses him.*]

GEORGES: Keep your distance. [*He laughs.*] So I've won in the end. Your progressive paper will publish an article by a crook. That won't make much of a change for me. I dictated to the father, and I'll dictate to the daughter.

VERONIQUE: I'll go with you. It'll be safer.

[BAUDOUIN *and* CHAPUIS *come in through the window.*]

CHAPUIS: Good morning, Nikita.

BAUDOUIN: Inspector Goblet is looking for you.

CHAPUIS: But don't be afraid. We are going to protect you.

VERONIQUE: It's all up!

GEORGES: Who knows? I have found my genius again. Perhaps my star is not dead.

BAUDOUIN: Come with us, Nikita. You are in danger.

CHAPUIS: This girl is in with the Communists.

BAUDOUIN: Perhaps they've given her the job of murdering you.

GEORGES: I am Georges de Valéra, the swindler, and I demand to be handed over to Inspector Goblet.

CHAPUIS [*to* VERONIQUE]: Poor Nikita!

BAUDOUIN [*to* VERONIQUE]: Your Russian friends have just arrested his wife and his sons.

CHAPUIS [*to* VERONIQUE]: His mind has been unhinged by sorrow, and he doesn't know what he's saying. [BAUDOUIN *goes to the front door and opens it. Two* MALE NURSES *come in.*]

BAUDOUIN [*to the* NURSES]: There he is. Be very gentle.

CHAPUIS: You need a rest, Nikita.

BAUDOUIN: These gentlemen are going to take you to a nice clinic.

CHAPUIS: With a lovely sunny garden.

GEORGES [*to* VERONIQUE]: You see what they've thought up. It's even worse than the suburban villa.

BAUDOUIN [*to the* NURSES]: Take it away!

[*The* NURSES *come forward, leaving the door open. They seize* GEORGES. GOBLET *comes in.*]

GOBLET: Naturally, ladies and gentlemen, you haven't seen a man five feet ten in height. . . .

GEORGES [*shouts*]: Here I am, Goblet! I am Georges
de Valéra!

GOBLET: Valéra!

GEORGES: I confess to two hundred swindles! You will
be Chief Inspector before the end of the year.

GOBLET [*coming forward, fascinated*]: Valéra!

BAUDOUIN [*blocking his way*]: A mistake, colleague. It's
Nekrassov.

GOBLET [*avoiding him and throwing himself on* GEORGES,
whom he pulls by one arm]: I've been looking for
him for years!

CHAPUIS [*taking* GEORGES *by the other arm*]: We tell
you that this man is a lunatic who thinks he is Valéra!

GOBLET [*pulling on* GEORGES'S *arm*]: Let go of him! He's
my property. He's my living, my man, my game.

CHAPUIS [*pulling*]: Let go of him yourself!

GOBLET: Never!

BAUDOUIN: We'll have you suspended.

GOBLET: You try! There'll be a row!

GEORGES: Courage, Goblet, I'm with you.

BAUDOUIN [*to the* NURSES]: Take them both away!

[*The* NURSES *fall on* GEORGES *and* GOBLET.]

VERONIQUE: Help!

[CHAPUIS *gags her with his hand, and she struggles
violently. At this moment,* DEMIDOFF *appears, fighting
mad.*]

DEMIDOFF: Where is my member?

GEORGES: Help, Demidoff!

DEMIDOFF: My God! My member! Give me my member! I want my member!

BAUDOUIN [*to* DEMIDOFF]: Who asked you to interfere?

DEMIDOFF: Interfere? [*He knocks him down. The others
throw themselves on him.*] Long live the Bolshevik-
Bolshevik Party! Keep it up, member! Down with
the cops! [*He knocks down a* NURSE.] Ah, you want
to split the Bolshevik-Bolshevik Party! [*He knocks
CHAPUIS over.*] You'd try to stop the onward march of
the revolution! [*He knocks* GOBLET *over.* GEORGES *and*

VERONIQUE *look at each other and get away through the window.* DEMIDOFF *knocks out the other* NURSE, *looks around him and goes out through the door shouting.*] Hold on, member, I'm coming.

GOBLET [*coming to, sadly*]: Didn't I say I wouldn't catch him! [*He falls back unconscious.*]

CURTAIN

SCENE VIII

PALOTIN'S *office. Dawn. Gray light. The electric lights are on.* NERCIAT, CHARIVET, BERGERAT, LERMINIER, *and* JULES *are present.* NERCIAT *is wearing a paper hat.* BERGERAT *blows into a toy trumpet.* CHARIVET *and* LERMINIER *are seated, helpless, with streamers twined around their dinner jackets.* JULES *is walking about, a little apart. They all look tired and lost. They are wearing the badges of the Future Firing Squad Victims—large rosettes on which the audience can see, in letters of gold,* FFSV. *During the scene it becomes gradually lighter, becoming fully lighted only after* JULES *has left.*

CHARIVET: I've got a headache!

LERMINIER: So have I!

BERGERAT: And I!

NERCIAT [*dryly*]: And so have I, my friends. What now?

CHARIVET: I want to go to bed.

NERCIAT: No, Charivet, no! We are waiting for Nekrassov, and you will wait with us.

CHARIVET: Nekrassov! He's still running!

NERCIAT: They promised to bring him back before dawn.

CHARIVET [*pointing to the window*]: Before dawn? It's dawn now.

NERCIAT: Exactly. Everything will soon be settled.

CHARIVET [*goes toward the window and recoils in disgust*]: How horrible!

NERCIAT: What is?

CHARIVET: The dawn! I haven't seen it for twenty-five years. Hasn't it aged! [*Pause.*]

NERCIAT: Friends . . . [BERGERAT *blows into his toy trumpet.*] For the love of God, Bergerat, don't blow that thing any more.

BERGERAT: It's a trumpet.

NERCIAT [*patiently*]: I can see that, old man, but would you do me a favor and throw it away?

BERGERAT [*indignantly*]: Throw away my trumpet? [*After a moment's reflection*] I'll throw it away if you'll take off your paper hat.

NERCIAT [*thunderstruck*]: My what? You're drunk, old man. [*He puts his hand to his head and feels the hat.*] Oh! [*He throws the hat away with disgust and pulls himself together.*] A little dignity, gentlemen. We're holding a meeting. Get rid of those streamers. [BERGERAT *puts his trumpet on the desk. The others brush themselves.*] Good! [JULES, *who has all this time been walking up and down, deep in thought, goes over to the desk, opens it, and takes out a bottle of spirits and a glass. He is about to pour himself a drink.*] No, my friend, not you! I thought you never drank.

JULES: I'm drinking to forget.

NERCIAT: To forget what?

JULES: To forget that I am in possession of the best piece of news in my whole career, and that I am forbidden to publish it. "Nekrassov was Valéra." Ha! There's a mouthful for you! Two celebrated men in one. Two headlines in one. The biggest plum in journalism!

NERCIAT: You don't know what you're saying, my dear chap.

JULES: I was dreaming. [*He goes on walking.*] Oh, to be a left-wing paper for one day! For a single day! What a headline! [*He stops, in ecstasy.*] I can see it. It covers the whole of the front page, continues on page two, invades page three. . . .

NERCIAT: That's enough!

JULES: All right. All right. [*Sadly*] After the Battle of Tsushima the editor of a leading Japanese paper was confronted with a similar dilemma. He committed hara-kiri.

NERCIAT: Have no regrets, my friend. Nekrassov is Nekrassov. He ran away just now because he thought he was the object of a Communist attack. [*Looking* JULES *straight in the eye*] That's the truth.

JULES [*sighing*]: It's less beautiful than the dream. [*There is a knock at the door.*] Come in.

[BAUDOUIN *and* CHAPUIS *enter. Their heads are covered in bandages.* CHAPUIS *has his arm in a sling.* BAUDOUIN *is on crutches.*]

ALL: At last!

NERCIAT: Where is he?

BAUDOUIN: We surprised him at Sibilot's . . .

CHAPUIS: . . . carrying on a gallant conversation with a Communist girl. . . .

JULES: With a . . . Sensational! [*He reaches for the telephone, but* NERCIAT *stops him.*]

NERCIAT [*to the* INSPECTORS]: Continue!

BAUDOUIN: He was about to sell his story to *Libérateur.*

CHAPUIS: "How I Became Nekrassov," by Georges de Valéra.

LERMINIER: To *Libérateur?*

BERGERAT: By Georges de Valéra?

CHARIVET: What a narrow escape we've had!

NERCIAT: Of course you arrested him?

CHAPUIS: Of course.

ALL [*except* JULES, *who is still dreaming*]: Excellent, gentlemen, excellent!

CHARIVET: Shut him up in a fortress!

LERMINIER: Send him to Devil's Island!

BERGERAT: Put him in an iron mask.

BAUDOUIN: The fact is . . . [*He hesitates.*]

NERCIAT: Speak up! Speak!

CHAPUIS: We had just captured him, when a score of Communists . . .

BAUDOUIN: . . . threw themselves on us and knocked us senseless.

CHAPUIS [*pointing to their bandages*]: Look at our wounds.

NERCIAT: Yes, yes. . . . What about Nekrassov?

CHAPUIS: He . . . he escaped . . . with them.

LERMINIER: Imbeciles!

CHARIVET: Fools!

BERGERAT: Idiots!

BAUDOUIN [*pointing to his crutches*]: Gentlemen, we have fallen victims to our duty.

NERCIAT: Not enough! I am sorry you didn't get your necks broken. We'll complain to the Prime Minister.

BERGERAT: And to Jean-Paul David.

NERCIAT: Get out! [BAUDOUIN *and* CHAPUIS *go out.*]

BERGERAT [*sadly takes off his rosette and looks at it*]: Finished! [*He throws it away.*]

LERMINIER [*same action*]: Finished!

CHARIVET [*same action*]: We'll die in our beds. [*Pause.*]

JULES [*to himself, sadly*]: He's lucky!

NERCIAT: Who?

JULES: The editor of *Libérateur*.

NERCIAT [*violently*]: That's enough. [*He takes the bottle and glass from* JULES *and throws them on the floor. To the other three*] Buck up, my friends. Let's consider the future with clear heads.

BERGERAT: There is no future. Tomorrow is the day of execution. *Libérateur* will publish Valéra's confession, and our evening rivals will take great pleasure in reproducing it in full. We shall be drowned in ridicule.

CHARIVET: In shame, my friend, in shame!

LERMINIER: We'll be accused of having played the game of the Communists!

BERGERAT: We are ruined and dishonored.

CHARIVET: I want to go to bed! I want to go to bed! [*He tries to go out, but* NERCIAT *holds him back.*]

NERCIAT: What a mania for getting to bed. There's no hurry, since you're sure to die there. [BERGERAT *blows his trumpet.*] As for you, my friend, for the last time, stop blowing that thing . . . that trumpet!

BERGERAT: At least I have the right to drown my sorrows in music. [*At a look from* NERCIAT] All right, all right. . . . [*He throws the toy away.*]

NERCIAT [*to* ALL]: Nothing is lost, but we must think. How are we going to save the paper? [*Long pause.*]

JULES: If you would allow me . . .

NERCIAT: Speak!

JULES: We could steal a march on *Libérateur* and publish the news in our afternoon edition.

NERCIAT: What?

JULES [*reciting his headline*]: "Bigger Than Arsène Lupin! Valéra Hoaxed All France."

NERCIAT: I ask you to be quiet.

JULES: We should sell three million copies.

ALL: Stop it! Stop it!

JULES: All right, all right. [*He sighs.*] This is the torture of Tantalus!

[*Pause.*]

NERCIAT: On second thoughts, I support Palotin's idea, but I would take it a step further. Our revelations will arouse public anger. . . .

BERGERAT: That's true.

NERCIAT: We'll appease it with a human sacrifice. We'll say that our good faith was abused. One of us will

take all the blame. We'll denounce his criminal care-
lessness in the paper and dismiss him ignominiously.
[*Pause.*]

CHARIVET: Who were you thinking of?

NERCIAT: The Board of Directors does not handle news
as such. None of its members is guilty.

ALL: Bravo! [*They applaud.*]

JULES [*stops clapping*]: In that case I don't see . . .
[*He stops. Everyone looks at him. He walks up and
down. Their eyes follow him.*] Why are you looking
at me?

NERCIAT [*coming up to him*]: My dear Palotin, courage!

BERGERAT: We regard this paper, in a way, as our child.

CHARIVET: It won't be the first time that a father has
given his life for his child.

JULES: Ah! Ah! You want me to . . . [*Pause.*] I accept.

ALL: Bravo!

JULES: I accept, but that won't help much. What am
I? A humble employee. The public doesn't even know
my name. But if you want to create a real sensation,
my advice is sacrifice your Chairman.

BERGERAT [*taken aback*]: Well!

LERMINIER: Well! Well!

CHARIVET: Palotin is not altogether wrong.

NERCIAT: My dear friend . . .

CHARIVET: Ah! You would be making a real gesture!

NERCIAT: And you'd take my place as Chairman? I am
sorry, but it was Palotin who introduced Valéra to us.

CHARIVET: Yes, but you accepted his statements without
verifying them.

NERCIAT: So did you.

CHARIVET: I was not Chairman of the Board.

NERCIAT: Nor was I. Mouton was Chairman.

CHARIVET [*walking toward* NERCIAT]: Mouton was suspicious, poor chap!

LERMINIER [*walking toward* NERCIAT]: It is not his fault
that we fell into the trap.

BERGERAT: It was you, Nerciat, who drove him out with your intrigues. [NERCIAT, *stepping back, knocks against the attaché case.*]

CHARIVET [*with a cry*]: Look out!

NERCIAT [*turning round*]: Eh?

ALL: The case! [*They look at it with terror, at first. Then suddenly, they become angry.*]

NERCIAT [*to the attaché case*]: Trash! [*He gives the case a kick.*]

BERGERAT [*to the case*]: I'll give you radioactive powder! [*Kicks the case.*]

CHARIVET [*pointing to the case*]: That's the cause of all the trouble!

LERMINIER: Death to Valéra! [*A kick.*]

ALL: Death! Death!

[*They go on kicking the case.* MOUTON *enters, followed by* SIBILOT.]

MOUTON: Bravo, gentlemen! Take some exercise. You're just the age for it.

NERCIAT: Mouton!

ALL: Mouton! Mouton!

MOUTON: Yes, my friends, Mouton, your former chairman, to whom honest Sibilot just confessed everything. Come in, Sibilot, don't be afraid!

SIBILOT [*coming in*]: I ask you all to forgive me.

JULES: Blundering idiot!

MOUTON: Silence! My good Sibilot, don't apologize. You have done us a great service. If we save the paper, it will be thanks to you.

CHARIVET: Can it be saved?

MOUTON: If I doubted it, would I be here?

BERGERAT: And you know the way?

MOUTON: Yes.

CHARIVET [*grasping his hand*]: It was criminal of us. . . .

BERGERAT: How can you forgive us? . . .

MOUTON: I never forgive. I forget, if you know how to make me forget. *Soir à Paris* is a cultural asset. If it disappears, France will be the poorer. That is why I am prepared to let bygones be bygones.

CHARIVET: What do you suggest?

MOUTON: I don't suggest anything. I demand.

BERGERAT: Demand, then!

MOUTON [*first demand*]: It goes without saying that I remain your Chairman.

NERCIAT: Allow me, my friend, a proper vote was taken . . .

MOUTON [*to the others*]: Think only of the paper. If Nerciat can save it, I'll withdraw.

CHARIVET: Nerciat? He's incompetent.

NERCIAT: I insist that . . .

ALL [*except* JULES *and* MOUTON]: Resign! Resign! [NERCIAT *shrugs his shoulders and leaves the group.*]

MOUTON [*second demand*]: You dismissed seven innocent employees. I expect them to be reinstated and compensated.

LERMINIER: Certainly!

MOUTON: Gentlemen, now I come to the main point. For the past year the paper has been on the downgrade. We have thought only of increasing sales. The staff has been engaged in a frantic search for sensational news. We have forgotten our stern and splendid slogan: The Naked Truth. [*He points to the poster on the wall.*]

LERMINIER: Alas!

MOUTON: What is the root of the evil? Gentlemen, it is because we entrusted the editorship of our paper to an adventurer, a man without principles and without morals. I mean Palotin!

PALOTIN: There we go! Of course, you've always wanted to get rid of me.

MOUTON: Gentlemen, you have to choose: him or me?

ALL: You, you!

JULES: I was the heart of the paper and my pulse was felt in every line. What will you do without the Napoleon of the objective press?

MOUTON: What did France do after Waterloo? She
lived, sir, and we shall live.

JULES: Badly! Beware! [*Pointing to* MOUTON] There's
Louis XVIII. There's the Restoration. I'm off to
St. Helena. But beware the July Revolutions!

MOUTON: Get out!

JULES: With pleasure! Stagnate, gentlemen! Stagnate!
From this morning the news is on the left. The daily
sensation is on the left! The new thrill is on the left.
And since they are on the left, I'll go after them. I'll
found a progressive daily that will ruin you!

SIBILOT: Chief, chief, forgive me, the lie was choking
me, and . . .

JULES: Stand back, Judas! Go and hang yourself!
[*He goes out.*]

MOUTON: No regrets! It was a public cleansing opera-
tion. [*Pointing to the window*] Look! Palotin leaves
us, and the sun comes out. We shall tell the truth,
gentlemen, we shall shout it from the housetops.
What a fine profession is ours. Our paper and the
sun have the same mission: to enlighten mankind.
[*He approaches them.*] Swear to tell the truth, the
whole truth, and nothing but the truth.

ALL: I swear it!

MOUTON: Come here, Sibilot. I ask you to entrust this
great and honest man, our savior, with the editorship
of the paper.

SIBILOT: Me?
[*He faints.*]

MOUTON: Here is my plan. I telephoned the Minister
just now. Naturally, he is dropping the charge against
Duval and Maistre. There are no clear grounds.

CHARIVET: He must be furious.

MOUTON: He was, but I calmed him down. We agreed
on the steps to be taken. At dawn tomorrow, three
thousand people will mass in front of the Soviet
Embassy. By ten o'clock there will be thirty thousand.

The police cordon will be broken three times, and seventeen windowpanes will be broken. At three o'clock in the afternoon a question will be raised in the Chamber of Deputies by a government supporter. He will ask that the Embassy be searched.

CHARIVET: You're not afraid of a diplomatic incident? . . .

MOUTON: I hope for one.

CHARIVET: We'll risk a war!

MOUTON: That's what you think. The Soviet Union and France have no common frontier.

NERCIAT: Where's the sense in all this and why all this fuss?

MOUTON: To smother in advance the fuss that *Libérateur* will make. For it is we, friends, who will start the dance. Today's issue of our paper is going to stir up public anger and the anti-Soviet demonstrations. [*He shakes* SIBILOT.] Sibilot!

SIBILOT [*coming to himself*]: What?

MOUTON: To work, my friend. The front page must be reset. Put first, as a lead-in: "Georges de Valéra Sells Out to the Communists." The main headlines must take up half the page: "Nekrassov Kidnapped by the Soviets during a Reception at Mme Bounoumi's." Then you'll have another subheading: "After spending twelve hours in the embassy cellars, the hapless victim was sent off to Moscow in a trunk." Understand?

SIBILOT: Yes, Mr. Chairman.

MOUTON: Take six columns and pad it out as you fancy.

CHARIVET: Will they believe us?

MOUTON: No, but neither will they believe *Libérateur*. That's the main thing. [*To* SIBILOT] By the way, my friend, the police found a further list among Nekrassov's papers. . . .

CHARIVET: A list of . . .

MOUTON: Of Future Firing Squad Victims, of course.

[*To* SIBILOT] You will publish the principal names on
the front page: Gilbert Becaud, Georges Duhamel
and Mouton, your Chairman.
[*He bends down, picks up an FFSV rosette, and pins
it to his buttonhole.*]

CHARIVET: Can I go to bed now?

MOUTON: Certainly, my friend. I'll look after things.
[*He pushes his colleagues toward the door.* NERCIAT
shows signs of resisting.] You too, Nerciat, you too.
When you have your head firmly on the pillow, I
know that you are not doing anything stupid. [*On
the threshold* MOUTON *turns toward* SIBILOT.] If you
need me, Sibilot, I'll be in my offices.
[*They go out.*]
[SIBILOT *gets up and walks up and down, at first
slowly, and then more and more quickly. Finally he
takes off his jacket, sends it flying onto an armchair,
opens the door, and calls.*]

SIBILOT: Tavernier, Perigord—front page conference!
[TAVERNIER *and* PERIGORD *come running in, see* SIBI-
LOT, *and stop, amazed.* SIBILOT *looks into their eyes.*]
Well, boys, do you love me?

CURTAIN

JEAN-PAUL SARTRE, who has been ranked as a playwright of genius, was born in 1905 in Paris, where he still lives and works. His first play, *The Flies* (*Les Mouches*), was produced during the German occupation of France in spite of its underlying message of defiance. Before World War II was over, his *No Exit* (*Huis Clos*) had also been staged in Paris and brought Existentialism into the vocabularies of the world. Sartre has made living theater out of his philosophy, and his plays, in translation, have stirred intellectuals everywhere. When *The Devil and the Good Lord* was first produced in Paris in 1951 it aroused a storm of controversy; it was the last production of Louis Jouvet's life, and Pierre Brasseur, who was later to play the title role of *Kean*, headed a cast of over ninety. In recent years Sartre has put aside the last novel of his universally famous tetralogy, *Road to Freedom*; he has worked primarily on non-fiction and devoted a year and a half to the writing of his most recent dramatic work, *Les Séquestrés d'Altona*, which was produced in Paris in September 1959.

THIS BOOK was set in ELECTRA, printed, and bound by THE COLONIAL PRESS, CLINTON, MASSACHUSETTS.

A free catalogue of VINTAGE BOOKS *will be sent at your request. Write to* Vintage Books, 457 Madison Avenue, New York, New York 10022.